SMYTHE LIBRARY

Stamp this label with the date for return.
Contact the librarian if you wish to renew this book.

— RELLING STACK —

0 4 JUN 2018		

BLOOD, SWEAT AND ARROGANCE

BLOOD, SWEAT AND ARROGANCE

and the Myths of Churchill's War

Gordon Corrigan

WEIDENFELD & NICOLSON

First published in Great Britain in 2006
by Weidenfeld & Nicolson

1 3 5 7 9 10 8 6 4 2

A CIP catalogue record for this book is available from the British Library.

ISBN-13   978 0 297 84623 9
ISBN-10   0 297 84623 X

Printed in Great Britain by
Clays Ltd, St Ives plc

Weidenfeld & Nicolson

The Orion Publishing Group Ltd
Orion House, 5 Upper Saint Martin's Lane, London, WC2H 9EA
www.orionbooks.co.uk

The Orion Publishing Group's policy is to use papers that are natural, renewable
and recyclable products and made from wood grown in sustainable forests.
The logging and manufacturing processes are expected to conform to the
environmental regulations of the country of origin.

Contents

List of Illustrations

Grant Tank (American)

Sherman Tank (American)

Sherman DD Tank (Allied)

Firefly Tank (British)

SOMUA Tank (French)

Char B1 bis Tank (French)

Mk 1 Tank (German)

Mk III Tank (German)

Mark IV Tank (German)

Panther Tank (German)

Tiger Tank (German)

88 mm Anti Tank Gun (German)

Swordfish Torpedo Bomber (British)

HMS Ark Royal

Fairey Battle Bomber (British)

Lancaster Bomber (British)

The Observer Corps

Neville Chamberlain

Winston Churchill

Field Marshal Sir Claude Auchinleck

General Charles de Gaulle

Field Marshals Viscount Alanbrooke and Viscount Montgomery

Generals Montgomery and Ritter von Thoma

List of Maps

Introduction

IN 1939 BRITAIN WENT to war to save the world from fascism and dictatorship. Let down by the perfidious Belgians and French, greatly outnumbered by swarms of German tanks, the British army fought its way back to the French coast. The miracle of Dunkirk, made possible by hundreds of little ships sailed by their patriotic civilian owners, brought the soldiers back to England to fight another day. Now Britain stood alone against the whole might of the German Wehrmacht and their cowardly Italian poodles. The people of Britain girded themselves for total war. They threw out the appeasers and the disarmers, sacked the incompetent generals and brought Winston Churchill, soldier, sailor and statesman, to power on a tide of public acclaim. He could offer nothing but blood, toil, sweat and tears, but, as King George said, at least we no longer had to worry about allies.

Through the Battle of Britain the Few – young public schoolboys to whom the game was the thing – held at bay the far more numerous Luftwaffe, while the people stoically withstood the Blitz, as death rained from the skies. Meanwhile the Prime Minister was cutting out the dead wood. Gort, Dill, Ironside, Wavell, Cuningham, Auchinleck all went: tired old men consigned to the dustbin of history until at last a new star appeared in the military firmament. Before Montgomery there was only defeat, after him there was nothing but victory. There is no God but Churchill, and Montgomery is his prophet.

After Britain had been the sole standard bearer for freedom for over two years, the New World came at last to the assistance of the Old, and with American entry into the war Britain no longer stood alone. In 1944 she returned to Europe, as she always knew she would, and under the National Treasure Montgomery, her army and air force fought on until final victory in Europe, followed by the defeat of Japan in the Far East. It was the end of a great struggle for the rights of man, and it was to Britain, which had fought for longer than any of the Allies, that much of the credit was due. Or so popular British opinion of the Second World War would usually have it. To most of the British public the First World War is generally thought of as unnecessary at best, mismanaged and a wholesale slaughter of British youth at worst. The Second War, on the other hand, is seen as a moral crusade where plucky Britain stood up to the evil dictators and won great victories. Having learned the lessons of the First War, the Second was far more competently conducted and the death toll a mere fraction of that incurred in 1914–18. The Kaiser was not such a bad chap, while Hitler was an evil monster; the causes of going to war in 1914 were not understood by the United Kingdom populace at large, while in 1939 everybody knew why we had to fight and supported the decision wholeheartedly. In 1914 we had the dithering Asquith as Prime Minister, and could not get rid of him until 1916, while we very quickly replaced the weak Chamberlain – whose appeasement of the fascists led to war in the first place – by the great war leader and strategist Winston Churchill in 1940.

The Second World War has become heroic myth in Britain. Criticism of the conduct of the First War began a mere twelve years after it ended, but even with the passing of the sixtieth anniversary of the ending of the Second, Britain is thought to have gone to war for the right reasons, and to have fought well after initial setbacks. The political and military leadership is considered to have been good, and better than during the First War.

This perception makes it difficult to face the fact that in 1940 the British and the French between them had more and better quality tanks than the Germans, and more infantry divisions; yet in the Battle of France they were constantly outmanoeuvred by fast moving German columns of all arms. Holland, Belgium and France all fell, and Britain was bundled unceremoniously out of Europe. At about the same time the hastily executed Norway invasion was abandoned and the troops withdrawn.

How could the nation which in 1918 had the best and most techno-logically advanced army in the world, the biggest navy and the only inde-pendent air force perform so badly a mere twenty years later, and against the same enemy that she had resoundingly defeated in 1918? In the approach to the Second War the British army was the only army made up of long-term regulars, volunteers all. It was the only army that had considerable experience of active service – against third-rate enemies it is true, but a ball from a home-made Pathan rifle will kill as surely as that from a modern machine gun, and with more discomfort. Of the original belligerents only Britain had a fully mechanised army, having long accepted that there was no place for the horse on the modern battlefield, and yet with all this, in 1940 it was outfought and outgunned and forced into a humiliating scuttle in a mere three weeks.

This book argues that the very nature, purpose and experience of the British armed forces militated against their performing well at the beginning of the Second World War. Unlike their German opponents, which had nothing to do except prepare for war on the continent of Europe, the British had an empire to police. The British army, navy and air force were spread around the world in penny packets, and priorities in methods, training and equipment reflected that – for very practical reasons. Britain had invented the tank, but inter-war development in Britain had gone down a blind alley, and instead of the tank being seen as only one element – albeit an important one – in a coordinated effort by all arms, it was regarded either as something which could be slow and ponderous to support the infantry, or the land equivalent of a destroyer, roaming the battlefield at will and operating independently. The Germans took a different view, and Blitzkrieg was the result.

In arguing that the British armed forces did not do well in the Second World War – or at least not as well as they might, and not as well as they had done in previous conflicts – I have no wish to be considered an iconoclast. I spent most of my adult life in the British Army and I am proud of its past and of what it has done. I spend a great deal of time studying its history, and that of the Royal Navy and the Royal Air Force. I find that most of our military history is deserving of great pride, and I have no intention of biting the hand that fed me for over thirty years. All that said, we can only learn how to manage future conflicts by examining the lessons of previous ones, and while a major world conflict may be some way off, it was that assumption in the years up to the mid 1930s that contributed in large part to our failures when war did come.

In this book my aim has been to re-examine some of our parameters, and ask what effect appeasement and financial constraints prior to 1939 had on our war-making ability; whether we really could have stopped Hitler short of war; what we actually went to war for, and then how we conducted that war once we found ourselves with no option but to wage it. My original intention was to look at the British waging of the war as a whole. When I realised that the result would be a door-stop of impressive proportions, I decided to consider only the war in the West: that waged against Germany and Italy, and to leave the Far East for another occasion. Of course the war in the West and that in the East were not fought in isolation; Britain's military assets were finite, and the hard decisions as to which theatre should have priority and when would merit a study in themselves. Far Eastern neglect and underfunding was even worse than that nearer home, and the Malayan campaign was at least as incompetently managed as that in Norway, but it was the Far East that produced the general whom I believe future historians will consider the best British general of the war – Field Marshal Sir William Slim. In neglecting the Far East in this book I do not in any way underestimate the significance of that theatre and of the men who fought there.

Conventional wisdom ascribes British failure in the early days to lack of funding between the wars, a mistaken faith in the League of Nations and collective security, the pusillanimity of the French, the duplicity of Hitler and the blindness of the 'appeasers'. Others blame the British class system (although if that had worked in previous wars, why should it break down so suddenly now?); yet others say that the admirals and generals and air marshals in post when war started were incompetent, proved by the number that were sacked as the war went on (but one has to ask whether the sacking or rustication of a large number of admirals, generals and air marshals by Churchill was wise). There is some truth in all of these views; in some quite a lot, in others only a grain, but there is more to it than that. There are factors inherent in the democratic system that make it very difficult ever to be ready for war – electorates simply will not allocate defence a priority over the things that are of immediate concern: education, health, housing and taxation. Elections in peacetime are never won on foreign or defence policy, and a party that advocated the spending needed to be ready for any eventuality would fail at the polls.

Should a war then arrive, the politicians and the generals cannot win. In the Gulf campaign of 2003 there were insufficient desert combat suits and desert boots to equip every soldier deployed. An outcry in press and television resulted. This was little more than a storm in a mess tin, for apart from dismounted infantry nobody actually needs a sand-coloured combat suit – a green one will do just as well. Desert boots, too, are but a fashion statement, as good old Boots, Combat, High are equally good and harder wearing, even if they do make your feet sweaty. Governments, advised by their military professionals, have to assess threats, and allocate priorities. In the years between 1992 and 2003 the British services – for very good reasons – did not place desert warfare near the top of their likely deployments. Some desert equipment was held, but not sufficient for everyone who was actually deployed in 2003. To have held sufficient against an unspecified requirement would have cost a very great deal, and in other circumstances would have led to strident criticism from the Commons Audit Committee. If the next campaign is in northern Norway (unlikely just now, but you never know) there will be accusations of unreadiness when only the infantry are issued with snowshoes.

Governments that have to rely on popular support find it difficult to embark on military adventures without a reason that sounds obvious and convincing to the public. No doubt it was easier to sell the Trojan War as just vengeance for the dishonourable seduction and kidnapping of the Queen of Sparta, rather than admitting that it was all about trade rivalry in the Aegean. Had Mr Pitt and his successors announced that the French Revolutionary and Napoleonic wars were being fought for control of oceans, markets and colonies the British people might not have remained belligerent for twenty-three years, whereas a titanic struggle against a bloodthirsty monster intent on enslaving the world was ample justification for fighting.

There were very good reasons for going to war in 1939, but they were not necessarily the ones trumpeted at the time, nor those generally trotted out now. So why did Britain go to war in 1939? To save the Czechs and Slovaks? Not quite: most Britons, if they thought of Czechoslovakia at all, saw it as an artificial state 'far away and of which we know nothing', to which might have been added 'and care less', and in any case if Britain had really cared about preserving it she would have gone to war in 1938, not more than a year later. Was it to save the Poles? Well, hardly. There was no British interest in Poland, a state with only occasional and fleeting appearances on the world stage as a country at all, and governed by a quasi-fascist regime that had gleefully grabbed a chunk of Czechoslovakia when Germany dismembered that country in 1938. Fond memories of Polish pilots in the Battle of Britain,* and the Polish Armoured Division in Normandy, should not blind us to the fact that the Poles were every bit as anti-Semitic as the Germans; the only difference was that Germany institutionalised it. Germany had more than a little justification for fearing and resenting the Poles, which is why the British attempted to persuade the Poles to come to the table only twenty-four hours before war broke out. Even so, if Britain declared war on Germany because that country's troops invaded Poland on 1 September 1939, then why did she not declare war on the USSR when Russian troops did exactly the same thing on 17 September?

Perhaps, then, Britain went to war to save the Jews? Well, no, not that either, because the Wansee Conference, which formalised the decision to dispose of Europe's Jews by killing them, did not take place until

---

*While of undoubted courage, the Poles were sometimes more trouble than they were worth. Many could not understand radioed instructions from English-speaking fighter controllers, and they were responsible for far too many crashed aircraft through attempting aerobatics beyond their flying skills. That said, however, some Polish pilots achieved very high scores in the Battle of Britain, particularly those who had experience of fighting the Luftwaffe over Poland.

January 1942, when Britain had already been at war for over two years. In any event, no country declares war to protect people for whom they have no responsibility. The British government may or may not have known the extent of the German policy of extermination of the Jews, but it would not have been regarded as a reason for going to war, nor could Britain, before or after 1939, have allowed unrestricted Jewish immigration to Palestine. Pre-war Jewish terrorism was directed not only against Arabs but against British soldiers too, and did not stop for the war.

Self-determination and the rights of small nations is often touted as justification for the war, but as the possessor of a huge Empire, the less developed parts of which were ruled fairly, efficiently and wisely, but certainly not democratically, Britain was not an advocate of unbridled self-government.

Did Britain go to war because Hitler was a tyrannical monster? Many of Hitler's policies were certainly abhorrent, but Britain does not declare war because she dislikes someone else's head of state, otherwise we would have gone to war with Stalin's Russia and Chiang Kai-Shek's China.

IT TOOK HITLER AND THE NSDAP hierarchy a long time to realise that they could not form an alliance with Britain. Certainly the British had, in many ways, far more in common with the Germans than with the French. In the previous two hundred years the British had spent thirty-eight years at war with the French[*] and only four fighting the Germans, who had hitherto been traditional allies. The Queen was British, the first non-German consort for well over two hundred years,[**] but the King (whose surname was Saxe Coburg Gotha until changed to Windsor in

---

[*] The Seven Years War 1756–63, the French-supported American rebellion 1775–83, and the Revolutionary and Napoleonic wars 1793–1815.

[**] Her predecessors were Mary of Teck (George V's queen – German), Alexandra of Denmark (Edward VII's queen – German, or at least Germanic), Albert of Saxe Coburg & Gotha (Victoria's consort – German), Caroline of Brunswick (George IV's (uncrowned) queen – German), Charlotte of Mecklenburg-Strelitz (George III's queen – German), Caroline of Ansbach (George II's queen – German), Sophia of Zell (George I's queen – German) and as George I was himself a German that takes us back to 1714. George I's predecessor, Queen Anne, was married to Prince George of Denmark – another German – and her Stuart predecessors generally took French spouses. Our next king is, of course, three-quarters German.

1917) was as German as a bratwurst, even if since the Great War the royal family had rather played down its German antecedents. The English language had far more in common with German than with French, and the average Englishman saw Germans as being disciplined and straightforward, compared to the effete and unhygienic French.* To Hitler, and to many Germans, it made complete sense for Britain to give Germany a free hand in Europe – after all, England's interest was in her Empire and in mastery of the oceans, and she could not possibly object to Germany's eradication of Bolshevism.

What Hitler and his satraps could never understand was that regardless of kinship, like or dislike, Great Britain could not and would not allow one power to dominate Europe and thus threaten her interests. She would always seek for a balance, and if that could not be achieved by diplomatic means then in the last resort restraint would be exercised by force. That was why Britain had fought the Dutch, the Spanish and the French in the seventeenth, eighteenth and nineteenth centuries, and why she had fought the Germans in 1914. It was why she saw France as a potential threat in the 1920s, and why she would go to war in 1939. Even if Britain had possessed the military assets and political will to restrain Germany from 1936 onward, which of course she had not, she would almost certainly have tolerated – or even approved of – much of what Hitler wanted. The remilitarisation of the Rhineland, the waiving of reparations, border adjustments with Poland, some revision of the Polish Corridor and a modest measure of rearmament would all have been acceptable, provided they had been arrived at by agreement – which with British support could have been achieved. Even Anschluss and the incorporation of the Sudetenland might have been swallowed, although the latter would have been a difficult mouthful as it removed Czechoslovakia's natural mountain frontier.

What no British government could accept, however, was that Hitler's ambitions were not going to stop at mere boundary adjustments to bring all Germans into his Reich, but that he actually meant all those things that he had laid out in *Mein Kampf*. What inspired the British to guarantee

---

*Times change. Only recently a French family staying with this author as part of a village twinning celebration, complained vociferously about the state of the lavatories in one of the village pubs!

Polish territorial integrity was the reluctant acceptance that the only way to stop complete German domination of Europe and beyond was by the threat of military action. To borrow a later statement by Churchill, if Hitler had been threatening Hell in 1939, Britain would have given a guarantee to the Devil, and no doubt, like Britain's to Poland, Hitler would not have believed it.

Britain went to war in 1939 for the reasons that great powers always go to war: because it was in her interests to do so. No one power could be permitted to dominate Europe; there had to be a balance between France and Germany, and France could not be allowed to be destroyed. Like it or not, Britain had given certain guarantees which embroiled her in European affairs to a much greater extent than had been the case in 1914, and all other methods having failed, only military force was left. It was not what Britain wanted, and it was not the time that she would have chosen, but Britain's vital interests were now threatened and she had no option but to go to war.

Not only does democracy hinder preparedness for war, but so too do the traditions of an island nation. Historically the British have had a very small army and a very big navy. The British army was a missile fired by the navy; the army existed to garrison the Empire and to provide expeditionary forces. At its best, the combination of a powerful navy and a small volunteer army allowed the British to intervene almost anywhere, by landing troops, supplying them and removing them to be used again if necessary. In the twenty-first century, with the end of the Cold War, we are reverting to an expeditionary strategy: it is what we do well and what we are comfortable with. In both world wars, however, we perforce had to engage on land. This meant the raising of an army far larger than existed in peace, and from a population with no inherent military experience gained by compulsory service in peacetime. Such expansion will inevitably lead to many errors and a large number of deaths while the services learn their trade. It happened on the Somme, it happened in Normandy and it will happen again in the future. If we do not want to spend a very large proportion of our national wealth on defence in times of peace, then we had better accept that there will be a difficult learning period when we do go to war, and live with the consequences.

In August 1914 the British army numbered just under a quarter of a million regulars, around 200,000 reservists and rather more than a quarter of a million in the part-time Territorial Force. The British element of the British Expeditionary Force despatched to the Western Front in 1914 was initially four infantry divisions, a cavalry division and an independent brigade. Eight months later in March 1915 it was eleven infantry and five cavalry divisions.[*] By 1918 this had grown to forty-eight infantry and three cavalry divisions, with further deployments in Italy, Palestine and Mesopotamia, or seventy-one infantry and eight cavalry (including cyclist) divisions in total.

In September 1939 the regular army was about the same size as it had been in 1914, the reservists rather less and the Territorial Army (the successor to the Territorial Force) considerably smaller. Again, we sent out four infantry divisions, but eight months later the British Expeditionary Force could field only nine infantry divisions and an armoured division. There were, it is true, a further three Territorial divisions in France, sent there as humpers and dumpers to build defences, but while they did get involved in the fighting they were without the material wherewithal or the training to play any meaningful role. At its peak the British army worldwide deployed thirty-four infantry divisions, eleven armoured divisions, two airborne divisions and ten armoured brigades, or rather less than two-thirds of its strength in 1918.[**] Of course the Royal Air Force had many more men in 1945 than it had in 1918, but the Royal Navy had rather less, and all this from a larger population, for although present-day Eire was part of the United Kingdom in the First War, and neutral in the Second, she made no attempt to prevent recruitment of her citizens into the British armed forces.

Winston Churchill is firmly embedded in British mythology as the man who won the war. Churchill often said that he was a soldier, and that soldiering was his first love. When he was forced briefly out of government in November 1915 he announced that he would return to what he knew best – soldiering. He fancied himself as a great strategist; able

[*]There were also two Indian and one Canadian infantry divisions, and two Indian cavalry divisions.

[**] Armoured divisions were a mix of armour, artillery, infantry, and engineers. An armoured brigade had the same amount of armour as an armoured division, although not the same engineer, artillery or infantry support. It had however the same shock effect as a division in the attack.

to see a military option or solution far more clearly than those who had spent their lives doing it. In the Second World War, in his correspondence with President Roosevelt, he styled himself a 'Former Naval Person' and genuinely thought that time spent as the politician put in charge of the navy was equivalent to having been an admiral. He was the honorary air commodore of a Royal Air Force reserve squadron and often wore an air commodore's uniform. Throughout the Great War Churchill, like Lloyd George, had never really understood that it was only on the Western Front that the main enemy – Germany – could be defeated. Like his master, Churchill had constantly looked for the easy option: the props that could be knocked away, the soft underbelly. In the Second World War his attitudes did not change. As First Lord of the Admiralty for the first eight months of the war, he insisted on personally commanding the movements and actions of individual ships from the Admiralty in London, and once installed as Prime Minister, with unfettered power to dictate to the service chiefs, he ran the war almost single-handedly, directing not only broad strategy but often detailed tactics as well, hiring and firing senior officers as he pleased.

The truth is that for all Churchill's claims to be a soldier and a sailor, he had actually done very little of it. He passed the examination for the Royal Military College Sandhurst in 1893 aged nineteen, and was commissioned in 1895. Originally destined for the infantry, he chose instead to join an expensive and gorgeously caparisoned cavalry regiment, the 4th Hussars. In the four years that he spent on the army list as a regular officer, before leaving to enter politics, he spent little time with his regiment, wangling six months' leave to accompany a Spanish contingent to Cuba, and then getting himself attached to General Sir Bindon Blood's Malakand Field Force expedition against the Pathans on the North-West Frontier of India, where he spent more time writing than fighting.[*] In 1898 he again pulled strings to get himself attached to the army in the Sudan, despite Kitchener's misgivings, where he took part in the famous cavalry charge of the 21st Lancers at Omdurman. Famous it undoubtedly was, but so

---

[*] On one occasion he accompanied a Sikh hill piqueting force, and being rather portly even then, almost got caught by the wily Pathan when the time came to withdraw. He was undoubtedly brave, but one suspects rather naive as well.

inept and unnecessary that the commanding officer was sacked after it, and of the thirty or so British deaths at the battle, twenty-one were from the Lancers.

Churchill left the army in 1899, failed to get elected for Oldham and went to the South African war as a newspaper correspondent, where he was captured by the Boers and escaped under circumstances that are still in doubt. He then joined the South African Light Horse, a local yeomanry regiment, which gave him the protection of a uniform if captured again, but he continued to act as a war correspondent. His first experience as a soldier was thus confined to less than five years as a subaltern, during which time he never commanded troops other than in barracks. Instead, he used family connections to have himself attached to expeditions that he thought might be exciting or that would give him a stage on which to posture, or provide a market for his writings. His next brief experience of wearing uniform was sixteen years later, when he was forced to resign as First Lord of the Admiralty in November 1915 as a result of the Gallipoli caper, itself a perfectly reasonable concept to begin with, but which should have been abandoned once the Royal Navy was unable to force the Narrows.

Out of political office, Churchill announced that he was returning to what he knew best: the army. When he was denied the appointment of Commander-in-Chief in East Africa, an extraordinary suggestion, the Commander of the British Expeditionary Force on the Western Front, Sir John French, in an even more extraordinary suggestion, promised him command of an infantry brigade, once he had completed a brief period attached to the 2nd Battalion Grenadier Guards to familiarise himself with conditions on the Western Front. Churchill's own letters and papers[1] claim that from a rather bad start, when the battalion were not keen to take him on, he rapidly charmed the Grenadiers until he was standing in for the commanding officer, was consulted by all and was much missed when he completed his six-week attachment. In fact, the battalion war diary[2] makes only one mention of Churchill, in an entry of 20 November 1915 which reads: 'Major the Rt Hon Winston Churchill who has just resigned from Government, arrived to be attached to the battalion for instruction, and accompanied the battalion to the trenches.' He is not mentioned again, even when leaving, and he certainly did not stand in for the commanding officer. During his period of attachment the battalion was in the trenches on and off for eighteen days north of the La Bassée Canal and had five men killed, two who died of wounds, thirteen wounded and seven men slightly wounded. It was not a time of great activity.

Now the War Office stepped in, and the notion of Brigadier General Churchill was vetoed. Instead Churchill reluctantly, and with some ill grace, accepted command of a New Army battalion, 6 Royal Scots Fusiliers. He wangled the transfer of a great friend, Sir Archibald Sinclair, from the Life Guards to be his battalion second-in-command, and then spent five months pretending to be a lieutenant colonel and battalion commander, most of it in Ploegsteert Wood, south of Ypres, a relatively quiet area at that time, wearing for some inexplicable reason a French steel helmet, and irritating his officers and the brigade commander by constantly rushing off to London when an opportunity arose to do a bit of political lobbying. For most of the 120 days that Churchill was in command the battalion was on a twelve-day cycle, six days in the trenches and six in billets. Although the war diary for April 1916 is missing, from what records remain it is apparent that nothing very much happened. Churchill unashamedly used the military communications system to bring him political gossip from London, and described his corps commander as a 'villain' when he refused him leave on the very sound grounds that if a battalion was in the trenches then its commanding officer should be there too.

To appoint an inexperienced outsider to command a battalion, and then to allow him to bring in a chum who was not even an infantryman as his second-in-command, was nothing short of disgraceful. It denied a professional officer of the regiment a command, and exposed the soldiers to the whims of a military dilettante. The war diary[3] of 6 Royal Scots Fusiliers is remarkably restrained, and mentions Churchill only once, in the entry for 7 May 1916: 'Colonel W. S. Churchill left the battalion today'. Churchill decided that politics was, after all, his first love, and was permitted to leave the army provided that he did not apply for military command again – a stipulation insisted on by the Secretary of State for

War, Field Marshal Lord Kitchener. His friend Sinclair turned down Churchill's offer to leave with him and make a career in politics, having the decency to reply that as he was young and unwounded, his place was at the front. Churchill returned from his self-imposed exile and resumed life as a politician.

By 1939 his actual military experience was therefore almost nil, woefully out of date and none of it bestowing any qualification whatsoever to expound on matters of strategy. There is no question that Churchill was personally brave and completely unafraid of death. The trouble was that he was not afraid of anyone else's death either, and his fascination for the minutiae of war made him very dangerous when he insisted on taking matters into his own hands, as he far too often did. As First Lord of the Admiralty during the Norwegian campaign of April to June 1940, Churchill's constant interference with the admirals was almost catastrophic, and when he became Prime Minister his old wish for the easy, or clever, option resurfaced. Soft underbellies were constantly searched for; military decisions were made on the basis of emotion; and commanders whom he disliked or who refused to pander to his foibles were sacked on a whim. It may be unfair to describe him as a drunk, but he certainly consumed more alcohol than was wise for a man of his age and physical condition, and to keep his professional advisers up half the night listening to his ideas on strategy when they, but not he, had a full day's work to look forward to on the morrow, was nothing short of selfish indulgence.

Had British military performance improved rapidly after the Battle of France in 1940, one could excuse that debacle as an uncharacteristic blip, to be remedied by the sacking of a general or an air marshal or two, but while the British, when they next fought on land, did well against ill-equipped Italians, they did not do quite so well against Vichy Frenchmen in Syria, and very badly against Germans in Crete and North Africa. Even after the Battle of El Alamein, three years into the war, an outgunned, outnumbered and logistically impaired Axis army, in a theatre then regarded by the Germans as peripheral, managed to avoid defeat all the way back to Tunisia, and that despite British codebreakers keeping Montgomery aware of almost every move Rommel intended to make.

In Sicily and Italy, too, British progress was ponderous and slow, and while Operation Overlord, the invasion of Europe in 1944, was a resounding success, many of the subsequent operations were not, with perhaps the epitome of incompetence being displayed at Villers-Bocage, when one understrength German tank company stopped a British armoured division in its tracks and forced its withdrawal.

Things got better but only very slowly. In the advance through Holland towards Germany, Operation Market Garden, the airborne assault on Arnhem, was an extraordinary concept, quite out of character for the British army so far, and even if misconceived planning and faulty execution had not caused the operation to fail, what on earth made the British planners think that a German army commanded by a man like Field Marshal Model would simply pack up and go home if it succeeded?

Armies depend on manpower, and navies on ships. Ships are more expensive than men, and take longer to build, and it was pure political expediency that surrendered British naval supremacy in the Washington Treaty of 1922, and which slashed all three services with the Geddes Axe in 1921. It had become apparent during the Great War that the battleship was increasingly vulnerable to aircraft, and many admirals considered that the aircraft carrier would be the capital ship in the next war. That view was not universally held – and certainly not by Winston Churchill – and while the Royal Navy planned to build seven new fleet carriers in the 1930s, lack of funds meant that only two appeared. Nevertheless, on the outbreak of war in 1939 the Royal Navy had twelve battleships and seven aircraft carriers, compared to the eight battleships (including two pocket battleships) and no carriers of Germany and Japan combined. The German invasion of Norway in 1940, the sinking of HMS *Hood*, the loss of HMS *Prince of Wales* and *Repulse* to Japanese aircraft, the 'channel dash' of the *Scharnhorst* and the *Gneisenau*, the U-boat menace that sank eight million tons of shipping in 1942 alone, all came as severe embarrassments. On paper the Royal Navy should have been able to deal with anything Germany and her allies could have thrown at it, but many of its ships were old, and, initially at least, it was unable to prevent Axis advances on the Atlantic coast, the Mediterranean and in the Pacific.

In the air Britain was, marginally, better prepared, largely because the effect of German bombing of the British mainland in the First War had led to the erroneous conclusion that 'the bomber will always get through'. The air staff had provided for the air defence of the United Kingdom, and had secured agreement for the formation of an offensive bomber force, but on the outbreak of war it had far too many different types of aircraft that could not carry enough bombs, and until well into the war there were no long-range fighters to act as escorts. The Battle of Britain was a salvation, but only just, and was lost by errors of the Luftwaffe high command – who failed to realise the importance of the Chain Home radar stations, and switched to targeting cities just when Fighter Command was on the brink of destruction – rather than by British superiority in the air, although the British command and control system was undoubtedly a factor. The UK's bomber offensive against German cities had no more success in breaking German civilian morale, nor in destroying her war production, than had German bombing of British cities, despite horrific casualties in Bomber Command.

In the end, Britain did emerge on the winning side, but years of neglect between the wars; Britain's position as a superpower without the economy – nor perhaps the will – to sustain it; the lack of incentive to military progress and a failure to realise that in the event of war France was defeated before she even started, all contributed to Britain entering a major war with fewer and less effective warlike assets than ever before in her history.

Not all about the British effort in the Second World War was bad: British troops were generally excellent at small unit special operations – commando raids and the like – but the efforts expended on the Special Air Service, the Long Range Desert Group, the Commandos and the various private armies that seem to proliferate whenever the British go to war, might perhaps have been better spent improving the whole, rather than just a small part, of the British military effort. British artillery was generally better, both technically and in the way it was used, than were German guns, but German tanks consistently outgunned and outperformed British ones, and it has to be asked how it was that an Allied army could be launched into an invasion of Fortress Europe equipped with tanks that were not only inferior to those of its enemies, but markedly inferior and known to be so since the Sherman's first deployment in North Africa in 1942.

The Royal Navy did fulfil one of its traditional roles at Dunkirk in 1940 – the evacuation of a British army by sea so that it could be used somewhere else, and it did, eventually, regain command of the oceans around the British Isles – although it should never have been allowed to lose it in the first place. By the time of the Normandy invasion the Royal Air Force was considered to be superb, particularly in operations in support of ground forces, but even here there was often more fuss and feathers than substantive results, and claims as to the number of tanks killed by Typhoon fighter bombers are not always borne out by the squadron war diaries.

IN THE SECOND WAR, unlike the First, the British did not deploy their main weight on land against the main enemy in the main theatre. Having been driven ignominiously out of Europe in 1940, most of the army sat around in England defending against an invasion that never came, or preparing to return to Europe some time in the future. Campaigns in Eritrea, North Africa, Crete, Italy and even the Far East were important, but they were never critical to the survival of this nation, nor to the outcome of the war; they were fought with relatively small numbers of troops, and were heavily reliant on the Empire – the Far East over-whelmingly so. The British army was never given the time and the opportunity to learn the hard way, as it had in the First War, in continuous fighting against a first-class enemy.

There are very good reasons why the period of history taught in schools and universities stops well before the lifetime of the students, for an objective assessment of people and events is impossible, or at least very difficult, until those events are far enough in the past for all the evidence to be available and for passions to have cooled. An oft-quoted story about the long view taken by China relates that when visiting Europe the late Chou En-lai was asked what he thought were the major effects of the French Revolution. He is said to have replied that it was too early to say. When I was a schoolboy in the 1950s the history syllabus came to an end in 1918, on the grounds that anything since was too recent for objective study, and should come under the classification of current affairs.

Certainly the more recent the field of scholarship, the more difficult it is to arrive at a valid historical balance. Partly this is because not all the information is available, and partly it is due to personal prejudices. Even now it is difficult to find an unbiased judgement of Attila the Hun, and impossible to find one of Hitler. Despite some excellent recent biographies, it may take another fifty or a hundred years before an objective assessment of Adolf Hitler appears. Distaste for him and his regime, and the evil things that they did, is just too embedded in the human psyche, here and abroad, for a proper and unbiased weighing of the man's life and times. Demonising one's opponents is all part of making war acceptable to the nation, and if the enemy leader can be made to look ridiculous as well as evil, then so much the better. But Hitler was not illegitimate; his real name was not Schikelgruber; there is no evidence whatsoever that he was a sexual pervert; he was not a house painter;* the transcripts of his military conferences up to the last week of the war show no signs of madness. He was a man of enormous personal charisma, was by no means lacking in military judgement, was elevated to power in as democratic an election as Germany had ever experienced, and retained the support of the vast majority of his countrymen to the bitter end. The so-called German resistance is a myth, created by post-war German politicians to elevate for their own purposes the activities of a very few disgruntled officers and intellectuals. Certainly Hitler's regime was autocratic and open opposition could lead to swift repression and even death, but it could not have survived had not the overwhelming majority of the German people believed in it.

And who can blame them? Hitler stabilised the currency, enacted laws to protect workers that were far in advance of anything in British legislation; introduced a public health service long before Britain's National Health Service; fixed old-age pensions at a higher level than Britain's; built the autobahns and achieved full employment by a massive programme of public works. All that was undeniably good. It was in his attempts to remove the shackles of Versailles and to give Germans back

---

* He did paint pictures in which there were houses, but that is a far cry from being an interior decorator.

their dignity that Hitler's policies are controversial, but even here much of what he did up to the dismembering of Czechoslovakia was seen by many in Britain as not unreasonable, even if they were irritated by Hitler's recourse to threats for what he might equally well have achieved by negotiation.

But any suggestion that Hitler may not have been all bad is likely to draw howls of protest even sixty years after his death. In Germany today it is illegal to make the unlikely claim that the state-sponsored wholesale killing of Jews did not take place during the National Socialist era, and it is illegal to publish or sell Hitler's turgid and largely unreadable *Mein Kampf*. One has to ask whether it can be right to prevent unpopular views being expressed, however offensive they may be, or however much we may disagree with them.

Criticism of the British military effort during the Second World War is fraught with pitfalls. Many of those who took part are still with us, are rightly proud of what they did and are resentful of what they see as uninformed criticism. One can opine that the actions of Marlborough's cavalry in Bavaria during the War of the Spanish Succession would have him in front of a war crimes tribunal today, pontificate about the King's Hard Bargains who made up most of Wellington's army, or be as rude as one may wish about incompetent commanders and soldiers in the Crimea, and not much dust will be raised. To suggest that Dunkirk was far from a glorious deliverance, that the campaign in North Africa after Alamein was ponderous, that progress in Normandy after D-Day was pitifully slow, that Montgomery was not a great general, that Wavell should never have been sacked, that the Royal Navy should not have been caught out by the Channel Dash, that the tank-busting capabilities of the RAF Typhoon were grossly exaggerated, that Combined Operations raids were often badly planned and unnecessarily careless of men's lives, carries with it the certainty of an eruption of anger by those who were there against he who was not.

There are lies, damned lies and regimental histories. Some years ago, as a serving officer, I had a paper published in a professional journal in which, in passing, I said that there was evidence to indicate that the time of H-hour (the time that an operation begins) for the British breakout from the Anzio beachhead in Italy in May 1944 was betrayed to the Germans by a deserter from a certain battalion of a regiment of British infantry. My sources were pretty good – the German intelligence officer of an SS Panzer Grenadier Regiment and the British brigade commander (both now dead). I omit the name of the regiment here as I have no wish to undergo a second bombardment of unsigned letters in block letters and green ink, with bits underlined, accusing me of traducing the memory of brave men. When Correlli Barnett first published *The Desert Generals* in 1960 the press demanded to know how Sergeant Barnett could possibly criticise the great Field Marshal Montgomery. Now that the relevant papers and documents not available to Barnett have been released, he is shown to have been absolutely correct.

In modern media-speak anyone who served in the war is automatically a 'war hero' and any campaign or service medal has been translated into a 'decoration'. A cook who was conscripted in 1944 and spent his war dishing up all-in stew at Aldershot, and who received the war medal along with everyone else who served for at least twenty-eight days, no doubt did a thoroughly good job, and was an important and valued member of the team, but he is not a decorated war hero.

I spent thirty-eight years as a regular soldier but all I know about the Second World War, and my opinions on it, are based not on personal experience but on reading and listening to accounts by those who were there; from trawling though reports written by friend and foe at the time and from looking at the ground and assessing what options might have been open to commanders on the day. I was born when the Battle of Stalingrad was in full swing and six weeks before Alamein, and I have no memories of the war except of relatives and neighbours showing me what I now know to have been looted German medals and badges; the sight of regular columns of men dressed in grey walking along the road (German prisoners of war, although I had no idea who they might be); and the ringing of church bells and great excitement – I was told it was for the end of the war, but I had no idea what a war was. Growing up in the late forties and early fifties I do remember rationing; that virtually every labourer wore an army greatcoat, and that everyone doing their gardening wore army boots to do it. I joined the army fifteen years after the war had ended, so warrant officers and senior NCOs, some captains and all majors and above wore war medals. The very fact that they had medals gave them great status in the eyes of we officer cadets and young officers, and it took me some considerable time to realise that war service did not necessarily imply great competence.

This book is the distillation of forty years of talking to people who fought in the Second War, and of reading memoirs, official histories and numerous documents in the National Archives. I have walked the ground of many, if not all, of the actions I relate, and where that has not been possible I have consulted those who have. I owe a huge debt of gratitude to the many historians who have shared their thoughts with me, or have been kind enough to offer criticisms of my own arguments, to the ever-patient staffs of the National Archives and the Prince Consort's Library and to Miss Elizabeth Selby of the Photographic Archive of the Imperial War Museum in London. Ted Rawes and Arnold Harvey have pointed me in some dark and fascinating corners, and Brian Nicholls has been kind enough to share his encyclopaedic knowledge of animal transport. I have been particularly fortunate in being given access to the unpublished research of an international team of four extraordinary men: Mr C. H. Whistler CBE, lately Head of the British Council and Cultural Councillor in Her Britannic Majesty's embassy in Brussels and wartime officer in British Naval Intelligence; Major Michael Archer MC, late of the Buffs and veteran of the Battle of France in 1940; Géneral de Corps d'Armée (lieutenant general) Jean Robert of the French army and lately Commandant of the Cavalry School at Samur, and Generalmajor (brigadier) Jan Christian of the German army, lately of NATO headquarters in Copenhagen, and as a Hauptmann (captain) commander of an anti-tank company in Rommel's 7 Panzer Division in 1940. These four, coordinated by Claude Whistler, who also translated the French and German documents into English, set out to investigate the background to the astonishing lightning victory of the German army and air force in the Battle of France. I have made much use of their deliberations, although the conclusions (and any errors) are mine. I must particularly thank Dr Mark Connelly of the University of Kent, who represents all that is best in the modern academic school of War Studies, and who has been kind enough to fill the role of sounding board and critic, usually over some very good lunches. As always, Ian Drury, Barry Holmes, my editor John Gilbert, and all the staff of Weidenfeld & Nicholson have been unfailingly supportive, as has my wife Imogen who has assisted me enormously in the production of the book.

Finally, for all my criticisms of the British war effort between 1939 and 1945, one must never forget that the German was always very hard to beat. From at least the time of the Great Elector, father of Frederick the Great of Prussia, until 1945, the German soldier was the best in Europe. His traditions stretched back to little Brandenburg, which if it could not fight would cease to exist, and came forward in time via Prussia, Britain's staunch ally for most of the Napoleonic Wars, to unification in 1870, and through two world wars. Germany lost those two world wars, but it was not due to incompetence by soldier, sailor or airman. One loves and prefers the company of the gentleman, but one has to respect the player.

NOTES

1. Martin Gilbert, *Winston S. Churchill, Vol. III*, Companion Volume Part 2, Documents May 1915 – December 1916, Heinemann, London, 1972.

2. The National Archives (henceforth TNA) Kew, WO/95/1215, War Diary 2 Grenadier Guards.

3. TNA Kew, WO/95/1772, War Diary 6 Royal Scot Fusiliers

1

Lessons Learned?

FOR WEEKS NOTHING very much had been happening along the front. German infantry peered through binoculars at French and British infantry peering back. Occasionally an aircraft would scoot rapidly into enemy territory and even more rapidly scoot back. Occasional raids would take place, desultory shelling by both sides killed a few of the unwary, and as usual the poor bloody infantry on both sides were firmly of the opinion that they were in for a long period of waiting.

And then, at 0420 hours, with an hour or so still to go before that first faint glimmer on the horizon that the army calls first light, all hell broke loose. As if as one, 620 artillery field guns opened fire, 200 of them laying down a creeping barrage and the rest seeking out enemy gun batteries, likely forming-up places and routes by which reinforcements might come, while nine divisions supported by 400 tanks erupted out of the mist. By the time it was light they had taken their first objectives and were streaming on, bypassing anything that looked like fighting a determined defence, leaving it to be mopped up by the follow-on units. Overhead 376 fighter aircraft engaged enemy infantry on the move, shot up vehicles and defensive positions, and kept the skies clear of enemy aircraft, while 147 bombers attacked enemy airstrips, railways and stores depots. Close up behind the infantry came the engineer bridging units, throwing temporary bridges across obstacles or repairing damaged ones to allow the artillery to advance. Motorised logistic units pressed ahead with resupply of ammunition, rations, petrol and all the paraphernalia needed to wage modern war, and behind them loaded railway trains awaited the order to move forward to restock mobile depots. All the while ambulance units stood ready to evacuate the wounded. By 1130 hours the tanks and their accompanying infantry had passed through their second set of objectives, and the pilots of the close-support aircraft could see small groups of infantry using fire and movement to close with the enemy, and then move on, with long columns of prisoners trailing back towards the 'cages' already prepared for them. As the lead battalions and brigades became exhausted, fresh troops were fed through them and the seemingly unstoppable advance continued, with the defenders now disorganised and ready to break. By last light the attack had secured all its objectives for that day, had taken 36,000 prisoners of war, 634 artillery pieces and innumerable machine guns and other war-making equipment.

It was a staggering and overwhelming success, mounted in great secret with assault troops moved up by night under strict radio silence, with all civilians moved out of the area, and all orders disseminated on a strict 'need to know' basis, with a minimum of written instructions. Blitzkrieg had arrived.

But this picture is not of the Battle of France 1940, nor a description of German panzers driving through French and British defences like the proverbial hot knife through butter.[*] Rather, it took place on 8 August 1918 when General Sir Henry Rawlinson's Fourth British Army initiated the Battle of Amiens, the first of the great Allied offensives that would win the First World War.

Of course nobody called it Blitzkrieg then, and the Germans didn't call it Blitzkrieg in 1940: that nickname was invented by the Allied press, but there was nothing particularly magical about it. Blitzkrieg was simply the coordination of all arms: the combination of infantry, armour, engineers, artillery and the air to produce shock on the battlefield. The aim of Blitzkrieg was not merely to kill enemy soldiers (although of

---

[*] The Americans have a much more colourful expression, 'like shit through a goose'. For those who cannot see the analogy, may I suggest observing geese?

course it did) but to catch the enemy off-balance – get inside his decision-making cycle, get him on the back foot and keep him there. It was what we today call manoeuvre warfare. It was the British who invented Blitzkrieg, but the defeated enemy who took the lessons away and remembered them, refined them, trained in them and applied them. By 1940 what the Germans practised in the Battle of France was nothing new; they were simply using principles that the British and the French knew perfectly well: the difference is that the Germans had made themselves significantly better at putting them into practice.

In 1918 it was the British army which was the cutting edge of the Allied offensives that led to victory in November. The French army was worn out, still fragile from its mutinies of 1917, and incapable of displaying the élan and the offensive spirit *à l'outrance* that had characterised it in 1914; the Americans were inexperienced and still going through the learning process that the British had begun on the Somme two years before. The British army of 1918 was not, of course, anything like the army of 1914. It had metamorphosed from a small, long-term regular force made up of volunteer professionals into the first citizen army that the British had had since the Civil Wars. It had been a long, hard haul, first undertaken by the old regular battalions which after Mons, First Marne, the Aisne, Ypres and the battles of 1915 culminating at Loos, had little regular about them save for their standards and battle honours. It continued with the arrival of the Territorial Force, originally never intended to reinforce the field army, but rather to release it by replacing regular units in the UK and in other relatively peaceful stations. To these were added the fiercely patriotic New Armies, and finally the conscripts from 1916. The original BEF had been a superb organisation, man for man by far the better of any ally or enemy; but it was tiny, and performed the role that has always been that of the British regular army: to hold the barbarian at the gate until the nation mobilises its resources. Once the unprecedented expansion of the BEF began, standards inevitably fell, and the nadir of the British army was probably on the Somme, when under-trained and totally inexperienced New Army battalions were thrown against defence lines that had been eighteen months in the making. In a nation that relies on a small regular army and then has to expand massively in war, huge casualties are inevitable while that army learns its trade, and there will always be a Somme (or, as we shall see, a Normandy). That is the price for being a power that matters in the world, and there is no easy way round it. The British army learned from the Somme, however, and next year, beginning in the Battles of Arras, those lessons were put into practice. The Battle of Third Ypres in 1917 would have seen off any other army in the world, but the British came through it stronger and with morale undamaged.

By the end of the war the British army was the most technologically advanced fighting machine on land anywhere. The British had invented the tank, and by 1918 they were very good at using it; they had promoted and developed military aviation when those great innovators, the Americans, who invented powered flight in the first place, dismissed flying as nothing more than a circus attraction, and by 1918 the British had the world's only independent air force. They were front-runners in the development of military communications, artillery methods and military medicine, and they still had by far the largest and most powerful navy.

As with any great undertaking, governments and military leaders sought to extract the lessons from 1914–18. What had gone well, and why; what had not gone well and might be improved next time, and what might be done to prepare for the next great struggle, should it come. Britain, at war for so much of her history, had never fought a high-intensity conflict before. Traditionally, she waged war with her navy, using blockade and intervention, a largely maritime strategy that saw the army as a missile to be fired by the navy, which could put soldiers on land anywhere there was a coastline, and take them off again to fight another day. In the Great War, for the first time, she found herself fighting the main enemy in the main theatre for the whole of the war, and she found that the Asquithian 'business as usual' methods of waging war simply would not work. As the war went on Britain found that increasingly government had to intervene in all sorts of fields that before the war would never have been considered any of government's business. Gradually, while not every aspect of national life necessarily ended up being run by government, the government almost certainly had an interest in it.

Total war may be defined as war in which the total resources of the nation – economic, industrial, demographic, military and political – are directed to one primary aim: the winning of that war. The Great War was the first total war in which Britain had ever engaged, and the methods needed to win it were drastic, authoritarian and only capable of being introduced gradually. It was all very un-British and certainly illiberal, but by the end of 1918 ministers, generals, civil servants and planners had a pretty good idea how to mobilise for total war, albeit they had arrived at that understanding by improvisation, trial and error, experimentation and forays down all manner of blind alleys.

One of the major lessons of the First War was the use, or misuse, of available manpower, and it was found that direction of manpower was necessary. Conscription for the services is the obvious example, but direction of labour was also necessary for industry; and industry had to be compelled to produce the goods needed for the war at a price that the country could afford. Alone among the powers of the Old World, Britain had never previously implemented conscription, which would have been seen as an unacceptable infringement of an Englishman's rights. When Asquith's government made the decision to deploy an army to Europe to fight beside the French, it was hoped that the necessary expansion could be undertaken by voluntary enlistment. The initial response to the call for men to fight for King and Country was overwhelming; the first hundred thousand enlisted within ten days of asking, the second by 28 August 1914 and the third by mid September. The trouble was that too many of these eager volunteers had left civilian jobs where they would have contributed far more to the war effort than by wielding a rifle and bayonet; and the munitions industries, already only large enough to provide for the relatively modest needs of peace with a bit over for export, began to lag even further behind in their efforts to equip the expanded army.

In an attempt to curb indiscriminate volunteering to the detriment of essential industries, from early in 1915 the government introduced the War Service Badge scheme, whereby those considered essential to the war effort in their civil occupations were given a badge, which protected them from white-feather profferers and importunate recruiters. It was not terribly successful, largely because the Admiralty handed them out to anyone who wanted one – 400,000 by July 1915 – while the War Office was more selective at 80,000. With the setting up of the Ministry of Munitions the two-tier badge scheme came to an end, and the ministry became the sole badge-awarding agency, but only to those working in the munitions industries. This too was open to abuse, and until a national register was drawn up, putting everyone into an occupation that could be classified as being essential or otherwise, the ministry could only rely on employers' views of who was and who was not an essential war worker.

By the end of 1915 the risk of losing essential workers to the services (overwhelmingly the army, as the navy was already far bigger than anyone else's) was outweighed by the stark fact that the weekly intake of recruits for the army was 30 per cent below that required. It now seemed that conscription into the services was inevitable, but, because of objections by trade unions,[*] one more chance was given to the system of voluntary recruitment. When this, too, proved incapable of reconciling the needs of the army with those of industry, the National Service Act was put into law in January 1916, and shortly afterwards all voluntary enlistment ceased.

It was hoped that this act would, with a national register and a schedule of protected employments, enable manpower to be made available for the army while still ensuring that essential industries could be manned. There were teething problems, principally over what was and what was not an industrial occupation essential to the war effort. For a while the government simply threw up its hands and passed to the trade unions the responsibility for deciding whether a man should be classified as being in a 'starred' (i.e. protected) trade or whether he could be taken by the army. This governmental opt-out fell apart in a very short time: to ask trade union leaders to take what might turn out to be life or death decisions affecting the men who had elected them to office as

---

* The unions had no great objections to compulsory service as such, but they had problems with the proposal that anyone who was in protected employment (such as a munitions worker) and then left that employment could not take another job for six weeks unless he had a certificate showing that the employer had consented to the worker leaving. This, said the unions, meant that an employer could decide whether or not a man was taken for the army.

their protectors against the wicked employers, was unreasonable and unworkable.

The system continued to be refined, and by the winter of 1917 the Ministry of Munitions was able to produce a Schedule of Protected Occupations, which provided a graded immunity for conscription according to age, trade and medical category. At the same time the various badges and certificates were replaced by exemption certificates. These certificates, however, could be withdrawn by simple administrative action, to satisfy the varying needs of the services and of industry; so to meet trade union concerns, local tribunals were established to hear appeals from workers, or employers, who felt that certificates had been wrongly withdrawn or wrongly granted. Medical examinations were instituted so that time was not wasted by decertifying a man unfit for military service. The system was now reasonably flexible. In August 1917 the Ministry of National Service was set up, with overall responsibility for the direction of manpower, and when at the end of the year it became obvious that the army would not get the number of recruits it needed, it was a relatively simple procedure for the ministry to raise the age of protection and make numbers of those previously exempt available for conscription. By 1918, and the passing of the Military Service Act that refined and embodied various separate acts and orders in council, the government was in a position to meet the needs of the army, despite the ever-increasing output of war materials – and the consequent need for skilled labour – from industry.

On the declaration of war in August 1914 the total manpower available to the army – regulars, reservists and Territorials – was 733,184.[*] By the end of 1914, less than five months after war had been declared, the strength of the army was 1,684,700, and thereafter:[1]

YEAR	MONTH	STRENGTH (all theatres)
1915	December	2,640,800
1916	December	3,397,100
1917	December	3,773,100
1918	November	3,759,500

[*]At least on paper. There was a limit as to what could be withdrawn from overseas garrisons, and much of the Territorial Force was not yet trained or equipped for war, or signed up for overseas service.

The varying systems, or lack of them, had at least managed to keep the army up to strength despite battle casualties, but it was clear, in reviewing the lessons of 1914–18, that such haphazard recruitment and manning procedures were not the best way to do it, and that plans should be in place for the introduction of conscription and a schedule of reserved/exempt/protected occupations as soon as war was declared, or even in the run-up to war.

Another lesson – drawn mainly from the Western Front – was that the impact of casualties in units, mainly infantry battalions, recruited from small or limited areas is far greater than if the same number of casualties are spread chronologically and geographically over the whole country. Territorial and 'Pals' battalions made up of men recruited from a few streets, the same factory, a couple of villages, had all the strengths that homogeneity of race, culture, language and tastes provided; they drank in the same pubs, went out with one another's sisters and supported the same football team. There was a strong sense of not letting down one's chums. The disadvantage, of course, was that when those battalions took casualties, they all happened at the same time and they all impacted upon the same area, producing the (erroneous) belief that Britain lost a generation in the First World War.

The solution was to adopt the American post-civil war system, where by deliberate policy regiments of infantry were drawn from right across the Union, rather than from a particular territorial area. It was all very well to recognise this, but the British infantry (and it was mainly the infantry that would be affected) were (and are) wedded to what they saw as the regimental system, with a high price being put on territorial loyalty and with a great reluctance to change cap badges. Conscripting men and posting them so that battalions would be composed of men drawn from across the nation might be logical and cost-effective, to say nothing of reducing the impact of heavy casualties, but it would be opposed by the regiments, and perhaps by the men themselves.

It was not just the allocation of manpower between industry and the armed services that would have to be addressed before the next war came along, but also how that portion of the population directed to industry should be treated and managed, and here too there were lessons to be learned from the Great War. It is easy to forget, in post-Thatcher Britain, that there was a time when industrial disputes were a regular occurrence, and when trade unions could hold governments to ransom. Strikes and associated action did not cease on the outbreak of war, although to be fair they did reduce. In 1913 a total of 9,800,000 working days were lost by industrial stoppages; in 1915 this dropped to 2,950,000, but by 1917 it was up to 5,650,000 days.[2] It may be thought rather odd that a soldier at the front could be sentenced to death for refusing to obey a lawful command, whereas a worker at home, probably paid more than the soldier, could go on strike without suffering any penalty – certainly a lot of soldiers thought so. Dictatorships rarely have to worry about keeping organised labour happy, but in a democracy, particularly in a democracy at war, labour has to be kept on side or it will not produce the goods needed at the front. Making all strikes illegal in 1914–18 would have been unenforceable, and unacceptable to the mass of the population, even if any political party could have been persuaded to try to get such a measure through the House.

If industrial disputes were to be prevented, or at least kept to a minimum, it was clear that government would have to control industry and employment in a way that had never been contemplated before. Pre-war wages and working conditions were a matter for negotiation between employees, via their unions if such existed, and employers, usually, although not always, at local level. When war broke out in August 1914 employers and trade unions declared an 'industrial peace' which agreed to leave outstanding differences in abeyance until after the war, and promised to try to find an amicable settlement to any new dispute. The difficulty was that the peace agreement had been negotiated on a national level, and trade union national executives had little or no control over local officials. This lack of grip by the centre, combined with a rise in the cost of living and rumours that employers were pocketing huge profits from war contracts, soon led to the collapse of the peace agreement and a strike over wages in that hot bed of workers' militancy, the Clyde. In defiance of national trade union leaders the Clyde strike went on for a month, and while a face-saving formula was eventually cobbled together to end it, local militants knew that they had the upper hand.

If the entire resources of the nation really were to be harnessed to the war effort, then many hallowed industrial practices – or malpractices – would have to be reformed. These ranged from job demarcation to wages to the resolution of disputes. Demarcation meant that only men classified as skilled were allowed to do skilled jobs. It was the unions that decided whether or not a job was skilled, and whether or not a man was qualified to do it. With the expansion in industry and the departure of workers who had volunteered for the army, there was a shortage of skilled men. Many of the jobs were not particularly skilled anyway, but any thought of bringing in semi-skilled men, or downgrading the jobs to unskilled, had to be negotiated with the trade unions. Again, the shortage of workers led to employers poaching men from other firms by offering higher wages or, when wages were brought under control, by bogus allowances. All this was happening against a background of a general rise in the cost of living, and if inflation was not to get out of hand then wages would have to be brought under control. In March 1915 the Treasury Agreement was signed between government and engineering and associated unions. Under the agreement the unions surrendered the right to strike in exchange for a system of arbitration and a promise that the government would limit employers' profits. Like the Peace Agreement before it, the Treasury Agreement fell apart because national executives could not control union officials and members at local level.

At last, in July 1915, the government moved to make strikes illegal by the Munitions of War Act. The act not only made it unlawful to strike but also introduced compulsory arbitration and a control on wages. It only applied, however, to munitions factories, and not to other fields – such as coal mining – which could directly affect weapons production (no coal – no coke – no steel), although there was a provision for strikes in those other industries to be brought under the act by royal proclamation, should it be considered that such secondary action affected the war effort. Two weeks after the act came on to the statute book, 200,000 miners in South Wales went on strike, and that strike was declared illegal by proclamation.

While it is true that there were one or two politicians – and not a few soldiers[*] – who would have quite liked to send a battalion or two into Wales to show the miners the error of their ways, this was hardly an option at this stage of the war, and would anyway have been counter-productive. The strike was settled, but not before the government was shown to be all but toothless as far as stopping mass strikes was concerned. There were other strikes, and the lesson that came out of those was that attempting to make strikes illegal was simply not enforceable, short of resorting to methods of coercion that we purported to deplore when employed by our enemies. Compulsory arbitration, however, was useful, as even if it failed to resolve strikes it did settle many disagreements that could have led to strikes, and was an instrument that could be redeployed for another war.

Like strike control, wages control was another desirable power that the government was never really able to exert. It tried, and had some influence over pay awards, but was never able to institute the widespread controls on wages, and hence inflation, that it would have wished. The conclusion was that wage control was a good thing, and should be attempted, but exactly how that could be done was another matter.

Perhaps the most extraordinary piece of legislation ever to be passed by a British government – and a Liberal government at that – was the Defence of the Realm Act (DORA), by which the government conferred upon itself powers that in a later age the Gestapo would rather like to have. Originally intended to deal with spies and traitors, DORA authorised trial by court martial for any person whose actions were deemed to jeopardise the success of His Majesty's forces or to assist the enemy. Fair enough, one might think, although why a court martial – with exactly the same rules of evidence and a rather greater reluctance to convict – should be chosen rather than the well-established civil courts is a mystery. Soon DORA's tentacles spread wider, and on 28 August 1914 it became an offence under the act 'to spread reports likely to cause disaffection or alarm': note the absence of the word 'untrue' before 'reports'. DORA

*There was a belief in the army that the Welsh were not joining. In fact by 1918 21.52 per cent of the male population of Wales had enlisted, voluntarily or by conscription, compared with 24.02 per cent in England. Some of that (not huge) discrepancy will be explained by the large numbers of Welsh miners exempt from conscription.

was of course a marvellous instrument for social control, and as ordinary crime decreased so she was used more and more.[3] Demonstrations likely to cause undue demands on local police forces, failing to observe the blackout,[*] lighting bonfires or having pigeons without a permit (which might be signalling to the enemy), throwing rice at weddings and selling jam tarts on a sugar-free day (hindering the war effort by wasting food), and infecting a soldier with venereal disease were all offences punishable under DORA. More drastic were the rights to detain suspects without charge, to search without warrant, to remove from any area any person deemed hazardous to the war effort and forbid that person's return. The act also allowed the revocation of British naturalisation by erstwhile citizens of an enemy power, and the detention of enemy aliens. All in all, DORA was an excellent weapon in the government's armoury, and one that would be wheeled out again in 1939.

While various government departments set up all sorts of committees and subcommittees to examine how they might prosecute the next war by learning from the last, the armed services were doing the same. The difference was that civil servants and politicians could not be seen to be taking the likelihood of war for granted – which might turn out to a self-fulfilling prophesy – whereas the soldiers and sailors and airmen were paid to prepare for war, or at least to draw up theoretical plans for it, and if they did not seriously consider the lessons from the last war they would be considered to have failed in their duty.

The army, and to a lesser extent the navy and the air force,[**] began to assimilate lessons from the Great War within days of any particular action. The change in the army between 1914 and 1918 was not just an increase in the numbers and the social composition of its manpower, but also the development of its tactics based on what had gone before. Training directives and manuals were constantly updated to reflect

---

* There was a quite unnecessary panic reaction to raids on the British mainland by Zeppelin airships and Gotha bombers, resulting in the imposition of a blackout. As a rehearsal for the Second War, however, when it was needed, it was useful.

** To a lesser extent because once the Royal Navy had chased off or sunk German commerce raiders, and had established its blockade of Germany, there were few naval engagements of note, so that the vital contribution of the navy to the defeat of Germany and her allies is often overlooked. New problems for the navy were, of course, posed by aircraft and submarines.

experience, and this process continued in the inter-war years, with doctrine amended to take into account government policy, the latest technology and the perceived threat.

Mindful of the distrust and intrigue that had marred civil/military relations between 1914 and 1918, the army wanted it recognised that the government must have confidence in its generals. Changing the Chief of the Imperial General Staff, the professional head of the army, and sending most of his staff to the front in 1914, thus having only a second eleven to provide central direction of the conduct of the whole war, had been very damaging. In a reference to the difficulties caused by having the Mesopotamian campaign directed by the Indian government rather than from Whitehall, one report[4] insisted that central direction of the war was essential, and recommended the formation of a national government, to coincide with the beginning of mobilisation, in order that the whole nation could devote its resources to the prosecution of the war, regardless of political affiliations. In view of the possibility of air attacks on London, the seat of government should be moved north as soon as mobilisation was ordered.

Most military thinkers realised that the days of trying to fight a major war with an entirely voluntary system of recruitment were over. Noting that the British army had never been large enough to finish any war quickly, they recognised – as had the government – that direction of manpower would be necessary to ensure that the needs of both the armed forces and industry could be met. Large numbers of potential officers had been killed in 1914–15, having been allowed to enlist as private soldiers in the New Armies, rather than having their quality recognised early on and diverting them into officer-training units; and only direction of manpower right from the beginning could prevent this happening again. The syllabuses of the Officer Training Corps in schools and universities[*] were questioned, as not being as up-to-date as they should be, and not interesting enough to attract and

---

[*] Today OTCs still exist at many universities. The school version is now the Combined Cadet Force. The CCF, along with the Army Cadet Force (based territorially) are officially youth organisations which happen to be sponsored by the Services, but in fact are a major source of recruiting officers (from the CCF) and other ranks (from the ACF).

train the large numbers that would be needed in a future major war.

Considerable discussion, at all levels of the army, was devoted to tactical lessons that might be applicable to a future war. Accepting that the size of the British army necessitated its being a rapier rather than a bludgeon, much thought was given to the achievement of surprise, which had been very difficult in the last war, particularly on the Western Front. Smoke, use of ground, operating by night and deception operations were all considered, and as late as 1932 the army was regretting 'losing the invaluable help of gas'.[5]

It is often forgotten that while it was the Germans who initiated the use of gas as a weapon, in 1915, and suffered the opprobrium of so doing, it was the British who became the experts in its use and reaped what military advantage there was to be had from it. Gas warfare escalated from chlorine to phosgene and its variants to mustard gas between 1915 and 1918, but the British always waited until the Germans took the next step up and then replied with their own, rather better, version. With improved means of delivery and vastly superior protection, the British became masters of chemical warfare, and in looking to a future war the military would dearly have loved to compensate for numerical weakness by the employment of this relatively inexpensive weapon, particularly as Germany – by 1933 the most likely enemy – was forbidden by the Versailles Treaty from manufacturing or possessing chemical weapons. As it was, the British government held to the provisions of the Hague Convention of 1907 and the Geneva Convention of 1929, and eschewed the offensive use of chemical warfare. In the event, although all belligerents in the Second World War did stockpile gas and developed detection and protection capabilities, in the west only Soviet Russia had an admitted offensive capability at the outset, which she did not use. In Germany Hitler forbade the use of gas offensively, although development took place, but one can only assume that the failure of Russia to use it in 1941–2 was due to the fear of retaliation.

Any soldier who had been anywhere near the Western Front understood the importance of firepower, particularly artillery, as the only way to reduce an enemy's ability to resist if surprise could not be achieved, and as an essential adjunct if it could. Interestingly, the Kirke Report of

1932 thought that the solution was either to increase the amount of artillery, or to augment the number of armoured fighting vehicles, or to improve mobility of the infantry, or to provide the infantry with its own covering fire in the form of mortars. What it should have said, of course, was that all those were needed, but post-war underfunding and constant pressure to save money had made generals reluctant to ask for anything that smacked of extravagance. Experience had shown that the shrapnel shell was of little use in modern war and should be replaced by high explosive, and there was a general recognition that firepower saved lives.

Even those generals (most) opposed to peacetime conscription (most) recognised that a professional army, such as the British, ran the risk of not being in touch with up-to-date scientific thought, something that would not be the case in a conscript force where all sections of society were represented. Thinking generals (again, most) were keen that developments in technology should be harnessed for military purposes, and they particularly favoured the extended use of armoured fighting vehicles because these could provide firepower without elaborate fire plans (they could not, but the idea was sound). One view, however, held that any expansion of the tank arm should wait until the outbreak of war, on the grounds that technology was forever changing, and improvements in design were coming along almost daily (one can see the hand of the Treasury in that one!). All-arms cooperation had been the basis of the BEF's success in 1918, and most soldiers saw that as something to be continued and developed. The concept of armoured infantry – infantry carried in its own integral armoured vehicles – was being talked about forty years before it became a reality, and there were suggestions that the only way to avoid the exhaustion which had often prevented initial success being exploited was to have strong reserves of all arms, including mechanised artillery, tanks and lorry-borne infantry, ready to pass through and drive deep into enemy territory.

Another avenue examined was one that has been trodden by soldiers since – and doubtless before – the time of Julius Caesar to the present day: the load carried by the infantryman. An infantry soldier must perforce be like a snail, and carry his house with him. He need not, however, move at the same speed as the snail, and armies have always sought to lighten the load on the man's back in order to enable him to move farther and faster, and to enable him to arrive on the objective fit to fight. The difficulty has always been that as one particular item is made lighter, or is superseded as unnecessary, something else comes along that has to be carried. The total weight carried by the average infantryman has thus remained very much the same for at least two thousand years, albeit that he carries different items which are better distributed about his body and that he is much more comfortable than his predecessor. It is probable that the infantryman will always carry around 60 lbs weight, as this is the load that can be carried by the average man without undue discomfort. He will become ever more effective with what he carries, however, as individual items become lighter, thus allowing him to be given yet another piece of kit deemed useful.

A good example is field service clothing. The British were the first to introduce a uniform that was practical for wear in the field and which provided the soldier with a measure of camouflage – khaki service dress. This, with some modification, remained in use for a century and a half until replaced by a dark green combat suit, followed by a disruptive pattern combat suit, and then (in 1998) by a layered system which catered for extremes of climate. Each piece of clothing is lighter, but there are more items, so the overall weight stays the same. The soldier of the Great War had a semi-waterproof groundsheet and a blanket issued for sleeping purposes – a system that remained unchanged until the 1980s when sleeping bags came along, shortly followed by the Goretex revolution.[*] The soldier now carried a sleeping bag, a liner and a 'bivvie bag' (a small individual tent), far more than his single blanket and groundsheet, but the weight stayed the same. Much the same applied to ammunition – the 7.62mm Self Loading Rifle was replaced by the 5.56mm SA80; ammunition was far lighter so much more could be carried – again the total weight was unchanged.

Inevitably the army looked at organisations post-1918, and as the

---

[*] Considered by this author to be the greatest advance in warfare since the invention of gunpowder, Goretex, like Hoover, gave what was a trade name to the whole field. Goretex is a man-made combination of fibres which is waterproof, keeps you warm, allows moisture to escape (which no previous waterproof did) and is light, comfortable to wear and takes up little space. Jackets, trousers, boot liners, gloves, bivvie bags all came to be made from Goretex.

machine gun had been proved to be a major support weapon both in attack and defence, there were many opinions on how it should be employed. In 1914 each infantry battalion had its own integral machine-gun section of two medium guns (Maxim, followed by Vickers-Maxim followed by Vickers, essentially the same gun with modifications). In late 1915 battalion medium guns were withdrawn and the Machine-Gun Corps was formed, thus enabling these assets to be concentrated and used more effectively, on the German model. As part of the post-war reductions, the Machine-Gun Corps was disbanded and the guns went back to infantry battalions. Many soldiers felt that this did not offer the fire support wanted, and while rejecting a return to the Machine-Gun Corps, advocated the conversion of some infantry battalions into machine-gun battalions, on the scale of one per division. Similarly, while expansion of the tank arm was being recommended, so it was recognised that infantry battalions would need some form of anti-tank weapon.

Communications, very much a problem in the Great War, came in for much study after it. This subject went hand-in-hand with command and control, because in order to influence the battle commanders had to know what was happening, which meant being able to receive information in real time, not hours or days after the event. Until the advent of modern artillery, machine guns and barbed wire, a commander could sit upon his horse and be able to see pretty well the whole battle area. He knew what was going on and could send his gallopers, his aides-de-camp and his runners to tell subordinate commanders what to do next. He could keep his reserves close up, to be deployed at the critical moment, to take advantage of an unforeseen opportunity, to reinforce success or to avert disaster. By 1914 technology had forced dispersion on the battlefield and those likely to influence the battle could no longer see what was going on. For information they relied on communication by telephone, runner, galloper, pigeon, flags and flashing lights – some, or even all, of which might work in static defence positions, but which were inevitably subject to long delays or even complete breakdown when the troops attempted to manoeuvre.

The army recognised the need for reliable communications, but, perhaps surprisingly, not all were sold on wider use of radio, or W/T (wireless transmission) as it was then known. Radio did exist, and by 1918 each division had one, but long before the invention of the transistor and the printed circuit these were huge, fragile and far from portable. While it was accepted that portable and reliably soldier-proof radios would eventually be produced, and some advocated that all communications forward of brigade headquarters should be by radio once such sets became available, there were others who thought that these might be jammed by more powerful enemy devices. In 1932 the Kirke Report made a quite startling suggestion for the time. Pointing out that if enemy jamming, or the simple failure of radios to work, were likely, then there were only two options. One was to revert to the wartime system of rigid plans which laid down in great detail exactly what everyone had to do in all given circumstances, with all the disadvantages that entailed, while the other was to issue broad directives, give complete discretion to junior commanders and let them get on with it. This latter was what the German army called *auftragstaktik*, which would enable them to run rings round the British and French in the Battle of France in 1940 and which the British would belatedly adopt as Mission Command and then Manoeuvre Warfare long after the Second World War was over and (almost) forgotten.

The fighting on the Western Front had convinced most who had experienced it that horsed cavalry could not operate against machine guns and barbed wire. The British, as a result of their experience in South Africa, had recognised this long before the French or the Germans did, and thus British and Indian cavalry on the Western Front was in practice if not in name mounted infantry, equipped with the same rifle (as opposed to an inferior carbine) as the infantry. In the immediate post-war years there were those who considered that the march of technology had now left no role for cavalry in battle against a sophisticated enemy, but even they had difficulty in finding an alternative. Everyone accepted a scenario where attacking forces had broken through enemy positions and fresh troops had to be moved rapidly up to exploit. As men could not march fast enough, and as the lorry had as yet little or no cross-country capability, and as armoured personnel carriers, while envisaged in theory, were considered to be beyond the peacetime budget, perhaps cavalry would still be needed. It was an argument that would continue throughout the inter-war years, and the proponents of a role for horsed cavalry were not all military dinosaurs baying at progress from their intellectual caves.

Prior to the outbreak of war in 1914 there had been no expectation that the army would expand to the size that actually became necessary. The army reserves existed to bring the regular army up to war establishment, while the Territorial Force would assume the defence of the United Kingdom and man some overseas garrisons to release regular units for the front. In the event, Lord Kitchener, appointed Minister for War at the outbreak, realised that existing arrangements could not produce the mass armies that would be needed, and raised the New Armies, battalions of existing regular regiments manned by voluntary enlistment. As we have seen, this had great advantages but also serious weaknesses, and the general view of the army was that in a future war the second line should be the Territorial Force, renamed the Territorial Army, with such legal changes as would be needed to allow it to be deployed overseas. As the standards and experiences of Territorial soldiers would inevitably lag behind those of the regulars, it was intended to bolster such units with regular officers and men rotating through them, with Territorials being given the option of occasional service with regular units. Expansion beyond the existing strength of the Territorial Army would be achieved by units splitting in two, thus retaining at least some experience in the newly created battalions or regiments.

The Royal Navy had found the Great War less traumatic than had the army. For centuries Britain's defence had been her navy, and while the very existence of European powers depended on the possession of an army, Britain without one might have had to give up her Empire, but would still have endured as a nation. The roles of the Royal Navy in the Great War were those that had directed its activities since at least the reign of Elizabeth I: the defence of the homeland (and now of the Empire); the preservation of the freedom of the seas for British trade; the delivery of the British army to, and its removal from, theatres of operations; the blockade of enemy coastlines; and the prevention of enemy fleets from doing any of these.

From 1914 to 1918 the Royal Navy had performed those tasks

admirably. The blockade was in place from the outset, and by preventing Germany from importing food and raw materials it contributed greatly to her inability to continue the war beyond 1918. It was the Royal Navy which ensured that it was the Allies and not the Germans who could take advantage of the slack in American industrial capacity, and the Royal Navy that made it possible for the American army to have one million men in Europe by the end of 1917. In the only major fleet-on-fleet naval battle of the war, Jutland on 31 May 1916,[*] the British Grand Fleet lost more ships and more men than the German High Seas Fleet; but next day the Grand Fleet was ready for action, whereas the High Seas Fleet had fled back to port and never came out again.

There was less public scrutiny of naval affairs after the war, partly because pre-war the Royal Navy had been maintained to the two-power standard – at least as big as the two next largest navies combined – and did not have to manage a massive expansion into a citizen force; partly because naval casualties did not attract headlines in the way the Somme or Third Ypres did for the army; and partly because the Royal Navy was generally considered to have done all that it was asked to do, and out of sight at that. The muted mutterings of the cognoscenti as to why there had not been an annihilation of the German fleet at Jutland; the occasional remonstrance from the mayor of a seaside town subject to German shelling; and the real threat to British imports in 1917 until the convoy system was instituted, went largely unnoticed. There were, however, two major fields of naval warfare where there were lessons to be learned, and in which the Royal Navy took a great interest: aviation and submarines.

The Royal Navy had been interested in aviation since the inception of powered flight. It was the first navy to establish an air branch, when in 1909 the naval estimates included the sum of £35,000 for the purchase of airships. At first the navy was interested in aircraft as being able to act as the eyes of the fleet, looking well beyond the horizon to give warning of the presence of enemy vessels. As dirigibles gave way to fixed-wing machines, larger naval vessels carried one or two seaplanes, and HMS

---

[*] In this huge naval battle, in which 265 warships took part, the combined death total was only around 3,500. The entire Royal Navy death toll for the whole of the First World War was 32,000, or less than 5 per cent of total British deaths.

Ark Royal became the navy's first seaplane carrier. These aircraft were winched over the side and the pilot took off from the sea, landing alongside to be winched inboard again when his sortie was complete. The problem with seaplanes, which instead of wheels had floats enabling them to land on water, was that to winch them into and out of the sea the ship had to stop – making it a target for submarines – and they could not achieve the altitude necessary to take on the huge German Zeppelin airships, which not only acted as scouts for German naval forces but also on occasion bombed the British mainland. The answer was to use fighter aircraft; but while a fighter could be launched from a makeshift platform on a cruiser or a battleship, given a bit of luck, it could not land back on, and so had eventually to crash-land in the sea, from which the aircraft and its pilot might or might not be recovered by the mother ship.

The first aircraft carrier converted for aircraft landings, as well as take-offs, was HMS *Furious,* which joined the fleet in the summer of 1917. On 2 August 1917 Lieutenant Commander E. H. Dunning RN became the first pilot to land successfully on *Furious,* and indeed the first to land on any ship at sea, and although he managed to kill himself when trying to repeat the operation a few days later, the concept was sound. In July 1918 a modified *Furious* launched seven Sopwith Camels to attack airship sheds in northern Germany. They destroyed two airships and returned safely to the mother ship. By the end of the war Britain had two aircraft carriers in service and plans for more. The battleship was still the capital ship of the fleet, but many sailors began to wonder whether the dreadnought might not now be superseded by the aircraft carrier.

The other major innovation to affect war at sea was the submarine. The Royal Navy commissioned its first submarines in 1902, and the Imperial German Navy in 1906. Originally seen as coastal defence vessels, improvements in engines and batteries allowed submarines to become truly ocean-going, and with the addition of an effective torpedo powered by a compressed air engine, equally capable of offensive action. In 1914 the Royal Navy saw the role of the submarine as being in conjunction with the surface fleet, its main task that of reconnaissance. As the war went on, this changed. British submarines that penetrated the Dardanelles and got into the Sea of Marmora achieved results out of all proportion to numbers and cost; but it was in the Atlantic that submarine warfare reached an intensity that, for a brief period, threatened Britain's ability to continue the war.

One of the reasons for Britain entering the war in 1914 was German insistence on developing a blue-water fleet. Because Germany had no overseas colonies of note, and was not dependent upon imports from abroad, as Britain was, there could only be one reason for her to develop a navy, and that was to take on Britain. Although by 1914 Germany had the world's second largest navy it was still considerably inferior to Britain's, and German admirals knew that it could not directly challenge the Royal Navy. If Germany could not command the seas on the surface, she might, however, be able to achieve much below it, and with a total of twenty-four submarines at the beginning of 1914, she built another fifteen that year and eventually disposed of 140 by 1917. Of all the Allied and neutral shipping sunk by Germany during the war, 88 per cent was sunk by sub-marines, rather than by surface craft, mines and aircraft. Eventually the British overcame the U-boat menace by instituting the convoy system, which had worked against surface raiders in the Napoleonic wars. The lesson for the future was there to be noted: a hugely expensive surface warship could be sunk by a torpedo costing relative pennies, and a nation that relied for survival on command of the seas could not ignore the submarine threat.

On 1 April 1918 the Royal Flying Corps and the Royal Naval Air Service merged to become the Royal Air Force, the third of Britain's fighting services and the world's first independent air force. Not everyone wanted that to happen: Major General (later Marshal of the Royal Air Force Viscount) Sir Hugh Trenchard, commanding the Royal Flying Corps in France, thought it 'quite unsound', as did Field Marshal Haig, otherwise a staunch advocate of military aviation.[6] The reasons for forming the RAF were as much political as military: Prime Minister Lloyd George saw hiving-off military aviation into a separate service as a way to diminish the power of the Commander-in-Chief of the BEF, and Lloyd George was no friend of Haig's.

Despite the political chicanery that surrounded the formation of the RAF, there were very sound reasons for taking aviation away from the army and the navy and putting it into a separate independent service. It had originally been intended that the Royal Flying Corps, founded in 1912, would be an inter-service organisation, with army and naval pilots and crew. It would provide aviation support wherever and however needed, and while for convenience it would be administered by the army, its loyalties would be to its function, divorced from petty inter-service rivalry. Inevitably, perhaps, this was not to be. When the role of aircraft was seen as reconnaissance it worked well enough, but as the capabilities of aircraft expanded, and with the Royal Navy forming its own Royal Naval Air Service in 1914, very much egged on and enthusiastically supervised by the First Lord, Winston Churchill, there was increasing competition between the army and the navy for aircraft, engines and spares.

For most of the war the British managed to maintain at least air parity, and often air superiority, more by aggression in taking the action to the Germans, than because British aircraft were better – often they were not.[*] As the war continued, tasks came to be identified that could be discharged by aircraft but which were not necessarily of direct interest to either of the two services. An example was the air defence of Great Britain. The possibility of death and destruction being delivered from the skies had been recognised, and in 1915 Admiral Lord Fisher, the First Sea Lord,[**] had produced a paper that was seen as alarmist but was in fact merely twenty-five years ahead of its time, in which he suggested the possibility of a ton of high explosive being dropped from an aircraft on to Horse Guards Parade, killing all manner of generals, civil servants and politicians.[7] In the summer of 1917 German bombers raided London and while little damage was done and only a few killed, there was widespread panic

---

[*] This might be a convenient opportunity to dispose of the old canard that British pilots were not issued with parachutes in case they were thus encouraged to bale out. It is true that in the early days of military flying parachutes were not issued, because the aircraft had neither the lift capacity nor the space in the cockpit for anything other than the pilot, and at the heights and speeds flown it was usually safer to crash with the plane than bale out. Once aircraft could carry more weight, were roomier and could reach greater altitudes, parachutes were issued, as they always had been for balloon crews.

[**] For those who have not been lucky enough in the DNA lottery to have had the benefit of a British upbringing, the political head of the navy – the navy minister anywhere else – is the First Lord of the Admiralty, who may be a lord but often is not. The professional head of the navy – the chief of naval staff anywhere else – is the First Sea Lord, who is rarely a lord when he starts the job, but often is when he ends it. It is not the intention of this book to explain the laws of cricket and it will attempt to keep well clear of the regimental system.

and demands that 'something must be done'. Two squadrons of the RFC
were detached from the Western Front, one stationed near Canterbury
and the other at Calais, to defend London, while the RNAS was given
responsibility for the air defence of the rest of the kingdom. No more
raids occurred, until the RFC squadrons were recalled to their primary
duty of waging war against the German army, when the weather
improved and another raid took place. Consideration was given to retal-
iatory raids against German cities, and although this was decided against
on the grounds that it would only provoke the Germans and that there
were not sufficient aircraft anyway, it was certainly seen as a possibility
for the future and something that could be embarked upon independently of the army or the navy.

The government then set up an inquiry under General Smuts,[*] which
recommended that the RFC and the RNAS should be combined under
an Air Board, which in due course became the Air Ministry. After that an
independent air force was just a matter of time. The potential of air power
was clearly recognised, even if it was often exaggerated. The Smuts report
remarked:

> ...the day may not be far off when aerial operations, with their devastation
> of enemy lands and destruction of industrial and populous centres on a vast
> scale, may become the principal operations of war, to which the older forms
> of military and naval operations may become secondary and subordinate.

The lessons that airmen took away from the war were that protection
of the home base could no longer be the sole preserve of the Royal Navy,
and that air power could be wielded independently of the other two
services.

At the end of the greatest war in human history, the most intensive
that Britain had ever engaged in, it must have seemed that politicians,
administrators, soldiers, sailors and airmen had absorbed the lessons.
The need for the mobilisation of all the nation's resources from the
beginning, the requirement for government to control and direct

---

* Quite why a Boer lawyer, whose only military experience was as a guerrilla leader during the South
African War, and who failed to defeat much smaller German forces in German East Africa in the First War,
had so much influence over British policy in both world wars remains an intriguing mystery.

manpower and industrial output seemed clear and unquestionable. The military had learned the dangers of indiscriminate voluntary recruiting, absorbed the need for more firepower and an increase in the mobility of the infantry, seen the potential of the tank, and grasped the importance of communications. The navy bent its mind to the impact of aviation and the submarine on war at sea; while the newly created air marshals debated the air defence of the United Kingdom and the possibility of projecting power over distances never previously possible. Doctrinally at least, Britain was very well placed to fight the next war.

It was one thing to identify the lessons, and quite another to implement them.

NOTES

1. *Statistics of the Military Effort of the British Empire During the Great War,* The War Office, London, 1922.

2. H. M. D. Parker, *History of the Second World War–Manpower,* HMSO, London, 1957.

3. For a discussion of how crime rates in WWI fell, see Gerard J. DeGroot, *Blighty: British Society in the Era of The Great War,* Addison Wesley Longman, London, 1996.

4. *Report of the Committee on the Lessons of The Great War,* The War Office, London, October 1932, TNA WO33/1297.

5. Ibid.

6. Brigadier General H. E. Edmonds, *Military Operations France and Germany 1918, May–July,* War Office, London, 1939.

7. Cited in David Lloyd George, *War Memoirs Vol. II,* Odhams Press, London, 1936.

2

An Indecent Haste

'IT SHOULD BE ASSUMED, for framing revised estimates, that the British Empire will not be engaged in any great war during the next ten years, and that no expeditionary force is required for this purpose.' So announced the British cabinet on 15 August 1919, a cabinet that included that scourge of appeasers and standard-bearer for British military might, Winston S. Churchill, combining the posts of Secretary for War and Secretary for Air, and that scion of the conservative squirearchy, Walter Long, as First Lord of the Admiralty. The ten-year rule, extended year by year, was to govern British defence policy for the next thirteen years, and effectively prevented any meaningful military expansion, nor allowed any expenditure beyond immediate needs. By the time it was abandoned, in 1932, it was far too late.

A mere nine months before the adoption of the ten-year rule, Britain disposed of the mightiest, most technologically advanced and most capable military machine ever seen. It had soundly trounced the world's foremost military power on land, destroyed the remnants of one empire (the Ottoman) and made a major contribution to the disappearance of another (the Austro-Hungarian). It included the world's largest navy by far, and its only independent air force. Now it was to be dismantled just as soon as the men could be paid off and the ships, airplanes and tanks sold, scrapped or put into mothballs. The government could, said Prime Minister Lloyd George, take some risks in defence, but none in social and economic affairs.

At the end of the First World War the victorious British army, not including Empire and Dominion forces, fielded worldwide sixty-seven infantry divisions, or 804 battalions, and twenty-six battalions of tanks, supported by artillery, engineers, the Machine-Gun Corps and the logistics and communication units to back them up. The Royal Air Force deployed 155 operational squadrons, or about 1,800 aircraft, as well as those used for training in Canada (around 400) and those awaiting issue, in workshops being repaired or in the resupply chain. In addition there were the forces of the Empire, although of these only India could be expected to retain units of any significance in peacetime.

With the armistice in November 1918 and the eventual Versailles Treaty the following year, Britain began to divest herself of the trappings of war as quickly as she decently could. Residual obligations such as the partial occupation of Germany, military assistance to the White Russians and absorption of former Turkish and German colonies would have to be discharged, but otherwise there was a rush to get back to whatever passed for normal. The Prime Minister announced the end of conscription, without even discussing it with the CIGS, and much resentment was caused by the early release from the army of men needed in industry ahead of less qualified men who had been in the service longer. Whatever the lessons learned, not very much attention was paid to the possibility of another world war, and while sergeants major did not exactly find themselves unemployable except as crossing sweepers,[*] as they had following the wholesale reductions after Waterloo, Field Marshal Sir Douglas Haig (Commander-in-Chief of the British Expeditionary Force from December 1915 until April 1919) had to chivvy and threaten and bully to get the government to do anything for the welfare of disabled ex-servicemen.

Why would anyone want to consider the possibility of another war?

---

[*] Until the regrettable replacement of the horse by the internal combustion engine as the principal means of transport in towns, crossing sweepers took post on the pavement armed with a broom. Those who wished to cross the road paid a penny (or sixpence if very rich) for the crossing sweeper to ensure that they did not have to tread in horse droppings.

The German beast was safely caged, with restrictions as to the size and composition of her army, Alsace and Lorraine were French again and a demilitarised buffer zone between France and Germany was established. The aspirations of the remnants of the polyglot Austro-Hungarian Empire had been met, in so far as that was possible; there was an independent Poland, and Germany was going to pay for all the damage she had caused. Admittedly Bolshevik Russia was a concern, but even if Allied troops could not win the civil war for the Whites, Russia was far too riven by her own internal problems to pose any threat to Britain or France. In any case, collective security was the new flavour, and the newly established League of Nations would preserve world peace at little cost to anyone.

All this was nonsense, but it is the sort of thing that politicians like. After all, they only have to think as far as the next election, and money saved on defence can be used to bribe the electorate. Should they be caught out when a requirement actually to use military force comes along, then they can always blame the admirals, the generals and the air marshals for their lack of preparedness. It is akin to not bothering to insure one's motor car against accident or one's home against burglary, in the pious hope that it will never happen. The continually extending ten-year rule was a clever ploy to stop the professional warmongers badgering the government for more money for defence.

It was now planned to reduce the army to 135 infantry battalions and two tank battalions, with commensurate reductions everywhere else. Of the infantry battalions, forty-five would be needed in India (along with eight regiments of horsed cavalry and no fewer than fifty-five batteries of field artillery),* twenty-seven in other theatres abroad (including the occupation force in Germany), and fifty-three in the United Kingdom. By 1922 it was government policy that, as the ten-year rule precluded any major war, the army need only be prepared for a minor conflict, and not in Europe. To meet that threat, one cavalry and five infantry divisions could be despatched, with the fourteen Territorial divisions as a second

* There was still a fixation about India that dated back to the Mutiny of 1857, despite the unquestioning loyalty shown by Indian troops in all theatres of war since. There was a tendency to maintain more British troops in India than were really needed (although as India paid for them, it was a way of keeping more British battalions in existence than might otherwise have been justified), and there was still a reluctance to put other than mountain artillery in Indian hands.

line if required. Lord Derby, Minister for War in Bonar Law's 1922–3 cabinet, conceded that while the chances of war in Europe were indeed 'remote', if it did occur Britain could provide one cavalry brigade and two infantry divisions after a fifteen-day mobilisation period – rather less than half her 1914 contribution.

Fifty-three infantry battalions at home (or considerably more than the thirty-six battalions worldwide in 2005) may seem a lot, but two divisions (or twenty-four battalions) were needed in Ireland until 1921, and in any case home-service battalions were used as drafting units to keep battalions stationed overseas up to strength. The Chief of the Imperial General Staff, Field Marshal Sir Henry Wilson, the professional head of the army, would have preferred to retain conscription at least until immediate post-war commitments – such as in Ireland and Russia – had been reduced to a manageable level, but politicians wanted to make a point by ending it as soon as hostilities ceased. Conscription in peacetime would not have been acceptable to a Britain that had traditionally relied for her defence on a powerful navy and an expeditionary army. Unlike European armies, Britain's had been professional and volunteer, except for the period 1916–18, during the most intense war in her history, and a wish to return to a small regular army was perfectly natural and cannot be faulted. What can be criticised, however, was the stated assumption that there was no need for an expeditionary force. There were sufficient troops in the United Kingdom to form one at least as large as that existing before the First War, which had given such a good account of itself in 1914, and although it would have cost a little more to create and maintain such a force, the extra expenditure would have been manageable. The permanent existence of an expeditionary force from 1919 or 1920 would not necessarily have allowed the deployment of larger numbers or better equipment in 1939, but it would have given the army something to hang its doctrinal hat on, something to train towards, and a real reason for existing. While such an expeditionary force would, like its First War predecessor, have had to be prepared to fight anywhere in the world, its existence would have stimulated professional debate and thought, and concentrated military minds on matters such as mechanisation and cooperation with aircraft, both of which had been well understood in 1918 but which thereafter were in danger of becoming the province of the military missionary and the iconoclast.

The intention to reduce the Tank Corps to but two battalions was seen by advocates of the tank as a disaster, but the Corps was lucky to survive at all. The tank was not the war-winning weapon that the British press claimed it was in 1916, although there were those who could see that it might well become such in the future. In the initial post-war euphoria it had been proposed to retain the Tank Corps at twenty battalions, until factors of cost and an uncertainty as to what the tank was actually for began to bite. It is often claimed that it was opposition by officers of horsed cavalry that inhibited tank development between the wars, but whereas there were undoubtedly some officers who wanted to 'get back to real soldiering', few really believed that cavalry had a major combat role on the modern battlefield, although until the reliability and cross-country performance of engine-powered vehicles improved it most certainly had a role in underdeveloped parts of the Empire and in liaison, reconnaissance and escort duties. The extreme Luddite view was typified by Major General Sir Louis Jackson, who in giving a talk entitled 'Possibilities for Future War' at a meeting at the Royal United Services Institution chaired by the Under Secretary for War, Lord Peel, said: 'The tank was a freak. The circumstances which gave rise to its existence were exceptional, and are not likely to reoccur. If they do, they can be dealt with by other means.'[1]

Jackson's view was not typical, and to be fair he pushed very hard for tracked transport as part of the supply services, but there was much genuine confusion as to where tanks fitted into the post-war army. Should they be in a separate corps, called upon for specific tasks; should they replace horsed cavalry and take on its roles; should they be mounted infantry; should they be part of the Royal Engineers?[*] Perhaps, thought some advocates of mechanisation, there should be two sorts of tank unit: one to act in direct support of the infantry, and one to act independently, as cavalry had. It was not until 1922 that the Tank Corps was finally established as a permanent arm of the service, and, in a rare example of an

---

[*] Before the advent of REME in 1942 there was a tendency to regard anything mechanical as lying in the province of the Royal Engineers.

increase in military assets, at four battalions rather than two. Some of the reasons for the survival of the Tank Corps were illusory: the army of occupation in Germany thought they were very good for overawing recalcitrant Germans; tanks, for example, had quelled civil disturbance in Silesia (and incidentally the Tank Corps, representing the British Army, had soundly thrashed the American Army of Occupation in an international military athletics meeting). Nearer home six tanks had managed to put down a riot in Glasgow in January 1919.* The Battle of Stalingrad is generally thought of as beginning in August 1942 and finishing with the surrender of the German Eighth Army in February 1943, but there was another battle for Stalingrad, then called Tsaritsin, on 1 July 1919, when a lone tank manned by seven British soldiers outflanked the defences, and drove into the town** as the spearhead of the White Russian General Deniken's offensive against the Bolsheviks. The Bolshevik defenders surrendered or fled, and the White Russian cavalry took 40,000 prisoners.

In the Middle East armoured cars provided mobility and firepower otherwise lacking since the demise of the Machine-Gun Corps. In a forerunner of what would, eventually, become standard tactics, in Iraq in 1921 Lieutenant Colonel George Lindsay kept a force of sixteen armoured cars in the field for three weeks, covering six hundred miles and supplied entirely by air. All communication was by radio, and aircraft were guided to the armoured force's position by radio. In a report, Lindsay advocated combined battle groups of aircraft, tanks, armoured cars, motor machine-gun units and trench mortars, adding as an afterthought that some infantry would also be needed to deal with obstacles. Shortly afterwards Lindsay was in dispute with a Colonel Alan Brooke, about the tactics that the latter was teaching at the Staff College. Lindsay accused Brooke of using tanks in 'penny packets', thus diluting their effectiveness, and in treating them as an appendage to artillery instead of using artillery to

---

* We would not now consider armoured vehicles as anything other than protection for troops on riot control duties, and there would be a reluctance to take them anywhere near crowds, but this author recalls a locally produced system whereby Ferret Scout Cars could be electrified. When surrounded by an angry mob the system was switched on with most gratifying results.

** This campaign was noted for incompetence and a reluctance to fight on both sides. The British were under strict instructions not to take part in the fighting but to confine themselves to training the Russians. The latter proved completely incapable of learning how to use tanks, and so the British tended to ignore orders and lead the armoured attacks themselves.

support penetration by the tanks. Brooke would be CIGS in the next war, and seems to have absorbed Lindsay's (absolutely correct) points about the employment of tanks.

While the influence of Liddell Hart on military thinking is much exaggerated (largely by Liddell Hart), he did, as early as 1919, advocate integrated infantry and armour units, with the infantry moving in armoured carriers.[2] He was forty years too early. Another proponent of armoured warfare, J. F. C. Fuller – known to his friends as 'Boney' because he was supposed to look like Napoleon – in a lecture at the RUSI in 1920 prophesied a fleet of ships landing amphibious tanks off the coastline of an enemy country. Ridiculed at the time, this was not all that different from what actually happened in June 1944. Fuller started life in the infantry, became a staff officer in the Tank Corps and did most of the planning for the Battle of Cambrai in 1917. An officer of great originality and intelligence, in his enthusiasm for the tank he rather tended to over-egg the pudding, making many enemies as he did so. He was retired as a major general in 1930 and never re-employed, although he continued to advocate the cause of the tank by lectures and writing. Nobody paid much attention to him in England – partly because, showing almost incredible political naivety, he joined Mosley's British Union of Fascists – but his views were studied in Germany, not least by Heinz Guderian, one of the fathers of the German panzer arm.[3]

In a logical world an army would decide what they wanted a tank for, and then design one to fit. The difficulty was that there were all sorts of conflicting views as to its function and likely specifications. Some very promising machines were proposed and prototypes produced. The Medium D, trialled in May 1919, had a sprung suspension, improved tracks that enabled it to drive rather than skid round corners,[*] and it could reach 20 mph. Even more – it could swim, propelling itself backwards and forwards across the River Stour in Hampshire, entering and exiting the water unaided. Unfortunately, although the idea worked, the engineering did not, and the Medium D suffered breakdowns too frequently to be put into production just yet. Another 'Light Infantry Tank' weighing seven

---

[*] Prior to that tank crews got their beasts round corners by applying the brake to one track and full power to the other.

tons could reach 30 mph, used far less fuel than any previous model and had an impressive swimming ability. Sadly, it too suffered from so many mechanical failures that it could not be issued. Again, a logical organisation would set up a programme of experimentation, try out all sorts of ideas, and decide which one worked and which did not. The British army is (usually) logical, but the Treasury is not, and at this time any money granted for a particular purpose (such as tank design) had to be spent in the financial year for which it was allocated, otherwise it reverted to the Treasury.[*] By 1921 the army had established a requirement for a tank to support mobile operations, but no tank was yet available. A tank designed by Vickers was looked at, and although not as good as the Light Infantry Tank produced by the Tank Corps' own designers, it was less liable to break down. Half a million pounds had been allocated for tank construction and the financial year was well advanced. Unless swift action was taken that money would be snaffled by the Treasury, and so Vickers was asked to produce an improved version of the machine that they had already demonstrated.

The Vickers Light Tank – later upgraded and designated the Vickers Medium Mark I – was not exactly what the Tank Corps wanted, but it was not a bad effort withal. It weighed twelve tons, had a crew of five, an official top speed of 15 mph (although Liddell Hart claimed to have clocked some doing 30 on roads) and its frontal armour was one-third of an inch thick. Its armament was one 3-pounder gun, four Hotchkiss machine guns in the turret, and two Vickers machine guns in the hull. It could travel for 150 miles without refuelling.[4] Significantly, it was the first tank ever to have a traversing turret (that is, while not able to revolve 360 degrees, it had some movement right and left), which improved enormously its ability to produce meaningful fire support. Stripped of its turret and armament, it was also used as a tractor, to pull medium artillery pieces, in which role it was named the *Dragon*.

All tanks are a compromise between firepower, protection and

---

[*] Although less rigid than it once was the system is still with us. This author recalls being accosted by worried quartermasters annually, usually about a month before the end of the financial year, with pleas to spend whatever was left in various budgets. We usually ended up buying something we didn't need, or getting some luxury which we had always wanted but could never afford.

mobility. The size of the main armament (the gun) decides the size of the turret (which must be big enough to allow the recoil), which in turn decides the size of the chassis. The size of the chassis and the amount of protection (armour) determine the weight of the tank and hence how powerful the engine must be to propel it at a particular speed. It is not possible to have a tank that combines great speed and manoeuvrability with enormous firepower and complete protection, but designers do the best they can. The Vickers engine was air-cooled, so that it could operate in tropical stations, and the large cooling fan absorbed a considerable proportion of the power output; the petrol tank was located in the fighting compartment (just below the turret) which offered a fair chance of the crew being roasted if the tank took a hit anywhere near the turret; its armour was thin, and the track mileage (the distance that could be travelled before the tracks needed replacement) was a problem. All in all, however, the Vickers was probably as near to the ideal compromise as could have been reached, given the technology of the time and the need for the tank to be in production immediately, without time for further study and development. It gave the Tank Corps and the army a tank that was an excellent stopgap; one that they could use to develop tactics and procedures. Moreover, as the first fast tank in service with any army, it would allow experimentation in the use of armour as the visionaries maintained it should be used – in wide sweeps, finding gaps in enemy defences, punching through enemy lines to exploit in rear areas, and as the vanguard of mobile war that would render obsolete the stagnation and siege conditions of the past.

Where the army, or rather the Treasury, got it badly wrong was in retaining the Vickers in service long after it had itself been rendered obsolete. It was still in front-line service in 1938, by which time it had long been overtaken by ally and enemy alike. The only other tank proper (that is one with a gun as opposed to a machine gun only) taken into service before the ending of the ten-year rule was the Vickers Medium Mark II, basically the Mark I but with thicker armour, slightly increased speed and, significantly, a fully revolving turret. This tank came into service in 1926 and was still with some front-line units until 1941.

Coming into service at about the same time as the Vickers Mark I was the beret. The service dress cap, worn by everyone, had proved unsuitable for wear in tanks unless it was worn back to front, not at all acceptable to a sartorially minded army. Officers of the Tank Corps noted that the French Chasseurs Alpins wore a beret, but their version was considered far too large and floppy for the British. The Basque beret, also worn by some French units, was too small and so the British version was a compromise between the two. The Tank Corps adopted it in black. From 1940, in khaki or navy blue, the beret became the standard headwear for the whole army – as it is today, although in a more exotic range of colours.[*]

Along with the development of an armoured doctrine for the British army came advances in transportation generally. The internal combustion engine was now sufficiently robust to allow thought to be given to replacing the horse and wagon with some sort of mechanical vehicle. Whether administrative transport should be on tracks or on wheels was eventually decided by the Treasury. Tracked vehicles could cover any type of ground, could cross ditches and could even be made amphibious. Six-wheeled lorries, being developed by the Royal Army Service Corps, had a good cross-country performance except over marshy ground, and were faster than tracked vehicles on roads. Wheeled vehicles were attractive to the road haulage industry, which had no interest in tracks, and so British administrative transport would be wheeled, and from 1927 onwards the horse and cart was rapidly being replaced by the motor lorry.

To show what might be achieved by mechanisation there was a demonstration for Dominion prime ministers and British politicians and senior officers in November 1925. The British army is very good at demonstrations, which are rehearsed down to the smallest detail. The results are entirely predictable and prove what the army wants them to prove. There is of course nothing wrong with that – it would be a bit pointless, not to say silly, to allow a demonstration to indicate other than the doctrine of the day, but this demonstration was seminal. It was important as it encouraged supporters of mechanisation, and encouraged the politicians to agree to the setting up of an armoured formation in the British army. It displayed a form of warfare that would not become standard in the

---

[*] The author's regiment wears a dark green beret, which occasionally caused mirth amongst the Chinese, where the Cantonese slang for cuckolding a man is 'giving him a green hat'.

British army for another forty years, and one that Britain's enemies would employ against her in fifteen.

It was a wet and windy day as the invited dignitaries arrived at the Camberley training area and were shown to their seats to witness the mock attack. The whole area was reduced to a sea of mud, and yet in swarmed a screen of light reconnaissance tanks to identify a route for the main assault which was made by Mark IIs supported by self-propelled artillery and aircraft, followed closely by infantry machine gunners in half tracks to take possession of the conquered ground. It had all the elements of Blitzkrieg.

The proposal to create an 'Experimental Armoured Force' in the Salisbury Plain area was first mooted in 1926. There were all sorts of stumbles on the way. The CIGS, Milne, initially keen on the idea, grew lukewarm; the original command and control arrangements were unsatisfactory and took time to get right; the commander first appointed, Fuller, was rude to too many people and lost the job; and there was institutional opposition from some who suspected (rightly) that if the army was to have more tanks they would have to lose infantry to pay for them. At last, though, on 1 May 1927 the force came into being. It had a reconnaissance battalion of armoured cars of various types (3rd Bn Royal Tank Corps); a tank battalion with forty-five Vickers Mark II tanks and four wireless tanks* (5th Bn Royal Tank Corps); a machine-gun battalion with thirty-six Vickers medium machine guns mounted in half tracks and six-wheeled lorries (2nd Bn Somerset Light Infantry);** a field regiment of four batteries of 18-pounders, all guns towed or self-propelled (9 Field Brigade Royal Artillery);*** a light battery of 3.7-inch howitzers in half tracks (9 Light Battery RA), and a field engineer company in six-wheeled lorries (17 Field Company Royal Engineers). In support were 16 (Army Cooperation) Squadron RAF, 3 (Fighter) Squadron RAF and 7 and 11 (Bombing) Squadrons RAF. Looking at the order of battle with a twenty-

---

*The battalion was organised into battalion headquarters and three companies. One radio tank would be with Bn HQ and one with each of the companies.

** The Machine-Gun Corps had been disbanded and to replace it a number of infantry battalions had been converted into machine-gun battalions on a scale of one per division.

*** An artillery unit was a lieutenant colonel's command but still, confusingly, called a brigade rather than a regiment because it supported an infantry brigade. The designation changed to regiment before 1939.

first century eye one is struck by the absence of anti-tank artillery and infantry, but it was a start, and as the very first armoured formation in the world, well worthy of note.

In the mid to late 1920s, therefore, despite the ten-year rule, prospects for the modernisation of the British army were by no means bleak. The Tank Corps – now the Royal Tank Corps – had a permanent existence; a reasonable stopgap fast tank was in service; ideas about armoured personnel carriers for infantry were actively discussed; proposals for all-arms battle groups supported by aircraft were under serious consideration; the experimental force was in being and mechanisation of transport was under way. Two factors, however, would combine to prevent the advances in thought being translated into practicality, and these were lack of money (or lack of political will to find money) and innate conservatism within the army itself.

General Sir George Milne (later Field Marshal Lord Milne), known as Uncle George, was appointed CIGS in February 1926 at the age of sixty. During the Great War he had commanded British troops in Salonika[*] from 1916–18, and then in Constantinople from 1919–20. He was not the first choice for the post, but the front-runner, Rawlinson, died suddenly. As CIGS for seven years, until 1933, he was unfortunate in presiding over the lean years of defence. A man of considerable charm and wit, and initially receptive to ideas of modernisation and mechanisation, he backed off in later years, and never challenged the ten-year rule. No doubt there is much merit in the maxim that it is pointless to go into a battle that you cannot win, but that rather depends on whether you are concerned about your place in history. Milne, like the other chiefs of staff, was constantly constrained by lack of funding for defence and lacked the strength of character to slap down entrenched vested interests within the regimental system of the army itself. There were officers who believed – quite genuinely – that the horse was superior to the armoured car or tank for

---

[*]One of Lloyd George's more impractical ideas. In his search for a mythical prop to knock away from under the Germans he insisted, against military advice, in getting involved with the French in operations against Bulgaria from Salonika. This caper achieved almost nothing, tied up a quarter of a million Allied troops to little purpose, and led to 30,000 British casualties (including 10,000 deaths), mainly from disease rather than enemy action. It also led to a huge VD rate amongst French troops there, which, when one looks at Mrs Boris the Bulgar, is rather surprising.

reconnaissance, and that it was more mobile. There were officers who objected to any move towards mechanisation because they realised – correctly – that mechanisation would mean the disappearance of hallowed old infantry regiments to fund the process.

Armies by their nature are conservative – they have to be. Civilian entrepreneurs whose experiments fail may find themselves in the bankruptcy courts; generals who fail may find themselves forced to witness foreigners holding victory parades down Whitehall. A reluctance to experiment is particularly apparent when money is tight: there is insufficient cash to try anything new without giving up what is known to be tried and true. Such conservatism is particularly common in the British army, which is always small and always strapped for cash. We cannot blame the generals for trying to hold on to what they know works, rather than invest in something that may not. We can, however, blame them when they fail to point out to their political masters, emphatically, vociferously and with their resignation if necessary, the folly of spending money on bribing the electorate rather than in paying the national insurance policy. Milne has gone down in history as a nice man who failed.

The cause of mechanisation was not helped by the views of the man chosen to command the experimental armoured force, Brigadier R. J. Collins, who when asked to comment on the results of various exercises carried out with infantry divisions to test the concept of an armoured force, was less than enthusiastic. He reported that cavalry could search ground better; that armoured vehicles were too restricted by terrain and that supply and maintenance would be a major problem. His exercise opponents, on the other hand, were much more positive. Colonel Archibald Wavell (later Field Marshal Lord Wavell), the senior operations staff officer in one of the divisions to which the armoured force had acted as enemy, felt that the moral force of armoured units was considerable; that it was impossible to defend properly against them; and that they could use their mobility to decide whether they wished to give battle or not. He was firmly in favour of expanding the armoured force, and making full use of armoured vehicles' mobility, firepower and protection. Wavell thought that these three factors should take priority in precisely that sequence, which is not the order in which the British army would put them today – because of its small size and consequent need to avoid wasting tank crews, the current British order of priority is protection, firepower and mobility – but which was probably about right in 1929.

As always happens when any major reorganisation of the services is mooted, whole flocks of dinosaurs emerged from their caves to bay at progress, including hosts of MPs, most of whom knew nothing at all about modern defence needs. It is true that some of the MPs had served in the Great War, but military technology had moved on, and most of them were more concerned about the position of the hallowed country regiment that recruited in their constituency, whose long traditions and battle honours might be cast away by disbandment to fund mechanisation. That the hallowed traditions dated from as recently as 1880, when Cardwell began to link numbered infantry battalions into regiments with territorial affiliations and a name, was lost on the protesters, whose arguments were as logical as to demand the return of archers in the British army on the grounds that they had done jolly well at Agincourt in 1415. For 1929 the army's budget for horse fodder was £607,000, while for petrol it was £72,000.[*]

An apathetic CIGS, lack of money, parliamentary protests, vested interests within the army and innate resistance to change all conspired against the move to mechanisation, but the argument was not entirely lost. Most thinking commanders saw that armoured fighting vehicles could be an advantage, and wanted them to support their infantry or cavalry formations. The problem was that there could not be enough tanks both to support the infantry and cavalry and to act independently, as the real protagonists of armour wanted. The result was an unhappy compromise, but better than nothing.

The armoured force was disbanded, to be replaced by two 'experimental infantry brigades', the title soon changed to 'mechanised infantry brigades'. At the same time the War Office proposed three types of armoured formations: for reconnaissance, offensive action and long-range operations. The light armoured brigade would have one regiment

---

[*] This is not an entirely fair comparison, as petrol did not then attract the punitive tax that it does now, but is included to show that the army still had an awful lot of horses – and rightly so, until money for mechanisation could be made available.

of armoured cars, two battalions of light tanks, and anti-aircraft and close-support artillery. For offensive operations the medium armoured brigade would have one battalion of medium tanks, two battalions of light tanks, and anti-aircraft and close-support artillery. For the third role envisaged for armour – long-range operations – the medium brigade would be augmented by infantry, engineers and more artillery. All this was good stuff – although the Second War, when it came, would demonstrate that armoured formations were always short of infantry – but to implement it the money would have to be found.

In 1928 the conversion of some cavalry regiments from hoof to track began. In one of his few sensible pronouncements on defence matters (made with an eye to saving money rather than with the good of the service in mind, but right nevertheless) Winston Churchill, as Chancellor of the Exchequer, said the cavalry must be ordered to mechanise, or be disbanded. This did not happen, and mechanisation of the cavalry was slow and hesitant. The CIGS decided that the first two regiments to lose their horses would be the two most junior who had not already been amalgamated in the rundown from 1919. These were the 11th Hussars and the 12th Lancers, who gave up their horses and converted loyally and, if not overenthusiastically, at least competently and with a reasonable modicum of keenness, to armoured cars. In hindsight, it might have been better to make the senior regiments of cavalry, the Life Guards and the Royal Horse Guards (The Blues), go first, but at least it was a start; and as the 12th Lancers were in Egypt, it gave some scope for the development and testing of armoured vehicles in that theatre. In 1929 Chancellor Churchill once again cut the army estimates, although he was prevailed upon to cut by £500,000 rather than the £2 million that he had initially demanded. That year the general election replaced the Conservative government with one formed by the Labour Party.

Surprisingly, perhaps, in view of its pacifist and anti-war traditions, the incoming Labour administration was not wholly averse to modernisation of the services, and made only a token cut (of £45,000) in the 1930 defence estimates. The new Secretary for Air, the wholly unsocialist-like and former regular soldier, Brigadier General Lord Thompson, pressed the case for mechanisation of the army until his untimely death in the crash of the airship R101 in 1930; and Emmanuel Shinwell, at the Treasury, despite a background not conducive to spending on defence, was also helpful. The plan now proposed was for three armoured brigades, the extra tank units to be partially funded by the disbandment of four infantry battalions, to be selected on the basis of lack of efficiency or failure to recruit. It was probably this suggestion that the hallowed regiments should be cut, as much as lack of money, that caused the plan repeatedly to be deferred. Despite the fact that the estimates for 1930 were much the same as the previous year, many cuts still had to be made, and these fell mainly on new equipment. The building of new tanks had been repeatedly postponed to meet Churchill's demands for economy, and if these were to be provided in 1930 then an increase would be needed. This would not sit well with those who had voted the new government into power, and did not happen. In 1930 the army received twenty-five new light tanks and the grand total of just three medium tanks – and even then this was only achieved by a process of creative accounting that would get a twenty-first-century officer jailed.

Political instability was another reason for inaction. In 1931 the administration was replaced by a coalition. The new National Government was led by Labour's Ramsay MacDonald, but was Conservative-dominated. The search for savings went on, and little progress was made in modernising the army. That year a brigade of the Royal Tank Corps was formed, but for six months only, and while valuable lessons were learned – not least about the need to develop battle drills until the shortage of radios could be overcome – only the minimum in new equipment, and nothing that might convey the impression that the British army was increasing its striking power, was sanctioned. The next year, 1932, a tank brigade was again formed, and again it was for training purposes only and soon disbanded. In both years, considerable attention was paid to the various exercises by observers from Germany.

AN AIR COUNCIL AND AN AIR MINISTRY had been established in January 1918, followed by the amalgamation of the Royal Flying Corps and the Royal Naval Air Service to form the Royal Air Force, the third service after the Royal Navy and the Army, in April that year. During the latter part of the First War the RAF had maintained and operated strategic bombing squadrons. We would not now describe the activities of Trenchard's 1918 squadrons, with bomb loads of a few hundred pounds delivered fifty or a hundred miles away, as strategic, but in that they attacked targets well behind enemy lines and not directly related to what the army was doing on land, they stimulated men of vision to see the air not merely as another dimension of the battle, but as a medium in which independent operations might be carried out by aircraft alone. Even so, in the headlong rush to disarm after the war, the RAF was to be reduced from around 2,500 aircraft and 155 operational squadrons to only 360 aircraft and twenty-nine squadrons. Over the next few years the fledgling RAF would have to fight not just to keep a realistic number of aircraft, but for its very existence as an independent service.

The generosity of spirit that persuaded admirals and generals to accept the formation of an independent Royal Air Force did not survive the financial cheese-paring that began to bite ever deeper into the post-Great War defence budgets. Few now would argue against the concept of an independent air force – although to include it in the Royal Navy's own air arm was a mistake that would have serious consequences at the beginning of the next war – but this was not universally agreed once peace returned. The war had ended before the RAF could show what it could achieve as an independent service, and now the generals saw no point in the RAF's army cooperation squadrons belonging to a separate service: they worked with and for the army, so why should they not be part of that army? The admirals, with perhaps more justification, thought that only naval officers and ratings could fully understand the aviation needs of the Royal Navy, and resented the loss of their own integral flying arm. The Royal Air Force itself, while paying lip service to the needs of the other two services, was much more interested in air control (actually air and armour control), whereby aircraft and mobile columns kept order in Jordan and Iraq and in parts of northern India, and in the development of a bombing force, because these roles supported the justification for an independent air force. The government was at first indifferent, and when Lloyd George gave the job of Secretary for Air to Winston Churchill, in addition to his appointment as Secretary for War, he said 'You might

as well take it [Air] with you, I'm not going to keep it as a separate department.'[5] By virtue of being Secretary for War Churchill had a seat in the
cabinet, but in April 1921 the air portfolio was taken over by Churchill's
cousin, F. A. Guest, who did not. Most politicians, many admirals and
generals and even a few airmen, thought that it was only a matter of time
before the RAF was reabsorbed into its original components.

And then: enter the man whose framed photograph ought to hang
above the bed of every officer of the Royal Air Force – Sir Samuel Hoare.
A professional statesman rather than a mere politician, Hoare's reputation has been tainted by accusations of so-called appeasement – about
which more later – but he was a truly remarkable man, whose support
for the RAF against the acquisitive tendencies of the army and the navy
was based on hearing and weighing the arguments, rather than by any
vested interest in the new service. An MP before the Great War and a
soldier of sorts during it,[*] he was appointed Secretary for Air (not in the
cabinet) by Prime Minister Bonar Law in November 1922, with the
warning that his tenure would almost certainly be short. A separate air
force, he was told, was too costly and its roles would soon be returned
to the army and the navy. At this time the strength of the RAF in the
United Kingdom had fallen to a mere hundred front-line aircraft. When
Baldwin replaced Bonar Law in May 1923 he wanted Hoare (rather than
his job) in the cabinet, and this allowed Hoare to press the case of the
RAF with increased authority.

The Chief of Air Staff from 1919 was Air Chief Marshal (later Marshal
of the Royal Air Force Viscount) Sir Hugh Trenchard, who had cut his
teeth with the RFC in France and who had pioneered strategic bombing.
On a professional level he was fighting hard for his service, and had
frequent and legendary rows of the blazing variety with the First Sea
Lord, Admiral Beatty, who thought (with some reason) that the RAF was
neglecting the navy's needs. Trenchard, initially dismissive of the concept
of an independent air force, had become its passionate advocate, and a
firm believer in long-range bombing of an enemy's heartland. He knew
all the arguments, but was not necessarily expert in their articulate

---

[*]He was medically unfit for active service, learned Russian and did much useful work as a member and
later head of a liaison mission to Russia.

advancement. Hoare *was* articulate, and the combination, which lasted until the Conservatives lost the election of June 1929 and Trenchard's retirement from the RAF the same year (he would be recalled in 1939) was a formidable one. Their first major battle was in early 1923 when the Sea Lords, en bloc, threatened to resign unless they got their air wing back. Hoare and Trenchard responded in less dramatic fashion, and in a cabinet paper Hoare argued that the concept of two separate air forces, with a small air ministry to coordinate aircraft procurement, might indeed be feasible. It might even cost less, but, tellingly:

> ...only by a centralised air force can we undertake the strategic operation
> that is likely to be the crisis in a continental war ... the present moment
> would be peculiarly inappropriate to abandon our strategic unity when we
> are admittedly defenceless in the face of France.[6]

It may seem odd that France was cited as a potential enemy, but, as Palmerston had observed, great powers have neither friends nor enemies – they only have interests. With Germany shackled by Versailles the strongest military power in Europe was France and so British defence policy, such as it was, had to take that fact into account.

A committee under the chairmanship of Lord Salisbury was convened to examine 'Inter Service relations in the context of National and Imperial Defence', with a subsidiary task of looking at RAF relations with both the army and navy, and, critically, of making recommendations as to what expansion would be required to ensure the air defence of the United Kingdom. The committee's report saw off the Sea Lords, with some weasel wording to persuade them not to resign, and recommended a home defence force 'of sufficient strength adequately to protect against air attack by the strongest air force within striking distance of this country.'[7] This was put at fifty-two squadrons totalling 204 fighters and 394 bombers, compared with the previous policy of bringing the existing total of 371 aircraft up to 575 worldwide – not just for home defence.

The chances of getting 600 aircraft for home defence at a time of retrenchment and parsimony were remote, but the very fact that the word 'expansion' should be uttered at all in the period of the ten-year rule sprang from a concept that would eventually be proved to be entirely erroneous

– but to which many, if not most, air staffs and many politicians and journalists around the world subscribed. Put simply it was the notion that 'the bomber will always get through'. During the Great War bombing raids on the British mainland by German Zeppelins and aircraft had killed 1,709 people, civilian and military, and injured another 2,050. This was a mere bagatelle, a drop in the ocean (unless you happened to be one of them) but in a nation unaccustomed to attacks on the homeland, they caused great alarm and foreboding as to what a future war might bring.

To reinforce this gloomy view of the consequences of bombing were the writings of General Giulio Douhet and his disciples, who had considerable influence in military circles. The Italians are not universally known for their military prowess, but they were innovators in military aviation.* Douhet commanded the Italian army's very first air unit, and pioneered aerial bombing in Libya during Italy's war with Turkey in 1911–12. Court-martialled and sacked during the First War for criticising the Italian high command (he was quite right – the Comàndo Suprèmo at that time was a joke), he was recalled after the disaster of Caporetto in 1917. In 1921 he published *Il Dominio dell'Aria* (*Command of the Air*), in which he argued that there was no practical defence against aircraft, and that sufficient machines would always get through to attack an enemy heartland. Moreover, Douhet argued, bombing of cities would so destroy industry and shatter civilian morale that governments would find it impossible to go on fighting, and the war could be won by airpower alone. This argument was, of course, attractive to advocates of airpower and to those who saw a way to avoid heavy expenditure on ships, armies and overseas bases. Giving evidence to the Committee for Imperial Defence in 1922 Arthur Balfour wrote:

> Only the Air Force can protect us from invasion by air. Even anti-aircraft guns, however numerous and however well directed, will never prevent invading aeroplanes working their will upon a city like London. Aircraft must in such cases be met by aircraft.[8]

* Modern Italians (the country dates from 1861) show little aptitude for conventional military operations, but they do seem well suited to individual enterprise. In the Great War they were good pilots and in the Second War the crews of their manned torpedoes and midget submarines performed deeds of great initiative and daring.

Trenchard was very much a believer in the Douhet mantra, and in 1923 in a statement to the parliamentary committee on air power he said:

> It is on the bomber that we must rely for defence. It is on the destruction of enemy industries and above all on the lowering of morale caused by bombing that the ultimate victory rests. Army policy was to defeat the enemy army; our policy was to defeat the enemy nation.[9]

As it happened, the Douhet argument was proved false. In the Second World War neither the Luftwaffe nor the Royal Air Force, despite bombing of an intensity far greater than Douhet ever envisaged, were able to destroy civilian morale – which does not mean that they were not effective in other ways – but the argument had sufficient strength in the 1920s for the British government, while not exactly smiling on the RAF, to at least grimace in its direction.[*] It was one thing to agree to improve the air defence of the United Kingdom, however, and quite another to actually spend money to do it. The plan recommended by Salisbury and accepted by government was still incomplete by the time the ten-year rule was cancelled in 1932.

Sir Samuel Hoare was instrumental in the setting-up of University Air Squadrons, which, although intended to provide a supply of pilots for the RAF in time of war, were cleverly organised on deliberately unmilitary lines, in order to attract students, and he at last secured funding for the RAF college at Cranwell to be housed in purpose-built accommodation instead of the temporary huts they had been forced to occupy as long as the Treasury refused funding for permanent buildings, on the grounds that the RAF would soon disappear. All in all, the RAF owes a great debt to Hoare: he was wrong in his insistence on keeping the Fleet Air Arm as part of the RAF, but without him and the redoubtable Trenchard by his side, there might not have been an RAF at all.

The air defence of the UK depended on fighter squadrons, but the Salisbury plan for a metropolitan air force included bombers, as it was bombers that could project power beyond national borders, and also act as a deterrent. Unfortunately, there was insufficient money to have enough

---

[*] Whether Douhet's theories might be right in a guided missile war remains to be proved.

of both fighters and bombers, and the result was a fudge that fulfilled neither requirement properly. Even the intention to have the home defence air fleet in place by the 1928–9 financial year was soon revised. In November 1925 a cabinet committee reported that the risk of war among the great powers of Europe was sufficiently remote to justify postponing the date by which the air defence of the homeland plan was to be implemented until 1935–6. Four years later, in 1929, the date of implementation was postponed yet again, to 1938.

Attempts to put the air defence of Great Britain on a sound footing in the 1920s were not helped by RAF doctrine as expounded by Trenchard. Great man though he was, Trenchard's ideas, which he pursued with single-minded determination, were not all sound. He firmly believed that the RAF should concentrate on offensive action, with the smallest possible proportion of its assets devoted to defence. When Trenchard retired in 1929 there were no fighter squadrons overseas, and suggestions that the bombers might need long-range fighters to escort them were dismissed. Even Trenchard's advocacy of bombers was to an extent nullified by lack of funding. In 1929 the RAF had eight types of bomber, ranging from the Vickers Virginia with a range of 900 miles and a bombload of two and a half tons, to the Westland Wapiti with a range of 362 miles and a bombload of a quarter of a ton. It was not until 1935 that serious consideration began to be given to air defence, regardless of what the Salisbury Committee and stirring speeches in parliament might promise.

FOR THE ROYAL NAVY, the cornerstone of Britain's defence, and indeed of her very existence as a nation, the post-war cuts came deep and fast. In 1918, even after losing fifteen battleships during the war, either from enemy action, accident, conversion into monitors or disarmed as obsolete, the Royal Navy still had fifty-five battleships in commission. Of these, thirty-four were all-big-gun Dreadnought type, and twenty-nine were less than ten years old. In addition there were nine battlecruisers, twenty-five other cruisers of 9,000 tons or more, 432 destroyers of various types with eighty-four light cruisers as destroyer flotilla leaders, two aircraft carriers and three seaplane carriers. It was a huge and impressive force, dwarfing anything else afloat, but Britain's main rival, Germany, which started the war with forty-one battleships had been defeated and her fleet scuttled. No thinking sailor denied that reductions could be made, but command of the seas was still seen as an essential plank of British defence policy, and there could be no question of relinquishing it.

With Germany out of the way there were four other navies worth considering: those of the United States, France, Italy and Japan. While the two-power standard had effectively been abandoned before the Great War, and could not be reimposed, the Admiralty drew up an eminently sensible plan for a post-war navy of thirty-three battleships, eight battle-cruisers, sixty cruisers and 352 destroyers, the whole to cost £171 million annually. Ideally, thought the British, there should be one Imperial navy, which would enable savings to be made in training and administrative costs, but this was not acceptable to the Dominions (Canada, Australia, New Zealand and South Africa), who were beginning to see themselves as nations in their own right, rather than as mere appendages of Britain. A navy is a symbol of nationhood.

For the Far East, a report prepared by Admiral Jellicoe recommended a Far East Fleet centred on eight battleships and based in Singapore. This would cost £20 million per annum, with the costs shared between Britain, paying 71 per cent, and the Dominions who would find the rest. This relatively modest fleet would, it was considered, be able to contain the Japanese at a manageable cost.

It was all very well for the admirals to make recommendations based on what they saw as the nation's long-term interests; they could afford to take the long view and were not dependent upon public opinion to keep them in office. The politicians saw things rather differently, and here there was the beginning of a real shift in the way that Britain was governed, a shift that continued in the inter-war years and is still with us today. With a limited franchise, Britain had for a very long time been governed by the middle classes, who, regardless of party, could talk about the 'national interest' without too much concern for the workers. As the franchise was steadily extended, however, and as workers became better organised through trade unions, while the proletariat did not reject grandiose ideas of empire, and they were all for Britannia ruling the waves, they did, however, become less inclined to acquiesce on the spending of public money on the armed forces rather than on things that affected them directly – health, education and pensions. During the Great War this trend had been temporarily halted, but now that the war was over politicians of all hues realised that if they did not pander to the wish for social spending they would be out of office, and this inclination increased as the Liberals were eclipsed by the Labour Party. Labour politicians between the wars were not uncouth class warriors, indeed they were very largely from the same background as their Conservative opponents (as they are today) but to retain the support of those who voted for them they had to push money their way, at the expense of defence.

In any case Britain was no longer the world's largest creditor nation – that was now the United States – and while by no means in the parlous financial state that she found herself in after the Second World War, she was not able to recoup many of the loans she had made to other allies (Italy could not and Russia would not repay), yet still had to repay those she had herself negotiated from the United States.

The imposition of the ten-year rule put paid to any hope of the thirty-three-battleship post-war navy, and of Jellicoe's Far East Fleet. Far from getting the £171 million that the navy wanted, they were given just £84.5 million for the year 1920/21. If this went on, then not only would the Royal Navy be overtaken by other navies, but expertise would be lost as designers and skilled men drifted away from employment in the shipyards.

Briefly, in 1921, it looked as if the decline of Britain as a naval power might be reversed. Of the world's other sea powers France was even more reluctant to spend money than was Britain; the Italian navy was largely confined to the Mediterranean, and Japan was allied to Britain. In the United States, however, animosity that had been set aside for much of the Great War began to re-emerge.

At the outbreak of war in 1914 President Woodrow Wilson and the American east coast establishment both, for different reasons, saw a German victory as being contrary to American interests; and America bent the rules of neutrality almost to breaking point to help the British, before entering the war themselves in 1917. Helping the British to win the war was not, however, the same thing as actually liking them. Many influential Americans resented what they saw as British arrogance, and were jealous of British naval supremacy. During the war the British blockade, although perfectly legal, caused great resentment in the USA, as indeed did American attempts to poach British markets cause resentment in the UK. President Wilson made it clear that once the war was over British dominance of the world's oceans would not be acceptable to the USA, and there were many senior officers in the US navy who were openly anti-British and who wanted to build a fleet that would rival the Royal Navy. One, Admiral Benson, even endorsed a report pointing out that historically the British had always gone to war with their trading rivals eventually, and they had always won.[10] In 1915, well before America's entry into the war and egged on by Anglophobe admirals, the President proposed to build a navy 'second to none'. As it happened, this '1916 standard' navy was not then built; after entering the war the need was not for capital ships – the Royal Navy had enough for all the Allies – but by 1918 the US had sixteen battleships in commission, or more than France, Italy and Japan combined. Relations between the two navies at working level were good, and in a gesture of solidarity on entering the war, in 1917 the US navy had put a battleship squadron under command of the British Grand Fleet, although the American Chief of Naval Operations had little time for the British policy of blockade, believing that more direct action would yield speedier results.[*]

At the end of the war one of President Wilson's Fourteen Points (perhaps one of the more extreme examples of how naive world statesmen can sometimes be) was absolute freedom of the seas in peace and war. This would render the British weapon of blockade useless at a stroke, and it was the only one of Wilson's points that the British refused to accept.

By August 1919 and the adoption of the ten-year rule, Britain had already scrapped 400 vessels of various types (including forty battleships), but even the only post-Jutland ship she possessed, the battlecruiser HMS

---

* Shades of the Second Front in the Second War. It was not always apparent to the Americans, in either World War, that the British were cautious and looked to the longer term for very sound reasons. The blockade from 1914 was unspectacular but had an enormous, and even to this day often unappreciated, effect on Germany's ability to continue the war.

Hood (fated to be sunk by the German *Bismarck* in May 1941) irritated the Americans, who now proposed to build the 1916 standard fleet. For the 1920–21 financial year the US government placed orders for six battle-ships and six battlecruisers, knowing full well that Britain must either bankrupt herself in trying to outbuild the USA, or concede command of the seas. It is difficult to see this as other than unadulterated American spite directed against a nation that wanted to be America's friend and ally.

Another source of American resentment was the Anglo-Japanese Treaty. At the turn of the century Britain was concerned as to the possible domination of Far Eastern waters by the combined fleets of France and Russia. Should Britain be threatened there she would have to reinforce the China Fleet from home waters – a risk in itself – and if she did not reinforce she risked losing Hong Kong, Singapore and the China trade. The answer was an alliance with Japan, herself concerned about possible Russian expansionism in the Far East, and this was signed in January 1902. The treaty was useful to Britain, and even more so to Japan, whose officers were trained by the Royal Navy and ships built in British yards. The treaty was revised and amended in 1905, and renewed in 1911. It was helpful to Britain during the Great War as the Japanese – by now known as the British of the Far East – were able to mop up German colonies in China and the Pacific (thus incidentally bringing them closer to the American mainland), deal with commerce raiders and keep trade routes open to allow the British to concentrate on home waters. It is ironic that the Japanese Naval Air Force, which would eventually wreak such havoc upon the American Pacific Fleet at Pearl Harbor in December 1941, was orig-inally set up and trained by the British.

America had been worried about the Japanese since long before the Great War. The provision of the Anglo-Japanese Treaty that really annoyed her stated that if one party were attacked, the other would come to her assistance. The Americans saw this as a direct threat to themselves (or rather as inhibiting them from implementing a pre-emptive solution to the Yellow Peril). A Japanese decision to embark on what they called their 'Eight-Eight' construction programme of eight battleships and eight cruisers, announced shortly after the Americans had ordered their new ships, only heightened US worries about Japan and suspicion of British motives. However hard the British tried to assure the Americans that they would never go to war allied with the Japanese against America, it remained an unstated aim of US foreign policy to get the Anglo-Japanese Treaty scrapped.

Despite British reluctance to spend – and the government was terrified of a naval arms race with the USA – the new American and Japanese building programmes were a direct threat to the Royal Navy's supremacy. National prestige was at stake, and if Britain did nothing she would quickly go from being the world's first to the world's third navy. After intense lobbying by Admiral Beatty, the First Sea Lord, even the most obdurate opponent of defence spending was forced to accept that an island nation, particularly one with an empire, could not concede command of the seas. Shipbuilding for the Royal Navy must recommence, and plans were approved for four new battleships, four battlecruisers and new or converted aircraft carriers.

It was at this point that the Americans sprung their trap. President Wilson was out of office and America out of the League of Nations, but determination to wrest control of the seas from the British remained, and now President Harding, he of the Teapot Dome scandal, saw a way to achieve that by guile rather than by spending. The United States invited the representatives of Britain, France, Italy and Japan to attend a conference on the limitation of naval armaments. The Washington Treaty of February 1922 agreed a ratio for battleships of 5:5:3 respectively for the UK, the USA and Japan, with each country agreeing to reduce their overall tonnage to 525,000 tons each for the UK and the USA, 315,000 for Japan and 175,000 tons each for France and Italy. There were limits on the size of replacement vessels, and rules as to how existing vessels could be converted. Despite British attempts to have the submarine banned altogether, there were no restrictions placed on their size or numbers, largely due to French insistence.

Where the Americans had boxed exceedingly clever was in getting agreement to the overall tonnage, as they could cut back by giving up ships planned for but not yet built (as could the Japanese), while the Royal Navy had to scrap existing vessels, and would have great difficulty in modernising what was left. A combination of the Washington Treaty and the ten-year rule meant that there could be no increase and precious little modernisation to the fleet until the abandonment of the rule in 1932, and by then time was running out and future enemies were building apace. For five hundred years Britain had regarded mastery of home waters, and by stages of the world's oceans, as a non-negotiable essential to her survival as a nation and to the security of her Empire. Now it was being taken away from her, not by defeat in battle but by the machinations and urgings of the country that would become her closest ally. For the first time in centuries Britain accepted parity rather than mastery, and for the first time ever, Britain was to allow her naval strength to be decided by international treaty, rather than by her own assessments of her needs.

It was what the academics like to call a canonical paradigm shift – a turning point of huge historical significance and directly relevant to naval weaknesses when the Second War came. Why on earth had the British agreed to it? The chief reason was that it was very tempting. It allowed the government to avoid making unpleasant decisions about taxation to pay for new ships and to escape the risk of electoral damage that might result from putting keels before public health. It pacified the Dominion governments, who feared being caught in the crossfire of an Anglo-American arms race; and it just might, if you were very optimistic and very naive, contribute to world peace.

A side effect of the Washington Treaty, and one very much intended by the United States, was the ending of the Anglo-Japanese alliance. By persuading the British to agree to the 5:5:3 ratio, rather than the 10:10:7 which Japan asked for, the Americans ensured that the Japanese left the conference convinced that they had been let down and snubbed by the British. At the urgings of the Americans, the Anglo-Japanese Treaty was dissolved, its abandonment camouflaged by a five-power agreement high on rhetoric about respecting one another's interests and low on substance. Whether the continued existence of the alliance would have acted as a brake on Japanese ambitions is doubtful. Japan was already exhibiting traits that were causing the British concern, but as Britain would not have gone to war against America under any circumstances, renewing the treaty might have allowed the British to moderate Japanese policy to some extent. On the other hand, of course, feeling in the USA was running so high that had the UK not abandoned the Japanese, then American support against Germany in 1939 might not have materialised to the extent that it did – although perhaps that support would not have been as vital as it was had America not sprung the naval limitations ambush in 1921.

In 1918 the Royal Navy was the world's leader in naval aviation, but the amalgamation of the Royal Flying Corps with the Royal Naval Air Service to form the Royal Air Force had meant that 2,500 aircraft and 55,000 men which had belonged to the Royal Navy now belonged to the RAF. The RAF had its own agenda and was not very interested in the navy's problems. The Fleet Air Arm, established in 1923 as part of the RAF's Coastal Area, was controlled by the RAF with the Royal Navy specifying the types and numbers of aircraft and providing the funding for them. Of the pilots, half were navy men, but all had RAF ranks and wore RAF uniform. The aircrew other than pilots were all sailors, while the maintenance technicians were airmen. When embarked on ships, all were subject to the Naval Discipline Act, but ashore to the Air Force Act. It was all an unsatisfactory dog's breakfast, and competition for resources led to the fleet's aviation needs being very much neglected. In the years 1929 to 1932 the Fleet Air Arm received a grand total of eighteen new aircraft, and it was not until 1937 that the Admiralty at last recovered control of its own aircraft,[*] by which time the Royal Navy was a long way behind its rivals.

ONE OF THE CHIEF SUPPORTERS of the ten-year rule and thus with a share in the responsibility for the unreadiness that it engendered, and indeed a man who found it difficult to look beyond what he knew and was familiar with, was Winston Churchill. In 1921 as Secretary for War and for Air he argued vociferously for the battleship, at a time when many thought it had come to the end of its reign as the capital ship of the fleet, and should be replaced by the aircraft carrier. In 1925, as Chancellor of the Exchequer, he opposed upgrading the Singapore naval base, on the

---

[*] Once naval aviation reverted to the Admiralty the designation 'Fleet Air Arm' was abolished, but as everyone continued to refer to naval aviation by that name, it was officially reinstated in 1952.

grounds that it was quite impossible for Japan to mount an attack on Britain without such a long period of warning that there would be plenty of time to prepare to receive it. 'I do not think,' he said, 'in our lifetime or in that of our children, you are going to see an attempt to invade and colonise Australia by force.'[11] In 1927 he ferociously campaigned for a reduction in the Naval Estimates, and in 1928 he recommended to cabinet that the ten-year rule should continue:

> It should now be laid down as a standing assumption that at any given date there will be no major war for ten years from that date; and that this should rule unless or until upon the recommendation of the Foreign Office or one of the Fighting Services or otherwise, it was decided to alter it.[12]

Churchill did not, of course, invent the ten-year rule, although he had been part of the cabinet which introduced it, and he never challenged it. Up to 1928 the rule had been reconsidered each year (and extended) but what Churchill now did was to turn it into a rolling assumption – tomorrow never comes – thus making it even more pernicious than it already was. Churchill's statement quoted above was, it has to be admitted, made when the warm glow engendered by the Locarno Pact had not yet faded entirely. Signed in December 1925 by Britain, France, Belgium, Italy and Germany this supposedly imposed upon the signatories obligations to accept the western border of Germany as dictated by Versailles, to alter the eastern borders only by arbitration, and to refrain from attacking one another except in legitimate defence or in response to a League of Nations resolution. Additionally France (but not Britain) guaranteed the security of Poland and Czechoslovakia. In return for Germany's signing the pact, the Allied army of occupation would withdraw from the Rhineland in 1930, rather than 1935 as had been intended. It was all hot air, fuss and feathers, but again allowed politicians to reduce defence spending.

Churchill was out of office from 1929 until recalled as First Lord of the Admiralty at the outbreak of war in 1939. During the so-called wilderness years it was easy for him to criticise government policy, and later to create the impression that only he had seen what was coming, and that only he had been a constant supporter of Britain's armed forces. The facts were that he was as guilty as anyone, and more so than some whom he castigated as appeasers.

While Britain was sheltering behind the illusory shield of collective defence and the League of Nations, her naval supremacy given away in Washington, and ideas and plans coming to nought due to lack of will to spend, other powers were less reticent.

NOTES

1. Quoted in B. H. Liddell Hart, *The Tanks, Vol. I*, Cassell, London, 1959.

2. See RUSI Journal, November 1919.

3. Heinz Guderian, *Achtung Panzer!* (tr. Christopher Duffy), Arms & Armour Press, London, 1992.

4. Specifications from Christopher F. Foss (ed), *The Encyclopedia of Tanks and Armoured Fighting Vehicles*, Spellmount, Staplehurst, 2002.

5. Quoted in Sir Maurice Dean, *The Royal Air Force and the Two World Wars*, Cassell, London 1979.

6. TNA Kew, CAB/24/158, *Air Policy and a One Power Standard*, quoted in J. A. Cross, *Sir Samuel Hoare*, Jonathan Cape, London, 1977.

7. TNA Kew, CAB/24/161.

8. N. H. Gibbs, *History of the Second World War – Grand Strategy, Vol. I*, HMSO, London, 1976.

9. Quoted in Robin Neillands, *The Bomber War*, John Murray, London, 2001.

10. Bernard Ireland, *War At Sea 1914–45*, Cassell, London, 2002.

11. N. H. Gibbs, *History of the Second World War – Grand Strategy, Vol. I*, HMSO, London, 1976.

12. Ibid.

3

The Other Side of the Hill

THE TREATY OF VERSAILLES, signed between the Allies and Associated Powers and Germany on 28 June 1919, brought the First World War to an end. Its provisions were savage.[1] Germany accepted sole responsibility for the war and agreed to pay for all the damage; the Kaiser was deemed personally responsible and was to be put on trial before a court composed of judges nominated by the victors (including a Japanese judge); her boundaries were adjusted (in some cases drastically) to the advantage of the Allies, and there were severe restrictions placed on her armed forces. The Kaiser had abdicated before Germany sued for peace in 1918 and had removed himself to neutral Holland whose government, to their great credit, faced down the British and French governments and refused to hand him over for trial.*

Abroad, Germany forfeited all her colonies and surrendered her rights in China, Siam (modern Thailand), Liberia and Morocco. In Europe Germany had to return Alsace and Lorraine, annexed from France in 1871 after the Franco-Prussian war; she lost disputed territory on the Danish and Belgian borders; she was forbidden to erect any fortification along the Rhine from the frontier with France, Luxembourg, Belgium

---

* Which was probably just as well as there was no legal framework under which a head of state could be put on trial. Even the stupidest English barrister could have had the case thrown out on Day One.

and Holland to a line thirty miles east of the river and was not allowed to station any troops or hold military exercises there, on pain of being declared to have committed a hostile act. The Saarland was to be detached from Germany and administered under the auspices of the League of Nations, while ownership of its coal mines was to pass to the French state. Even more draconian were the provisions for Germany's eastern borders, where an area fifty miles across and fifty miles north to south was ceded to Poland – the 'Polish Corridor', which in allowing the newly consti-tuted state of Poland access to the sea cut off East Prussia from the rest of Germany. The hitherto German coastal city of Danzig, now in the Corridor, became a 'free city' with its own administration guaranteed by the League of Nations but at the disposal of Poland as its seaport.

The German armed forces were severely restricted by the treaty. Not only was the army to be reduced to 100,000 men by 31 March 1920 (a mere nine months after the signing) but the treaty went into minute detail as to how many formations could be maintained (seven infantry and three cavalry divisions in no more than two corps), and even stipulated the estab-lishment. An infantry regiment (three permitted in a division) was to consist of three battalions, each battalion of three companies and a machine-gun company, a total of seventy officers and 2,300 other ranks. A pioneer battalion (one per division) was to have two companies of pioneers, a pontoon detachment and a searchlight section, with a strength of twelve officers and four hundred men. A signal (sic) detachment (one per division) was to comprise one telephone detachment, one listening section and one carrier pigeon section, and twelve officers and three hundred men.

The 100,000-man total was to include no more than four thousand officers, of whom no more than three hundred could be employed in state or national war ministries, and there could be no General Staff. Manning was to be by voluntary enlistment only, and officers already serving and retained in the new Reichswehr were to serve until at least the age of forty-five, and new entrants for a minimum of twenty-five years. Other ranks were to serve for a minimum period of twelve years. No more than 5 per cent of officers and soldiers could be discharged in any one year; there were to be no provisions for mobilisation and all schools and training establishments except those essential to the manning of the

100,000-man army were to be closed. The numbers of policemen, forest guards, coastguards and customs officials were to be the same as in 1913 except that increases could be made in direct proportion to any increase in population (which, as a result of war deaths and the loss of large chunks of territory, was unlikely in the foreseeable future). All these officials were strictly forbidden to receive any form of military training. Germany was not to send military attachés or military missions abroad; her citizens were forbidden to join other armies and the Allies agreed not to enlist them, with the exception that 'The present provision does not, however, affect the right of France to recruit for the Foreign Legion in accordance with French military laws and regulations.'[2]

All this dotting of i's and crossing of t's was designed to make sure that the crafty Germans did not somehow bypass the restrictions by creating a short-service army, whereby men would be discharged after only a few years of service, thus quickly building up a reservoir of trained manpower. Even the number of rifles Germany was permitted to own was stipulated (84,000), and the number of rounds of ammunition for each class of weapon (eight hundred for each of the eighty-four 10.5cm howitzers allowed) was laid down. No armoured vehicles of any kind and no chemical weapons were to be made, imported or owned.

The German navy was to hand over all its ships and those not in German ports were automatically the property of the Allies.[*] For the future Germany could have six battleships, six light cruisers, twelve destroyers and twelve torpedo boats. Replacements could not be built for twenty years (battleships and cruisers) or fifteen (smaller ships), and when they were, nothing was to exceed 10,000 tons displacement. No submarines could be built or owned. The maximum strength was to be 15,000 men, of whom not more than 1,500 could be officers, and there were rules about length of service similar to those for the army.

As for air forces, Germany was not to have any at all, except that until 1 October 1919 she was to provide one hundred seaplanes fully equipped for mine detection, but unarmed, which were to be used to assist in the

---

[*] The German High Seas Fleet was under arrest in the British naval base at Scapa Flow, when on 21 June 1919 it was scuttled by its crews, thus rendering irrelevant the bickering amongst the Allies as to who should have its various components.

clearing of German minefields laid during the war. To ensure that Germany adhered to these restrictions, an Inter-Allied Military Commission was established which would be based in Germany with the right of inspection anywhere it chose.

The early days of the post-war German armed forces were little short of chaotic. Many senior officers wanted to oppose the Versailles terms and resented those such as General Groener who had been deputed by Hindenburg to advise the Kaiser to abdicate and who had then to accept the terms. The army was under attack from the left, which wanted a far more democratic body than even a defeated army was prepared to become, and from the right, which thought that the army should overthrow the Weimar Republic with its Social Democrat government. There were those among the victorious Allies who thought that Germany should not be permitted any armed forces at all, but wiser counsel pointed out that in that case the republic would fall to the Communists: the new Germany needed some military capability to keep order internally and to guard her frontiers. In fact the 100,000-man army was initially incapable of doing any such thing, and the putting down of Communist revolutionaries internally and Polish dissidents on the eastern frontier was delegated to the Freikorps, ex-officers and soldiers who formed what were in practice mercenary bands, tolerated by the government because they needed them to restore order, and by the army because they constituted a reserve which the army might be able to use in better times.

Very quickly the German army began to seek ways of getting round the restrictions imposed upon it by Versailles. Colonel General Hans von Seekt, head of the army under various titles from 1919 until 1926, was an officer of the old school who had little time for a republican form of government but who recognised that the only chance of restoring the army to what he saw as its proper place in Germany was to keep it strictly out of politics and to adhere as far as possible to the old imperial traditions. Despite the inclinations of some officers to support the abortive Kapp putsch in 1920, Seekt made sure that the army obeyed the government, and the putsch was short-lived.[*]

---

[*] Wolfgang Kapp, a right-wing politician, and Generals von Lutteritz and Maercker, supported by some of the Freikorps, attempted to overthrow the republic and restore the monarchy.

In some ways the army became even more elitist under the Weimar Republic than it had been under the Kaiser, for despite the Social Democrats' wish to have more officers commissioned from the ranks, 35 per cent of the officers of the Reichsheer of the period 1921–34 were themselves the sons of officers, compared to 24 per cent for the pre-Great War years; and of the officers commissioned into the German army in 1922 22 per cent were from the nobility,[*] rising steadily year by year to 36 per cent in 1932, before the social levelling of the Nazi years began to reduce the figure.[3]

Seekt's policy was to maintain the German military virtues and the integrity of the army until such times as expansion could be carried out. He was not in any sense a warmonger nor did he seek to reopen the Great War, but he did begin to outflank the Inter-Allied Military Commission. He civilianised anything that was not directly concerned with military matters, such as some of the administration and the historical, archive and library functions, which enabled him to fill the vacancies created with combatants. There was far more cavalry in the new army than Seekt needed, and so infantry and artillery officers and men were hidden in the cavalry; an air-planning cell was set up which, even if it had no aircraft, could at least consider air-support procedures; much technical work and experimentation was farmed out to the Charlottenburg Polytechnic in Berlin; the Intelligence Directorate was given the innocuous title of Statistics Section; cavalry squadrons and transport units were secretly 'double-hatted' as artillery observation units and signals sections, and other transport units experimented with tank tactics despite not having any tanks. On the eastern frontier the Border Force East, a paramilitary organisation composed of ex-servicemen, was set up in secret. Intended to deal with Polish guerrillas, it was commanded by regular army officers and armed from stocks of Great War weapons which were supposed to have been handed over but had in fact been stored in hidden dumps.

The Great General Staff (the operational staff) was illegal under Versailles so staff officers were trained covertly under divisional

---

[*] I take German nobility to be Freiherren and above, the equivalent of knights baronet in our system. There was of course also a plethora of officers with a *von* to their name, which merely means that they are (or their ancestors were) equivalent to our untitled landed gentry.

arrangements, rather than in a central staff college, and staff officers were appointed but given the title of 'command assistants'. Whereas up to 1913 officers volunteered to take the examination for the staff college, and it was the examination results coupled with reports on their performance at duty that got them selected to attend, from 1921 all middle-piece lieutenants were required to take a written examination, whether they wanted to be staff officers or not, and were selected to attend on the basis of the exam marks alone. To British eyes this had the disadvantage of producing military technicians rather than long-range planners, and although it worked well enough, it may account for the very high standard of operational planning when war came, coupled with a seeming lack of coherent long-term aims and a complete inability to decide what to do once the battle was won.

With only 100,000 men the army was not, of course, typical of German society, and nor did Seekt wish it to be. Soldiers were recruited directly by regiments (equivalent to brigades in British parlance) and volunteers had to be between seventeen and twenty-one years of age, unmarried, not less than five feet five inches in height and medically fit; they had to produce employers' and school reports and have no criminal record. For officers the system was exhaustive. On selection as a potential officer the candidate served for fifteen months as a private soldier and, if still considered suitable for officer training, took an examination for fahnenjunker or officer cadet, which, if passed, got the boy promoted to lance corporal (Gefreiter) and sent on a junior NCOs' course at the School of Infantry at Dresden. After that he took another examination which made him a senior officer cadet, or Oberfahnrich, which allowed him to be a member of the officers' mess although still legally an other rank. After a probationary period he was finally accepted – or not – for commissioned rank by a vote by the officers of the regiment, after which he attended a course at an officer school. It thus took between four and five years from enlistment before an aspiring officer actually became one, and the standard was high. The British, then and now, would consider so much other-rank service as making it unnecessarily difficult for the young officer to make the huge leap – socially, intellectually and professionally – from the status of a private soldier or a junior NCO to that of an officer; but it worked for the Germans between the wars, and the products of the system were generally high-grade commanders when the Second War arrived.

All ranks were forbidden to marry before the age of twenty-seven, and then permission for other ranks was only granted if the man could show that his intended wife was free of debt, came from a respectable family and had an unblemished reputation. Officers did not have to justify their intended's background, as it was a presumption that anyone an officer wished to marry would be suitable.

Von Seekt considered Poland (allied to France) as a permanent threat to Germany – as other German generals did later – and in this he found common cause with Russia. Both Russia and the Weimar Republic thought that Poland should not exist and that the frontiers should be restored to those existing in 1914.[*] As hardly anyone else would have anything to do with Bolshevik Russia, Lenin was happy to cooperate with Germany – both were, after all, the world's pariahs. As early as 1921 negotiations began in Moscow between von Seekt's representatives and the Red Army, and, entirely contrary to the provisions of Versailles, arrangements were put in hand for German military training and the manufacture of weapons to take place in Russia. Parallel to these secret negotiations was the Treaty of Rapallo of 1922,[**] whereby Germany and Russia agreed to drop claims against each other arising out of the war, and restored diplomatic relations. At a time when most of the western powers, including Great Britain, did not recognise Soviet Russia, Rapallo had advantages for both sides.

Training in Russia was the responsibility of the Special Group Russia, in Army Headquarters, which arranged for German officers and men to begin flying training from 1922, while the manufacture of aircraft, poison gas and ammunition was looked after by the Company for the Promotion of Industrial Enterprises, a German concern with offices in Berlin and Moscow. By 1924 there was a fully fledged German Military Mission – Centre Moscow – and command of the flying training programme was in the hands of a full colonel. All German officers serving in Russia were technically 'retired', in case the Allies should stumble across their existence.

---

[*] Which is pretty well what happened in 1939 when Germany and Russia divided Poland between them.

[**] Not to be confused with the Treaty of Rapallo of 1920, which resolved territorial questions between Italy and Yugoslavia.

Proposals for mechanisation were the province of the Inspectorate of the Army Service Corps, and beginning in 1922 each of the seven infantry divisions permitted by Versailles established a motor transport battalion. This battalion's primary, and only admitted, role was supply, but men like Captain Guderian were already experimenting with the movement of infantry by transport, the use of transport for reconnaissance, and running map exercises to test procedures for air- and motor-transport cooperation. Guderian, an infantry officer by trade, had commanded a radio communications centre during the latter stage of the war. In January 1922 he commanded the 7th (Bavarian) Motor Transport Battalion, from where he was posted to the Inspectorate of Motor Transport. German officers had studied the lessons of tank warfare in the Great War, and particularly the use of them by the British in 1918. At this stage there could be no tanks in Germany, so in 1924 the first dummy panzers appeared, made of cardboard, plywood and canvas and fixed on a chassis of two bicycles, the whole contraption powered by two pedalling soldiers inside.

Colonel General von Seekt was in favour of mechanisation, but only up to a point. By keeping it out of politics Seekt was undoubtedly good for the army, but in some ways he was a stultifying influence. In 1925 Colonel (later Field Marshal) Werner von Blomberg, head of army training, suggested that the lance had no place in modern war and should be withdrawn from the cavalry. Seekt refused, on the rather odd grounds that when he himself had suggested the withdrawal of lances during the war, it had been refused. Similarly, Blomberg's request for cyclist units to be issued with motorcycles fell on deaf ears.[4] Once Seekt retired, however, in 1926, progress speeded up. By April 1927 the 6th Motor Transport Battalion in Hanover had received thirty-two dummy tanks made from sheet metal on a motor-car chassis, and shortly all motor transport battalions had a company similarly equipped.

In Russia a German armoured school was opened in December 1926 in what had been a Red Army artillery barracks at Kasan, three thousand miles away from Germany, and there tests were carried out on various types of armour, and guns of different calibres, the aim being to decide what form the future German tank should take. The quid pro quo for the Russians in all this was that they were permitted to send Russian students on courses at the German School of Infantry at Dresden, and Russian warships were granted the use of German ports on the Baltic.

In 1928 the first German tank appeared – or rather did not, for it was built in great secrecy in the Krupp and Rheinmetall factories, designated the Light Tractor as a cover name and shipped off to Russia for testing. Shortly afterwards came the Heavy Tractor, six of which were made and sent off to Kasan. Although only intended for training and testing, these tanks compared with the contemporary British tanks incorporated in the Experimental Armoured Force as follows:

NATIONALITY	TYPE	FRONTAL ARMOUR	MAIN ARMAMENT	MAX SPEED	WEIGHT
British	Vickers Mk I Medium	8mm	47mm gun	15 mph	12 tons
German	Light Tractor VK 31	14mm	37mm gun	21 mph	10 tons
British	Vickers Medium Mk II	12mm	47mm gun	18 mph	14 tons
German	Heavy Tractor I	14mm	75mm gun	25 mph	17 tons

Already the German tank designers were looking at faster and better-protected armoured vehicles, but it was not only tanks that were being manufactured contrary to the provisions of the Versailles Treaty. Heinkel had opened an aircraft factory in Sweden, ostensibly to build civil aircraft but all designed so that they could quickly be converted for military purposes; Dornier had factories in Switzerland and Italy, and the Junkers plant in Germany that had been permitted to supply the needs of civil aviation, was in fact testing military applications. The British military attaché, Marshall-Cornwall, was convinced that there were more men in the Reichsheer than were authorised, and noted that wheeled vehicles with canvas screens were representing tanks on German army exercises. Occasionally the obituaries of officers killed on training or in aeroplane crashes in Russia appeared in the German newspapers, and when the War Ministry was asked by French or British embassies to explain, they affected complete ignorance and claimed that while these people had formerly been officers in the German army, they were no longer so, and sure enough scrutiny revealed that their names had been removed from the

German Army List. This fooled few, but it was difficult to prove otherwise.

The next illegal tank was acquired in 1932, its cover name Neubau-fahrzeug, or 'Newly Built Car'. It weighed nearly twenty tons, had a maximum speed of 19 mph, mounted 75mm and 37mm guns and had frontal armour of nearly one inch. Only six prototypes were built, but they were used in the Norwegian campaign of 1940. To train German army tank crews there was now a two-year course in Berlin, attended by officers in civilian clothes, and with two interim visits of five months each to Kasan. The first course, in 1929, had ten German lieutenants and ten Russians, the Russian element progressively increasing until the 1932 course had a hundred Russian students. It may be that the German army's surprise when they met the Russian T34 tank in 1942 was largely of their own making.

By 1927 Major Guderian was teaching armoured tactics at the School of Transport, without ever having been in a tank, but using manuals based on the British Provisional Regulations for Armoured Fighting Vehicles. It was established by now that the Motor Transport Inspectorate would be the nucleus of the future panzer arm, and the first armoured training battalion was raised, with one motorcycle company, one company with dummy tanks and one company with dummy armoured reconnaissance vehicles. From this unlikely acorn grew the most feared military machine of the twentieth century, and already officers were being transferred into Motor Transport units. They could be from any arm but the preference was for infantry, and some very high-grade officers were attracted by the (unwritten) prospect of being in at the ground floor when the pretence of being supply units could be dropped. In 1929 Guderian was sent on attachment to the Swedish army's armoured battalion, where he could crawl over and drive a tank and generally test low-level tactics. On return, in February 1930, he was placed in command of the 3rd Motor Transport Battalion in Berlin, organised with one armoured recce company (dummy light tanks), one tank company (dummy tanks) and one anti-tank company equipped with wooden guns. As the standard infantry model '98 rifle had the same trajectory as a proposed 37mm anti-tank gun, by mounting rifles on the wooden barrels of the dummy guns some idea could be got as to the capabilities of a real anti-tank gun.

In March 1931 the now Lieutenant Colonel Guderian became Chief of Staff at the Inspectorate of Motor Transport, and now began the debate on future armoured tactics. Guderian and his commander, General Lutz, believed that tanks could be employed autonomously, in panzer divisions, while others, concerned about the cost, saw the tank as an infantry support weapon. It was agreed that each infantry division needed a mechanised anti-tank company, but there was much argument about the best calibre for the gun on the light tank (or armoured reconnaissance vehicle), when it was produced. Motor Transport officers wanted a gun of 50mm to be mounted, while the Ordnance and Artillery departments favoured the smaller 37mm. Finally cost was the deciding factor and the 37mm was selected, but the Motor Transport Inspectorate managed to have the turret of the light tank designed so that it would take the 50mm gun if in the future finance became available.

It was this latter tank that eventually became the Panzer Mark III, while a medium tank being designed at the same time and with a 75mm gun became the Panzer Mark IV, eventually the German main battle tank until replaced by the Mark V Panther, but which with various modifications remained in service throughout the Second War. The Mark IV was designed to have an all up weight of 24 tons, as this was the maximum weight that standard German road bridges could take; it had a crew of five, a top speed of 25 mph, and had radio communications fitted as standard. It had two inches of frontal armour. The Panzer Marks I and II were intended to be stopgap vehicles for training purposes only, until the Marks III and IV came into service. The Mark I was based on a British Carden-Lloyd chassis and had two medium machine guns in a revolving turret, while the Mark II had one heavy (20mm) and one medium machine gun, also in a revolving turret. These two vehicles did not come into service until after Hitler came to power, and although originally intended for training only, in practice very large numbers of Marks I and II were deployed during the Battle of France in 1940.

In 1932 the Reichsheer produced its own Combined Arms Manual and its first Armoured Reconnaissance Battalion, with two armoured recce companies (dummy light tanks), one motorcycle company and one heavy company consisting of a platoon each of field engineers, anti-tank guns (wooden) and mortars.

Clandestine training, manufacture of prohibited items and secret stockpiling of weapons were by no means an activity of the army alone or of the political right: all German governments from 1919 onward turned a blind eye or actively supported the Reichsheer in its attempts to outmanoeuvre Versailles. In February 1927 a report to the German cabinet on secret weapon stocks led to a procedural device to avoid illicit military expenditure being subject to Reichstag scrutiny, and to conceal it from the Allies. That this planning was extensive is shown by the Reichsheer's intention to have enough weapons, equipment and ammunition to be able to equip a sixteen-division army by 1932, and a twenty-one-division army by 1938. This, and approval to build a pocket battleship (that is, one up to the treaty limits), was approved by the Social Democrat cabinet.[5] Had the matter of rearmament been put to the general public, which of course it could not be, then an overwhelming majority, regardless of political allegiance, would have supported it.

Within the army there was much analysis of the lessons of the Great War and discussion as to how future wars might be fought. Few officers doubted that there would be a future war – threats were identified from France and from Poland – but unlike the situation in 1914, which was predicated on a German war of conquest, debate in the twenties and early thirties assumed that Germany would be the victim of aggression. In a directive to senior commanders in 1930, the Defence Minister listed the possible tasks of the armed forces with the codewords applicable to each scenario. Attack by a foreign state was 'Case Pilsudski'.[*] In general most soldiers realised that future war would be total, and that the armed forces would be but one part of the national effort. Groener thought that modern wars would be so expensive that they could only be of short duration, while others reverted to the classic German problem: wars have to be won quickly, to avoid having to fight on several fronts. The German navy, meanwhile, considered that they should now move from coastal defence to planning for a more active role, and began to give some thought as to how they could attack sea routes between a western and an eastern enemy. Their planning assumption was that in the worst case Germany would be under attack by France and Poland simultaneously.

* Marshal Pilsudski had led a coup in 1926 and ruled Poland as a dictator until his death in 1935.

By the time Hitler would repudiate Versailles, the German army was ready for expansion. It had absorbed and studied the lessons of 1914–18, had recognised that in modern war the tank would play a major part, understood the necessity for all-arms cooperation and had training for it well under way. By using the Reichsheer as a cadre, and by training everyone in it to operate two or three ranks up, there was sufficient high-quality expertise to expand several fold without any dilution of standards.

Outside the barracks the German republic staggered on, not helped by the Allies presenting the bill for war damage, a total of £6.7 billion, to be paid in the ratio of 52 per cent to France, 22 to Britain, 10 to Italy, 8 to Belgium and 5 to Serbia, with the remaining 3 per cent going to minor participants. America, which had declined to sign the Versailles Treaty, and Russia, where the Bolshevik revolution had led to the murder of the Tsar and his family and an exit from the war, got nothing (although the Treaty of Brest Litosvk, which gave huge chunks of western Russia to Germany, was cancelled). In 1921 another Communist uprising in Germany was put down, but most anti-government agitation came from the right. It was claimed that 40,000 ex-officers were behind anti-republican and pro-monarchy riots and assassinations. Unemployment, poverty and the humiliation of defeat all fuelled nationalism and there was a whole raft of political parties, many of them with only a few hundred members, ready to propagate the myth of the 'stab in the back', which insisted that Germany had not been defeated on the battlefield but betrayed by faithless politicians, socialists and Jews. The army was well aware that it had been defeated in the field, but naturally made no attempt to dissuade those who claimed that it had not.

One of the many little parties jockeying for the support of the disaffected, the ex-soldiers, the unemployed and the anti-Semites was the Nationalsozialistische Deutsche Arbeiterpartei, or NSDAP, the National Socialist German Workers Party, founded in 1919. A rising star of the party, and one of its earliest members, was Adolf Hitler, a twice-decorated wartime lance corporal, who based his appeal on denunciation of the Versailles Treaty, hatred of the constitution of the republic and dislike of Jews. In Britain, where there has not been an anti-Jewish pogrom since the early thirteenth century,[*] it is easy to forget that anti-Semitism has a long history in Europe, especially in France, Germany and Russia. British Jews tended to be British first and Jews second, and while there was the occasional golf club that refused them membership, in general there were few bars to Jewish progress socially, politically or in the professions. In Europe Jews were more easily identified and attacked. Demagogues who wish to unite a crowd of (mainly) 'have-nots' behind them have always found it easy to encourage hatred of a group who are thought to be 'haves'.

The NSDAP, of which Hitler soon became chairman, set up its own uniformed wing, the SA, supposedly to protect its meetings from attacks by Communists. To get round the prohibition on paramilitary organisations SA originally stood for Sports Abteilung (sports department), later openly becoming the Sturm Abteilung (storm troopers). The *Volkische Beobachter* was purchased as the newspaper of the party (soon banned by the government in Berlin, but not in Bavaria) and the German eagle with the swastika adopted as its sign.[**] The party, with its impressive symbols and simple ideology that glorified the Germanic race, denied defeat and promised order and a return to greatness, was attractive to many, and there is no doubt that Hitler was an inspired orator, with the gift of catching the mood of his audience and bending it to his own will.

In 1922 the German government had obtained a postponement of part of the reparations payments, and for 1923 she asked for a further delay. The facts were that Germany simply could not pay without risking such hardship in the population that revolution would be a real possibility. The British were sympathetic but the French decidedly not. President Poincaré announced that if the Germans did not pay up then France would seize German industrial plants and exploit them for herself until Germany did pay. On 10 January 1923 French and Belgian troops marched into the Ruhr, took over the factories and ordered German workers to

---

[*] They could not have been persecuted in England after 1290, when they were expelled from the country altogether, but even after Cromwell asked them to return during the Protectorate they remained generally unmolested.

[**] The swastika (Sanskrit *Swas* – life, and *Tika* – sign) is an ancient symbol long predating Germany or even Christianity, and still found in India, Nepal and Tibet. It variously represents the sun or the eternal wheel of life. The NSDAP, by some rather selective thinking, saw it as being an Aryan symbol.

remain at their posts. The results were strikes, riots and confrontation, and a stop to all reparation payments, the situation being particularly provocative to the Germans by the French using black colonial troops. In Essen French troops opened fire on protesting German workers and killed thirteen of them; the German government began to print money to pay out-of-work and striking workers, inevitably triggering the collapse of the currency and an inflationary spiral that by the end of the year would reduce the purchasing power of the German mark to one-million-millionth of its value in 1914.[6]

All over Germany separatist movements were springing up, ranging from Marxists on the extreme left to monarchists and nationalists of varying hues on the right. In Bavaria the threat to stability was seen as so serious that the Bavarian government abrogated its powers to a former prime minister, von Kahr, a monarchist and firm believer in provincial autonomy. Kahr was determined to stamp out Marxism, but had no intention of letting extreme nationalism in the shape of the NSDAP fill the gap, and he banned a series of meetings at which Hitler was to speak. Elsewhere in Germany Seekt was able to ensure that the army remained loyal to the government, but in Bavaria the local army commander, General von Lossow, openly supported von Kahr, and intended to order the troops under his command to swear an oath to the provincial government. This would have been the first step in outright secession, and Seekt ordered Lossow to resign, which he refused to do. All this suited Hitler, who saw advantages for the NSDAP in what Kahr and Lossow were getting up to; but they were intending to do it without Hitler, and so the NSDAP decided to launch their own coup. They would first take over Bavaria, and then use that state as a launch-pad for a march on Berlin, in a copy of Mussolini's march on Rome the previous year. The difference, of course, was that Mussolini was an established political figure and had been invited to take power; Hitler was unknown outside Bavaria and had not a single parliamentary seat.

The so-called beer-hall putsch was launched by the NSDAP on 8 November 1923, the ostensible aims being to end the occupation of the Ruhr, overthrow the republic and deal with the Jews and the Communists – the alleged perpetrators of the stab in the back of 1918. Despite the support of General Erich von Ludendorff, a hero of the military pantheon, the putsch was a complete failure. On 9 November Hitler and Ludendorff, leading a crowd of several thousand brown-shirted SA members and supporters, marched towards Munich's main square. They were ordered to halt and disperse by a police roadblock and when they refused the police opened fire. Ludendorff ignored them and marched on, unscathed. Hitler fled and fourteen marchers were killed. The coup was over and subjected to much ridicule in the press. The NSDAP was banned in Bavaria and Hitler was tried on a charge of treason and sentenced to five years' imprisonment. He actually served nine months, during which time he wrote *Mein Kampf*.

Modern Germany is so terrified of a resurgence of National Socialism that *Mein Kampf* is banned (banning of books was something that the Nazis did quite a lot of, too). A more certain way of ensuring there is no backsliding to the bad old days would be to make it mandatory for all Germans to read what must be one of the most constipation-inducing tomes ever penned. That said, for those who bothered to read it, *Mein Kampf* laid out exactly what Hitler intended to do and did do, as far as he could, when he achieved power.

1923 was also the year when the limitations of the League of Nations, the shining hope of those who believed in collective security and the solving of international problems by negotiation, were first exposed. The League was set up in January 1920. It was fatally flawed from its inception by the refusal of the USA to join, concerned lest collective security might draw her into overseas commitments that she did not want to undertake; initially, however, it seemed to be working. The League had delineated the boundaries of the free city of Danzig and the Saarland; and it resolved problems between Yugoslavia and Albania, and on the border of Silesia. It mediated successfully between Sweden and Finland and between Poland and Lithuania, even though it had done nothing to halt the fighting between Poland and Russia when Poland saw an opportunity to grab bits of a Russia weakened by its own civil war. The difficulty faced by the League, like its successor the United Nations, however, was that it was not a power in its own right, but merely a club, which could only take such action as its members would agree to. In dealing with minor players on the world scene the League coped well – after all, the price of eggs was unaffected by whether Sweden and Finland went to war, or by where exactly the border between Poland and Lithuania lay. But once the League touched upon the interests of the great, or medium, powers, it was much less free to act.

In 1923 three officers of an Italian boundary commission delineating the border between Greece and Albania were murdered. There was no evidence that the perpetrators were Greek, and there was certainly no official Greek support for the killings. Nevertheless, Mussolini, recently in power and flexing Italy's muscles, delivered an ultimatum to the Greek government in such terms that no independent nation could have accepted it. In retaliation for Greece's rejection of the ultimatum Italian troops occupied the Greek island of Corfu after a bombardment by the Italian navy. The League was outraged and at the instigation of the British delegation Italy was roundly condemned and ordered to withdraw. Mussolini now said that if the League continued even to discuss the matter Italy would leave the League. The League promptly backed off. The matter was resolved by the French and the British persuading the Greeks to make, and the Italians to accept, apologies and reparations rather less severe than those originally demanded, but the incident and the cracks in the League that it exposed did not go unnoticed.

With the failure of the Munich putsch Hitler and his acolytes realised that the only sure way to obtain power in Germany and to keep it must be by legal methods, which would mean winning elections. Hitler had made a study of propaganda as used by the Allies in the war, and also of American commercial advertising, which was largely based on constant repetition of slogans. He asserted that the only way to get the populace to vote for the NSDAP would be by mass propaganda. While other political parties tried to appeal to the electorates' ability to discriminate, and to make a decision based on examination of the various manifestos on offer, Hitler saw propaganda as aimed at emotion rather than logic, as appealing to faith rather than to reason. As he said, 'Propaganda must appeal to the feelings of the masses rather than to what is called their understanding.'[7] By mass meetings and newspapers (radio was forbidden to the party until 1933) the NSDAP hammered home their message: only Hitler could make

Germany great again; only Hitler could restore full employment and stabilise the currency; only Hitler could smash the shackles of Versailles and restore Germany to her rightful place in the world; only Hitler could deal with the 'criminals of 1918'; only Hitler could stop the Jews and the Communists. It was all heady stuff, and by promising each group what it wanted to hear, without going into too much detail about how it was to be achieved, support began to grow.

The appeal of Hitler could only be enhanced by the continued French occupation of the Ruhr. It was not lost on the Germans that France had refused even to enter into discussions about her own loans owing to the United States, but did not hesitate to keep up demands for reparations payments from Germany. Eventually the Dawes Plan, drawn up in 1924 under the auspices of the Allied Reparations Committee, was agreed, with the British pressurising the reluctant French to sign. Under the plan a central bank with a board composed equally of Germans and representatives of the Allies would be set up. It would be the sole note-issuing bank and from it reparations payments would be made. The amount to be paid would depend upon the strength of the German economy and the value of the currency, and as well as an international loan the bank would have a lien on certain industries, railway rolling stock and consumption taxes in order to have the wherewithal to pay. French troops evacuated the Ruhr.

At this point there did appear to be some hope for democracy, as represented by the Weimar Republic, in Germany. With the adoption of the Dawes Plan, repayments would now be manageable, and secessionist movements in Bavaria were brought under control. In September 1926 Germany was invited to join the League of Nations. Despite von Lussow in Bavaria, the Reichsheer had so far managed to distance itself from involvement in politics. The Geneva Protocol of 1924, where signatories were to renounce war except as instructed by the League, and were to combine against an aggressor, was a step towards collective security. A proposed Treaty of Mutual Assistance was rejected by Britain, under pressure from the Dominions who were concerned lest they might be dragged into a war for some obscure part of eastern Europe, but on the face of it the Locarno Treaty of 1925 seemed to give France the assurance of security that she needed.

In 1925 the first president of the German republic, Friedrich Ebert, died. The election for a successor was won by a reluctant Field Marshal Paul von Hindenburg, hero of the Great War, who at seventy-eight years of age and neither a radical nor an extremist of left or right, was seen as a safe candidate. There were still ominous signs, however. The German-Soviet non-aggression pact of the following year, 1926, while on the surface pointing towards a more peaceful world, annoyed the Allies as it had been concluded bilaterally, and they were worried that it might contain secret clauses – as indeed it did.

In 1927 the ban on Hitler (now released from prison) speaking at meetings was lifted, but in the 1928 elections, much to the relief of many inside and outside Germany, the NSDAP won only twelve seats in the Reichstag, the federal parliament. The Social Democrats were the largest party returned with 153 seats, while the Communists got fifty-four. The new government tried very hard to negotiate a French withdrawal of the occupation troops from the Rhineland, but failed due to French insistence on any withdrawal being linked to increased reparations payments. Squabbles over reparations and rising unemployment in Germany, along with general dissatisfaction at the continued application of Versailles, all helped to increase Hitler's support both in Germany and in Austria, where ever since the collapse of the Empire in 1918 there had been a strong movement for union with Germany – Anschluss – specifically forbidden by Versailles.

The Kellogg-Briand Pact, signed in 1928 by all the great and many of the not so great powers, outlawed war as an instrument of national policy. It encouraged the British to believe that collective security really could work, and confirmed Hitler's belief in the decadence of the West. Communist-inspired riots in Germany in 1929 and rising unemployment saw the NSDAP gain ground, and now they united with the various other nationalist parties in demanding not just a reduction in reparations, but their cancellation altogether, along with a repudiation of the war guilt clause, whereby Germany accepted the entire blame for the war. On this latter point Hitler was on sure ground; there was hardly a German of any political hue who did not agree. It had only been signed at Versailles in 1919 at the last minute, and then only after the German Chancellor had sought the advice of the German army as to whether an Allied invasion subsequent to a refusal to sign could be resisted; he was told that it could not be.

Another unintended boost to NSDAP support was the US stock market crash in 1929. Driven largely by overproduction, there had been sharp falls in the prices of basic commodities, and this sparked off a panic and huge falls in the prices of shares. Between September and November the market fell by nearly 50 per cent, affecting not just rich plutocrats but small savers too. American factories found orders cancelled and had to lay workers off; the reduction in American purchasing power led to fewer orders in overseas markets, and in Germany unemployment reached the three million mark, while NSDAP membership reached two million.

Under the provisions of the Young Plan of 1929, the complete evacuation by France of the Rhineland (though not of the Saar) took place in 1930. This, however, did little to help German moderate opinion, and in 1930, when the Social Democrat government was unable to get its budget through the Reichstag and called an election, the NSDAP stood on a programme of cancellation of reparations, removal of the war guilt clause, readjustment of Germany's eastern boundaries (living space), a return to conscription, and the removal of Jewish influence on public policy. As a great many people were attracted by at least one of these points, the NSDAP vote climbed from 810,000 in 1928 to three million, and their seats from twelve to 107, making them the second largest party in the Reichstag, behind the Social Democrats with 143. In Britain, Churchill remarked gloomily that if Hitler ever did get into power he would resort to armed force as soon as he was able to do so.

As the second largest party, the NSDAP would normally have formed part of a coalition government, but Hitler refused all blandishments unless he was appointed Chancellor with no restrictions placed on whom he might appoint to his cabinet. In the country, support for Hitler continued to grow after the League of Nations vetoed a plan for free trade between Germany and Austria, on the grounds that this was but a prelude to Anschluss under another name, as of course it was. In order to make sure that the customs union could not be implemented, the French government withdrew her deposits in the main Austrian bank, thus precipitating its collapse and a banking crisis in Austria and Germany, which in turn intensified anti-French sentiment, never far from the surface in Germany at the best of times. In the 1932 German presidential elections, Hitler came second to Hindenburg with 37 per cent of the vote. While the powers met at the League of Nations disarmament conference, a German general election – the first of two that year and called because the NSDAP had made the normal functioning of parliament almost unworkable – returned the NSDAP as the largest party with 230 seats to the Social Democrats' 133. This time Hitler was offered the chancellorship but Hindenburg was not prepared to meet his conditions, and another election was called in November of the same year. Once again the NSDAP were returned as the largest party, albeit that their seats were reduced to 197.

THE COUNTRY WITH MOST to fear from a reinvigorated Germany was France, and many German soldiers saw a pre-emptive war launched by France as a real possibility. In fact, although France emerged from the Great War on the winning side, it was in many ways a Pyrrhic victory. In both blood and treasure France had paid a high price. With a population six million less than that of Britain, she had suffered almost twice as many deaths, and in an ageing population the men of military age were already a smaller percentage of the population than they were in the UK. Altogether 66,000 miles of roads and 31,000 miles of railway line had been destroyed or damaged; 320,000 houses, 20,000 factories, 2,000 bridges and 600 railway stations had to be rebuilt. The national debt had soared to 150 billion francs, compared to 35 billion in 1914. The country was exhausted, and so was the economy. The cost of rebuilding was supposed to be met from German reparations, but of the 132 billion gold marks that were due, only ten billion were ever paid. Germany considered the terms of Versailles harsh, but Prime Minister Lloyd George and President Wilson had watered them down from the original French proposals, and even after the signing in 1919 Marshal Foch was still complaining that the provisions were too timorous. One has some sympathy for the French position: Prussia had been a major participant in the defeat of Napoleonic France and in 1870 had not only defeated France but humiliated her. There were many in the France of the Great War who remembered 1870, and they were determined that Germany should never again be in a position to threaten France as the dominant continental power.

Like England, France was determined to demobilise and disarm as quickly as possible. The French army would still be vastly bigger than Britain's, but then France was a land power and needed an army big enough to defend her borders. Large in numbers it might be, but the cost was to be kept to a minimum. The French army was a conscript force but the three years' compulsory service before 1914 was reduced to two years in 1919, to eighteen months in 1923 and to a year in 1928. Also in 1928 the fifteen tank regiments in the army were reduced to ten. Ten tank regiments, each of two or three battalions, was far more than the British could even dream of in 1928, but aside from fifty British Mark Vs of First War vintage, French tanks were mainly the light Renault FT17, with a two-man crew and a top speed of just over 2 mph. It first appeared in 1917 and was still in service in 1940. In addition to a general shortage of funding, political instability, with French governments changing at an alarming rate, meant that there was a lack of direction and no consistent policy in national defence. Politicians found it easier to procrastinate – after all, they would not be in office when the chickens came home to roost – and if they did make a decision it would be overruled by the next administration.

Many of the influential French military leaders were too old, too tired and too self-satisfied to look further than the methods in use in 1914–18. In 1925 Joffre was seventy-three, Foch seventy-four, Fayolle seventy-three and Pétain sixty-nine. Even in the normally conservative British army these generals would have been long retired and with no power to affect current doctrine, but in France they sat on the Military Advisory Council and could, and did, exercise considerable influence. None was prepared to think laterally, or to promote original ideas. There were, however, certain French generals who were thinking ahead. General Estienne, in a lecture to the Conservatoire National in 1920, and repeated in Brussels before the king of the Belgians, described a future war as being waged by massed tanks and armoured infantry, supported by self-propelled artillery and aircraft; he saw no place for the horse on the battlefield, and advocated each tank having two crews, so that battle could continue without pause; he considered that surprise and mobility would be the key factors in any future war. Estienne went further and described how 100,000 men could be moved fifty miles in a single night using 8,000 lorries and 4,000 tanks manned by an elite corps of 20,000 men. Having arrived at their destination, heavy tanks, weighing fifty to a hundred tons each,[*] would break through the enemy defences, after which light tanks and armoured infantry, supported by mobile artillery, would pour through the gap and fan out, destroying a confused and disorientated opponent. General Estienne had his disciples – Charles de Gaulle being one – but there was no possibility of obtaining the expenditure to fund such grandiose ideas, and those tanks that were available were seen as supports for the infantry, rather than being employed as an independent arm, as Estienne wished. He retired in November 1922 but was re-employed as Director General Armoured Studies, with declining influence, for another ten years.

General Maxime Weygand, Chief of the General Staff (professional head of the army) until 1931, was initially also in favour of the tank, but saw it as working in conjunction with horsed cavalry; as did the Director of Cavalry, General Flavigny, who saw tanks as providing the cavalry with surprise and offensive capability. Despite this support from on high, there was resistance to development of armour: it was too expensive and it was resisted by many cavalry officers. Even Weygand had to admit: 'It costs too much to mechanise and anyway, supplies of petrol are limited.' A plan to form an armoured division in 1927 was shelved, and such armoured doctrine as there was concentrated on the need for a heavy tank to support the infantry, with a lighter and much faster machine to work with the cavalry. An Inspector General of Mechanisation was set up in 1927 but he could achieve little: no one could agree on exactly what was wanted, and there was no money for experimentation. In 1931 the so-called 'Petrol and Oats' solution was adopted, whereby cavalry divisions were given some armoured elements, including a regiment of dragoons (motorised infantry) to replace one of the regiments of horsed cavalry. In any case, the French army was thinking increas-

---

[*] He was away with the fairies here; there was hardly a bridge in France or Germany that would take such a weight, and no army had compatible bridging equipment.

ingly not of attack, but of defence, personified by the Maginot Line.

In 1870 France had been defeated, and her military theorists decided that the culprit was a reliance on defence. In 1914, therefore, French military doctrine placed its faith in offensives of such fury as to drive the larger and better-equipped Germans out of their prepared positions and defeat them. The result was that the war was still fought on French soil, with huge casualties. After 1918, French analysts, noting how difficult it had been to break into or break through defensive positions on the Western Front, judged that the only way to prevent another invasion of France was to construct massive fortifications along her frontier. No soldier pretended that any defence system could be impregnable (although many politicians did), but it would be such that it would deter any attacker, or if deterrence failed would be so powerful that the cost in time and blood to breach it would soon prove unacceptable. André Maginot, the Minister of Defence from 1929 to 1932 who initiated the building of the Line, had been at Verdun in 1916, and had seen the strength of fixed defences and the difficulties of getting through them. The Maginot Line was planned and designed between 1920 and 1930, and built between 1930 and 1937. The Line was a series of highly sophisticated forts and defensive positions running from southern France to the Belgian border. It did not extend from the Franco-Belgian border to the coast because of the difficulty of construction in the low-lying wetlands of Flanders; and while from time to time there was discussion about continuing the Line along the German-Belgian border, the finance was never available. After 1936, when Belgium cancelled her defence agreement with France and proclaimed her neutrality, she refused to accept any fortification through the country or along the frontier as compromising that neutrality (which of course did them no good at all in the long run, as neutrality rarely does). Received opinion tells us that the Maginot Line was a complete white elephant, that it was useless and achieved nothing. That is not entirely true – it proved a very effective obstacle to any attacks on it – but it did encourage soldiers and politicians to rely far too much on its defensive qualities at the expense (and the Line was very expensive) of modernisation and mechanisation of the French army.

In 1931 the 61-year-old General Maurice Gamelin succeeded the

64-year-old General Weygand as Chief of the General Staff. Unlike Weygand, Gamelin was not in favour of the tank and did little to advance the cause of mechanisation. Gamelin, and most of the political and military hierarchy of France, were now totally defensively minded, mesmerised by the Maginot Line. The development of a new tank – the Char B – which had been authorised, was now delayed, almost cancelled altogether, and the tank was not finally put in service until 1935. It would be the French army's main battle tank in 1940, weighed thirty-one tons, had a crew of four, a top speed of 17.5 mph and frontal armour of two and a half inches.

If the French army was in a poor state by the early 1930s, the French air force was even more so. Ostensibly much larger than Britain's, its aircraft were obsolete, many of them grounded though lack of spares or fuel, and it was short of pilots. All in all the underfunded French armed forces, with their poorly paid conscript soldiers and their elderly, defensively minded generals, in a country with weak political institutions and still suffering from the First War, were in no state to cope with a newly resurgent Germany, soon to arise from the ashes of defeat.

IN GERMANY, ON 30 January 1933, having exhausted all other possibilities, President Hindenburg offered the chancellorship to Adolf Hitler, who accepted. Nothing would ever be the same again.

NOTES

1. *The Treaty of Peace between the Allied and Associated Powers and Germany*, HMSO, London, undated.

2. Ibid., Article 179.

3. Karl Demeter (tr Angus Malcolm), *The German Officer-Corps*, Weidenfeld & Nicolson, London, 1965.

4. Albert Seaton, *The German Army 1933–45*, Weidenfeld & Nicolson, London, 1982.

5. Research Institute for Military History, Germany (ed), *Germany and the Second World War*, Vol. I (tr Falla, McMurry and Osers), Clarendon Press, Oxford, 2003.

6. Martin Gilbert, *A History of the Twentieth Century*, Vol. I, HarperCollins, London, 1997.

7. Adolf Hitler, *Mein Kampf*, Munich, 1930.

4

Rearmament

IN 1929 THE BRITISH government confirmed the ten-year rule. They did the same thing again in 1930, but now the Chiefs of Staff Committee (the professional heads of the three services) warned that many nations were increasing, rather than decreasing, their arms budgets, and pointed out that Britain was less ready to fulfil her treaty obligations now than she had been in 1914 when there were no such obligations. The world economic situation was giving cause for concern, as were conditions in Germany where it was becoming increasingly apparent that the full sums due as reparations would not be forthcoming. In 1929 the Young Plan, whereby reparations would be reduced to a sum that could be afforded and be paid as a final settlement, had been signed but had done nothing to stifle nationalist agitation. There was worry about Japanese aggression in Manchuria, and the League seemed unable to do very much about it short of war with Japan which the British, as the dominant naval member of the League, were anxious to avoid.

Not until 1932 did the government begin to doubt the wisdom of the years of allocating funds to social services rather than defence, and even then, while it took the bullet into its collective mouth, it declined actually to bite it. That year the Chiefs of Staff Committee produced their annual report to the Committee for Imperial Defence, a subcommittee of the cabinet. In an era when we have become accustomed to having one Ministry of Defence to direct the activities of all three services, and one Chief of the Defence Staff, an officer who can be of any service, as the government's principal military adviser, it may seem incongruous that a unified ministry dates only from 1964, and that there was no Chief of Defence Staff until 1957 (Marshal of the Royal Air Force Sir William Dickson). Until then each service had its own minister and fought the other two for such resources as might be available. The Chiefs of Staff Committee, comprising the professional heads of each service, the First Sea Lord, the Chief of the Imperial General Staff and the Chief of Air Staff, dated only from 1926 and was chaired by whichever of the three chiefs was the senior. Often the two senior services, the Royal Navy and the army, ganged up on the junior, the Royal Air Force, and this was particularly true of the period before rearmament. In 1932, however, inter-service rivalry and squabbles were set aside, and the report was unanimous and damning.

The world, stated the report, was a dangerous place and Britain's armed forces were completely incapable of meeting her various League and international treaty obligations, never mind the defence of Britain and her Empire. In the Far East war with Japan was a possibility and Hong Kong and Singapore were so weak that they might be captured long before the British fleet could get there; the coasts of India, the southern hemisphere Dominions and bases abroad were wide open to attack. The RAF was unable to defend the homeland; the army was far too small and ill-equipped to fulfil the tasks allotted to it. Since the end of the war in 1918 the services, particularly the army, had been consuming accumulated stocks of ammunition and spare parts and now these were running out, with no provision having been made for their replacement. Ship-building skills had diminished, and the munitions industry had declined alarmingly, to a size where it could not, without a long period of regeneration, meet the needs of a future war.

The fault, said the chiefs, was the ten-year rule. The assumption, repeated year after year, that there would be no war for ten years inhibited expansion, re-equipment, modernisation and morale, to the extent that the nation was now dangerously vulnerable. The report recommended that

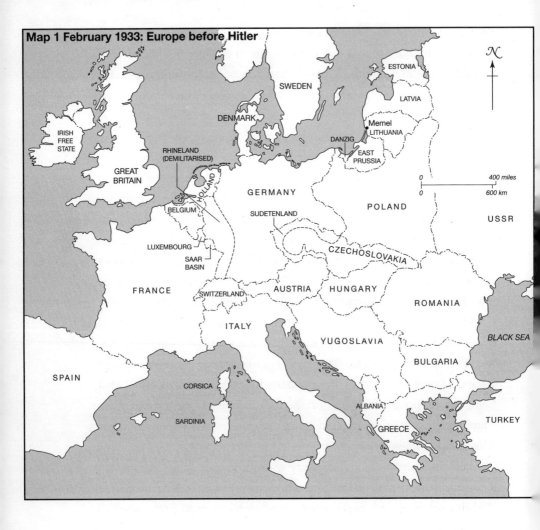

Map 1 February 1933: Europe before Hitler

IRISH
FREE
STATE

GREAT
BRITAIN

SWEDEN

DENMARK

ESTONIA

LATVIA

Memel
LITHUANIA

DANZIG

EAST
PRUSSIA

RHINELAND
(DEMILITARISED)

HOLLAND

GERMANY

POLAND

USSR

BELGIUM

SUDETENLAND

LUXEMBOURG

SAAR
BASIN

CZECHOSLOVAKIA

FRANCE

SWITZERLAND

AUSTRIA

HUNGARY

ROMANIA

ITALY

YUGOSLAVIA

BULGARIA

BLACK SEA

SPAIN

CORSICA

SARDINIA

ALBANIA

GREECE

TURKEY

0   400 miles
0   600 km

the rule should be scrapped, and that arrangements for purely defensive improvements (such as the fortification of the Singapore naval base) should be put in hand immediately. The report was considered by the cabinet in March 1932, and accepted. Having agreed the recommendations of the chiefs, however, the government now did nothing for eighteen months. Admittedly the disarmament conference was in full swing at Geneva; admittedly the reparations conference was about to open in Lausanne and as it was intended to reduce reparations to the absolute minimum tension in Europe might diminish; admittedly Britain's economy was not in good shape; admittedly the public mood was not conducive to increased defence spending, but with all that, it was an incredible and inexcusable lapse by the national government. The service estimates for 1932 were less than those for 1931, and those for 1933, passed after Hitler had come to power in Germany, were even lower still.

At the disarmament conference British representatives found themselves in some degree of sympathy with Germany, who pointed out that the provisions of Versailles limiting German armaments were supposed to be the prelude to general disarmament, which had not happened. That being the case, Germany felt that she should have the right to rearm to a level of those powers surrounding her – by which she meant the French. The British found themselves irritated by the French, who were prepared to make no concessions to Germany without some practical guarantee against yet another invasion, and whose intransigence led to German withdrawal from the conference, only to be coaxed back again in December 1932.

The Chiefs of Staff Committee report to the Committee for Imperial Defence for 1933 said that while matters in the Far East had improved slightly by the signing of a treaty between Japan and China, yet the threat of war with Japan still remained. Germany, thought the chiefs, was once more showing the potential to become a 'public menace'; she was rearming and would doubtless continue to do so until she again posed a threat to peace and stability. The provisions of the Locarno Treaty (guaranteeing European borders) could well drag Britain into a war with France against Germany. The chiefs noted that apart from some relatively modest speeding-up of the programme to put the defences of

Singapore in order, nothing practical had been done in response to their report of the previous year. While the ten-year rule had been abandoned, no statement of doctrine or intent had replaced it. If the current disarmament negotiations failed, said the report, then the situation would become much worse.

The disarmament talks did fail, for not only did Japan give notice of leaving the League, but in October 1933 Germany gave notice of leaving both the League and the disarmament conference. By the time the cabinet considered the reports of the Chiefs of Staff and the Committee for Imperial Defence, in November 1933, it was evident that the situation was indeed much worse. Reluctantly, and parsimoniously, the British cabinet accepted the Chiefs of Staffs' strictures, and declared that henceforth British priorities would be the defence of interests and possessions in the Far East, followed by defence needs in Europe, followed by the defence of India. Japan and Germany were identified as the possible enemies, while France, the United States and Italy were considered friendly powers. The Chiefs of Staff, along with representatives of the Treasury and the Foreign Office, were to prepare for cabinet scrutiny a programme to remedy the worst deficiencies This programme was to put right the decay that had arisen from fourteen years of neglect occasioned by the ten-year rule, and was not to be a programme of rearmament, nor to lead to any new commitments by any of the three services. While the bullet was still not yet bitten, at least governmental teeth had closed over it.

The Defence Requirements Subcommittee began work at once, its first task being to identify the threat. While the Chiefs of Staff were quite clear that Japan and Germany were the potential enemies, Sir Warren Fisher, the Treasury representative on the committee, disagreed. He was adamant that friendship with Japan was the only way to preserve British interests and possessions in the Far East, and as good relations with both the USA and Japan were mutually incompatible, Britain ought to risk a break with the US – hostilities even – in the interests of a rapprochement with Japan.[1] This was not as far-fetched as it seems today, when for sixty-three years the US has been Britain's major ally, both within the North Atlantic Alliance and bilaterally. Fisher's argument was that whereas the US did not threaten and could not attack British territories in the East, Japan did and could. Friendship with Japan, and a return to the close and amicable relations that had existed prior to the Washington Naval Conference, would ensure the security of the British Empire in the East, and if it did come to war, then the combined British and Japanese navies would have no great difficulty in seeing off the United States. Logic there may have been in Fisher's arguments – which were supported by the British ambassador in Tokyo – but to forsake America, with its commonality of language and race, and a shared religious and cultural background, for an uncertain Asiatic ally whose behaviour in China was increasingly difficult to justify, was never a realistic option. That was probably just as well, for however close Anglo-Japanese relations might have become, the concessions required by an expansionist and militarist Japan would have been more than Britain would have been prepared to make.

The committee predicted that Japan was seeking naval parity with Britain and the US, and that this should be resisted by all means short of war. As for Germany, she was seen as needing five years to rearm to the extent of posing a credible threat, which predicated a five-year period for the UK to put her house in order. For the Royal Navy this should involve modernisation of capital ships, the building-up of naval stores and the modernisation of naval bases, particularly those in the Far East. For the army, which had been allowed to run down even more than the other services, the air defence of the UK dictated that a potential enemy (Germany) should be kept out of bomber range of the UK, which meant that the Low Countries of Holland and Belgium must be defended, which in turn meant an expeditionary force. This, thought the committee, should consist of four infantry divisions, one cavalry division, one tank brigade and two air defence brigades. Apart from the tanks and the air defence units this was what the UK had contributed in August 1914. As for the Royal Air Force, the committee wanted the 1923 plan, agreed then but never implemented, of fifty-two squadrons for home defence to be activated as soon as possible. The problem here was that the 1923 plan was drawn up to counter a French attack, and only provided defence for the south of England. Now, with Germany as the potential enemy, if the north was to be included, and if the army's expeditionary force was to have air cover, then another twenty-five squadrons would be needed for home defence and another nineteen again for the expeditionary force. As this was a new requirement, rather than correcting deficiencies, it was decided to pass the problem to the cabinet, and let them decide.

A major problem foreseen by the committee was what they termed the moral disarmament of the British people. After years of exposure to propaganda from pacifists, League supporters and so-called war poets, a series of disarmament conferences, and the experience of unemployment and economic retrenchment, public opinion had become so opposed to war that it was quite unready to accept the expenditure that even modest rearmament would entail. A by-election had recently seen a Labour candidate, standing on a pacifist programme, win what had been seen as a safe Conservative constituency.[*] That the senior serving officers could see what is normally only picked up by a political antenna, shows how serious the situation was.

By mid 1934 the British government found itself still attending the disarmament conference, despite it having been rendered meaningless by Germany's withdrawal, and making ludicrous and quite impractical proposals that all air forces should be abolished or, if that could not be accepted, that bombing of cities should be outlawed. At the same time the British were trying to find some common ground between the German wish to rearm and the French refusal to countenance it. German rearmament was inevitable, and already taking place in secret, so would it not be best to recognise that fact and broker some sort of agreement whereby the French would disarm and the Germans rearm until something nearer parity might be achieved? Unsurprisingly this found no favour with the French. When the British air estimates for 1934 showed a modest increase, they were roundly attacked by Winston Churchill as being too small, which was a bit of a cheek as it had been he, when in office, who was largely responsible for the parlous state of the nation's defences in the first place.

---

* East Fulham, in October 1933, when a Conservative majority of 14,000 was transformed into a Labour majority of 4,000.

The man who pushed hardest for rearmament was the Chancellor of the Exchequer, Neville Chamberlain, later reviled by the Churchill lobby as the arch-appeaser. Chamberlain insisted that Britain should have a powerful air force and an army capable of providing defence in depth by defending the Low Countries. Referring to the long-ago agreed but never implemented plan for fifty-two RAF squadrons for home defence, he proposed ninety, with a further eight for the Fleet Air Arm and overseas. The army should have an expeditionary force capable of deploying to the Continent within one month of mobilisation, its composition to be the often recommended one cavalry and four infantry divisions plus air defence and a tank brigade. Where Chamberlain found himself in disagreement was in his and the First Sea Lord's assessment of the naval threat. The Royal Navy, supported by the navy minister, was of the view that the main threat was, at least in 1934, Japan, but that if a fleet had to be sent to the Far East then there would be insufficient warships to meet a threat from the largest European naval power, France. That France was not considered a threat was not the point: Germany was a threat, and she was demanding naval parity with France. The Royal Navy should, therefore, modernise its capital ships, increase its building programme, build up enough stocks of fuel to last for the first year of war and put the defences of naval bases in order, particularly that of Singapore, where heavy guns were essential. Chamberlain's view was that while both Japan and Germany posed threats, the country could not afford to fight a war against both simultaneously, and as Germany was the greater menace the main thrust should be to rearm against her, with only the minimum being done in the Far East to satisfy Australian and New Zealand opinion.

When all this went to the cabinet the result was generally unsatisfactory. Ministers and MPs were concerned that public opinion was so against any form of land war that any increase for the army might result in the government being voted out of office; the only form of defence which the public might tolerate was air defence and so a modest increase to seventy-five squadrons, rather than Chamberlain's ninety, for home defence was approved. Although the requirement to replace the army's ageing tanks, and its shortages of ammunition and all manner of kit was recognised, only half the money needed to put the situation right would be provided in the first five years. The navy got virtually nothing.

The cabinet were encouraged in their wish to retain as much financial stringency as they could by the events of 30 June 1934 in Germany. There the SA, originally the NSDAP's uniformed bully-boys and increasingly a private army, had begun to advocate policies that diverged from those of Hitler. In particular they wanted to implement socialist measures that went much further than Hitler – with the need to placate big business and the middle classes – was prepared to go, and saw themselves as rivals to the army as the armed instrument of the state. This was naturally unacceptable to the Reichsheer, and as part of its unofficial bargain with the NSDAP it provided transport and communications while the SS, the praetorian guard of the NSDAP, rounded up and executed the leaders of the SA, so removing it as a threat to Hitler. All this, thought the British government, indicated internal weaknesses in the regime, and made it less likely that Germany would develop aggressive policies. What it actually meant, of course, was that Hitler was far stronger, rather than weaker, having eliminated a potential rival organisation and bought the support of the army, which was now the sole bearer of arms in the state.[*]

While the British government was havering about rearmament and worrying what modest improvements the electorate would stand for, the new German government had no doubts. Already, in 1932, the Minister of Defence had agreed to a plan to raise an air force of six fighter, three bomber and thirteen reconnaissance squadrons – 140 aircraft and 4,630 officers and men – and anti-aircraft units, the whole to be paid for with secret funds not subject to parliamentary control. At first this was to be a branch of the army, but once Hitler came to power in 1933 an air ministry was set up to raise, train and equip a separate service – the Luftwaffe. Also, in 1932, a staff college had been secretly formed in Berlin, under the cover name of 'Officers' Course Berlin'. With the death of President Hindenburg in August 1934 the offices of President and Chancellor were combined into one, and what has been seen as the Nazification of the armed forces began. Despite the bleatings in self-serving post-war

* For the time being. The first armed regiments of the SS were created in 1938; by 1945 there would be thirty-eight divisions of the Waffen (armed) SS.

memoirs, many, if not most, service officers were more than happy to go along with the NSDAP. These military professionals had no great depth of political or economic insight, but here was a man who said he would expand the forces, release Germany from the clutches of Versailles, restore her to her rightful place in the world and establish law and order. He and his party had been democratically elected and had formed the government in accordance with the constitution, and even his assumption of dictatorial powers on the death of Hindenburg had been approved by thirty-eight million votes to five million in an apparently legitimate plebiscite. Why would they not support him? He was, of course, only an ex-lance corporal with no breeding and a hoarse, grating voice; some of his speeches were certainly inflammatory, and many of his party members were little more than thugs, but the realities of power would temper NSDAP ideology. Hitler would in time develop into a statesman, and anyway there was no one else who could command public support like he could.

It has generally been averred that it was Hitler and the NSDAP that ordered the Reichswehr – the armed forces – to take an oath to the Führer personally, in place of one to the constitution and institutions of the republic; to place the NSDAP logo of a German eagle carrying a swastika on every serviceman's right breast; and to use the Deutsche Gruss or Fascist salute when in uniform without headdress. Modern German historians, however, are of the view that it was the senior officers of the services, primarily of the army, who suggested it and implemented it through the new Minister of Defence, General von Blomberg.[2] With these trappings came an acceptance of the Aryan clause whereby Jewish officers and men were discharged and expelled from regimental associations. Many officers had reservations. Colonel (later Field Marshal) Erich von Manstein wrote to the minister in protest against the expulsion of Jews; the minister protested to Hitler but got nowhere; some disliked the NSDAP trimmings and the Hitler oath as a politicisation of the forces, but although there was some grumbling, officers saw the new regime as offering far more advantages than risks. It was only much later, when political interference caused the Wehrmacht to lose battles that it ought to have won, that generals began to doubt the wisdom of acquiescence with Hitler and the NSDAP; but even if they had not welcomed him in 1933 there was nothing they could legally have done about it, while an illegal putsch to remove Hitler might well not have been supported by the bulk of the army, and certainly not by the populace.

The first phase of expansion required the army to increase from seven infantry divisions to fourteen by 1934, and to twenty-one by 1935, increasing the strength from 100,000 to just over 300,000. Existing infantry regiments of the Reichsheer, Regiments Nos 1 to 21, had three battalions and a depot battalion. The first expansion was done by taking the third and depot battalions of each regiment to form a new regiment. Thus Infantry Regiment No 1 formed Infantry Regiment No 22, and IR No 21 formed IR No 42. As this expansion was still covert, there could be no conscription to provide the other two battalions now needed for each regiment, and recruits were obtained by the normal system of voluntary recruiting for the Reichsheer, and by a new one-year enlistment, for which priority was given to men who had served in the Great War or the police. In Phase Two each of the original and Phase One regiments provided their depot battalions to form the nucleus of a third regiment. Thus IR No 1 and IR No 22 between them formed IR No 43 and so on. These Phase Three regiments obtained their other two battalions by the transfer to the army of police battalions, no longer required as the various police forces were being filled up by disbanded SA members. A similar procedure was used to expand the artillery, engineers and supply and transport units. Because clandestine training in Russia had been stopped by order of Stalin on Hitler's accession to office (one of the planks of the NSDAP manifesto was virulent anti-Communism), it was difficult to hide what was going on, but outwardly at least, Germany continued to adhere to the provisions of Versailles. Existing divisional commanders became corps commanders, but given cover titles such as Infantry Commander Area I, or Commandant Area VII. The time for an open breach was not yet.

The German army was already well supplied with men of vision and technical understanding who saw armoured formations as being at the heart of the army of the future. Not all senior officers were convinced, but the protagonists of the tank found a powerful mentor in Hitler. Colonel

General Franz Halder, Chief of the General Staff of the army from 1938 to 1942, said in *Hitler als Feldherr*, published in 1949:

> It is true that Hitler had not only a vivid interest in, but also a distinct brain for, technical construction of all kinds. He was personally interested in weapon development as well as in engines ... nobody will dispute that this was in many cases a strong impulse which was of great benefit to the Armed Forces.

Hitler, having told the Minister of Defence that he wanted bigger and better armed forces capable of winning a defensive war by 1938 and an offensive one by 1941, generally then left the professionals to get on with it, rarely interested in the detail and not interfering in promotions and appointments. In the armoured field he made an exception, however, and took a close and personal interest in the development of the panzer arm. Most German officers saw the role of tanks as in support of the infantry, but even many of those who envisaged an independent role for armour rarely thought above regimental or brigade size. Hitler, however, pressed for panzer divisions and even corps, and there can be little doubt that the phenomenal success of the panzers in the Battle of France in 1940 owed much to Hitler's initial support. Without it the minority of officers who understood what armour could do – Guderian, Lutze, Manstein, Hoth, Reichneau – would not have got very far.

It had always been intended to form panzer units from the motor battalions of each infantry division. So far mechanisation had been carried out in secret or in Russia, but in March 1935, buoyed up by the plebiscite in the Saarland, where an overwhelming majority voted for return to Germany rather than incorporation in France, Hitler announced that Germany no longer considered herself bound by the Versailles Treaty, and that conscription would begin in two months' time. The German army would be expanded to thirty-six divisions plus three panzer divisions. All pretence was cast aside; the Truppenamt (troops office) was renamed the General Staff, the Chief of Army Staff became the Commander-in-Chief of the Army and the Reichswehr (the army and navy) became the Wehrmacht (army, navy and air force). Headquarters of the transport corps was renamed the Motor Combat Corps Command and then, in September

1935 Panzer Corps Command, with General Lutze as its commander and Guderian as Chief of Staff. Orders were placed for the construction of Panzer Marks III and IV and all their ancillaries with Krupp, Daimler and Maybach. A panzer division on the 1935 establishment had one panzer brigade with two tank regiments each of two battalions; one rifle brigade with a motorised infantry regiment of two battalions; an armoured reconnaissance battalion; a motorised artillery regiment of two battalions; a motorised signal battalion; a motorised engineer company and the usual logistic units. It was a well-balanced and powerful organisation.

It was not, however, the world's first permanent armoured formation. That honour, surprisingly, belongs to the British. Surprising because in 1933 Milne – who, while he had retreated from his earlier position of wholehearted support for mechanisation and modernisation, was at least still not positively against – was replaced as CIGS by the 62-year-old Montgomery-Massingberd, who assuredly was. An artillery officer like his predecessor, the new CIGS was a highly experienced staff officer but decidedly light on operational and command experience.[*] He was not convinced of the case for modernisation nor did he believe that a war was imminent, saying in a speech early in 1933: 'I venture to say that the army is not likely to be used for a big war in Europe for many years to come.'[3] He would continue to support the horse, and in 1933 the British army, with 136 battalions of infantry and eighteen regiments of horsed cavalry (plus another twenty-one in the Indian army), but only four battalions of (ageing) tanks and two (converted cavalry) regiments of armoured cars, did not look very different in equipment and organisation than it had in 1914.

Montgomery-Massingberd did, however, sanction the first permanent armoured formation in the world. It was only a brigade, but instead of being brought together for training and then dispersed, this would be a permanent part of the structure. The 1st Tank Brigade became operational in May 1934, commanded by Brigadier Percy Hobart, originally an Indian sapper and miner who had won a Military Cross at Neuve

---

[*] He had commanded an ammunition column as a subaltern in the South African war, and then spent the whole of the Great War as a staff officer on the Western Front, rising from General Staff Officer Grade 2 (major) in a division to Chief of Staff of an army (major general).

Chapelle in 1915 and who had since become an ardent advocate of the tank. It had three medium battalions and a light battalion of the Royal Tank Corps, and its logistic elements were all motorised. Each medium battalion had three companies, each company with one section of seven light tanks, one section of five medium tanks and a section of two close-support tanks. True, the light battalion had a plethora of different types of so-called tanks (such as the two-man Carden-Lloyd) which were little more than light tractors, but at least the brigade was in being and could begin to develop independent armoured tactics. The Germans took careful note, and their 1935 regulations for panzer units included what they had learned from the British experience.

The Western powers' reaction to Germany's renunciation of Versailles was the short-lived Stresa Front, whereby Britain, France and Italy aimed to take collective action to uphold the terms of Versailles. It achieved nothing. With rearmament by Germany now open and admitted, despite its illegality under Versailles, the British government was concerned to note that in March 1934 the German air force, the Luftwaffe, fielded 350 front-line military aircraft, and that her aircraft production was running at sixty a month. It was also noted that by October 1934 Germany would have 576 aircraft and be producing one hundred per month, and was aiming for 1,300 aircraft plus reserves by October 1936, or considerably more than the RAF's 880 worldwide, with 560 available for the defence of the UK.

The naval picture, too, was gloomy. The Washington and London naval agreements were due to expire in 1936 and as yet there was no plan to replace them. Japan had given notice of leaving the treaties and had increased her naval expenditure. The possibility of a war with Japan and Germany seemed ever more likely, and yet the Royal Navy had slipped below even the truncated limits permitted by treaty, both in the number of ships available for deployment and in the equipment that she carried. Even such replacement ships as could be funded for took longer and longer to build, such had been the emasculation of the once great industry which before 1914 had turned out ships of all sorts faster than anyone else in the world. Worse, by 1942 seven battleships, twenty-four cruisers, eighty-three destroyers, two aircraft carriers and a host of smaller ships would be so over-age that they would have to be replaced – and where was the programme to do so?[4] The Labour and Liberal parties opposed rearmament, still believing in the chimera of collective security through the League, and the Conservatives, previously the party of strong defence, were inhibited by being part of the National government. Neville Chamberlain, although a strong advocate of rearmament, had, as Chancellor, to recognise that the weak economy and high unemployment rate made any increase in defence spending unpopular with the voters. The exception was spending on the air force. The populace had swallowed the 'bomber will always get through' myth, and was genuinely concerned by the now public growth in German air power. What little cash that might be available would go to the RAF.

The Anglo-German Naval Agreement of 1935 astounded Britain's allies at the time, infuriated the French and has perplexed some historians ever since; but it was the only thing Britain could do if she were to attempt to hold Germany in the West while dealing with Japan in the East – still in 1935 seen as the most likely scenario. Had there been no agreement there can be little doubt that the Germans would just have gone on building until the entire Royal Navy would have been forced to stay in home waters. The agreement accepted that the German navy could expand until it was 35 per cent of the size of the Royal Navy (a fourfold increase over that permitted by Versailles), and 45 per cent in submarines (hitherto banned altogether). The Germans got the better of the deal, allowing them a breathing space in which to build until Hitler was ready to repudiate the agreed limits.

No sooner had the agreement been signed than yet another assumption – that Italy was a friendly power – had to be stood on its head. Italy had decided that she wanted to expand her colonial empire and had invaded Abyssinia. There was much fuss and feathers at the League, which instructed Italy to stop it, and whose members looked to Britain, with her powerful Mediterranean Fleet, to be the instrument of enforcement. There was particular outrage at the use by Italy of chemical weapons against the Ethiopians.[*] Britain could have closed the Suez Canal and

---

[*] But, to be fair to the Italians, very little outrage about the torture of Italian prisoners and mutilation of Italian dead.

GENERALOBERST HANS VON SEEKT (1866–1936) Commander-in-Chief of the German Reichswehr at a critical time after the First World War, von Seekt managed to keep the army out of politics, insisted on very high standards for both officer and other rank recruits, re-established staff training under various guises, and arranged for the training of tank and aircraft crews in Russia, forbidden by Versailles. Not always responsive to modern ideas, he did save the Weimar Republic from a number of attempted coups from right and left, (including Hitler's in Bavaria in 1923) and it is largely to his credit that while many aspects of the Republic were inefficient or corrupt, the army was not. Replaced as Commander-in-Chief in 1926, he was elected to the Reichstag in 1930 and grew increasingly close to Hitler and the NSDAP, despite having a Jewish wife. He was an adviser to the Chinese regime of Chiang Kai-Shek from 1934 to 1935. Here he is seen with Hitler observing German army manoeuvres only a few months before his death in 1936. (© Bettman/Corbis)

**GENERALFELDMARSCHALL
WILHELM KEITEL (1882–1946)** In
1938 Hitler became his own Minister of
Defence and ordered the setting up of an
Armed Forces Staff (Oberkommando der
Wehrmacht, or OKW). This was perfectly
sensible, but the supreme headquarters
was grossly understaffed, and could not
possibly do what it was supposed to do:
coordinate the activities of the three
services. Keitel, an artillery officer, was
appointed to head OKW, and found it
impossible to control Hitler. His fulsome
and wildly exaggerated praise of Hitler
devalued him in the eyes of many army
officers, and he became indelibly associated with the nastier aspects of the
regime. More sinned against than sinning,
he was sentenced to death by a war
crimes trial and executed at Nuremberg
in October 1946. (© IWM 1260)

**GENERAL DER INFANTERIE
ALFRED JODL (1890–1946)** Head of
the Land Operations Branch at OKW
under Keitel, Jodl was a competent and
professional staff officer who was considerably more intelligent than his chief.
While he rarely opposed Hitler directly,
he did sometimes manage to get the
Führer to change his mind by persuasion. Charged with war crimes at
Nuremberg, Jodl was executed after first
being thoroughly interrogated by the
western Allies anxious to discover his
views on defending Europe against the
Russians. While it is difficult now to see
any justification for Jodl's execution – he
concerned himself almost entirely with
operational matters – one has to remember that at the time the desire for
revenge was very strong and some of the
judgements of the International Military
Court would not have stood up in a
British court. (© Getty Images)

GENERALFELDMARSCHALL WALTER VON BRAUCHITSCH (1881–1948) (RIGHT) AND GENERALOBERST FRANZ HALDER (1884–1972) Von Brauchitsch was appointed Commander-in-Chief of the German army in 1938 until retiring on health grounds in December 1941. Unlike many senior officers he supported Anschluss and the dismemberment of Czechoslovakia, and while he must take some of the credit for the early successes of the war, he was unable to stand up to Hitler when his military training and instinct told him the Führer was wrong. Halder was Chief of the Army General Staff from 1938 until 1942, working very closely with von Brauchitsch and noting in his diary the constant wearing down of his master by arguments with Hitler. An archetypal staff officer of great and meticulous competence, Halder was dismissed in September 1942 for opposing the weight given to the ultimately disastrous Stalingrad operation. Although not involved in the plot of July 1944, he was thrown into a concentration camp and was lucky to survive the war. (© IWM MH 13141)

GENERALFELDMARSCHALL FEDOR VON BOCK (1880–1945) A Prussian who won Hohenzollern Germany's highest military decoration, the *Pour Le Mérite*, as the commander of a Foot
Guards battalion in 1917, von Bock commanded the troops that entered Austria on the declaration
of Anschluss, Army Group North in the Polish campaign and Army Group B in the Battle of France.
In the invasion of Russia he commanded Army Group Centre, but was sacked when the advance
against Moscow stalled. He was re-instated as Commander Army Group South in January 1942 but
sacked again in July after the disaster of Stalingrad. He held no further active command and was
killed in an air raid on 4 May 1945 – the day German forces in North West Europe surrendered.
(© Ullsteinbild)

Above Left **GENERALFELDMARSCHALL ERICH VON MANSTEIN (1887–1973)** Considered by many (including this author) to have been the best general of the war on any side, it was Manstein who, as Rundstedt's chief of staff, devised the startlingly successful plan for the Battle of France that included an armoured thrust through the Ardennes. As an army group commander in the Russian campaign, as late as 1943 he was convinced that the war in the East could still be won if only the army was allowed to revert to what it did best – rapid manoeuvre and deep thrusts – rather than trying to hold ground. Although he was one of the few generals of whom Hitler was wary, Manstein's constantly argumentative attitude to the Führer eventually got him sacked in March 1944. In 1949 he was sentenced to eighteen years' imprisonment by a British war crimes court, which his British barrister considered a disgrace, and was released in 1953. (© Getty Images)

Above Right **GENERALFELDMARSCHALL GERD VON RUNDSTEDT (1875–1953)** An old-fashioned Prussian officer of the best type, von Rundstedt retired in 1938 but was recalled for the Polish campaign where he commanded Army Group South. He strongly supported the Manstein amendments to Case Yellow and commanded Army Group A in the Battle of France. Although opposed to the whole concept of the invasion of Russia, he commanded Army Group South in that campaign, until being sacked in November 1941 for carrying out a tactical retreat contrary to Hitler's orders. Hitler eventually accepted that Rundstedt was right and recalled him. He was sacked twice more, and recalled each time. An aristocrat and one of the most intellectual of German generals, he frequently (as in this photograph) wore the uniform of the Colonel of the Regiment of the 18th Infantry, to which he had been appointed on his first retirement, rather than that of a colonel general or, from July 1940, that of a field marshal.

GENERALFELDMARSCHALL WILHELM RITTER VON LEEB (1876–1956) Von Leeb's knighthood (which was non-hereditary) came as part of a Bavarian gallantry decoration awarded him when an artillery officer in the First World War. He was highly respected as an author on tactics and strategy between the wars. Regarding the NSDAP policies with disdain, and Hitler as an upstart, von Leeb was compulsorily retired with the honorary rank of colonel general in January 1938, probably at Hitler's urging, but was recalled later that year to command an army for the occupation of the Sudetenland. He was opposed to the violation of neutrality inherent in Case Yellow, but commanded Army Group C in the Battle of France, and then Army Group North in the invasion of Russia. Sacked in January 1942 for advocating a tactical retreat from Leningrad during the winter, he held no further active command. (© Ullsteinbild)

GENERALOBERST HEINZ GUDERIAN (1888–1953) A gifted, far-sighted and highly intelligent officer who combined expertise in communications and a belief in the tank as the weapon of modern warfare, Guderian became the world's foremost exponent of armoured tactics in the years leading up to the outbreak of war. He showed tactical brilliance as Commander XIX Panzer Corps in the Battle of France, but was a difficult subordinate inclined to disobey orders that did not suit him. He commanded a Panzer Army in the invasion of Russia until being dismissed in December 1941 for insisting (wrongly, as it turned out) to Hitler that the German army could not hold its advance positions through the winter of 1941/42. Recalled as Inspector General of armoured forces in February 1943, he was promoted to be Chief of the General staff of the Army in July 1943, before being again dismissed in March 1945 for trying to persuade Hitler to seek peace with the Western Allies. In many ways a visionary soldier, he failed to fully realise the effect that Allied air superiority would have on the ability of armoured formations to move by day. (© IWM 30928)

GENERALFELDMARSCHALL ERWIN ROMMEL (1891–1944) As the only Second World War German general allowed to be lionised by the modern German army, Rommel's post-war reputation is a triumph of marketing over reality. While perhaps not himself a Nazi he was an early supporter of the NSDAP for his own ends, and used Hitler and the party to propel him rapidly upwards, moving from colonel in 1939 to field marshal in 1942. A charismatic and inspirational leader, he was only a moderately competent commander above divisional level, neglecting logistics and being far too keen on being up the front involved in minor tactics rather than in controlling the battle. His successes in North Africa were more due to British incompetence than to his own abilities. While his attitude to the anti-Hitler plot of July 1944 was almost certainly to remain distanced from it but to take advantage if it worked, he was suspected of involvement and given the option of suicide or disgrace. He should be remembered for his bravery and initiative as a junior officer in Italy in the First World War (where he won the *Pour le Mérite*) and as a most effective commander of a Panzer division in the Battle of France, rather than for his largely manufactured reputation as the German commander in North Africa. (© Getty Images)

GENERALFELDMARSCHALL ALBRECHT KESSELRING (1885–1960) Originally an artillery
officer, Kesselring transferred to the Luftwaffe in 1935 and commanded two air fleets in the Polish
campaign and in the Battle of France. As commander Luftflotte 2 during the Battle of Britain he was
well aware of the unlikelihood of a successful invasion of the UK and had no difficulty in seeing the
character flaws of his Commander-in-Chief, Göring. From December 1941 he was Commander-in-
Chief South, responsible for Italy, the Mediterranean and North Africa, where he ably supported
Rommel as far as the assets available to him would allow. After the Allied invasion of Italy in 1943
Kesselring conducted a most able defence until being transferred to the North West European theatre in the last months of the war, when it was far too late to affect the end result. (© TopFoto)

blockaded Italy, but there were difficulties. The fleet was vulnerable to attack by Italian aircraft; the anti-aircraft defences of Britain's Mediterranean possessions and Egypt were hopelessly inadequate; realistic sanctions would upset the Americans, who owned the oil and much else that Italy imported; and most of all, if the Japanese or the Germans – or, heaven forefend, both – now made a hostile move the Royal Navy would be quite incapable of meeting it. The British played safe, withdrew the fleet to Alexandria and forfeited Italian friendship without preventing them from behaving badly in Abyssinia. The Foreign Secretary, Sir Samuel Hoare, who had done so much to ensure the survival of the RAF when Secretary for Air, was forced to resign when a ploy hatched between him and the French Prime Minister, Pierre Laval, to let Italy have bits of Ethiopia was leaked to the newspapers. Cleverly, the Germans supplied arms to Haile Selaisse, the Ethiopian emperor, in order to prolong the conflict and widen the rift between Italy and the Anglo-French – thus encouraging Italy to move closer to Germany.[5]

And now, with the British distracted by the Italian crisis, Germany did make a hostile move – on 6 March 1936 she marched into the Rhineland. There were already considerable numbers of German troops in the Rhineland – the French estimated 40,000 – but their presence was either flatly denied altogether by Germany or they masqueraded as customs officials and police; this, however, was open and flagrant.[6] The remilitarisation was carried out by only three battalions of infantry, against the advice of senior generals and to the joyful acclaim of virtually every German, Nazi or no. Everyone in Germany held their breath: but the Allies did nothing and a further nineteen battalions, some artillery and some motorised units followed. This was a clear violation of Versailles and a direct threat to the security of France, who hoped that Britain would support her in expelling the Germans from the zone. The previous year Britain had refused to guarantee the demilitarisation of the Rhineland; that zone had been created as a measure of security for France and Belgium, it was not a vital British interest and it was up to those countries to decide what to do.

At a series of meetings between 13 and 16 March the British cabinet elected to do nothing. Despite the Foreign Secretary, Anthony Eden, stressing the French view that if Germany was not stopped now, then 'a very dangerous war would be loosed two years hence when Germany was likely to be no kinder and stronger', the cabinet recorded that 'public opinion in this country was more favourable to Germany than to France, and was definitely anti-war'. Furthermore, they considered that to demand that Germany withdraw would mean war, and 'the British people could not agree to fight a war in order to drive Germany out of the demilitarised area to which eventually she was to be allowed to return'. In any case, reported the CIGS on 16 March, in reply to a suggestion that British troops might be inserted as a buffer between France and Germany, 'British battalions were only 450–500 strong, very young men, hardly more than boys. Their physique would not compare with that of the Germans.' What an admission to have to make for the man who stood in the boots of Marlborough, Wellington and Haig!

In the event, devoid of British support, the French did nothing either, and thus began the period known as appeasement. In fact, of course, there was little that Britain could have done. Certainly she and France together could have sent the three German battalions packing, and, just, the rest of the Wehrmacht too, still only in the first throes of expansion. Many today consider that they should have done so. Had Britain and France taken decisive military action, the theory goes, Hitler would have received a blow to his prestige from which he could not have recovered; he would have been voted out or the army would have removed him. The course of aggression leading inexorably to war could have been halted before it began and the Second World War would not have happened. Quite apart from the fact that the Polish Corridor, or tension between Germany and Russia, or instability in the Balkans would have led to war eventually, whoever was in power in Germany, this argument fails to distinguish between what should have been done and what could have been done. Politics is the art of the possible, and neither the British public, nor the Empire, nor the French public, nor the important neutrals (notably the USA) would have approved military action to restore the demilitarised status of the Rhineland – which was, after all, indubitably and inalienably, German soil.

In the British general election of 1935 foreign policy was, unusually, a major issue. Each party stood on planks of collective security, negotiation and universal brotherhood, and any individual who suggested that there might be a real chance of Britain having to go to war in the near future tended not to get elected. Pacifism, or perhaps collective refusal to face reality, was still very much at the core of British public opinion even after the Germans had reoccupied the Rhineland, and there were those in England who saw Stalin's Russia as a far greater menace than Germany who had, after all, provided Britain with her monarchy and, except for the unfortunate events of 1914–18, had generally been her ally against the traditional enemy, France. A subsequent plebiscite in Germany, called to approve Hitler's actions, returned a majority in favour of 99 per cent, and was probably genuine. On Monday 9 March 1935 *The Times*, in a leader entitled 'A Chance to Rebuild', tut-tutted at Germany's breach of Versailles and Locarno, but observed that Locarno had only embodied the clauses of Versailles:

> …which imposed de-militarisation upon the German side only of the Franco-German frontier. Thus, having failed as the starting point of a process of appeasement it survived only, in German eyes, as an additional guarantee of one of the 'inequalities' in which the Nazi movement of resurgence and revolt had its birth. In the view, not of Nazidom alone, but of all Germans, the sacrifice offered in Germany's free acceptance of the 'inequality' had proved vain.

The next day, 10 March, under the sub-heading 'Facing Facts As They Are: An American View' *The Times* published a letter purporting to come from an American resident in England which said:

> The treaty [Locarno] has failed in its principal object, and nothing of it now remains but that one-sided restriction of German sovereignty which the German people resent with an intensity of bitterness that no one can fully appreciate who has not lived for some time in that country … but a new Reich has been established … with the entire German people behind him, certainly so far as the removal of limitations on the national sovereignty is concerned. Herr Hitler has taken action: his military forces are in the Rhineland … there they will undoubtedly stay unless driven out by superior

force. Is another war, which may engulf all Europe and perhaps America too, necessary because Germany has resumed her absolute sovereignty over the Rhineland?

The expansion of the Wehrmacht now proceeded apace, but it was not without its difficulties. Whereas a private soldier can be trained in a matter of weeks, or months if he is a technician, officers and non-commissioned officers have to be grown and nurtured. The training period for officer cadets was reduced from over four years to two and a half, and the 1938 intake was 2,000 compared with 180 in 1933, but this would only provide subaltern officers and there were still huge gaps in the middle-piece ranks. The problem was resolved, at least partially, by opening the officer ranks to former officers of the imperial army or the Reichsheer, by transfers from the police and by the commissioning of capable NCOs. The rein-stated staff system was little changed. Corps Headquarters were small and concerned only with operations: the divisions they commanded were responsible for their own supply and replenishment under army arrange-ments. The three main staff branches, Operations, Quartermaster and Personnel (equivalent to the British G, Q and A then, and G3, G4 and G1 now), should have been staffed by officers of the Great General Staff, but from 1919 these could only be trained in secret, so there were very few of them and in divisional headquarters only the senior staff officers in the operations and quartermaster branches (a lieutenant colonel and a major respectively) were of the Great General Staff, the others being perfectly competent but not, or not yet, graduates of what was probably the best staff training system in the world.[*] Staff officers had, and were expected to exercise, far more initiative and authority than they ever had in the British army, which partly explains why German units were able to go on fighting and reacting even when communications with their next higher headquarters were cut off. German orders tended to be expressed as intentions, or as missions, with the recipients left largely to their own devices as to how they achieved that mission. In the British army orders were far more detailed, and tended to spell out exactly what each sub-unit should do, with the result that when things went wrong

[*] Even by 1939 the German army had only 272 fully trained General Staff officers.

subordinate commanders were often left floundering.[*] At every German level of command from corps upwards there was a chief of staff, and the commander was obliged by army regulations to seek and listen to the advice of his chief of staff before coming to a decision. Once made, the decision was the responsibility of the commander, but until 1939 the chief of staff was entitled to communicate a dissenting opinion to the next higher headquarters. After 1939 only the chief of staff of an army retained this right.

The shortage of trained officers had advantages, however, for soldiering is a young man's game. In 1932 there were forty-two general officers in the German army; in 1936 there were 150. The number of colonels grew from 105 to 325. The average age of a colonel in 1930 was 52; in 1936 it was 43. The average age of lieutenant colonels dropped from 47 to 40, and majors from 41 to 35.[7]

While the British government were adopting a three-pronged approach of seeking some form of accommodation with Germany on the one hand, cautiously rearming on another and, at least in the case of the new Foreign Secretary, Anthony Eden, considering the possibility of a war with Germany at some stage in the future, the new Wehrmacht had found itself another training area. In July 1936 the Spanish army rose against the left-wing Popular Front government. The resultant Spanish Civil War between the Nationalists (Franco, the army, monarchists, big business and the middle classes) and the Republicans (Republicans, Socialists, Communists and the navy) went on until April 1939. The Germans and Italians helped the Nationalists, while the Russians tried, with limited success despite the presence of ten future marshals of the Soviet Union, to back the Republicans.

German assistance in the shape of the Kondor Legion commanded by von Thoma, later to command the Afrika Korps, was small in numbers of men (much less than the Italian contribution which included Mussolini's son as a pilot), but effective in that it was often able to tip the balance in favour of the Nationalists. The Luftwaffe learned a great deal, including the fact that fighter dogfights are possible, something that most

---

[*] For the past fifteen years or so the British army has been gradually moving towards the German system. We have very nearly got there.

air forces had rejected where speeds were in excess of 200 mph. They also gained experience of what was called strategic bombing. The Heinkel 111 and the Junkers 52 were only converted civil transport planes, able to carry eight bombs weighing 550lbs each, but as the first modern instruments of aerial attacks on cities they were impressive.[8] The bombing of Guernica, twenty miles north-east of Bilbao, by the Kondor Legion on 26 April 1937, has provided much raw material for painters, poets, novelists and peace campaigners over the years, but in truth the damage and the death toll was far less than the 1,500 dead announced by the Republicans at the time. There may have been as few as thirty dead, but as it was in the interests of both the Republic (to demonstrate the bestiality of the Franco forces), and Franco (to encourage other cities not to resist) to exaggerate the casualties, and as the dead were all Basques anyway, neither side really cared very much and there are no accurate statistics available. The actual damage, however, was irrelevant. The morale effect was enormous and only confirmed public opinion in Britain in its determination to avoid war.

The Spanish Civil War became a crusade for many idealists, romantics and democrats around the world. The International Brigade, which fought for the Republic, included 2,000 British volunteers, of whom 500 were killed, and many more French, Russians, Scandinavians and Americans. The British government remained neutral, largely because of Soviet support for the Republic and the Fascist tenor of the Nationalists, but also because it was reluctant to ally itself too closely with France, after a Popular Front government of the left had been elected in 1936. In January 1937 the Foreign Enlistment Act made it illegal for British citizens to enlist in foreign armies, the intention being to stop volunteers going to Spain.

In Britain the Chiefs of Staff and the Committee of Imperial Defence were increasingly concerned about the possibility of a war on three fronts: with Japan in the Far East, Italy in the Mediterranean and Germany in the West. They considered that in view of that possibility allies were essential, and despite its left-wing government the only possible ally was France, the United States being seen as increasingly isolationist. Even allied to France, the situation was parlous. In April 1936 Britain and France between them could muster nineteen battleships, against Germany's six, and ninety-three submarines to Germany's twenty; but in the air the combined Anglo-French bomber fleet of 306 aircraft compared with Germany's 405, only partly redressed by an Anglo-French superiority in fighters of 469 to 144. On land the Anglo-French could field fifty infantry divisions (only two of them British) compared to twenty-nine German; but Germany could produce three armoured divisions whereas the Anglo-French had none. Furthermore, the French army was ill-equipped and, in the opinion of its Commander-in-Chief, in no state to go to war with Germany. Winston Churchill attended French army manoeuvres, inspected the Maginot Line that autumn and wrote: 'the officers of the French army are impressive by their gravity and competence. One feels the strength of the nation resides in its army.'[9] At a time of much political idiocy it is difficult to think of a pronouncement that was to prove so utterly and completely erroneous in such a short time. The French army should have been in a better state than it was for, amazing though it may seem, due to incompetence of a high order, French military administrators had been unable to spend all the money allocated to them. For 1933 there had been an underspend of 59 per cent; for 1934 30 per cent and for 1936 a staggering failure to spend of 60 per cent!

In October Germany launched the battlecruiser *Scharnhorst* and in December the *Gneisenau*. At 32,000 tons they were well above the treaty limits, but no one seemed to care, nor to do anything about it. Hitler was putting the German economy to rights by a huge programme of public works, including not only increased rearmament but also the building of an extensive network of autobahns and the opening of the Volkswagen motor car factory, designed to produce a car that every German could afford. There was increased German agitation in the Sudetenland – German-speaking areas of Czechoslovakia – in the Polish Corridor, in Austria and in the free city of Danzig; membership of the Hitler Youth became compulsory; persecution of Jews and other 'undesirables' intensified, and the 1936 Olympics were staged in Berlin, giving an opportunity for the new Germany to show what she could do. Visitors were impressed and none more than David Lloyd George who, having visited Dachau concentration camp, expressed himself impressed by the services to the state being rendered by the inmates.

In Britain the Chiefs of Staff, in assessing Britain's preparedness for war in March 1936, used words like: 'perilously exposed', 'completely open' and 'utterly inadequate'.[10] It was clear that rearmament, embarked upon hesitatingly and nervously, must be speeded up. The government's ability to do this was helped by what was thought to be a slight shifting in public opinion towards some awareness of the danger, and by an improvement in the national economy. In the defence review of 1935 it was agreed that for the Royal Navy seven capital ships and fifteen cruisers should be built as replacements in the years 1936 to 1939, in addition to four new aircraft carriers and a flotilla of destroyers. This was at least a start; but it was only replacing ships in a navy that was already too small to fulfil its worldwide commitments, and in any event a decision was taken to mention only two capital ships when the estimates were debated in Parliament, partly for fear of being accused of warmongering and partly because the Royal Navy had not yet resolved the battleship versus aircraft carrier controversy. While the cabinet agreed that the Expeditionary Force should be reinforced from the Territorial Army, so that the regular contingent of four infantry divisions should be built up to sixteen (twelve Territorial), within eight months of the declaration of war, there was no money to provide the Territorial Army with modern equipment and training facilities to fit them for war. Such money as was available went to improving the first, regular contingent.

This acceptance that it would not be possible under existing arrangements to reinforce the Expeditionary Force did lead some observers (and some generals too) to the conclusion that a small force would be unable to exert any real influence, and could be easily destroyed if things went badly for the French. Better, some thought, not to send anything at all and concentrate on providing air and naval support alone. Although militarily this argument was sound, the reasons for not adopting it were the same as those in 1914 and those from 1945 to the present day: only a physical presence on the ground in Europe would convince ally and enemy alike that Britain was serious. The RAF did best of all out of the review, with a general recognition that the air defence of Great Britain (referred to by the acronym ADGB) needed to be improved, and as the government had assured Parliament that RAF strength in the UK would be at least equal to the largest air force within striking distance – the Luftwaffe – then the size of the metropolitan air force would be increased.

The cause of mechanisation of the army was helped by the relief of Montgomery-Massingberd as CIGS by Sir Cyril Deverell, a committed reformer, in 1936. Although those in favour of mechanisation were now in the ascendant, the Treasury would countenance no increase to the overall strength of the army. This meant that if the Royal Tank Corps was to be expanded, to provide more armoured units, then the manpower and the funding would have to come by disbanding some of the 'older arms', the cavalry and the infantry. As there was little enough infantry, the cavalry was the obvious target, but many cavalry officers were insistent that there was still a role for the horse and resisted conversion to a mechanised or motorised role. One of the reasons often given by both Milne and Montgomery-Massingberd for not increasing the already sluggish pace of mechanisation was a wish not to damage morale of the cavalry and infantry units! While the Royal Tank Corps, who had, after all, been the pioneers of mechanisation, would have preferred cavalry regiments to be disbanded and replaced by RTC battalions, the decision was taken to mechanise the cavalry, and in 1936 eight cavalry regiments were ordered to mechanise, five to be equipped with light trucks (and effectively to become vehicle mounted infantry) and three with light tanks. It was also decided to form a mobile division, based on the existing tank brigade, to be up and running in 1937. Announcing this in the House of Commons the Secretary for War apologised to the cavalry, saying that mechanisation was 'like asking a great musical performer to throw away his violin and to devote himself in future to the gramophone'.[11] This was hardly conducive to encouraging the cavalry to give up their horses. In 1937, in the teeth of considerable opposition, Deverell ordered the mechanisation of the entire cavalry. Although it should have been taken much earlier, it was a brave decision.

In May 1937, Prime Minister Baldwin resigned, exhausted with the abdication crisis of the previous year, and was replaced by Neville Chamberlain, hitherto Chancellor of the Exchequer. Chamberlain had been advocating rearmament for longer than anyone else – at a time when Churchill was advocating cuts in the defence vote – and as Prime Minister was quite clear about what he wanted. As both he and his successor as Chancellor, Sir John Simon, were convinced that public opinion would not stand for the level of expenditure that the Chiefs of Staff considered necessary – which could only be met by substantial increases in taxation and a reduction in social expenditure – the new Prime Minister had to find some way of improving Britain's military position without provoking national bankruptcy or serious social unrest. His priorities were clear: a strong RAF, a navy capable of fighting one war, and an army capable of meeting colonial and imperial commitments. What this meant was that the air defence of Great Britain was to be the overriding priority; the Royal Navy was to be prepared for a war against Germany but not against Italy and Japan as well, and the army was not to prepare for what Chamberlain called 'European Adventures'. The money to be allocated for defence and rearmament was decided not on the basis of what was needed, but on what could be made available, so once again defence policy was being made by the Treasury.

In hindsight, of course, the Royal Navy did have to fight against Germany, Italy and Japan, and the army did have to take part in European adventures, but in 1937 the only leading politician prepared to stand up and say that they might was Winston Churchill, and he was regarded by many as an untrustworthy troublemaker – which in some ways he was. In deciding what resources to allocate to defence, the Chancellor made the point that having invested in new and replacement equipment and increased aircraft and manpower, there would come a point at which the new model services could not be maintained out of government revenue. That point would come in 1941. While not expressly stated, the implication was that the threat must be removed by 1941 (by war or negotiation) or the whole costly apparatus would have to be dismantled.

Even after approving the extra expenditure needed to meet the Prime Minister's priorities, savings were still demanded. To find them, the army's reserves of ammunition for colonial campaigns were reduced, the number of anti-aircraft guns ordered for the defence of London was scaled back and the pool of equipment and ammunition to bring the Territorial Army up to war establishment was dispensed with altogether. All this less than eighteen months before the outbreak of war!

The new British policy in regard to the army and its expeditionary force brought the government into direct confrontation with the CIGS, Deverell, who was a convinced European and who was unshakeably of the view that Britain must stand with the French. After only a year and ten months of what was normally a three-year appointment, Deverell arrived in his office one December morning in 1937 to find a letter on his desk from the newly appointed Secretary of State for War sacking him. It was discourteous in the extreme, and typical of Leslie Hore-Belisha, who thought he knew more about the way an army does its business than those who had spent all their lives doing it. The reforms he demanded were, on the face of it, attractive. He wanted more and easier commissioning of other ranks, missing the point that sergeants and captains have quite different jobs to do and are rarely interchangeable. He also wanted younger generals, again failing to understand that in a small professional army promotion will inevitably be slow, and that the only way to get people to retire earlier, to make way for those below them, was to bring down the qualifying age for pension, which the Treasury refused to do. History will remember Hore-Belisha for the pedestrian crossing marker that bears his name, introduced when he was Minister for Transport from 1934 to 1937, but his behaviour towards the CIGS was only the beginning of a sustained attack on the senior levels of the army and what he saw as musty and outdated thinking in the War Office. Up to a point he was right, but it was his way of going about it that upset the army, to the extent that by 1940 he had attracted so much resentment that he had to be removed from office. He then fell back on the last resort of the discarded by claiming unfair discrimination (he was a Jew) when Chamberlain would not make him Minister for Information.

On the night of 11–12 March 1938 the German army marched into Austria. It was met by cheering crowds, not a shot was fired and there was no resistance. Austria was, after all, a German state. By now even *The Times* was running out of tolerance and in a leader of 12 March entitled 'A blow to Europe' it (almost) thundered:

> This, the latest and worst demonstration of the methods of German foreign
> policy can only deepen in this country the suspicion and indignation aroused…

> It comes at a time when, as most people have hoped, Herr von Ribbentrop's [the German Foreign Minister and ex-ambassador to the UK] visit to London was giving an opportunity for a new approach to a settlement of Anglo-German relations, and it deals a blow to the policy of appeasement by leaving it more than doubtful whether appeasement is possible in a continent exposed to the visitation of arbitrary force… the means by which the will of the Reich has been imposed upon a neighbour incapable of resistance requires no further definition… a British protest in the strongest terms has already been presented.

On 15 March the same newspaper gave wide coverage on its main page[*] to the declaration by the Prime Minister that events in Austria demanded a review of British defence requirements, and a call by the Home Secretary Sir Samuel Hoare (now rescued from political exile) calling for a million volunteers for the Air Raid Precautions programme.

Pro-monarchist officers having been removed, the Austrian army was incorporated into the Wehrmacht, and the full panoply of NSDAP administration was imposed. But even while it was to become abundantly clear that whatever assurances Hitler and his government might give, they would break them just as soon as it suited them to do so, there was a reluctance in Britain to abandon the cause of collective security and negotiation altogether, and go headlong for rearmament. While Britain did now have a Minister for Coordination of Defence, Sir Thomas Inskip, this was very far from having unified direction of the defence effort. In Germany, however, a scandal (possibly manufactured) led to the resignation of the Minister of Defence and Commander-in-Chief of the army, Field Marshal von Blomberg,[**] after which Hitler assumed the post himself, and created the Oberkommando der Wehrmacht, the Armed Forces high command, to coordinate the operations of the three services. After the war many German generals criticised this decision, and often blamed OKW and its officers for their defeats. In fact, it was not the concept but the individuals posted to it, and its taking on more responsibility than it had resources to discharge, that was wrong. The Chief of

---

* Not, of course, its front page. Some of us are old enough to remember with nostalgic fondness the days when *The Times* devoted its entire front page to the Personal Column and advertisements.

** Aged 60 and a widower, he had married a 24-year-old stenographer with the Reich Egg Marketing Board, who turned out to have had a racy past.

Staff of OKW, Field Marshal Keitel, an artillery officer, was by no means incompetent but he could not stand up to Hitler and soon stopped trying. The chief of the operations branch from April 1938, Major General (later Colonel General) Alfred Jodl, was a highly competent staff officer and more inclined to resist political interference than was his chief, but even he could achieve little once Hitler was persuaded that he was blessed with strategic talent and knew how to wage war better than his professionals did. Both men were executed as war criminals in 1946 after the Nuremberg trials, Jodl only after he had been extensively questioned by the British and Americans as to his views on the defence of western Europe from an attack by the erstwhile ally, the USSR.

Hitler's next target was Czechoslovakia, which, with the incorporation of Austria into the Reich, was now bordered on the north, south, and west by German territory. The Sudetenland of Czechoslovakia ran along Germany's eastern frontier and contained three and a half million Germans – or at least German speakers. While they considered themselves Germans they had never been part of Germany, and up to 1919 had been perfectly content as citizens of the Austro-Hungarian Empire. The Sudeten mountains were the natural defensive barriers of Czechoslovakia, and the area also contained much of the country's armaments factories – and Czechoslovakia had one of the most advanced weapons production industries in Europe. Germany began by claiming that the Sudeten Germans were being persecuted (they were not) and that they were under-represented in the Czech parliament (they were over-represented). As with Austria, German threats and pressure began to build up. Nothing less than complete cession of the Sudetenland to Germany would do, and when the Czech government announced a plebiscite whereby the Sudeten Germans could decide for themselves whether or not to join Germany, pressure from France, Italy and Britain forced the Czechs to concede without a vote. Germany occupied the Sudetenland, with no resistance, between 1 and 10 October 1938 and Poland took the opportunity to grab Teschen, a piece of Czech territory that she had long coveted and which contained 132,000 Czechs and 20,000 Germans, but only 77,000 Poles. She also grabbed the Czech rail junction of Bohumin, to stop the Germans seizing it first. It was, of course, a complete and utter sell-out of the Czechs, particularly so by the French who had a treaty of alliance with them, but also by the British who made it clear to the French that they could expect no help from the UK should they decide to honour their obligations to the Czechs.

It was all very well for the maverick Churchill to thunder from the back benches, and for the British Communist Party[*] to organise a protest march in London, but the facts were that Britain was quite incapable of going to war in October 1938, even if she had wanted to. At a cabinet meeting of 30 August the Minister for Coordination of Defence, Sir Thomas Inskip, announced that Britain could not be ready for war for at least a year. Rearmament had been for the defence of Britain, not for the projection of power abroad, and land forces could not be deployed for many months. It was too far to send an air force, and the only other alternative – a naval blockade of Germany – would take too long to save Czechoslovakia. Chamberlain flew to Germany on 15 and 22 September to discuss the Czech crisis with Hitler, and on 27 September he broadcast to the nation. Referring to the fact that air-raid shelters were being built and plans for the issue of gas masks dusted off, he said:

> How horrible, fantastic, incredible it is that we should be digging trenches and trying on gas masks here because of a quarrel in a faraway country between people of whom we know nothing... It seems still more impossible that a quarrel which has already been settled in principle should be the subject of war.[12]

Both Inskip and Simon argued in cabinet that Czechoslovakia was an irrelevance, an artificial state (which of course it was), and an instability in the heart of Europe. Many in Britain felt the same, and, while deploring Hitler's vulgar and threatening manner, thought it not unreasonable that he should wish to include all Germans within the boundaries of the Reich. On 29 September Chamberlain again flew to Germany and with the French Prime Minister Daladier and Mussolini met Hitler in Munich. Chamberlain returned home with his bit of paper to be greeted by

---

* Czechoslovakia was not Communist, and it is doubtful if many of the members of the British Communist Party even knew where it was, but international Communism at that time was anti-German.

cheering crowds, Czechoslovakia lost the Sudetenland, and Germany's population rose to seventy-nine million.

During the winter of 1938–9 German behaviour towards the rump of Czechoslovakia worsened. Demands were made for gold deposits in the Czech central bank to be placed under German supervision, and accusations were made that Czechoslovakia was intending to allow Soviet troops passage though Czech territory to attack Germany. It was all nonsense, of course, but already Germany was thinking in terms of territorial expansion to the east, and Czechoslovakia would do for a start.

On 15 March 1939, after agitation inside Czechoslovakia by the Slovak and Hungarian minorities, Germany marched into Czechoslovakia and the state ceased to exist. Bohemia and Moravia became a 'Reich Protectorate', the Slovaks got their own nominally independent client state, and Hungary annexed Ruthenia. For the first time Hitler had gobbled up territory without the excuse that he was only acceding to the wishes of the German inhabitants to be repatriated.

On 15 March, in the British House of Commons, where business that session included such exciting legislation as the China Currency (Stabilisation) Bill and the Wheat (Amendment) Bill, the Prime Minister, referring back to the Sudeten crisis, told members:

> We could have threatened to go to war with Germany… [that option] was rejected, and I do not believe that there was then or that there is now, any considerable body of opinion in this country which would have been prepared to support any other decision. We had no treaty with Czechoslovakia; we had always refused to accept any such obligations.[13]

The House then got on with weightier matters; Mr Gibson asked the Secretary of State for Scotland what was the number of convictions for drunkenness in Renfrewshire, Paisley, Dundee and Aberdeen respectively for the years 1932 to 1937, and Mr Eckersley provoked loud cries of 'Oh' when he demanded of the Secretary of State for War why pyjamas issued to British soldiers stationed abroad were made in Japan.[*]

---

* For those who cannot resist irrelevant trivialities, there were a total of 2,478 convictions in 1937 alone; and the Secretary of State for War said he would investigate the nightwear scandal.

NOTES

1. N. H. Gibbs, *History of the Second World War – Grand Strategy, Vol. I,* HMSO, London, 1976.

2. Research Institute for Military History, Germany (ed), *Germany and the Second World War, Vol. I* (tr Falla, McMurry and Osers), Clarendon Press, Oxford, 2003.

3. General Sir William Jackson & Field Marshal Lord Bramall, *The Chiefs,* Brassey's, London, 1992.

4. Paul M. Kennedy, *The Rise and Fall of British Naval Mastery,* Allen Lane, London, 1976.

5. Research Institute for Military History op. cit.

6. TNA Kew, CAB/27/603 of 13 March 1936.

7. Samuel W. Mitcham Jr, *Hitler's Field Marshals and their Battles,* Leo Cooper, London, 1988.

8. *Jane's Fighting Aircraft of World War II,* Random House, London, 2001.

9. Martin Gilbert, *A History of the Twentieth Century, Vol. II,* HarperCollins, London, 1998.

10. N. H. Gibbs, op. cit.

11. Capt B. H Liddell Hart, *The Tanks: The History of The Royal Tank Regiment, Vol. I,* Cassell, London, 1959.

12. Martin Gilbert, op. cit.

13. *Hansard,* 11th Series, Vol. 345, HMSO, London, 1939.

5

The Chickens Come Home

GERMANY'S DISMEMBERMENT of Czechoslovakia concentrated minds wonderfully. On 21 March 1939 Lithuania ceded Memel to Germany (lost at Versailles); on April 7 Italy instituted an almost bloodless invasion of Albania, King Zog fled and the Italian King Victor Emmanuel became King of Albania as well as Emperor of Ethiopia. Britain and France responded by giving guarantees of territorial integrity to Poland, Greece, Turkey and Romania.

In Britain the aftershock was felt by politicians, admirals, generals and even some of the public. At long last the realisation struck home that all the years of negotiation, reliance on the League and appeals to better nature had failed. War was inevitable: it was only a question of when. For Britain the twenty years since the last great conflict had been marked by dither, financial retrenchment, inconsistency, weak government and social and financial crises. The ten-year rule had not only prevented any improvement in British military strength, it had emphatically contributed in large measure to its decline. Within the navy and the army there was an inclination to keep quiet, avoid rocking the boat, stay below the parapet and hope not to be noticed. Even after the abandonment of the ten-year rule in 1932 there was no real commitment to putting things right, and new ideas were far too often ignored or stifled; iconoclasts were shunted sideways; men of real vision and talent became discouraged. This was perhaps worst in the army. The Royal Air Force, while not necessarily getting the resources the air staff would have liked, was at least getting something. A naval officer at sea is still faced with the challenges that he joined for, even if his ship has rather fewer companions than hitherto, but an officer in an army where new equipment never arrives, and if it does is unsuitable or unreliable having been ordered on the cheap, where there is no money for experimentation and where new ideas are regarded as subversive, is unlikely to maintain his youthful enthusiasm for long.

It is true that the decision to mechanise the army had been taken in principle, that a tank brigade was in existence and that a mobile division (initially commanded by Major General Alan Brooke, a gunner and later CIGS) was in the process of being organised in the UK, and from September 1938 another in Egypt. Tank production, however, was far too slow, there were too many light tanks and the army had gone down a blind alley in deciding that the infantry required their own tanks to provide intimate fire support and needing only be able to move as fast as the infantry could march. Equipment was in short supply, radios for the tanks were hard to come by, and many of those that were supplied did not have frequencies compatible with those used by the infantry. Some aspects of the development of Britain's armoured forces bordered on the absurd. In the headquarters of the 1st Tank Brigade when the brigade commander in his tank wanted to communicate with the brigade major in his, the message was written on a piece of paper and passed from tank to tank using a child's shrimping net on a bamboo pole.

In the 1920s in America a commercial engineer, J. Walter Christie designed a new type of suspension with a tank to fit it. This was offered to but rejected by the US army. The Russians were interested in Christie's ideas but as the US would not allow weapons to be sold to the Bolsheviks, they had to acquire a number by subterfuge. They copied the Christie suspension to produce the BT series, the forerunner of the excellent T 34, probably the best tank of the war. In 1936 British observers at Russian manoeuvres were impressed by the performance of the Russian BT7 light tank. The Royal Tank Corps, after much argument, managed to persuade the Treasury to provide the money to buy the one remaining Christie

tank in existence in America. Unfortunately, when the tank was transported to New York in October 1936 for shipment to England, the US
government, in the grip of one of its periodic fits of righteousness, refused
an export licence. The British military attaché in Washington was a man
of determination and resource. The tank was dismantled and the chassis
shipped to England as a tractor, while the parts moved as pineapples.

There were other shortages too. Priority for engines went to the RAF,
and the army's tanks and other mechanical vehicles had to wait; steel was
in short supply and priority went to the navy, so steel for the army's tanks
was bought from Austria, which supplied a high-quality product even
after Anschluss and right up to the outbreak of war.

It was not that nothing was happening, or that no progress was being
made: it was, but it was all taking place too slowly and in too little quantity.
Reorganisation of the infantry had started in 1938, when battalions each
received a platoon of ten carriers, open-topped and lightly armoured
tracked vehicles that could carry six infantrymen besides the crew of two,
or a medium machine-gun section. Initially named the Bren Gun Carrier
(because its armament was the new Bren light machine gun)* and then
the Universal Carrier, it had a myriad of roles and was quickly taken up by
other arms as well as the infantry. Battalions also got their own mortar
platoon, equipped with two- and three-inch mortars that could fire a
high-explosive bomb out to a range of 500 and 5,000 yards respectively.
The Royal Artillery was getting the excellent 25-pounder towed
gun/howitzer, the standard weapon of the British field artillery throughout the war and the best field gun of any of the belligerents. Everywhere
horses were being replaced by vehicles, but in a 1939 infantry division of
nine battalions in three brigades, there was only enough transport to
move a single brigade at any one time – the rest marched, as they had
always done.

After Munich a (yet another) reversal of policy decided that an expeditionary force would, after all, be needed. The Territorial Army was

* Taken from a Czech design made at the armaments factory at Brno, modified for the British army
and manufactured by Enfield (hence Bren) this was undoubtedly one of the best light machine guns ever
produced. First issues were made in 1938, originally in .303 calibre, and converted to 7.62 in 1960. It
continued in British service well into the 1980s, despite being supposedly replaced by the (belt fed)
GPMG in 1964.

ordered to be reorganised into twelve infantry divisions, of which three were to be motorised, and an armoured division. Then, after Germany's occupation of Bohemia and Moravia, a modest form of conscription was introduced in April 1939 (opposed in the House of Commons by the Labour and Liberal parties) and at the same time the Territorial Army was ordered to be doubled. Conscription – the Military Training Bill – made all males between the ages of 20 to 22 liable for six months' compulsory military service. They were to be known as Militiamen, and it was envisaged that they would be employed mainly in air defence. In fact, six months was barely enough to instil a limited understanding of military ways before returning the men to civil life, and only one intake was called up before conscription proper was introduced on the outbreak of war. Modest though this measure was, it is to the great credit of Hore-Belisha that he persisted in driving it through, at the risk of his own political career. Contemporaneously with the Military Training Bill, the internecine struggle between the Royal Tank Corps and the cavalry was partially solved by the creation of the Royal Armoured Corps, an umbrella organisation that would include the mechanised cavalry and the Royal Tank Corps, which now became the Royal Tank Regiment with its battalions changing their nomenclature to regiments.[*]

It was all very well to introduce conscription and to increase the Territorial Army – the measures had the advantage of telling the world that Britain was actually taking the possibility of war seriously, and they would avoid the chaotic recruiting muddles of 1914 and 1915 – but there was not enough modern equipment to clothe and equip all those called up or encouraged to join, and as is inevitable when a small regular army is suddenly expanded, there was a serious shortage of officers and senior NCOs. The expansion of the army was mainly of its infantry, but the UK's chief ally, France, had plenty of infantry. What was needed was armour, and while the British were now, very late in the day, talking about a field force of thirty-two divisions, four of them armoured, the propor-

---

[*] That is, 1st Royal Tank Regiment, 2nd Royal Tank Regiment etc. The cavalry won in the end, as today (2005) there are only two regiments RTR and only one is equipped with tanks (the other is the Nuclear, Biological and Chemical Warfare battalion, a role that regular soldiers will run several miles to avoid doing, so boring is it). All other armoured regiments of the British army were originally horsed cavalry.

tion of armour was not only too small, there was not the slightest hope of producing the tanks, never mind training the crews, in the immediate future. Even having taken what was for Britain a momentous and unprecedented step, by ordering a form of conscription in peacetime, the government was still nervous. A message from the Secretary for War (Hore-Belisha), classified 'Personal and Private', was sent to all commanders-in-chief:

> You will read the announcement made by the Prime Minister this afternoon. It may be useful letting you know that measures now announced are NOT, repeat NOT, relating to any immediate military measure. Indeed the military situation in Germany at present time is that the great majority of army formations have now returned to their peace situations [after marching into Czechoslovakia]. How long this relative quiet position will last one cannot foretell.[1]

On the basis of pure number-crunching, the Royal Navy was well prepared for war in the spring of 1939. The line-up of major warships was:[2]

	BRITISH EMPIRE	FRANCE	GERMANY	ITALY	JAPAN
Battleships	12	5	2	4	9
Battlecruisers	3	1	2		
Pocket battleships			2		
Cruisers	62	18	6	21	39
Aircraft carriers	7	1			5
Destroyers	159	58	17	48	84
Fast assault boats	11	13	16	69	38
Submarines	69	36	50	35	21

These, on the face of it, impressive assurances of Franco-British supremacy in everything except fast attack boats – which could never win a war at sea by themselves – concealed a number of weaknesses. After years of neglect many British ships were obsolescent, if not actually obsolete, and the building programme agreed to in 1936 would not show any results until 1940 or 1941. In 1938 the cabinet had turned down the First Sea Lord's recommendation that the Royal Navy should build to a two-power standard (i.e. able to take on Germany and Japan at once) and would not give an unfettered go-ahead for warship construction until August 1939. The figures also failed to take into account that Germany had to prepare for only one naval war – against Britain and France – whereas the Royal Navy had to worry about the Atlantic, the Mediterranean and the Far East. As it was, the Far East had virtually been abandoned, and while a large fleet was based on Alexandria, the navy could not guarantee to protect British merchant shipping passing through the Mediterranean. In hindsight, it is fortunate that the German naval expansion plan was predicated on war not breaking out before 1944. The one bright glimmer in the naval firmament was the return of the Fleet Air Arm to the Royal Navy from the RAF in June 1937. The navy should never have lost the Air Arm in the first place, and the neglect that it had suffered through being a very low priority for the air marshals would take time to put right; it would not all be righted by the time war broke out, but to return it to the navy was the correct decision.

The Royal Air Force had received a greater priority than the other two services during the inter-war years, but here too there were glaring deficiencies. Professional airmen had insisted that the RAF was an offensive arm, that bombers were what mattered, whereas politicians leaned towards the air defence of Great Britain, which meant fighters. The result was that there were barely enough fighters to protect the country against incoming bombers, nor enough bombers to project overwhelming destructive force against the German homeland, and there were no long-range fighters to escort those bombers that were available. Fortunately, from 1935, the Air Member for Research and Development, Air Vice Marshal 'Stuffy' Dowding (later AOCinC Fighter Command) had encouraged the development of Radio Direction Finding, or Radar, and in this the British were considerably in advance of the Germans, which would soon prove to be just as well.

The comparison of front-line strengths, that is aircraft available for immediate use, in summer 1939, shows that the much feared and expected discrepancy was perhaps not as great as believed, then and now. While authorities disagree as to exact numbers (the confusion is mostly between actual and deployable strength and reserves) it looks as if Luftwaffe and Anglo-French air forces compared in deployable (serviceable, that is capable of taking to the air and not part of the reserve) combat aircraft (fighters and bombers) as follows:[3]

	FIGHTERS	BOMBERS	DIVE BOMBER AND GROUND ATTACK	TOTAL
Germany	1,011	1,014	267	2,292
France	637	242		879
UK	615	280		895

Bearing in mind that at this stage no German fighter could reach the UK – for that they would need airfields in Holland, Belgium or France – the threat to the UK was from 1,014 bombers which should be able to be dealt with by 615 fighters. Once again, however, the figures concealed important weaknesses. Many of the French aircraft – around a third – were obsolete or obsolescent, and for those that were not there was a shortage of spares and of fuel. The RAF had based the ADGB on there not being an expeditionary force, whereas if there was now to be one – and the Air Staff continued to oppose it – then fighter squadrons would have to be deployed to provide it with air cover. Additionally no account had been taken of the need to protect the Home Fleet, nor for air cover for coastal merchant shipping, nor for the air defence of Northern Ireland, where Belfast was an important shipbuilding centre that might (and did) become a target for German bombers.

The inescapable fact was that while in the summer of 1939 Britain was a great deal stronger than she had been at the time of Munich, largely due to the removal of the expenditure straitjacket, she was still in a disgracefully weak position. She was completely unable to defend her empire worldwide; she had barely enough – some thought not enough – assets for the air defence of the homeland, and having rejected an expeditionary force was now forced into the uncomfortable realisation that if she did not produce one, then France might well not resist whatever aggression Hitler got up to next. There was grandiose talk of a thirty-two-division field force, including four armoured divisions, but the truth was that most of those divisions consisted of untrained men with no equipment, and there was not yet one armoured division, never mind four. Britain was a great power – she had been one of the victors of 1919, she had invented the tank, Britannia ruled the waves – what on earth had happened to the workshop of the world, the mightiest empire the world had ever seen? Who was to blame?

Conventional received opinion tells us that it was Chamberlain and the appeasers, the guilty men of Munich, aided and abetted by craven generals and tight-fisted bean counters at the Treasury who were to blame, and that picture is reinforced by those who won the struggle for political control of the nation in 1940, when disaster after disaster, as we shall see, prompted a change in government. It was in the interests of Winston Churchill – brought in from the cold as First Lord of the Admiralty in 1939 – and his adherents to propagate that view and to ridicule the little man and his umbrella.

In fact, Chamberlain was not ridiculous in appearance, and nor was he a coward, nor a lackey of the dictators, nor an unrealistic believer in universal brotherhood incapable of seeing the threat that Fascism posed. Chamberlain was repelled by National Socialism and was one of the first members of the cabinet to oppose the ten-year rule and, in 1934, one of the first to advocate rearmament. He wanted to fight the 1935 general election on a platform of improving Britain's defences but Baldwin thought this would distance the Conservatives from their Labour coalition partners. As Prime Minister his defence posture – a strong air force, a one-power navy and no expeditionary force – may have been unrealistic, but at least it was a policy, even if it had changed from when he had been Chancellor. Winston Churchill, in contrast, argued for battleships in the 1920s when the evidence favoured aircraft carriers; opposed any development of the Singapore naval base in 1925; recommended the automatic extension of the ten-year rule in 1928, and fought to reduce the naval estimates in 1928 and the army estimates in 1929. It was only when he was out of office, and increasingly unlikely to regain it, that Churchill underwent a conversion that makes the Black Death seem like a minor outbreak of the sniffles, and began to bang the drum of opposing the dictators and building up Britain's military strength. Of course Churchill was right, but he must also take the blame for contributing to that weakness in the first place.

Because of the ten-year rule, and the tortuously slow pace of re-armament after its abolition, the last time that Britain might have been able to stamp on Germany militarily was in 1936, but it is a pretty big 'might'. Had all been quiet in the Mediterranean, and had the situation in the Far East been favourable, and had France agreed to use her large army, then something might have been achieved; but all was not quiet in the Mediterranean, Japan was a real worry and, as we have seen, nobody in power in Britain or France was prepared to go to war. After 1936 appeasement was the only possible course for the Chiefs of Staff and the government to take until Britain's armed forces were capable of acting decisively. Even the Treasury, always the scapegoat for a lack of defence spending, then as now, was not being entirely unreasonable when it argued that Britain could not afford the military capability that the Chiefs of Staff recommended. In the French Revolutionary and Napoleonic wars Britain's strong economy had enabled her to keep hostilities going for twenty-three years and finance the series of coalitions needed to defeat France. From 1914–18 she had the deepest Allied purse, and that enabled her to purchase all manner of war-making equipment from the otherwise idle industrial plants of America. She was able to make loans to France, Italy and Russia and was never seriously in danger of economic ruin. Now, however, things were different. While Britain in 1939 was still, just, the world's largest creditor nation, her industrial capacity had reduced in line with a decline in global economic activity, and the basic rate of income tax had risen from 4s 6d in 1934 to 7s 6d in 1939, or from 22.5 per cent to 37.5 per cent. Britain was still a world power with a great empire, but for most of the inter-war years the emperor had very few clothes. Here was one of the great illusions laboured under by politician and chief of staff alike: that if Britain could avoid Germany's 'knock-out blow' then a long war would increasingly be to her advantage. That had been true when Britain's wealth was unassailable; it was far less true now.

In apportioning responsibility for the parlous state of Britain's military posture before the outbreak of war, the blame has to be spread very widely indeed. On politicians who preferred butter to guns (but in a democracy did they have an alternative?), on senior officers who knew what was wrong but were not prepared to resign and say so publicly (but the code of argument followed by loyal acceptance was strong), on news-papermen and self-styled experts like Liddell Hart (but were they just telling the public what it wanted to hear?), on Treasury mandarins who refused the money needed (but was the money there to be had?), on the electorate itself which would not have voted for a vigorous military stance (but should not politicians educate the electorate?); and finally on those people in and out of office, who had been persuaded that the slaughter of the Great War was so dreadful that almost anything was preferable to war (it was not). One hopes that the years 1920 to 1939 might be a lesson from history, but one suspects that the same mistakes are quite likely to be repeated again!

The disappearance of Czechoslovakia from the map removed thirty-five divisions which might or might not have been militarily effective but which would certainly have made the Germans cautious about their rear, which was of course one of the reasons for removing Czechoslovakia from the equation in the first place. The German army was now in the throes of yet another expansion, and comparative strengths in September 1939, before the outbreak of war were:

DIVISIONS	GERMANY	FRANCE	UK
Cavalry	1	3	
Armoured	8	2/3 (2 tank brigades)	1 (still forming) and 1/3 (Div + army tank brigade)
Mechanised infantry	6	2	
Infantry	70	81 (10 in N. Africa)	21
Mountain	3		
Airborne	2		
Fortification		13 (on Maginot Line)	

Of the British infantry divisions, five had been formed only in 1939, but the same applied to three of the German armoured and thirty-one of their infantry divisions. The French had only two armoured brigades, with a plethora of tanks of different types, but they had 430 of the excellent Somua (Societé d'Outillage Mecanique et d'Usinage d'Artillerie). This was the first tank to have a cast hull and turret, and with frontal armour of 1.57 inches, a 47mm gun, a top speed of 25 mph and a range of 143 miles, it was probably the best tank of the time. On paper, therefore, the situation, should it come to a trial of strength, was by no means hopeless.

So far Germany had remilitarised the Rhineland, absorbed Austria, incorporated the Sudetenland and gobbled up Czechoslovakia. She had created an air force, expanded the Wehrmacht, repudiated Versailles, and, at the end of April 1939, denounced the Anglo-German naval agreement and the German-Polish non-aggression pact. All this had been done without firing a shot. It consolidated the position of Hitler and the NSDAP at home, which became stronger with every success, and, until the dismemberment of what was left of Czechoslovakia, there were many outside Germany who, though they regarded the German government as composed of upstart bullies, were prepared to admit that Versailles had been unfair, and that all Hitler had done was include in his Reich peoples and territories that were German anyway. In Britain most people found Hitler's threatening methods objectionable, particularly as he could have got most of what he wanted by negotiation, but they would have been reluctant or downright opposed to supporting war before 1939.

It is worth pausing, in the last few months of what passed for peace in Europe, to ask what were Germany's long-term aims. The short-term objectives were obvious: escape from the restrictions of Versailles and reparations, international recognition of her as an equal, and frontier adjustments to right the wrongs done in 1919 would have been part of the policy of any German government, Nazi or not. Once the anti-Republican and nationalist plank was removed, however, National Socialism was a muddled mixture of Fascism, including the corporate state and the leadership principle, and a rather woolly and unscientific belief in the superiority of the Aryan race (however that was defined). Underneath the hyperbole about the Thousand-Year Reich saving the world from Bolshevism and the Jews, it is not easy to see exactly how National Socialism intended Germany to develop: policy seemed to be made on the hoof, with little consistency and less coherence. Perhaps one of the few realistic tenets was a conviction that Germany's expanding population needed living space – lebensraum – and as this could not be obtained by going south or west, it would have to be to the east, to lands presently inhabited by Poles and peoples incorporated into the USSR.

It does seem that this was National Socialist Germany's long-term aim, and that everything before the invasion of the USSR in June 1941 was preparation for that. It is clear that Hitler did not want a war with France and Britain, and by the summer of 1939 he thought that the guarantees to Poland were empty rhetoric. Today we see the German invasion of Poland as aggression pure and simple, but there were many in Germany who saw behind the Nazi propaganda yet still believed Poland was a threat to Germany. The Poles are a tough, hard people, but they disliked both the Germans and the Russians and had an unfortunate tendency to be rude to both at the same time, which, bearing in mind their geographical location, may partly explain why Poland has been an independent country for only brief periods of history. Poland had taken advantage of Germany when that country was weak; had waged an economic war against her from 1925 to 1934, and had ordered partial mobilisation in March 1939. In 1939 she had a population of 35 million (including six million Russians) and could mobilise forty infantry and three mountain divisions, eleven cavalry and two mechanised brigades. Additionally Poland had 156 serviceable bombers and around 150 serviceable fighters, and a small navy of four destroyers and five submarines. Admittedly Polish equipment and tactics were out of date and they relied far too much on horsed cavalry, but in the view of many German generals Poland could pose a serious threat. Field Marshal Erich von Manstein, perhaps the most competent general of the war, on either side, certainly thought so:

> Poland was bound to be a source of great bitterness to us after she had used
> the dictated peace of Versailles to annex German territories to which neither
> historical justice nor the right of self determination gave her any claim ...
> every time we looked at the map we were reminded of our precarious
> situation ... a nightmare that disturbed us all the more whenever we thought
> of the aspirations for German territory still harboured with such ill-
> concealed longing by wide circles of the Polish people.[4]

At first German demands on Poland were for the return of the Polish Corridor and Danzig, with their predominantly German populations. The situation was not helped by the Poles issuing an ultimatum to the

Danzig city senate on Friday 4 August giving them twenty-four hours to stop their refusal to recognise Polish customs regulations, and to regulate their open border with East Prussia. On Monday 5 August *The Times* published a letter from Major C. B. Ormerod:

> As long as the Corridor separates East Prussia from the German mainland the peace of Europe will be insecure. If Pomerania [the Corridor] were ceded to Germany Poland could be provided with an outlet to the sea through East Prussia and Memel-land. It would be a comparatively simple matter to arrange for the exchange of Poles and Germans occupying Pomerania and Memel-land respectively, under conditions beneficial to both, under a general plan of redistribution of population. Thus racial rivalries and oppression of minorities would disappear.

Even at this late hour the British government thought that some accommodation might be arrived at, and urged the Poles to negotiate. Simultaneously both British and German representatives were negotiating in secret with the USSR. The British aim was to line up Russia and Italy alongside Britain, France and Poland in urging and if necessary enforcing restraint upon Germany. The German aim was to persuade Russia to stand aside while Germany dealt with Poland, and with France if the Franco-Polish treaty of alliance actually came to anything. There was little in it for Stalin in an agreement with Britain, which might very well involve Russia in a war against Germany, but with Britain unable to provide very much in the way of assistance; and anyway the talks stalled on the refusal of the Polish government to agree to Russian troops crossing Polish territory to get at the Germans if it came to war.

An agreement with Germany, however, once ideological differences were discarded by both sides, offered Russia a great deal. Presented to the world as a commercial agreement and non-aggression pact, the secret clauses of the Molotov–Ribbentrop Pact promised that Finland, Estonia, Latvia (despite the sizeable German minorities in the latter two states), the eastern half of Poland (which had been lost by Russia in 1921) and Romanian Bessarabia would be in the Russian sphere of influence, while Lithuania and western Poland would be in that of Germany. The secret clauses went on to say: 'The question whether the interests of both parties make the maintenance of an independent Polish state desirable, and how the frontiers of this state should be drawn, can be definitely determined only in the course of further political development.'[5] Additionally, Russia would supply Germany with certain raw materials and foodstuffs that she could not produce in sufficient quantities herself. It is impossible to overemphasise the importance of this agreement to Germany and to her war effort. It rendered ineffective any blockade that the British might impose, thus removing the main concern of German admirals and economists, and made war with France and Britain seem far less risky than it would have been had Germany not been able to rely on the benevolent neutrality of the Soviet Union at her back.

The pact was announced on 23 August, and on 25 August Britain converted her guarantee to Poland into a formal alliance, obliging Britain to go to war in defence of Polish territorial integrity. In the early hours of the morning of 1 September 1939 the Luftwaffe and German naval units opened hostilities against Poland, and these were followed by the army, striking westward from Germany, south from East Prussia and north from Slovakia. In all, German land forces involved in the Polish campaign consisted of six armoured (panzer) divisions, forty-five infantry, four motorised, four light and three mountain divisions, with a further five infantry divisions following on. Apart from the armoured units this was not all that much larger than the Polish forces opposing them (1.5 million against 1.3 million), and even the preponderance of armour (3,600 armoured vehicles against 750) is not as overwhelming as it may seem: while a German armoured division of 1939 was established for 312 tanks, 268 were Panzer Is and IIs, armed only with machine guns.[*] Except in the armoured and motorised divisions much of the artillery and transport was horse-drawn. A German infantry division of 1939 had over five thousand horses on strength, and still had 4,656 in 1944.

Supporting the German land forces engaged were a total of 810 bombers, 405 fighters of various types and 324 Stuka dive bombers. This latter, more properly the Junkers Ju 87D, could carry up to 3,000lbs of bombs, depending on configuration, and had a range of 370 miles. The

---

[*] Today (2005) a British armoured division fields 216 Challenger II main battle tanks each armed with a 120mm gun.

advantage of a dive bomber was its ability to place a bomb accurately on target, and the fitting of a siren to the Stuka made it a terrifying weapon against inexperienced troops. It was effective in Poland (and initially in the west too) but was technologically obsolescent, its impact being psychological rather than merely destructive. German naval forces in the Polish campaign were centred round the battleship *Schleswig Holstein* and included destroyers, minesweepers, motor torpedo boats, eight submarines and naval aviation.[6]

On the morning of the day German troops invaded Poland, 1 September 1939, the French and British governments demanded a German withdrawal, and ordered general mobilisation, while Italy declared herself a non-belligerent and Switzerland declared neutrality.[*] The next day Prime Minister Chamberlain formed a war cabinet, with Winston Churchill back from the wilderness as First Lord of the Admiralty. Chamberlain offered the Labour and Liberal parties a coalition government; they refused but did not vote against any war legislation. That afternoon ten bomber squadrons of the Royal Air Force began to move from England to airfields in France. At 0900 hours British Summer Time on 3 September the British government issued an ultimatum to the German government saying that if Germany did not halt operations in Poland and agree to withdraw, then Britain would declare war. The French issued a similar ultimatum. At 1100 hours British time (1200 hours German time) the British ultimatum ran out and the Prime Minister announced that Britain was now at war with Germany. At 1700 hours the same day France, too, declared war on Germany, and ten RAF bombers dropped five million leaflets over German cities along the Rhine telling the Germans how naughty they had been. The next day the British sent another ten bombers on a rather more warlike mission – to bomb German shipping in the harbour of Wilhelmshaven. Seven of the bombers were lost, three to anti-aircraft fire and two shot down by German fighters, and the only damage inflicted by the RAF was to the (neutral) Danish town of Esbjerg, a hundred miles away from the target and bombed in error by a navigationally challenged bomber crew.

* The British had assured the French that if Germany invaded Switzerland and France therefore declared war on Germany, Britain would declare on the side of France.

When Britain had last declared war, in 1914, the legal position was that the whole of the Empire was also automatically at war, the logic being that if the King was at war then so were all his Dominions and territories. After the First War the British had said that the self-governing Dominions (Canada, Australia, New Zealand and South Africa) could in future decide for themselves whether they wished to partake of a war entered into by Britain, and if they did could themselves declare war accordingly. Protectorates could in general make up their own minds. The position as regards colonies was, of course, unchanged as these were ruled by the mother country and not by any indigenous administration. India was neither a dominion nor a colony, but as the Governor General was the head of the administration as well as being the King's representative, she too was assumed to be at war.

Australia and New Zealand announced themselves as being at war with Germany on 3 September, the day the British ultimatum ran out, taking the 1914 view that there was no need for a separate declaration of war. South Africa, mindful of the sympathies of a section of its Boer population, took a little longer. The Prime Minister, the 73-year-old Boer General Hertzog, was about to declare his country neutral, but was outnumbered in cabinet by the 69-year-old Boer General Smuts and his supporters, and declared war on Germany on 6 September. Canada waited until her parliament reassembled and declared on 10 September, not through any lack of patriotic fervour but to a far more practical purpose. As the Neutrality Acts forbade the USA from exporting any war materials to a belligerent, Britain could not now take delivery of contracted military equipment built in the USA. By delaying her declaration of war by a week, Canada could take at least partial delivery of much useful war-making materials before she too became a belligerent.

The National Service (Armed Forces) Act, passed on the same day that Britain declared war, rendered all males between the ages of eighteen and forty-one liable for conscription into the armed forces. Those in reserved occupations were exempt depending on their age, and in practice men were called up by years, the youngest first, and single before married men. The length of service was for the duration of hostilities or 'so long as His Majesty may require'. Men called up could state their preference for service (navy, army or air force) and regiment or corps if volunteering for or directed to the army. Of the first intake of 200,000 men who registered in October 1939, half opted for either the Royal Navy or the Royal Air Force, and as the service which most needed manpower was the army, many of them were disappointed. The first stage of the selection process involved a medical examination, to which crippled or limbless men were not called. As might be expected, older men were the more likely to be turned down on medical grounds. Throughout the war the percentage of men aged under twenty who were placed in Medical Category III (only capable of very limited duties, known to the army as 'excused breathing') or IV (unsuitable for any form of service) was 8.3 per cent, rising to 35.2 per cent for those aged thirty-six and over. Despite the general public antipathy to any form of military endeavour during the 1930s, only about a thousand men are recorded as being deliberate column-dodgers who refused to register for service, and only 59,162 men applied to be treated as conscientious objectors.[7]

Neither Germany, France nor the Soviet Union recognised grounds of conscience as an excuse for avoiding military service. The British had always been tolerant of conscientious objectors, those people who claimed that reasons of principle or religion forbade them to fight (but presumably did not forbid them to accept the protection of those who did?). During the whole of the Second World War, of the 59,192 applicants 3,577 had their applications accepted unconditionally, 28,720 conditionally (that is, they were required to take up and continue in approved civil employment), 14, 691 were accepted for non-combatant duties in the armed forces, and 12,204 had their applications turned down.[8] There were also exceptions from conscription on the grounds of hardship (509,878 applications, 163,372 turned down) and, after November 1939, men could have their call-up deferred if they were temporarily engaged in work of national importance.

While the full panoply of control of manpower and industry, a lesson identified from the First War, was not fully implemented until the spring and summer of 1940, nevertheless many of the mistakes of that war were avoided by the early imposition of conscription and a list of reserved occupations that only needed minimal amendment before promulgation.

Northern Ireland, as in the First War, was excluded from the provisions of the National Service Act, as it had been from the Military Training Bill before it. Northern Ireland was then effectively internally self-governing, although part of the United Kingdom rather than a Dominion, and thus subject to laws passed in Westminster unless specifically exempted in the act. Ever since the separation of Northern Ireland from the Irish Free State, in 1921, the northern administration had been overwhelmingly Protestant and Unionist, and had made little effort to integrate the substantial Roman Catholic minority. Unionists were concerned that conscription would provide military training to Roman Catholics (assumed by Unionists to be disloyal), while the British thought that many Roman Catholics, who (not unreasonably) felt themselves excluded from the structures of the state, would object to being conscripted to fight for it. As it was, around 37,000 residents of Northern Ireland volunteered for the British forces during the war; so did 38,544 residents of the neutral Irish Republic, as the Free State had been styled since 1937. Enlistment figures for Irish citizens living or working in the UK who volunteered are not known, but must have been considerable.

Despite Ireland's neutrality – which infuriated Churchill – Ireland was very definitely neutral against Germany. Downed RAF crews were put in detention camps near the border with Ulster and the gates left open; German crews and German spies were securely locked up. IRA members were interned without trial and six of them were executed. At one stage the Irish representative in London asked the British government if they could please discourage southern Irish soldiers from going home on leave in uniform, as the sight of British soldiers wandering around Dublin rather compromised Irish neutrality. A system was instituted whereby soldiers passing through the ferry ports of Liverpool and Holyhead handed in their uniforms and drew civilian suits, to be exchanged for uniform again on return from leave.

While the battles for Poland raged there was little that the French and the British could do to help, despite increasingly shrill Polish pleas. British bombers could have reached German cities (they had already done so, dropping leaflets), but the cabinet was resolutely opposed to bombing cities, even indisputably military targets in or near cities, partly because of the effect it might have on neutral nations (the American President Roosevelt had appealed to all belligerents not to bomb civilian targets), and partly because of the fear of retaliation. As the Chancellor of the Exchequer, Sir Kingsley Wood, said at cabinet: 'It would be entirely wrong for us to bomb even German munitions works, as we would be bound to kill women and children and thereby provoke reprisals… to do anything that would lead to the bombing of Britain by Germany would be a fatal error.'[9] The Luftwaffe had no such inhibitions in Poland, but then they had destroyed most of the Polish air force on the ground in the first few hours of the war.

On 7 September the French did make a symbolic entry into Germany, at three points in the Saar over a frontage of about sixteen miles. There was hardly any fighting, the Germans in the area fell back, and having penetrated a few miles the French occupied some abandoned villages and stopped. The Germans were happy to leave them there.

Britain was definitely committed to sending an expeditionary force to the Continent, but even in the choice of commander of the land component there was dither and muddle. Secretary of State Hore-Belisha considered three candidates. On the outbreak of war the CIGS was the 53-year-old General John Vereker, sixth Viscount Gort. A Grenadier Guardsman, Lord Gort had won the VC, three DSOs and an MC and had been mentioned in despatches eight times in the First War, which he finished in command of a battalion of his regiment. Although he had been a staff officer during the First War, and a post-war student at the Staff College and Commandant there in 1936, he was far more of a field commander than a skulker in the corridors of Whitehall, as any credible CIGS perforce had and has to be. Hore-Belisha did not like him and was increasingly irritated by his blunt statements of the militarily (but not necessarily politically) obvious. Lieutenant General Sir John Dill was General Officer Commanding-in-Chief (GOCinC) Aldershot Command, a post that had long been accepted, albeit not formally designated, as Commander-in-Chief of the British Expeditionary Force should one be formed. Dill, five years older than Gort, had been passed over as CIGS after Deverall's dismissal because of Hore-Belisha's policy of reducing the age of members of the Army Council. He too had done well in the

First War, finishing it as a full colonel with a DSO and eight mentions in despatches. Like Gort he was both a graduate and had been Commandant of the Staff College, and unlike Gort was a far-sighted military thinker. To the publicity-conscious Hore-Belisha, however, Dill's undemonstrative nature made him unattractive.

The third actor in the September 1939 appointments game was General Sir Edmund ('Tiny') Ironside, 59 years old and six feet four inches in height. He too had had a good war from 1914 to 1918 before becoming Chief of Staff (and for a while commander) of the international force fighting on the side of the Whites during the Russian Civil War. Although he was a Staff College graduate, and had been Commandant there in 1923, Ironside was far more of a field soldier than a staff officer. A natural linguist, in the South African War he had disguised himself as a Boer ox-wagon driver to find out what German volunteers fighting for the Boers were up to, and the author John Buchan in *The Thirty-Nine Steps* modelled his hero Richard Hannay on Ironside. In July 1939 Ironside was Governor and Commander-in-Chief Gibraltar when Hore-Belisha brought him back to England as Inspector General of Overseas Forces with a promise (not legally binding) that he would be appointed Commander-in-Chief of the BEF if one were despatched. Ironside was an energetic Inspector General; he visited Poland and thought that the Poles would give a good account of themselves, but advised Marshal Smigly-Rydz, the Polish Commander-in-Chief, that his plan to hold with his main forces forward was faulty, and risked communications breaking down and formations being cut off and defeated in detail. In the event Ironside was wrong about the performance but right about the plan. Ironside had no delusions as to the muddle and incompetence at the top of his own government: 'They are all dreamers and thinkers and cannot turn them [military options] into orders. Not a good augury for war.'[10]

It is typical of the state of Britain's military affairs – comical if not so tragic – that the Commander of the BEF was not appointed until after war had been declared. On the afternoon of 3 September the ultimatum had expired and the Prime Minister had broadcast to the nation. Ironside's staff was in Aldershot, poised to take over the BEF, when Ironside was summoned to the War Office by Hore-Belisha. Expecting to be confirmed as Commander-in-Chief BEF, Ironside was told that he was to be CIGS in place of Gort, who was to command the Expeditionary Force. Dill was also to join the BEF as a Corps Commander, with a backdated promotion to general that would make him one day junior to Gort! This ludicrous situation was made worse by Gort being allowed to take the Director of Military Operations, Pownall, with him as his Chief of the General Staff of the BEF. Thus one of the major errors of the First War was repeated: the two men who knew what was going on and who were most familiar with the war plans (such as they were), the CIGS and the Director of Military Operations, were removed from the centre just when they were most needed. As it happened, Gort was not a bad choice for the BEF, but Ironside was out of his depth as CIGS, having never served in the War Office and being far too straightforward for his own good.

This situation should never have been allowed to happen. The selection of the Commander-in-Chief was a purely military matter, which should have been decided by the CIGS well before the outbreak of war, and with a staff nominated, in place and ready to go. The sensible solution would have been to leave Gort where he was as CIGS, appoint Dill to command the BEF and make use of Ironside's fluent French by using him as the principal liaison officer with the French, rather than the Duke of Gloucester, the King's brother, who had problems communicating in English, never mind French, and while a thoroughly decent man was one of the stupider examples of Hanoverian in-breeding. As it was, Hore-Belisha, who was far too fond of meddling in matters that should have been left to the generals, used this opportunity to get rid of a CIGS – Gort – with whom he did not get on, and to put in someone whom he thought (wrongly) would be his poodle. The generals should never have allowed him to get away with it.

It was not only the command of the BEF that was a source of muddle, but the status of the Advanced Air Striking Force (whose bombers moved to France on mobilisation) and the BEF's air cover. The Air Staff had never liked the idea of getting involved in support of ground forces: it detracted from the Trenchard doctrine of the offensive use of air power, and the knowledge that if the army deployed it would perforce demand air cover was one of the driving factors behind the staff's opposition to an expeditionary force. The Chief of the Air Staff at the outbreak of war, Air Chief Marshal Sir Cyril Newall, had said on his appointment in 1937 that ground-support operations (well demonstrated in Spain by the Kondor Legion) were 'a gross misuse of air forces', and his views had not changed.[11] Air Chief Marshal Sir Hugh Dowding, Air Officer Commanding Fighter Command, was in conflict with the Air Staff, but he too was against an expeditionary force. Contrary to the Trenchard doctrine, Dowding thought that the first priority of the RAF should be the air defence of Great Britain, rather than offensive operations with bombers. Any diversion of fighters from defence of the homeland was to be resisted, and that included anything for the BEF. Dowding was, however, honest enough to realise that if, contrary to the advice of the air marshals, there was to be a BEF then the only fighter that could give it adequate support was the Hurricane, and in March he had reluctantly earmarked four squadrons (sixty-four aircraft) for that purpose.

As for command and control, the Air Staff 'took the line that the army should not be allowed a fighter force the commander of which was subject to the orders of an army general officer. It was regretted that even four squadrons had been specifically allocated to the Field Force.'[12] They were even less happy in May when it became necessary to allocate a further six squadrons, as the proposed expeditionary force grew to four rather than the original two divisions. Should Gort need support from the Advanced Air Striking Force, he would tell the War Office, which would ask the Air Ministry, which, if it agreed, would tell Bomber Command who would issue an order to the air vice marshal commanding the AASF in France. The Air Component eventually grew to thirteen squadrons, but the army did rather push its luck by demanding another 250 aircraft for close-support operations by June 1940, and its own air force. When the RAF countered by pointing out that there was as yet no British equivalent of the Stuka because nobody had ever asked for one, and that to provide another 250 aircraft for the army would cripple Bomber Command, it was eventually agreed to combine the thirteen squadrons of the Air Component with the bomber squadrons of the Advanced Air Striking Force and put the whole thing under Gort. The bombers could then only be tasked by Bomber Command of the RAF in exceptional circumstances, and only with the approval of the war cabinet.

As it was, when the crunch came there was insufficient air cover for the BEF, but this was not the fault of the RAF. Between the wars the priority given to the RAF was directed towards the air defence of Great Britain (fighters – the politicians' requirement) and an air offensive arm (bombers – the Air Staff's requirement). Nobody had allowed for air cover for the BEF because for most of the time there was no intention of having a BEF. That said, the bickering between the generals and the air marshals over what the aircraft should be used for and who should command them was a sad precursor of what was to come. In these days of 'purple' training and jointery in operational headquarters, with one staff college for all three services, it is easy to forget that it is only a few years ago that the army and the air force (and to a lesser extent the navy) stopped regarding each other as a far greater threat to their own existence than the Russian hordes across the inner German border.

Despite staff talks between the British and the French since Munich the previous year, the Allied command arrangements were far from satisfactory. General Gort had the status of an army commander (albeit that two corps each of two divisions is a pretty small army), and as such he came under the French General Georges, commander of the Armies of the North-East (an army group commander in British parlance), who in turn was subservient to General Gamelin, the Commander-in-Chief of the French army worldwide. This was fair enough, but Gort was also a commander of a national contingent in a coalition, and therefore had to deal with political matters as well as purely military affairs both with his own government and with the French, and was the commander of every British soldier (and some airmen) in France, including those in the ports and on the lines of communication. Not only that, but General Gamelin frequently bypassed General Georges to try to give orders directly to General Gort. It was an impossible situation, and yet the answer was obvious. Later in the war command arrangements would take into account the impossibility – or at least the undesirability – of one man being both the head of a national contingent and a commander of fighting troops. In North Africa Montgomery would have Alexander to fly top cover for him, and in the Far East Slim would have Mountbatten. What was needed now, but what was not forthcoming, was an army commander responsible for fighting the battle, and above him a commander British forces, responsible for dealing with home and Allied governments and for command of all those troops not involved in the fighting.

It took five weeks to get the four-division BEF to France, considerably longer than it took to get a rather larger force there in 1914. Because of the fear of sea and air attack on the troopships, St Nazaire, Nantes, Brest and Cherbourg were used as the disembarkation ports, and the British then moved to the Belgian border where they took up position between the French Seventh Army on the left, and the French First and Ninth Armies on the right. Most of the French (and hence the British) effort was concentrated on the left wing, as the Germans, it was thought, would be most likely to attack through Belgium and/or Holland, rather than try to take on the Maginot Line. The BEF was divided into two corps. General Sir John Dill commanded I Corps, with 1 and 2 Divisions, while Lieutenant General Sir Alan Brooke commanded II Corps of 3 and 4 Divisions. Each division had one divisional cavalry regiment (mechanised reconnaissance); three field and one field-park companies Royal Engineers; infantry divisional signals (about 500 men and a lieutenant colonel's command, but not designated a divisional signals regiment until later); three field regiments and an anti-tank regiment of the Royal Artillery; an intelligence section, a supply column, a petrol company and an ammunition company, all motorised, of the Royal Army Service Corps; three field ambulances and a field-hygiene section of the Royal Army Medical Corps; a divisional provost company of the Royal Military Police; a postal unit and even a bath and laundry unit. The division commanded three infantry brigades, each of a small headquarters, an anti-tank company and three battalions of infantry. In this original BEF all the troops were regular, all the transport was mechanical and, small though it was, it should, like its 1914 predecessor, have been a highly trained and well-equipped force. The reality was somewhat different.

The British army went to war in 1939 with much the same kit as it had when it finished the last war, in 1918, but with rather less of it. The Vickers medium machine gun, the Lewis light machine gun, the Enfield rifle, the steel helmet, the web equipment, even the uniform the man wore, was either of the same pattern or almost identical to that on issue at the end of the Great War. The only major new items were the 25-pounder field guns, the Bren light machine guns, the carriers and the tanks. But the 25-pounder was not yet on issue to all field regiments, and some still had the 18-pounder introduced in 1904; the Bren was slow in coming into service, and each mechanised cavalry regiment was equipped with only twenty-eight Mark VI light tanks, with frontal armour of 0.65 inches and its main armament nothing more than two machine guns. Divisions had only a few medium machine guns; the Machine-Gun Corps had been disbanded in 1922 and none of the eight infantry battalions converted to machine-gun units in 1937 were yet available. Infantry battalions had only two 3-inch mortars each and there was no anti-aircraft artillery, all available guns being placed to protect civilian targets at home.[13] The only armour not allocated to divisions was provided by 4 Royal Tank Regiment, which moved to France on 19 September under command of Headquarters BEF with its Infantry Tanks Mark I. Weighing eleven tons and with frontal armour 2.6 inches thick, the Matilda was almost impossible to knock out with German anti-tank guns of the period, but its main armament was only one Vickers machine gun, and with a top speed of less than 8 mph it was useless for anything other than as a (moderately) mobile machine-gun platform.

Now that they were actually in France and alongside the French army, some of the British began to have doubts. Even Brooke, Commander II Corps, who had gone to school in France, spoke French and liked the French, was not impressed when he attended a French parade:

> Finally Corap [French general commanding their Ninth Army] invited me to stand alongside him whilst the guard of honour, consisting of cavalry, artillery and infantry, marched past. I can still see those troops now. Seldom have I seen anything more slovenly and badly turned out. Men unshaven, horses ungroomed, clothes and saddlery that did not fit, vehicles dirty and complete lack of pride in themselves or their units. What shook me most, however, was the look on the men's faces, disgruntled and insubordinate looks, and although ordered to give 'eyes left' hardly a man bothered to do so.[14]

Admittedly these men were conscripts, not British regulars, but even so it was an unhappy harbinger of what was to come.

The Royal Navy's first task in the war was to escort the BEF safely to France, and this they did, losing not a ship nor a man in the process. The Germans made only half-hearted attempts to prevent it, and once mines had been laid and three German submarines sunk, they abandoned the effort in October. Because of the inability of the RAF to provide sufficient air cover, the Home Fleet moved, as it had in the last war, to Scapa Flow. There too German submarines were a danger, and there too destroyers of the Royal Navy accounted for several. The U-boats did score one major success, however, on 17 September, when *U 29* sank the fleet carrier HMS *Courageous* in the Western Approaches. *Courageous* was unescorted and submarine-hunting at the time, something that went against all the admirals' experience which said (rightly) that rather than try to find and destroy submarines in the wide ocean expanses, where they could be anywhere, they should be destroyed when they came to attack convoys. That *Courageous* was doing what she should not have been was due entirely to pressure from that great naval strategist, the First Lord of the Admiralty, Winston Churchill, who insisted on the navy 'taking the offensive', however unwise that might be.

Meanwhile the Poles fought bravely and tenaciously, but while the Germans did not have it all their own way – they were still learning and practising techniques previously only tested in map exercises or on manoeuvres – professionalism, better communications, air power and mobility told; and when the Soviet army invaded on 17 September the Polish army collapsed. The Soviets had not told the Germans that they were intending to enter Poland, and by then German units were already well beyond the demarcation line agreed in the Molotov–Ribbentrop Pact. While troops fighting in soon-to-be-Russian areas could not just stop, the German army was ordered to withdraw through a series of report lines back to the agreed Russo-German border, and this was generally achieved without clashes, or indeed without German or Russian troops ever meeting. In Britain the cabinet debated whether the guarantee to Poland was directed against any aggressor, or only against Germany? Must Britain now declare war on the Soviet Union? Fascinating though it would be to speculate, the Attorney General, after some fast legal footwork, was able to assure the cabinet that they need concern themselves only with Germany.

The Polish government and high command crossed into Romania, and on 27 September hostilities came to an end. Germany and Russia amended the border agreed in the pact to give Germany rather more of Poland in return for Russia having Lithuania. Pomerania and West Prussia, previously German territory, were reincorporated into the Reich, while the rest of Germany's share of Poland became the *General-Gouverment* under a German governor general, Dr Hans Frank.

Poland dealt with, units of the German army began to move west.

NOTES

1. Quoted in Roderick McLeod (ed), *Time Unguarded: The Ironside Diaries 1937–1940*, David McKay, New York, 1962

2. Figures from Stephen Roskill,*The War at Sea, Vol. I*, HMSO, London, 1954.

3. Figures from John Ellis, *The World War II Data Book*, BCA, London, 1993.

4. FM Erich von Manstein (tr Anthony G. Powell), *Lost Victories*, Greenhill, Elstree, 1987.

5. Research Institute for Military History, Germany (tr McMurry and Osers), *Germany and The Second World War, Vol. II*, Clarendon Press, Oxford, 2000.

6. Ibid.

7. Central Statistical Office, *Statistical Digest of the Second World War*, HMSO, London, 1951.

8. H. M. D. Parker, *History of the Second World War – Manpower*, HMSO, London, 1957.

9. Martin Gilbert, *A History of the Twentieth Century, Vol. II*, HarperCollins, London, 1998.

10. Roderick McLeod (ed), op. cit.

11. John Terraine, *The Right of the Line*, Hodder & Stoughton, London, 1985.

12. Air Historical Branch, quoted in Terraine, op. cit.

13. For exact composition of divisions see Lt Col H. F. Joslen, *Orders of Battle: Second World War 1939–45*, HMSO, London, 1960.

14. David Fraser, *Alanbrooke*, Collins, London, 1982.

6

Inaction and Defeat

DURING THE FIRST WEEKS of the war the British government was floundering about, trying to decide a strategy. All that had been promised to the French was four divisions, and these were on their way, with a vague assurance of two armoured divisions later. These divisions did not yet exist, but the new CIGS, Ironside, for all his ignorance of the ways of Whitehall, was trying to get it into the heads of politicians that it was the German army that posed the greatest threat, and that only an army could defeat it. The French, Ironside said, had no intention of going on the offensive, nor of provoking the Germans. They would sit behind their fortifications for as long as they could, and wanted far more British troops than the British had. Ironside found that apart from the intention to send four divisions to France, the army had no war plans as such, and no thought had been given as to how the Empire could contribute, nor, indeed, how the Empire could be defended. In trying to impose some thinking and planning for the future, Ironside and his fellow chiefs, Admiral Pound and Air Chief Marshal Newall, were handicapped by having to attend the interminable meetings of which politicians are so fond. The Supreme War Council of the Allies (Britain and France), the war cabinet, the Chiefs of Staff Committee, the Military Co-ordination Committee and the Priorities Committee, required all three to attend, while the Board of the Admiralty, the Army Council, the Land Forces Committee, the Air Council and various promotion boards required at least one of them.

Service officers, by their very nature and training, are not good committee-men. They are accustomed to appreciating a situation, weighing up the factors and taking a decision. They spend little time in debate and discussion and they do not have to pander to a fickle and ignorant electorate. They issue orders and directives, not platitudes and cajolements. Politics, on the other hand, requires that everyone has his say, however irrelevant or impractical that say may be; politicians seek consensus, and a cabinet is not subject to a law requiring obedience on pain of imprisonment, or, in the extreme, death. All this means that the waging of war by a democracy is a very difficult business, and often tortuously slow, as politicians have to be persuaded of the advantages and disadvantages of military options that they do not understand. At least in 1939, unlike 1914, the cabinet was convinced relatively early on that this war would not be over by Christmas. In the Great War the British Empire had produced ninety-five divisions. Now, with the needs of the Royal Air Force and its associated aviation industries, the demands of the air defence of Great Britain and the fact that many modern weapon systems were manpower-intensive, the best that the British might be able to do in this war, thought the CIGS, would be fifty divisions, thirty-two of them British. Ironside saw these divisions being deployed in France (twenty), in the Middle East (twelve), and in the UK as an imperial reserve (eighteen). Little thought was given to the Far East, except for the strengthening of existing garrisons there. As the Suez Canal was the 'centre of the Empire', the troops there would ensure its security and, if Italy came into the war on the German side, would capture Italian colonies in Libya and East Africa. Additionally the CIGS thought that another ten division's-worth of equipment should be prepared, in order to arm allies who might appear (Turkey was one possibility). The Royal Navy, concerned that its supplies of steel for shipbuilding might be diverted to build tanks for the army, and the Royal Air Force, jealous of its own expansion plans, opposed Ironside, but on 17 September the war cabinet agreed to aim for a three-year war and a total of fifty-five divisions, although they would not endorse Ironside's proposals for their deployment.

Britain was, of course, a long way away from a fifty-five division army, and even further away from equipment for it.[*] In France the BEF dug in along the Belgian border, but despite overtures by both the British and the French, the Belgians would countenance no staff talks, no discussions, no joint plans and no construction of defences on Belgian soil. Any such measures, they thought, would only compromise their neutrality and make it more, rather than less, likely that Germany would invade them. Belgian politicians and generals had learned little from 1914.

Under pressure from the French, and from the CIGS, a build-up of the BEF from its original four divisions began. Ironside was at pains to point out that it was no use just sending men: they must first have the necessary equipment and training, which meant that the twenty-division BEF that the army aimed for would take eighteen months to come to fruition. Churchill disagreed: in another totally impractical flight of fancy he demanded that the twenty divisions be sent at once, and equipment borrowed from the French. Fortunately, wiser counsels prevailed.

In December 5 Division, mainly a regular formation, but with no armour and only two, rather than three, field regiments of artillery joined the BEF, and in January and February 1940 the first two Territorial divisions appeared, 48 (South Midland) and 50 (Northumbrian), the latter with no armour, only two regiments of field artillery, and only two infantry brigades. The newly arrived divisions went to I Corps (48) and II Corps (5 and 50). In April a third corps, III Corps, was formed under Lieutenant General Sir Ronald Adam, and this took on three more Territorial divisions, 42 (East Lancashire), 44 (Home Counties) and 51 (Highland) Divisions. Neither 42 nor 44 Divisions had any armour. In April too, three more Territorial divisions – 12 (Eastern), 23 (Northumbrian) and 46 Divisions – joined. These were second-line divisions, raised when the Territorial Army was ordered to be doubled. None had any armour or artillery, they had only skeleton communications and the most rudimentary administrative support. 23 Division had only two infantry brigades. These divisions were sent to France for labouring duties on the lines of communication and 'to complete their training'. Like the rest of

---

* In the event the British army alone managed forty-eight divisions by the end of the war.

the BEF they had few opportunities for training; defences had to be prepared where none were before, and the French insistence on radio silence meant that even CPXs* could not be held.

Meanwhile the German army was evaluating its performance in Poland. German losses in the campaign were 11,000 dead and 30,000 wounded, as compared with 70,000 and 133,000 Poles against Germany, and 50,000 killed and an unknown number of Poles wounded against the USSR.[1] The main lessons were the importance of the tank and the aeroplane. Without close air support of the land forces by the Luftwaffe, and without the mobility and shock action that armour gave, the German army could not have won the Polish campaign as swiftly as it did. Of the tanks employed the Mark IV was, the generals felt, undoubtedly the best. They identified the importance of having sufficient anti-aircraft artillery able to move with the army; in Poland this had not been so urgent, but it would be vital against the West, particularly the British. General Guderian reported to the Chief of the General Staff of the Army, Colonel General Halder, that the 15–20 per cent losses in tanks could be made up fairly quickly, but complained that there was insufficient pontoon bridging to sustain any operations in an area where there were many rivers. Motorised divisions needed to be reorganised into a two-regiment structure, as three regiments had proved unwieldy; more panzer divisions needed to be formed and some infantry divisions were still equipped with Czech weapons.

There was concern, too, about the quality of the infantry. Both Colonel General Feodor von Bock, Commander Army Group North, and Colonel General Wilhelm Ritter von Leeb, Commander Army Group West, were convinced that the infantry was not as good as it had been in 1914, and that the men did not show the same panache and aggressive spirit as had their fathers, so that officers were obliged to be further forward than they should have been, with the resultant disproportionate casualties.[2] Given the rapid expansion that the German army had undergone and the limited time there had been for training of police and border guard units trans-

---

* CPX: Command Post Exercise, where headquarters, but not whole units, are exercised in movement, communications and operational procedures. The CPX was and is an essential precursor to the FTX, or Field Training Exercise, where the entire unit or formation is exercised in the field.

ferred to the army this was hardly surprising, but it reinforced the generals' wish to remain on the defensive for the time being, regardless of their professional preference for quick wars and lightning blows.

The army was unhappy too about the behaviour of Nazi party officials and members of the General SS in Poland. What politicians called 'house-cleaning' (beatings, imprisonment and even executions of Jews and potential members of a Polish resistance) was seen by the soldiers as ill-treatment of civilians and contrary to international and German military law. As members of the Wehrmacht were punished for misbehaviour towards civilians or prisoners of war, the army expected that the Nazi functionaries and SS should be too, but their complaints to Hitler were ignored, and the only action taken was to remove responsibility for internal security in the occupied areas of Poland from the army and give it to the SS and Gestapo (the Geheime Staatspolizei, or State Secret Police).

While Hitler would now undoubtedly have preferred a peace settle-ment to a continuation of the war, he wanted it on his terms. Feelers to the Allies did go out, via Italy, but as the Allies would accept nothing less than a complete withdrawal from both Poland and Czechoslovakia there was an impasse that was unlikely to be bridged. Despite the submission by General Karl-Heinrich von Stuelpnagel, Oberquartermeister I at Ober-kommando des Heeres (OKH), the equivalent of the Director of Military Operations at the British War Office, that the German army could not be ready for an assault on the Maginot Line before 1942, it was Hitler who ordered preparations for an early strike against the West. Various start-dates were decided upon, only to be cancelled because of bad weather or pleas from the generals and airmen for more time. In the winter of 1939, 15 October and 15–20 November were all possible dates for an offensive, and plans ranged from Fall Braun, or Case Brown, a joint German–Italian attack across the upper Rhine (Italy was not yet in the war); Case Bear, an attack on the Maginot Line, and Cases Hawk, Green and Yellow, for attacks on France and the Low Countries. (The British precede the codeword for their plans with the word 'Operation'; the German term is Fall, which translates as 'Case'.) It was clear very early on that Holland and Belgium would be invaded, despite von Leeb's expressing to his fellow generals his belief that Germany would never be forgiven if she violated Belgian neutrality for the second time in twenty-five years.

Scandinavia was of interest to the Germans, the British and the Russians; the Germans because they imported around ten million tons of iron ore from Sweden and Norway, the British because they aimed to cut off that supply, and the Russians because they wished to improve their position on the shores of the Baltic. As a result of the Molotov–Ribbentrop Pact, Lithuania, Latvia and Estonia were now client states of the Soviet Union, which had established naval bases there. Now the USSR wanted bases at the mouth of the Gulf of Finland, on the Karelian Isthmus, which linked Leningrad with Finland proper, and on the Arctic Ocean. This meant obtaining territory, or leases on territory, from Finland, which the Finns were not prepared to give, knowing full well that if they did they too would be little more than Russian puppets. Negotiations in Moscow between Finland and the USSR came to nothing; the best Finland would concede was the lease of a few islands off Karelia, and the only concession from Russia was the offer of part of Eastern Karelia (useless to Finland, or indeed to anyone else). On 26 October 1939 an almost certainly Russian-faked attack on Russian border guards led to a Soviet cancellation of the Finnish–Soviet non-aggression pact of 1932, and demands for the withdrawal of Finnish troops from the border. On 29 October the USSR broke off diplomatic relations and the next day attacked Finland without a declaration of war. Despite overwhelming superiority – thirty Soviet divisions against eight poorly equipped Finnish ones; 2,000 tanks against fifty; 2,000 aircraft against 300 – the Russians found to their dismay that their hopes of a quick and inexpensive victory were swiftly dashed. Terrain and the weather helped the Finns, as did the fighting spirit of their Commander-in-Chief, the 73-year-old Marshal Baron Carl Mannerheim, and in the early stages the Russians got a very bloody nose indeed.

The Finns naturally expected help from Germany, and from the other Scandinavian countries. Germany stuck rigidly to her pact with the USSR, and repeatedly warned Finland that she could expect nothing from her. To do otherwise would have jeopardised the trainloads of grain, oil, cotton, iron and rare metals that were crossing the Russo-German border daily, and this attitude caused great resentment and anti-German feeling in Finland and Scandinavia generally. The next obvious source of assistance to the Finns was her neighbour, Sweden, but she was reluctant to get involved because she would have to obtain weapons and equipment from Britain and France, and that would involve her in the wider war, with Britain unable to offer her protection.

Britain was interested in helping Finland partly because, since the breakdown of the Allied-Soviet talks in August, Russia, having come to an accommodation with Germany, was once more a threat, and also because of her wider concerns about Scandinavia. Before the outbreak of war the British had made secret approaches to Norway and Sweden offering them protection in the event of a German invasion, the quid pro quo being that neither should export iron to Germany. No reply was ever received.

German imports of iron ore and other supplies from Sweden and Norway came via the Swedish port of Lulea, at the top of the Gulf of Bothnia in the Baltic, which the British could not get at, and from the Norwegian port of Narvik, which they could. Moreover, Lulea was iced up for four months of the year, whereas Narvik was ice-free. It would be a relatively simple matter for the Royal Navy to interrupt the shipment of supplies from Narvik, which travelled by merchant vessels down the Norwegian coast and into German ports on the Baltic via the Skagerrak. There was one problem: Norwegian neutrality, which meant that ships carrying iron to Germany could stay in Norwegian territorial waters all the way, and to attack them would be a breach of international law. The British were examining ways around this little difficulty, and as the Germans were well aware that they would, they too were looking at a takeover of Norway and Denmark – Case North – to pre-empt the British doing the same thing.

To begin with the British planners saw the solution to the Scandinavian iron ore problem as being purely a naval matter, either by the laying of mines in Norwegian waters or by the Royal Navy sinking ships bound for Germany, and to hell with Norwegian neutrality. Once the Winter War between Finland and Russia started, there was a risk that Russia might invade northern Norway with a view to establishing bases there.

Such a scenario was completely unacceptable to the British government, which instructed the Chiefs of Staff to consider the pros and cons of declaring war on the USSR. Finland then became the excuse for British intervention on land, and plans included landings of troops to secure the iron ore field themselves, then to provide help to Finland, and then to mount even more land operations to counter the inevitable German reaction. The British, with French agreement, stopped two divisions from moving to the BEF in France and earmarked them for Finland. The only way to get them there, however, was through Norway and Sweden, and as both those countries resolutely refused transit rights, this part of the plan stalled, and was finally overtaken when, eventually, vastly superior numbers told and the Finns were forced to sign a peace treaty on 13 March 1940. The only British participation in the Winter War had been by fifty-three aircraft of the RAF operating from Finnish bases; and these were removed once it was clear that the Finns were going to negotiate a peace settlement with the Russians. That nothing had been done to help the Finns was felt particularly keenly in France, and the government fell (a not unusual occurrence in that country) with Édouard Daladier being replaced as President of the Council of Deputies (Prime Minister) by Paul Reynaud, who was rather more aggressive than his predecessor.

Although the British had in fact abandoned their plans for landings in Norway once they realised the strength of Norwegian and Swedish opposition, they had not withdrawn their threats of such landings from the Norwegian and Swedish governments. They now decided that troops and ships should be kept at readiness for landings at key points in Norway should the Germans make a move to occupy that country or Sweden. The British Chiefs of Staff were of the view that to the Germans Norwegian neutrality was preferable to their having to occupy that country; and in any event, because of the Royal Navy, no German attempt at a seaborne landing on the west coast of Norway could possibly succeed. How wrong could they be?

Information obtained by German intelligence, and the *Altmark* incident of February 1940, when the Royal Navy destroyer HMS *Cossack* had followed a German tanker into Norwegian waters, boarded her and released British merchant seamen held prisoner, convinced the Germans

that the British would, given the opportunity, pay little heed to neutrality.[*]
The German naval staff were convinced that the occupation of Norway
was now a race between Britain and Germany, and German planning for
an occupation of Denmark and Norway began in earnest. On the night of
2–3 April 1940 the heavy equipment (vehicles and artillery) that would
be needed by the troops left German Baltic ports in disguised cargo ships.
Meanwhile, on 5 April, the British war cabinet had decided to mine
Norwegian waters, and on 6 April they told the Swedish and Norwegian
governments of their intention. The Swedish Foreign Minister's reaction
on receiving the British communiqué was to tell the British Ambassador
that 'our two countries are very near to war'. That same night, coinci-
dentally, German forces set sail for Narvik and Trondheim. On 7 April
the British Admiralty received reports that German warships were moving
north from Jutland, and as the day wore on the ships became a fleet. That
evening the British Home Fleet and the Second Cruiser Squadron sailed
from Scapa Flow to intercept.

Between 0430 and 0500 hours on 8 April the British laid their mines
in Norwegian waters off Narvik, while a landing force was ready aboard
ships in British ports ready to sail in case of any German reaction. Quite
independently, and unsuspected by the Allies, Case Weserübung began,
and at 0415 hours on 9 April the German army crossed the German-
Danish frontier, dropped parachutists at key points and sailed into Copenhagen harbour. At 0600 hours the Danish government ordered a ceasefire.
The Danish authorities collaborated until after Stalingrad and Alamein,
when it was realised that Germany might lose the war, at which point a
popular resistance sprang up. Meanwhile the British, who had closed their
minds to any possibility of German landings on the North Sea coast of
Norway, assumed that the reported naval activity was an attempted
breakout by the German navy into the Atlantic, and sailed to meet it. An
increasingly frenzied series of signals, many contradictory and emanating
from the great strategist himself, Winston Churchill, began sending ships
hither and thither. The First Cruiser Squadron, based at Rosyth with
troops embarked in readiness for landings at Bergen and Stavanger in

* The *Altmark* had resupplied the pocket battleship *Admiral Graf Spee*, which was on a commerce raiding
jolly, and had relieved her of the crews of merchant ships she had sunk.

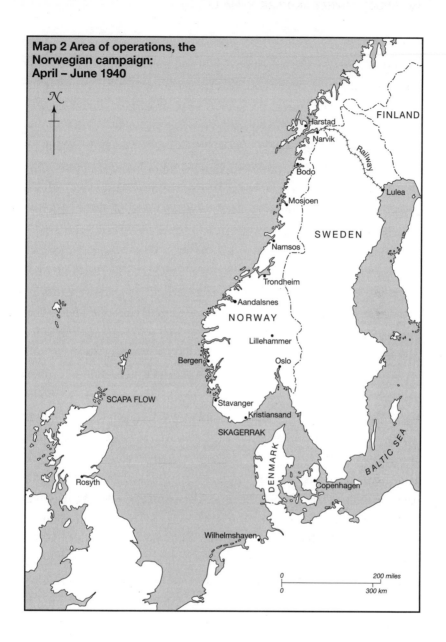

Map 2 Area of operations, the Norwegian campaign: April – June 1940

N

FINLAND

Harstad
Narvik

Railway

Bodo

Lulea

Mosjoen

SWEDEN

Namsos

Trondheim

Aandalsnes

NORWAY

Lillehammer

Bergen

Oslo

SCAPA FLOW

Stavanger

Kristiansand

SKAGERRAK

DENMARK

BALTIC SEA

Rosyth

Copenhagen

Wilhelmshaven

0   200 miles

0   300 km

Norway in case of just this eventuality, was ordered to leave its troops and join the Home Fleet. The men were hurriedly bustled off the ships but there was no time to unload their equipment, so those four battalions were of no use anywhere until the cruisers returned five days later. At the same time the escorts for the troopships earmarked for landings at Narvik and Trondheim were told to head from the Clyde to Scapa Flow, leaving the troopships in harbour behind them. A careful plan, prepared for this very situation, was thus jettisoned just as it might have achieved something, and all at the whim of a First Lord incapable of thinking beyond the immediate wish to do something – anything – as long as it looked busy.

In fact the Home Fleet was chasing a diversion, and on the same day, 9 April, the Germans succeeded in effecting seaborne landings, backed up by airborne attacks, at Narvik, Trondheim, Bergen, Egersund (south of Stavanger, the main airport), Kristiansand and Oslo. By 1900 hours that evening all landings were complete and the landing areas were under German control. Although the eventual occupation army in Norway and Denmark would grow to around 300,000 men, the forces initially deployed were modest. Denmark was taken by two infantry divisions and a motorised rifle brigade, while Norway was the responsibility of a mountain division (3 Mountain Division, Lieutenant General Dietl) and two infantry divisions (69 and 153, Major Generals Engelbrecht and Tittel) in the first wave, two infantry divisions in the second and one in the third waves. They were supported by a reinforced flying corps, eleven warship groups and eight transport squadrons.[3] Submarines provided reconnaissance and long-range security. German shipping losses in the Weserübung landings were extraordinarily light. The heavy cruiser *Blücher* was sunk by shore batteries in the entrance to Oslo fjord, and the heavy cruiser *Hipper*, heading for Trondheim with its escort of four destroyers and carrying 1,700 troops, was rammed by the sinking HMS *Glowworm*[*] and badly damaged. The Royal Navy had failed, while the German navy had tried something that its commander, Admiral Raeder, admitted 'violated all the rules of naval warfare' and had, for the moment at least, succeeded.

---

* The destroyer HMS *Glowworm* was part of the escort to the battlecruiser *Renown*, but had left her station to look for a man lost overboard when she chanced upon the *Hipper* at about 0900 hours on 8 April.

On receipt of a signal from *Glowworm* reporting the position of the *Hipper,* Admiral Sir Charles Forbes, commanding the Home Fleet, ordered the battlecruiser *Renown* (launched 1916), and later in the evening of the same day the battlecruiser *Repulse* (also launched 1916) and four destroyers, to cut off the *Hipper* group. At 0330 hours on 9 April, *Renown* chanced upon the two German battlecruisers *von Scharnhorst* and *von Gneisenau* (both launched 1936), which were supposed to lure the British away from the landing areas. In filthy weather, and despite being slower and outgunned, *Renown* managed at least three hits on the *Gneisenau*, at little damage to herself, before the German ships disappeared into the fog heading north-west. The Admiralty now told Forbes that his priority was to catch the *Scharnhorst* and the *Gneisenau* on their way back to Germany. As the Home Fleet was large enough to take on the whole of the German navy, never mind two, albeit modern, battlecruisers, Forbes ordered four cruisers and seven destroyers to go off and attack Bergen. Perhaps unwisely, Forbes told the Admiralty what he had done. The First Lord ordered him to cancel the plan, and the ships returned to the fleet. This was a pity: had Forbes' ships carried on they would have found an entire German squadron at anchor in Bergen harbour, and would have been able to sink the lot.

The Admiralty now had a sudden change of mind, decided that Bergen was, after all, a suitable target and sent out the aircraft carrier *Furious* (launched in 1917 but reconstructed three times since) from the Clyde with the aim of using her torpedo bombers against the German warships in Bergen. In the rush to obey Churchill's orders to sail, however, *Furious* had not been given time to embark her fighters, which meant that she could protect neither herself nor the fleet. When the Luftwaffe attacked the fleet on 9 April, damaging the battleship HMS *Rodney* and sinking the destroyer HMS *Gurkha*,[*] Admiral Forbes wisely decided that to send *Furious* within range of shore-based aircraft would be to lose her. The Royal Navy had a major success on that day, however, when the submarine HMS *Truant* attacked the German light cruiser *Karlsruhe* in the Kattegat, in the approach to Oslo harbour east of Denmark, and damaged her so

---

[*] In February *Gurkha* had sunk *U 53* in the North Western Approaches.

badly that her own escort had to sink her. The next day the recently restored Fleet Air Arm had an excellent day when fifteen Skua dive bombers from the Orkneys hit the light cruiser *Konigsberg* with three 500lb bombs and sank her.* This was a landmark in naval aviation: it was the first time in war that a major warship had been sunk by air attack. It would not be the last.

Farther north Admiral Forbes, now temporarily freed of his shackles by the First Lord, sent the Second Destroyer Flotilla up Narvik fjord. The flotilla commander, Captain W. A. B. Warburton-Lee, with his five destroyers, arrived at the entrance to the fjord late on 9 April, to discover from the Norwegian lighthouse keeper there that ten rather larger German destroyers had passed up the fjord that morning. Intending to attack at high tide, Warburton-Lee pressed on and arriving off Narvik in the small hours of 10 April in driving snow, found five German destroyers in Narvik harbour, sank two and badly damaged the other three. On their way out of the harbour the tables were turned, for the other five German ships, tucked away in adjacent fjords, sprang into action. One British destroyer was sunk, one driven ashore and one badly damaged. Warburton-Lee was killed but the other three British ships got away, sinking a German ammunition ship as they went. On 13 April, the battleship HMS *Warspite* and nine destroyers returned to finish the job. This time they found eight large destroyers and a submarine, all of which they sank. About sixty German sailors were killed, but the remainder – some two thousand – got ashore and were promptly formed into an ad hoc naval battalion armed, clothed and equipped from a Norwegian depot in Narvik. Despite their unintended augmentation, the members of the German garrison were now rather lonely, short of ammunition and without naval support. If only the British had had a force ready to land immediately, the subsequent history of the Norway campaign might have been different. Unfortunately, because of Churchill's anxiety to play at being an admiral, the landing parties had been forgotten and delayed.

In London the British now began the interminable sequence of meetings and discussions that characterise the waging of war in a

---

* The Skuas belonged to the aircraft carrier *Ark Royal* which had been sent off to the Mediterranean as fleet protection, hence she had a full complement of fighters rather than a mix.

democracy, what the CIGS, Ironside, described as 'committees sitting wobbling and havering'. All were agreed that something must be done, but there were only twelve infantry battalions in the UK capable of being sent anywhere, and four of these were currently unusable because their equipment was at sea with the Second Cruiser Squadron. The original plans for landings in Norway were based on their being unopposed: as the Germans had beaten the British to it, any landings would be opposed, requiring more troops, more fire support and different equipment. A Chiefs of Staff meeting at 0630 hours on the morning of 9 April recommended that as not all of the original landings could now be made, a priority must be decided upon. The chiefs recommended that from the purely military perspective the southerly ports (Bergen and Trondheim) were the most important. To the considerable irritation of the CIGS the war cabinet could not be persuaded to meet before 0830 hours, and they did little except discuss the agenda for a meeting of the Allied Supreme War Council later that day. In the evening the Military Coordination Committee met, and while accepting the chiefs' advice that only one Norwegian port at a time could be captured, decided that it should be neither Bergen nor Trondheim but Narvik, as troops there might still be able to take possession of the Swedish iron ore fields at Gällivare. On 10 April the war cabinet ruled that the objective would indeed be Narvik. Twenty-four hours had been wasted. As Ironside said, 'You cannot make war like this.'[4]

Of the twelve battalions in the UK that could be sent, reduced to eight until the Second Cruiser Squadron returned with the kit of the other four, six were ordered to embark on civilian liners in the Clyde and Scapa Flow, while the other two embarked on the cruiser *Southampton* at Scapa. At this stage they were all destined for Narvik. On 11 and 12 April there were more committees and more delay. Churchill wanted the CIGS to divert part of the Narvik force to Namsos, in order to 'stake a claim to Trondheim', seventy-five miles to the south. Ironside refused: as he put it, 'a convoy packed for one place is not suitable for another', and in any event there were going to be barely enough troops for Narvik, never mind Namsos as well. The suggestion and its countering once more delayed the arrival of the expedition by another twenty-four hours. On 11 April the liners with the main body sailed, heading for a rendezvous with their naval escorts, the cruisers *Manchester* and *Birmingham*, which they reached on 13 April.

The force commander for what was now entitled Operation Rupert was 57-year-old Major General P. J. Mackesy, a Royal Engineer, who had been nominated by the CIGS when the idea of invading Norway and Sweden had first been mooted earlier in the year. Mackesy's normal job was commanding 49 Division, a Territorial Army division still in the UK, and the troops to be used would be two of his brigades, 146 and 148, reinforced by a regular brigade, 24 Brigade, from Aldershot. Mackesy sailed from Scapa Flow in the cruiser *Southampton* on 12 April, with an advance party of two battalions and the commanders of the three brigades that made up the force. The intention was to land not at Narvik itself, but at Harstad, a small harbour on an island about sixty miles away, and there to sort the force out before mounting an attack on Narvik itself. The French had agreed to provide two demi-brigades (each of three battalions) of Chasseurs Alpins (mountain infantry), and two battalions of the Foreign Legion, but none of these could arrive before 23 April at the earliest.

As this was to be a combined operation one might suppose that there had been close cooperation and joint planning between the army and the navy beforehand, but this was not the case. Vice Admiral Sir Edward Evans had been nominated to command the ships involved, but, on 11 April, when Mackesy was on his way to Scapa Flow, Evans was abruptly replaced by the 67-year-old Admiral of the Fleet Sir William Boyle, 12th Earl of Cork and Orrery. It was most unusual for an officer of his rank (equivalent to field marshal in the army) to be nominated for an operation of this relatively small scale, particularly when he was senior to the Commander Home Fleet, on whom he relied for the provision of ships. Cork was instructed to report directly to the Admiralty, rather than to Commander Home Fleet; he had never met General Mackesy and the instructions he had been given from the Admiralty (act boldly) were quite different from those Mackesy had been given by the War Office (do not attempt an opposed landing). The reason for this extraordinary state of affairs, running contrary to all good sense, was yet again the First Lord, Churchill, who was a great personal friend of Admiral Cork's, admired Cork's aggressive nature and insisted on his appointment.

It got worse. At 0200 hours on 14 April, when the Narvik force was still at sea, General Ironside, the CIGS, was asleep on a camp-bed in his room at the War Office in London, when he was woken up by Churchill, accompanied by the Deputy Chief of Naval Staff, Rear Admiral Phillips.* Churchill announced that the navy was going to attack Trondheim (a plan that had been turned down on 11 April) and that he wanted a force of troops to follow up by making a pincer attack from Namsos and Åndalsnes (one hundred miles south-west of Trondhcim). Ironside explained (one wonders how on earth he kept his temper) that there were no troops available for such operations until Narvik had been taken, whereupon Churchill demanded that 146 Brigade, in the rear of the convoy, be diverted to Namsos and Åndalsnes. In vain Ironside explained that the loading of the ships had been for a single operation; to divide it now would mean that 146 Brigade, of Territorials, would land without much of its heavy equipment, with no anti-aircraft artillery and without its commander, Brigadier C. G. Philips, who was, quite correctly, with General Mackesy in the leading ship. Churchill would brook no discussion, and emphasised that he spoke with the authority of the cabinet's Military Co-ordination Committee. That statement was a lie. Churchill was chairman of the committee but it had authorised a diversion only if it was plain that Narvik could be captured without serious opposition – which was far from the case – and he obtained its agreement to his change of the plan retrospectively, and then only by browbeating the other civilian members who realised that it was too late to revert to the *status quo ante*.

Ironside tried without success to get the First Lord's orders rescinded, and 146 Brigade was duly informed of the change of plan, regardless of their not having any maps of the new location. Ironside did at least manage to have it agreed that the brigade would land at Namsos, rather than splitting itself between Namsos and Åndalsnes: the latter could wait. Farther north Admiral Cork learned of the success of the *Warspite* group in eliminating the German naval forces at Narvik on 13 April. Cork, who had originally arranged to meet General Mackesy at Harstad, now tried

---

* Phillips went down with the *Prince of Wales* off the coast of Malaya in December 1941.

to signal the troop convoy to urge a direct attack on Narvik. Communications failed and he could not contact Mackesy on *Southampton*. On the morning of 14 April Mackesy and Cork both arrived at Harstad. The two were of diametrically opposite temperaments: Mackesy a cool, quiet, thinking planner, already doubtful as to the wisdom of the operation due to the lack of air support and shortage of artillery; Cork red-headed, flamboyant, autocratic, aggressive and with a quick temper. The two discovered that they were operating under quite different orders and a shouting match began, made worse when the rather short Cork stumped off to carry out a personal reconnaissance of the ground, disappeared into a snowdrift and lost his monocle. Cork wanted an immediate attack direct on Narvik, and could not understand the soldiers' reluctance to attempt it. The soldiers, mindful of their orders not to attempt an opposed landing, for which the troops were neither equipped nor trained, found it impossible to get through to Cork that the terrain, the deep snow, and the lack of landing craft ruled out an attack from the sea. Next day what was left of the Narvik expedition began to arrive.

Muddle and confusion continued. The landing at Namsos was now to be called Operation Maurice and was to be commanded by Major General Sir Adrian Carton de Wiart VC DSO, an almost legendary officer seven times wounded and deficient of an eye and a hand as a result.[*] Warned on 12 April and briefed on the 14th he was flown out to Namsos on 15 April and discovered that facilities were totally insufficient to properly support a brigade, not least because everything was covered in four feet of snow. Nevertheless, the battalions of 146 Brigade landed at Namsos on 16 and 17 April. Mackesy lost another of his brigades on 18 April when 148 Brigade, another Territorial Army formation, was sent to land at Åndalsnes as a result of Norwegian pleas that they could not hold the Germans advancing from Oslo towards Trondheim. The Åndalsnes landings were now named Operation Sickle and for the time being would be commanded by Commander 148 Brigade, Brigadier H. de R. Morgan, who initially could only get two of his battalions on shore,

---

[*]Born in 1880, he had actually retired from the army in 1924 and settled in Poland. His military career was reactivated in July 1939 when he was appointed to the British military mission to Poland. He got back to England via Romania when Poland collapsed.

with the third still at sea and due to arrive two days later. He had no transport and only one battery of light anti-aircraft artillery. At this stage the plan was for a direct attack upon Trondheim, in which the navy would sail straight up Trondheim fjord and land two brigades, the as yet uncommitted 147 Brigade of Macksey's 49 Division and 15 Brigade, a regular formation in 5 Division that had been removed from France at short notice for this operation. The landing would be supported by the pincer attack from Namsos and Åndalsnes. This plan, Operation Hammer, was cancelled on 19 April by the Chiefs of Staff, to the great irritation of Churchill, whose wheeze it was, due to the threat from air attack, but not before yet another general had been appointed to command it, and an offer from Admiral of the Fleet Sir Roger Keyes, off the active list since 1931, to lead it in person had been turned down.[*] As the Luftwaffe had unchallenged mastery of the skies, cancellation was a sound decision. On 19 April the first demi-brigade of Chasseurs Alpins, three battalions of French mountain troops, landed at Namsos, and on 23 April 15 Brigade was sent there as well. Swift action by the Luftwaffe not only caused considerable damage to the port facilities at both Namsos and Åndalsnes, but also induced the French admiral who had landed the French troops to withdraw, taking his empty troopships with him. That in itself might not have mattered very much, but he also took his (British) anti-aircraft cruiser, leaving the troops ashore without any means of hitting back at the Luftwaffe. Both Carton de Wiart and Morgan had to signal that no more troops could be accepted at either location for the present.

Mackesy at Harstad was now reduced to just one brigade, 24 Brigade, a regular formation with two Guards and a line infantry battalion. He could make little progress against a determined German defence under Lieutenant General Deitl, commanding 3 Mountain Division, and when he signalled the War Office to say that he would not attack until the promised reinforcements arrived he got a rocket – rather unfairly as all his reinforcements had been diverted to Namsos or Åndalsnes.

---

[*] Major General Hotblack should have set out for Norway on 18 April, but was found unconscious at the bottom of the Duke of York's Steps that morning, without a mark on him. It transpired that he had had a stroke, and so Brigadier Berney-Ficklin was appointed in his stead. Berney-Ficklin and his staff took off for Norway by air and the aircraft crashed. No one was killed but all were rendered *hors de combat*.

The first clash of the Second World War between British and German soldiers took place on 21 April. Carton de Wiart's Mauriceforce had no transport and one of his battalions had been separated from its mortars, which were on a ship, somewhere. He sent two battalions forward to cover the road from Namsos to Trondheim, when the Germans began to probe up the road from Trondheim. The Germans were fully equipped for the country, they were prepared to fight and they were well trained. The British were none of these. When Germans came up against the positions of 146 Brigade they simply climbed up the sides of the valley and outflanked them. By the morning of 22 April it was apparent that the British could not hold, and that German infantry was infiltrating behind them. A withdrawal began, which without transport and in snow was not easy to coordinate. One battalion, in the words of General Sir David Fraser, withdrew 'in a way which their Commanding Officer found impossible to check'.[5] The brigade now took up defensive positions along the road running south from Namsos, incapable of any offensive action and only barely able to defend themselves. Fortunately the Germans were quite happy to leave them there.

The southern arm of the pincer had an even worse experience. Brigadier Morgan's instructions were contradictory and he was unsure whether he should obey the British military attaché to Norway, who turned up having got out of Oslo just ahead of the German arrival, or the signals coming from London, or his original instructions, such as they were. At one time or another, depending upon whom he listened to, he was to eject the Germans from Trondheim; prevent the Germans from reinforcing Trondheim; support the Norwegians trying to stop the Germans from advancing from Oslo, or all three. The attaché told him he was under command of the Norwegians, whereas London told him he was not but should do his best to help them. Morgan now yielded to Norwegian pressure and did just what he emphatically should not have done: he allowed his two battalions to be split up under Norwegian command and placed strung out in support of Norwegian units. Very shortly afterwards, on 21 April, they replaced Norwegian units south of Lillehammer, facing a German advance from Oslo. They had no chance, and when the Germans attacked under cover of heavy mortars the Norwegian general in command of the sector ordered a withdrawal. There was no transport and the men of the two exhausted battalions staggered off through snow, many being cut off and captured. Eventually, having thrown away much of their kit that they could not carry, the survivors regrouped at Faaberg, north of Lillehammer, in the small hours of 22 April.

That afternoon the Germans attacked again, using light artillery and mortars to support outflanking movements. Again 148 Brigade were forced to withdraw to Tretten, another ten miles to the north, being attacked by German aircraft on the way. The following day, 23 April, the Germans resumed the attack, this time supported by tanks (three Mk Is or IIs and a Mk IV) against which the British had no defence. What was left of the brigade withdrew in Norwegian buses another forty-five miles north, to Heidal. By now there were only nine officers and three hundred other ranks capable of doing their duty, the brigade commander and his headquarters had been captured, and the brigade was finished as a fighting force. German reports spoke of the British as 'retreating in complete dissolution'.[6]

While the German soldiers on the ground thought that they were doing pretty well, from Berlin the picture looked much bleaker. Colonel General Keitel, Chief of Staff of the Armed Forces high command (OKW) wrote to General of Infantry Nikolaus von Falkenhorst, Commander-in-Chief Norway on 23 April:

> The Führer's one great pressing anxiety is the situation at Trondheim… if now, after the appearance of the English, the resistance is stiffening the early reinforcement of Trondheim and the establishing of communications by this channel [by sea] will be impossible. Apart from U-boat supply the Trondheim group itself can only be reinforced and increased by air at present. The six field guns despatched in fishing boats constitute the only probable exception. Reinforcement via Sweden is unfortunately out of the question… I am informing you of our views and of the Führer's anxiety.

In Narvik, too, the Germans did not have it all their own way. There resupply was mainly by air, and with the typical German ability for military improvisation, the Luftwaffe managed to get two Norwegian anti-tank guns and fifteen Polish anti-tank rifles to Dietl's force, although some were so damaged as to be unusable. They also parachuted in ammunition, but the Germans reported that about 25 per cent was unserviceable.

They need not have worried. With three detachments in Norway, unable to talk to one another but all answering directly to London, the British decided to appoint a Commander-in-Chief of all land forces, except Narvik. Lieutenant General H. R. S. Massy was given the post, but neither he nor his staff ever left London – and it is difficult to see what good they could have done even if they had. Shortly afterwards, as if there were not enough generals in Scandinavia, London appointed yet another – Major General B. C. T. Paget – to command the remnants of Operation Sickle. Paget, having tried in vain to get some air cover for his force, sailed for Norway and arrived during the night of 25–26 April. One lieutenant general and three major generals were commanding what would normally be the responsibility of one major general at most. Paget's request for air cover might have received a more sympathetic hearing had it not been for the fate of the air assets that had already just been sent. On 24 April a squadron of Fleet Air Arm Gladiators had flown off the carrier HMS *Glorious* and had landed on a frozen lake forty miles from Åndalsnes. They might have done some good had their exploit not been trumpeted in the British press. The publicity inevitably came to the attention of the Germans, who promptly bombed the lake rendering the squadron incapable of doing anything.

Up north in the Narvik area, more and more stores began to arrive at Harstad, many of them intended for the brigades that had been diverted to Namsos and Aandalsnes, some even from the cancelled expedition to Finland. The limited port facilities became choked, while stores that were not wanted arrived and those that were did not. Admiral Cork was being bombarded by signals from Churchill in London demanding an immediate assault on Narvik, while Mackesy patiently explained yet again that deep snow to the waterline, blizzards, limited beaches covered by the Germans, no artillery and nothing more than open boats made an assault from the sea out of the question. Churchill, as First Lord of the Admiralty, could give orders to the navy, but not to the army. As chairman of the Committee for the Coordination of Defence, he could, however, and did, have a Commander-in-Chief for Narvik appointed, and nominated Cork for that post, which put Cork in charge of Mackesy. Cork announced that he was going to use the heavy guns of the fleet to bombard Narvik, after which the army could have no excuse for not landing. Mackesy demurred on the grounds that a bombardment would cause heavy civilian casualties, something that, at this stage of the war, the army was not prepared to permit. Cork then said that he would bombard only military targets. Mackesy was still unhappy because he did not believe that naval gunfire was sufficiently accurate, nor that British knowledge of the layout within Narvik was detailed enough to ensure that a house containing Germans was hit while one containing Norwegians was not; but he did agree that the bombardment could go ahead, at military targets only, and that if reconnaissance showed that it had been successful, and that the German ability to resist a landing had been seriously impaired, then the troops would attempt a landing. The affair was to happen on 24 April. The bombardment duly took place. It damaged little besides Norwegian goodwill, and the troops did not assault. An attempt to take Narvik from the west also failed when a battalion of 24 Brigade occupied the village of Ankenes, a few miles from Narvik, only to be driven out again by a German counter-attack.

The British now decided to evacuate central Norway: Mauriceforce and Sickleforce had achieved nothing and were unlikely to be able to do anything in the immediate future. Even if an up-gunned Operation Hammer were to be successful, there was insufficient anti-aircraft artillery to protect Trondheim against the inevitable German onslaught from the air. All this was a severe blow to British pride, and to Britain's standing with the Norwegians. London hoped, therefore, to hang on to the northern foothold, and take and keep Narvik. To this end another French demi-brigade of Chasseurs Alpins arrived at Harstad on 27 April, and three battalions of the French Foreign Legion and a Polish brigade in the French service three days later.[*] From British sources came a battery of field artillery and a troop of infantry tanks. It was also decided to withdraw

---

[*] After the fall of Poland a large number of Polish soldiers, sailors and airmen fled Poland. The French incorporated Polish units in their army and eventually (but not yet) the British would field one Polish armoured division, one Polish tank brigade and two Polish infantry divisions. The Russians would field five tank brigades and twelve infantry divisions, while the Germans too would enlist Poles whose hatred of the Russians was stronger than their dislike of the Germans (or to whom a uniform, pay and three meals a day seemed a better bet than life in a prisoner-of-war camp).

5 Division complete from the BEF in France and send it to Norway, although this never actually happened. If Narvik could be captured and held, then perhaps some British pride could be salvaged, and at least some part of Norway could remain Norwegian. The King of Norway and the national gold reserves were already on board a ship of the Royal Navy and making for Tromso, in the far north.

On 26 April the first British prisoners of war captured in Norway arrived in Germany. Hitler expressed a wish to see them personally, and it was evident that some sort of propaganda exercise was intended, probably interrogation in front of journalists. General Keitel, Chief of Staff of OKW, pointed out to Hitler that anything done in breach of the internationally accepted rules regarding the treatment of prisoners of war (and parading them in front of the press was illegal) would only rebound on German prisoners. Hitler backed off.[7]

On 3 May Admiral Cork once more demanded a seaborne attack on Narvik, and once more General Mackesy refused, despite the fact that Cork was technically his Commander-in-Chief. Mackesy pointed out that although the snow was melting the beaches were still covered by the fire of the German defenders, and he had no faith in a naval bombardment to keep their heads down while his men assaulted. It has to be said that Mackesy was now being dilatory. He was quite right that a seaborne landing was a very dubious endeavour, but as he seemed incapable of taking Narvik by manoeuvres on land, he might well have been better to risk it. The matter was now referred to London with a request for a decision, as if those far from the scene could possibly assess the factors for and against an attack better than those on the ground. London had already decided that an officer with some experience of mountain warfare should be sent out, with a staff, to assess the situation, and to take over the chief command from Cork and command of the troops from Mackesy. The officer selected was Lieutenant General Sir Claude Auchinleck, an officer of the Indian Army but currently commanding IV Corps in the UK, and the decision whether or not to launch a seaborne attack on Narvik was to await his assessment of the situation on his arrival, which was hoped to be by 12 May.

The remnants of Mauriceforce and Sickleforce were evacuated between 30 April and 3 May. At least the Royal Navy came out of the operation with credit, for they managed to get most of the troops – around six thousand altogether – on board and away by night, virtually unmolested. Churchill, not surprisingly, felt that the troops should stay, disperse into the mountains and carry on a guerrilla war. He did not explain how resupply, movement and casualty evacuation would be provided for these Territorial soldiers unversed in the skill of skiing, unfamiliar with the local language and untrained and unequipped for this inhospitable terrain where winter temperatures of over forty degrees below are common. While scuttle from central Norway was in full swing, the build-up of the Narvik force continued, to enable them to take and hold the town. This would include blocking the advance of the Germans from their strongholds in the south, partly to be carried out by five independent companies, Territorial Army units composed of volunteers from battalions based in the UK. They were as militarily ineffective as the idea was ludicrous.

While all this was going on, committees of various sorts came and went, British generals flew to France and French generals to England. Churchill demanded that he be made chairman of the Chiefs of Staff Committee, and on 1 May he got his way. Politicians were well aware that the Norwegian campaign had not gone well and, as Ironside wryly noted, were all busily composing speeches to explain why they were not to blame.

On 7 and 8 May the House of Commons debated the Norwegian campaign, including a passionate speech by Admiral Sir Roger Keyes in full uniform, who castigated the government and the naval planners, taking care to exclude his great friend Churchill. Such was the anger over the debacle that Scandinavia had become, and such was the fear of politicians anxious to save their skins, that on 10 May Neville Chamberlain was forced to resign as Prime Minister, replaced by Winston Churchill. So a debate on the mismanagement of the Norwegian campaign brought to power the very man who had been largely responsible for that mismanagement. But that was not all that happened on 10 May 1940: on that same day Case Yellow began, and the Germans invaded Holland, Belgium and Luxembourg.

The Norwegian campaign now became an unimportant sideshow. General Auchinleck took one look and recommended evacuation from

Narvik as well. On 22 May the war cabinet agreed, but not before Narvik had been captured first. On 28 May it was duly captured, by the French, the Norwegians and the Poles. The Royal Navy supported the attack, as did the Royal Air Force with land-based fighters delivered by the navy. Apart from anti-aircraft artillery British troops took no part: they were all deployed to cover the approaches from the south against any German thrusts to relieve the siege. Between 4 and 8 June the Royal Navy got 29,000 Allied troops away from Harstad and Narvik, leaving much of their equipment, such as it was, behind.

German manpower losses in the campaign were modest; at Narvik, between 9 April, when they arrived, and 10 June when the last British soldier was at sea, 3 Mountain Division had only ten officers and 120 men killed. In the entire campaign 1,317 Germans of all three services were killed, 1,604 wounded and 2,375 missing (mainly at sea and mostly in fact drowned). The Luftwaffe lost 242 aircraft, considered by them as a reasonable price to pay, but for the German navy the loss of one heavy and two light cruisers, ten destroyers, a torpedo boat, four U-boats and a number of auxiliary vessels was serious, and reduced even further the Kriegsmarine's options in any future plans for an invasion of England. The butcher's bill for the Royal Navy was about 2,500 men, the largest single loss being when the aircraft carrier HMS *Glorious* was sunk by the *Scharnhorst* on 8 June. *Glorious* and *Ark Royal* had delivered the RAF's fighters to Norway to support the attack on Narvik, and when that attack succeeded and the order to withdraw was given, the RAF were told to destroy their aircraft, Hurricanes and Gladiators. With considerable courage the air commander decided that rather than destroy these valuable machines, which might be sorely needed elsewhere, his pilots would fly them to the carriers, and this they did, despite hardly any of the pilots ever having made a deck landing before. *Glorious* was then permitted to proceed home independently by the fastest route in order to expedite a court martial, and was heading for England when she was caught by the *Scharnhorst*.[*] It will probably never be known why *Glorious*

---

[*]The official story was that she was sent home to refuel, but see Capt S. W. Roskill RN, *Churchill and the Admirals*, who says that a dispute between the Captain and his Commander (Flying) led to the latter being warned for court martial.

had no air patrols up nor torpedo bombers on standby (she had both Fleet Air Arm and RAF aircraft on board), for she and her two destroyer escorts were sunk, albeit not before inflicting serious damage on the *Scharnhorst*. Fifteen hundred men went down, and only forty-six sailors were saved, thirty-nine by a Norwegian fishing boat which landed them in the Faroe Islands, and seven by the Germans who made them prisoners of war. The Royal Navy's losses of warships, besides the *Glorious*, were two light cruisers, nine destroyers, six submarines and a number of auxiliary vessels. Between them the Royal Navy and the RAF lost 112 aircraft. The army had twenty-two officers and 191 other ranks killed, and a great many more were captured. But by this time a far more serious disaster had unfolded nearer home.

What had begun as a perfectly reasonable wish to deny Germany stocks of iron ore and other vital imports, which would have made a real impact on that country's ability to wage war, had become blurred by a wish to help gallant little Finland against the big red Russian bully. It is a very good thing that British troops were not deployed in Finland against the Russians, for apart from there being very few ski troops or troops trained in any form of winter warfare available to the British, thus running a real risk of ignominious defeat, subsequent Anglo-Russian cooperation against Germany, difficult as it was to be anyway, would have been even more tricky had we been at war with the USSR over Finland. There was no British interest whatsoever in Finland, and the government should never have allowed itself to be diverted into thinking that there was. Had the British acted against Norway and Sweden early enough it is quite possible that the Germans might have been forestalled, and that the Royal Navy could have prevented a German attack after the arrival of British forces. In that event the British might have been able to prevent Swedish and Norwegian exports reaching Germany, which would definitely have been in the British interest. Violations of Scandinavian neutrality would of course have attracted international criticism, which need not have concerned the British overmuch: after all, in the event, the Germans got away with it.

Having missed the bus in getting into Norway, the British might still have been able to spoil the German plan had the Royal Navy been less convinced that the Germans would not even try to land on the west coast by sea. The German convoys, had they been intercepted, would have been sitting ducks and much damage might have been caused. Unfortunately, the navy was deluded into thinking that the movement of ships was a breakout into the north Atlantic, and reacted accordingly. Even then something might have been achieved, particularly on 13 or even 14 April, after the Royal Navy had destroyed the German navy's ships in Narvik fjord. As it was, Churchill's impatience and short-termism had ensured that the troops were either not embarked or not escorted and not able to land that day. Even when the two battalions on the *Southampton* were in the area communications broke down and the troops could not be diverted from Harstad, even if General Mackesy had agreed.

To divert 146 and then 148 Brigade from the force sailing to Narvik was folly of the highest degree. The convoy had been briefed, loaded and equipped for one joint operation; to break it up and divert two-thirds of it while at sea was nonsense. Churchill was no strategist, whatever he claimed and may have thought, and the generals and the admirals should have been stronger in their objections. To allow the political head of the navy to sit in the naval operations centre in Whitehall and personally direct the movement and actions of warships should never have been permitted, and the admirals should have resigned rather than let this dilettante, no doubt after a good and well-lubricated dinner, meddle in matters that he did not understand, while contributing to the destruction of the King's ships and soldiers. Operations carried out by two or more services can often be difficult, even today when we have much more experience of joint warfare and are far more conversant with one another's problems than was the case in 1940. That briefings and instructions were carried out and disseminated by the army and the navy without reference to each other was a recipe for disaster from the start. There were far too many commanders all with their own channels to the War Office or to the Admiralty, whereas there should have been one overall commander from the outset, with the communications to control his forces and to be able to take decisions in real time based on up-to-date information. For Churchill to get away with replacing the naval commander by a chum on the day the operation started was nothing short of disgraceful, and did much to ensure the failure of the whole affair.

The troops were not up to the job. Territorials with only very limited training should not have been embarked on operations for which they had no training and no experience. It may be argued that there was no one else to send, and that is partly true, and even more reason for not splitting the force once it had sailed. Auchinleck said that the British troops were 'soft and callow', which infuriated the War Office who said that Auchinleck had been in Norway far too short a time to be able to come to any worthwhile conclusion. His critics had not been in Norway at all.[*]

Probably the worst aspect of this whole sorry story was the insistence of politicians on holding endless committee meetings and in demanding to know all the minute details of every operation, details that they could not understand and had no training to assess. Churchill was particularly bad here, behaving, in the CIGS's words, like a child who plays with something until he has had enough and then loses interest and turns to another toy:

> Too many damned strategists who all have a finger in the pie, all amateurs who change from minute to minute and are either very optimistic or very pessimistic. Very difficult to make war under such circumstances. We must get back to allowing the soldiers to make decisions... a real stupid wrangle about stupid little tactics. Every plan is taken and torn to pieces by a lot of civilian amateurs. We simply cannot get on with the work at all.'[8]

Every disaster has some positive aspects to it, provided one looks hard enough, and there were some advantages accruing to the British from the Norwegian affair. Although the German naval losses were roughly equal to those of the British, the Royal Navy could (just) afford them, whereas the Germans could not. A belief in Germany that the British regarded Norway as being much more important than they actually did, and a conviction that Britain would at some point invade Norway again,

---

[*] The real problem was that Auchinleck was an Indian army officer brought over to command a UK corps on the advice of Admiral Lord Chatfield when the CIGS had been complaining about a shortage of competent senior officers. British officers, many of whom were jealous of the Indian army with their long-service highly motivated soldiers, resented the fact that a British officer had not got the promotion and the job.

did keep a 300,000 strong German occupation force tied up for the whole of the war – far more than were needed to keep order, and who might much more profitably have been employed elsewhere.

From the German point of view the lessons of this first ever combined campaign by all three services of the Wehrmacht were the absolute importance of air cover for naval forces, and the fact that even a superior naval force could be denied freedom of movement in narrow waters (like those around Denmark) by the threat of air attack. This was the first time when significant use had been made of transport aircraft to support the army, by delivering supplies and reinforcements and by dropping parachute troops and free-dropping ammunition. The importance of joint planning was demonstrated, as much by how the Allies did not do it as by the way that the Germans did, but the Germans too had their complaints about interference by Hitler in operational detail. The Commander-in-Chief of the army, von Brauchitsch, is quoted by his Chief of the General Staff as returning from a Führer conference and saying 'one could cry if it were not such a farce',[9] and the German historian of Case Weserübung considered that:

> 'His [Hitler's] inclination to meddle and give orders regarding the details of military operations became evident for the first time. The success of the operation strengthened his tendency to place too much faith in surprise and readiness to take high risks as a prescription for victory. With this faith he could win individual campaigns but not the war.'[10]

The difference, of course, was that the German generals and admirals only had to convince one politician – Hitler – and not the plethora of committees of little men that the British had to put up with.

For the British there were lessons too, albeit that they were not necessarily heeded. The advocates of air power over the all-big-gun battleship thought their case proven, but the argument was by no means over, and the need for unity of command ought to have been demonstrated but was not yet accepted. There are many examples in Britain's long military history where muddle, indecision and mismanagement have led to defeat and disaster, but for a campaign that demonstrates gross incompetence at the very top of government, and spinelessness by the

War Office and the Admiralty for putting up with it, it is difficult to find a better example than Norway 1940.

It was certainly no way to run a war, and it would get much, much worse.

NOTES

1. Research Institute for Military History, Germany, (tr McMurry & Osers), *Germany and the Second World War, Vol. II*, Clarendon Press, 1991.

2. Charles Burdick & Hans-Adolf Jacobsen (eds), *The Halder War Diary 1939–1942*, Greenhill, London, 1988.

3. Research Institute for Military History, Germany, op. cit.

4. Roderick McLeod & Denis Kelly (eds), *Time Unguarded: The Ironside Diaries 1937–1940*, David McKay, New York, 1962.

5. David Fraser, *And We Shall Shock Them*, Hodder & Stoughton, London, 1983.

6. TNA Kew, CAB 146/3, Captured Enemy Documents.

7. Charles Burdick & Hans-Adolf Jacobsen (eds), op. cit.

8. McLeod & Kelly, op. cit.

9. Burdick & Jacobsen, op. cit.

10. Research Institute for Military History, Germany, op. cit.

7

Collapse in the West

AS THE DEBACLE OF the Norwegian campaign unfolded, the BEF in France was building up. There were virtually no attempts to interfere with the move of British men, vehicles and stores to the Continent, partly because at this stage the Germans had no wish to provoke major action in the west, and partly because the German navy was fully occupied with Scandinavia, where, despite their remarkable success in putting troops ashore, they had taken considerable losses. At the outbreak of war Germany had only thirty-two divisions in the west, and not all of these were combat ready. Hitler had thought that the western allies would do nothing if he moved against Poland. In this he miscalculated: Britain and France did declare war, but he was right in his assessment that militarily they would do little or nothing. In truth there was little or nothing that they could do, and the British had accepted that the fate of Poland lay in the eventual winning of the war against Germany, and not in anything that might be done in the immediate future.

Once the Polish situation was resolved, the German army and air force could regroup to deal with the west. By October 1939 the thirty-two divisions in Colonel General Ritter von Leeb's Army Group C had grown to two army groups and by May 1940 there were three: B in the north, stretching from the Dutch border down to the Belgian border east of Mons; A in the centre covering southern Belgium and Luxembourg; and C responsible for the zone running from southern Luxemburg to the Swiss border. Army Group B, commanded by Colonel General von Bock had twenty-five infantry and three armoured divisions; Army Group A, Colonel General von Rundstedt, had forty-four infantry and seven armoured divisions and von Leeb's Army Group C had seven infantry divisions. The huge discrepancy in the forces available to each of the three army groups reflected their roles in the forthcoming campaign.

Both the British and the French had to accept that it might be as late as 1941 or '42 before they could gather enough strength to take the offensive against Germany, and until then they would have no choice but to remain on the defensive. While Allied strength on land was building up, the Royal Navy would impose its traditional weapon, the blockade. Allied planners considered that the Germans, with their liking for short sharp wars (despite the German generals' reservations on this occasion) would probably attack first. When they did, thought the British and the French, they would try a rerun of the 1914 Schlieffen Plan. That plan had attempted to solve the two seemingly immutable German difficulties when making war: the risk of having to fight on two fronts, and the economic need for a quick victory. The plan had originally been drawn up by that archetypal staff officer Alfred Graf von Schlieffen, who died in 1913, and was revised several times. It held that if Germany went to war against France and Russia, France would mobilise much faster than could Russia. That being so, France should be dealt with first, after which the few German troops in the east could be reinforced by moving forces from the west, using the extensive German railway network. To defeat France rapidly, the Germans would merely hold along the Franco-German border, and put their maximum strength into a wheeling movement through Holland and Belgium, sweeping down the Channel coast, circling round to the west of Paris and then pinning the French armies against their own frontier defences.

When war was launched in 1914 the plan failed – albeit only just. The main reasons for failure were three: Schlieffen's successors held that violating Dutch as well as Belgian neutrality was a bit much (and anyway Holland could be a useful lung for Germany if the war did go on for longer than was expected); the German army could not march fast enough nor could its logistic tail keep up; and the plan had never worked out what to do with the garrison of Paris. This time the Allies counted on the Germans coming through Holland as well as Belgium; mechanisation would give them the speed they needed and they could bomb Paris. The German right wing would therefore be strong, and in any event the Maginot Line made it very difficult to attack other than in the north. There was, of course, a risk that the Germans might instead opt to make their main thrust through southern Belgium, through the Ardennes, a region of hills rather than mountains, between Liège and Luxembourg. Despite the subsequent claims in many accounts of the Battle of France, nobody ever said that the Ardennes were 'impassable' to tanks. Certainly the area was heavily wooded, there were few major roads, and there were many defiles and potential choke-points, but a cursory drive through the region shows that it was not and is not impassable to tanks nor to any other vehicles. What French, British and, initially, some German strategists did believe was that offensive operations could only begin once forces were balanced, that is, by formations where all the mutually supporting elements – field and anti-aircraft artillery, engineers, armour, infantry, forward air-control teams and communications units – were actually present. That being so, it would take much too long to pass any appreciable armoured, mechanised or motorised force through the Ardennes, and have it complete at the far side. As the Germans would be going all out for a swift decision, the Ardennes approach could be discounted.

On the assumption that the Germans would attempt an updated Schlieffen Plan, the French had, until 1936, agreed with the Belgians that once war was declared or even threatened, French troops would advance into Belgium and fight the Germans there. This had the advantage for France of keeping the fighting away from French territory and industrial centres, and for Belgium of giving her a powerful ally. Planners intended to base the defence of Belgium on the Albert Canal, which ran from Antwerp south-east to Maastricht and then along the River Meuse, southwest to Namur and then south to the French border at Givet. But when Belgium renounced her treaty with France in 1936 and decided to rely on the dubious protection of neutrality alone, the French and Belgian general staffs could no longer plan jointly, although some highly unofficial contacts were still maintained between individual officers.

Unable henceforth to pre-empt German aggression against Belgium, the French now intended to move into Belgium only once the Germans did. They abandoned any idea of defending along the Albert Line, and now resorted to two defensive Plans, E and D. Plan E involved defending from Mézières, west of Sedan, along the Franco-Belgian frontier as far as Lille and then turning into Belgium, going north and north-east along the River Scheldt (the River Escaut in French) to Ghent and then Antwerp. This was relatively safe for the French, as they would not need to advance very far from their own frontier, but it only preserved a small sliver of northern Belgium. Plan D envisaged a defence from Mézières north through Wavre and then along the River Dyle to Antwerp. This was riskier than Plan E, as it meant much greater inroads into Belgium, but it did leave about half of Belgian territory in the hands of its rightful owners and was about fifty miles shorter than the Plan E line. The only worry about Plan D was the so-called Gembloux Gap, twenty-five miles of open, rolling plain between Wavre and Namur with no rivers or canals and no natural obstacles. This would be difficult to defend against determined attackers with armour, and for that reason Gamelin, the French Commander-in-Chief, had favoured Plan E. Now, however, it was whispered that the Belgians were fortifying the gap, and that supposition, and pressure from the British, mindful of their historic obligations to Belgium as a creature of their making, persuaded the French to opt for Plan D.

As soon as Belgian and or Dutch neutrality was breached, Plan D, the Dyle Plan, with Gamelin's 'Breda Variant', would be implemented. The plan required the French Seventh Army on the extreme left (north) of the Allied line to advance along the Channel coast as far as Breda in Holland, there to link up with the Dutch army and secure the Scheldt estuary. At the same time twenty-two Belgian divisions would hold the Germans off as long as they could along the Albert Canal and then withdraw to the Dyle between Antwerp and Louvain. The BEF would hold the Dyle from Louvain down to Wavre, not far from its immortal victory at Waterloo in 1815; the French First Army would cover the

Gembloux Gap; the French Ninth Army would take up position in the Belgian Ardennes along the River Meuse from Namur to Sedan, while the French Second Army would defend from Sedan to Longuyon, the northernmost end of the Maginot Line.

Contrary to what the Allies believed, in September 1939 the German army had no plan for action in the west; the generals thought the army was unready for war against a major adversary, and were unhappy about being once more branded as aggressors. Rules of engagement were strict, aerial reconnaissance across the borders was limited and even the navy were only to conduct limited operations against British merchant shipping. An air-defence zone was established up to fifty miles deep all along the German frontier and work on the West Wall was accelerated. This system of defensive fortifications, although sometimes described as the German Maginot Line, was very far from being so. Started in 1938, it ran for nearly four hundred miles from Basle to Geilenkirchen, along the border but not slavishly following it. It used natural obstacles and made maximum use of easily defended features of the ground. Unlike the Maginot Line, however, it was designed to assist a battle of movement, rather than swallow up and immobilise troops inside it; and in order not to inculcate a defensive mentality, roofing was deliberately kept to a minimum. In areas of the frontier thought to be vulnerable, the population was removed and rehoused farther inside Germany. Here the military authorities came up against opposition from the NSDAP gauleiters, or district leaders (chairmen of county councils, in British terms, but with rather more power) who felt that removal of residents was bad for morale and implied that Germany would be invaded. The Germans removed far fewer of their people than did the French, who moved 250,000 from eastern Alsace Lorraine into central France. Unlike the situation in 1914, blockade was no longer a serious worry to the Germans, as the Molotov–Ribbentrop Pact had provided a back door that the British could not close. A long war might, unusually in terms of history, suit Germany after all, or so some of the generals thought.

Even in the Luftwaffe, a far more politicised service than the other two, there were doubts. The Commander-in-Chief was Hermann Göring, a First War fighter pilot, and holder of the Pour le Mérite, Hohenzollern

Germany's highest decoration for gallantry. A civilian stunt pilot and salesman after the war, he had joined the NSDAP early on and was placed in command of the newly raised (or at least newly admitted to) air force after the NSDAP formed the government, being promoted to field marshal in 1938. Far more realistic than many of his party colleagues, he understood the limitations of his air force, hoped for a political settlement with Britain and was against an early offensive in the west. Hitler had different ideas.

After the defeat of Poland, Hitler still hoped to come to terms with the Allies, or at least with the British, and only when this proved clearly impossible did his repeated chivvying of the Commander-in-Chief of the Army, von Brauchitsch, and his generals force them to produce a plan for offensive actions in the west. This first draft of Case Yellow (the codeword for operations in the west), was relatively mild, and even after several redrafts it still did not envisage a rapid defeat of France but only an advance into Holland and Belgium in order to establish air and naval bases for operations against Britain, and as protection for the Ruhr, which Hitler (rightly) thought would be vulnerable to attack from the RAF. There were certain political demands to be made on France: Alsace and Lorraine would revert to Germany, as would some areas of northern France that had once been German, or at least part of the Holy Roman Empire. Still Hitler insisted on more, and Yellow was recast as something very similar to Schlieffen, exactly as the Allies had suspected but rather more pedestrian. By late October 1939 the aim, as laid down by OKW Directive No 6 for the Conduct of the War, was:

> ...to defeat as much as possible of the French army and of the forces of the Allies fighting on their side and at the same time to win as much territory as possible in Holland, Belgium and northern France to serve as a base for the successful prosecution of the air and sea war against England and a wide protective area for the economically vital Ruhr.[1]

Dates for the attack in the west came and went, but apart from some tinkering with boundaries and the movement of a division or two from this corps to that, the plan remained very much the same, until Lieutenant General Erich von Manstein, Chief of Staff of von Rundstedt's

Army Group A, submitted a plan that was both radical and original and, he insisted, would force a quick decision in the west. Manstein initially put his plan to Army Headquarters, OKH, as he was entitled to do, but as at that time, December 1939, OKH was trying to dissuade Hitler from attacking in the west at all, his proposals got short shrift. It was only when Hitler had overcome the generals' resistance and they had accepted that an offensive was inevitable whether they liked it or not, that anyone was prepared to take the Manstein plan seriously. At the end of January 1940 one of Hitler's adjutants, Colonel Rudolf Schmundt, visited Headquarters Army Group A, and took the plan back to Hitler, who was delighted – it had many features that he himself had suggested at an OKW conference as long ago as November 1939.

The first phase of the new Case Yellow envisaged one army group in the north (B) driving into Holland and Belgium and enticing the Allied mobile and armoured formations north, where they would be encircled and destroyed (hence the alternative name of Operation Sichelschnitt or 'sickle cut'); a second army group (Rundstedt's A) would push its armour through the Ardennes, drive through northern France to the sea and cut the Allies in two, while in the south a third army group (C) would push up against the Maginot Line and fix its defenders in position. Phase Two would see Army Groups B and A turn south and deal with the French armies in central and southern France. Manstein had sent staff officers in civilian clothes to cycle through and around the Ardennes and he was convinced that the region could be traversed by armoured and mechanised formations. Hitler's preference for the Manstein plan was confirmed when on 10 January a Luftwaffe courier aircraft crashed in Belgium, and the officers on board were discovered to have been carrying the plans for (the pre-Manstein) Case Yellow. Although the officers insisted that they had burned the plans before the Belgians had arrived at the crash site, there was suspicion that they had said this to save their skins. They were safe from German justice by being interned in Belgium, but the Luftwaffe general commanding their Luftflotte (air fleet) was dismissed the service. Whether or not the Allies saw the plans (and they probably did not), Case Yellow was now amended to incorporate Manstein's ideas, and he – no doubt as a rap over the knuckles

Map 3 Area of operations, the Battle of France 1940 – opening phases

NETHERLANDS

NORTH SEA

Amsterdam

The Hague
Utrecht
Rotterdam
R. Lek
Arnhem
R. Waal

Moerdijk
Breda
R. Maas

Ostend
Antwerp
Albert Canal

Dunkirk
Ghent
R. Dyle
Brussels
Maastricht
Aachen
BELGIUM
Louvain
Liège
Eben
Emael
R. Scheldt
Wavre
Mons
R. Rhine
GERMANY

Arras
Namur
Dinant
Givet
ARDENNES

FRANCE
Monthermé
Mézières
Sedan

R. Meuse

Maginot Line

0   80 miles
0   80 km

for daring to argue with his elders and betters – was sent off to command XXXVIII Corps in the process of forming in Stettin. Instead of merely establishing bases in Holland and Belgium, plans now increasingly talked about the intention to 'annihilate' (vernichten) the French and British armies.

In support of the army for Case Yellow would be two air fleets commanded by Air Force General Albrecht Kesselring (Luftflotte II, in the north) and Air Force General Hugo Sperrle (Luftflotte III, in the west). As German airborne troops (at this stage neither the French nor British had any) and anti-aircraft artillery were part of the Air Force rather than the army, each Luftflotte had an anti-aircraft corps, and Kesselring's Luftflotte II had under command 7 Air Division (air-portable infantry) and 22 Airborne Division (parachute and glider troops). Also in support, but playing only a minor role, was the German navy, which initially could do little except lay mines along the Dutch and Belgian coasts.

Despite Hitler's wish to attack in the late autumn, then the winter of 1939, and again in the early part of 1940, the weather was such that the generals had their way, and after no fewer than twenty-nine postponements between October 1939 and May 1940, D-Day was fixed for 10 May 1940.[*] In the lead-up to the day for the attack, German propaganda attempted to lower morale and sow dissension among the Allies, using leaflet drops, radio and loudspeaker broadcasts, and rumours spread by agents. Very little of this was directed at the British, partly because, despite Norway, the Germans considered British soldiers to be tougher and more resilient than the French, and partly because they considered (correctly as it turned out) that French morale was more brittle. The main propaganda themes were that Germany had no territorial claims on France, Belgium or Holland; that French soldiers were going to be killed because of Poland, and stirring up the already existing French resentment of the British. Leaflets and broadcasts implied that the French were being tricked into doing England's work for her, while England's own

---

[*] I have used the British expression throughout. D-Day is the day an operation starts, and when planning all dates are either plus or minus of D-Day, which means that however many times D-Day is changed, the entire plan does not have to be retyped. The French call it J- (for Jour, day) and the Germans A (for angriff, attack).

contribution was tiny compared to that of France. Every French soldier could see the disparity of forces for himself, and that line of argument struck a chord with many. The city of London, the capital of international finance, came in for much verbal attack, as did Churchill personally. One leaflet showed John Bull standing at the edge of a cliff, displaying a swastika-emblazoned matador's cloak, being charged by the French bull. England was using hatred of Germany to lure France to her doom. The same leaflet was headed 'Pour la city [sic] rafle l'or On envoie les Francais a la mort': 'Frenchmen go to their deaths for the city which piles up the gold.'[2]

Unlike the Schlieffen Plan, which had been pored over, discussed, practised, war-gamed and worked out down to the last bootlace before 1914, Case Yellow (Sichelschnitt), was cobbled together in a few months, with staff officers taking decisions on the hoof, and with much of the detail passed up and down verbally. The Allied Plan D, on the other hand, had been four years in the making. The competence of the two sides would now be starkly contrasted.

On paper there was not a great gap in the relative strengths of the Germans and the Allies. On land the comparison on 10 May 1940 was:

RELATIVE STRENGTHS 10 MAY 1940[3]

	INFANTRY DIVISIONS	ARMOURED DIVISIONS	CAVALRY DIVISIONS	TANKS
Netherlands	8			
Belgium	20		2	10
UK	13			310
France	97	3	5	3,063
Allied total	138	3	7	3,383
Germany	131	10		2,445

The Allies had more divisions than the Germans, and although they had fewer armoured divisions they had more tanks. It is true that there had been no, or very little, joint planning between the Franco-British and the Dutch and the Belgians, that three of the British divisions were little more than very large fatigue parties and dumpers, neither equipped nor trained for battle, and that 51 (Highland) Division was locked up in the Maginot Line with the French. All that notwithstanding, the Germans had nowhere near the three-to-one superiority generally considered necessary for the attacker; their infantry divisions, with the exception of the four motorised divisions, were reliant on horse transport and there was still a great shortage of regular officers and NCOs. The French were also horse drawn, but this was less important for defenders, who were not expecting to rely on rapid movement. The initiative is always, or nearly always, with the attacker, as he can decide the timing, direction and point of main effort, but even so, in sheer numbers the Germans were the smaller force.

The Allies not only had more tanks than the Germans, they had better ones too. In the entire German army on 10 May 1940 there were 3,505 tanks, including those in armoured units, in workshops and in reserve. By type these were:

Panzer I	1,276
Panzer II	1,113
Panzer III	429
Panzer IV	296
Panzer 35/38	391 (Czech tanks taken over by the Germans)

As the Germans fielded 2,445 tanks on 10 May, including 627 Mk III and IV, this left only just over a thousand in reserve, under repair and on the eastern border. A panzer division had either four or three panzer battalions, depending on what stage of equipping it had reached, and a battalion had three companies of light tanks (Mk I, II and III) and only one 'medium' company, of Mk IVs. The Mk Is and IIs were obsolescent in 1940; the Mk I was armed with only a machine gun, and the Mk II with not much more, leaving only the Mk IIIs and Mk IVs able to operate as tanks proper.

The French in May 1940 fielded between 2,381 and 3,000 tanks, depending upon which source one consults. If we accept the lower figure, these were in fifty-one tank battalions, of which four were in each of the three armoured divisions, four in each of the three light mechanised divisions, and twenty-seven were independent battalions. Each French tank battalion had forty-five medium or light tanks, or thirty-three heavy tanks, depending on its role. The light tanks were the R35, H35, H39 and

HCM; the medium was the Somua and the heavy was the B1. In addition the French had about six hundred old First War Renault tanks guarding airfields. All the French light tanks (1,746 of them) had 37mm guns, rather than the German Mk I's machine guns or the Mk II's 20mm gun, and all had frontal armour of at least 1.5 inches, more than the German Mks I, II or III. Even if we discount light tanks, the French still had 635 Somua or B1 tanks.

Of the British armoured regiments with the BEF one was a cavalry regiment with armoured cars, six were mechanised cavalry each with twenty-eight Mark 6 light tanks, armed only with a machine gun, and one was 4 Royal Tank Regiment which, despite its name, was equipped with fifty Infantry Tanks Mark I, Matildas, armed only with machine guns. The only British unit with anything like a proper tank was 7 Royal Tank Regiment, which arrived in theatre only a few days before Case Yellow began, and which had twenty-three of the A12, the Matilda Mark II. If these are added to the French total of Somua and B1, then the Allies had 658 gun tanks to face 627 of the Germans. Qualitatively they compared as follows:

TYPE	WEIGHT	FRONTAL ARMOUR	MAIN ARMAMENT	SPEED	RANGE
British A12	27 tons	3.7-inch	2-pdr (40mm) gun	15 mph	160 miles
French Somua	19 tons	1.57-inch	47mm gun	25 mph	143 miles
French B1	31 tons	2.36-inch	75mm gun	17 mph	112 miles
German PzKpfw III	19 tons	1.97-inch	37mm gun	25 mph	102 miles
German PzKpfw IV	22 tons	1.97-inch	75mm gun	25 mph	130 miles

Admittedly there was one major design problem with all French tanks: the turret was designed for only one man. This meant that the tank commander had to control the driver, navigate, communicate, identify and acquire the target and operate the gun. If he was a troop or squadron commander he had to control his sub-units as well, and it was often far too much to ask. But even with this drawback, qualitatively and quantitatively in tanks the Allies were superior to the Germans. The difference lay in how they were used.

In the early hours of 10 May 1940 what came to be known as the Battle of France, but should more properly be the Battle of North-West Europe, began. German doubts about the morality of violating Dutch and Belgian neutrality were no doubt soothed somewhat by the capture of British documents in Norway showing that the British had every intention of violating that country's neutrality had the Germans not done so first, but German diplomats nevertheless sought some pretext for what they were about to do. On 9 May the Dutch and Belgian ambassadors in Berlin were each handed a note complaining about their own gross breaches of neutrality – failure to stop British aircraft using their air space, anti-German sentiments in the press, clandestine assistance to British intelligence and anything else that might be used to justify invasion.

In order to achieve surprise, the northern part of Case Yellow demanded the seizure in advance of forts, bridges and crossing points that might block the German advance. Paratroopers and glider infantry of 22 Airborne Division were to capture the area of the Hague, but many of the transport aircraft were shot down, crashed or got lost, and less than half the troops reached their objectives. Although those who did land managed to capture airfields at Valkenburg, Ypenburg and Olkenburg, these had to be given up during the day in the teeth of strong Dutch opposition. The lesson, not lost on the Germans – nor indeed on the British when they too eventually raised parachute troops – was that in planning an airborne operation one must always provide more troops than are needed, as not all those emplaned will actually reach their objectives. Farther south 7 Air Division, augmented by a regiment of 22 Airborne, did rather better. They landed in the Dordrecht–Moerdijk–Rotterdam area, where they captured the airfield at Waalhaven and seized and held bridges over the Rivers Meuse, Waal and Lek. Frantic calls for help from the Dutch to the British were answered by the RAF bombing Waalhaven, to little effect.

For the advance into Belgium in the direction of Brussels it was considered necessary to seize bridges over the River Meuse at Maastricht, on the Dutch–Belgian border, and also to force a crossing of the Albert Canal, an extension of the Meuse which ran to Antwerp. From the German point of view Maastricht was a failure. It was intended that the bridges should be captured in a *coup de main* by German special forces dressed in

Dutch uniforms (a breach of the law that rendered them liable to execution if captured). As it happened, the Dutch blew the bridges long before the Germans could get there, and imposed a twenty-four-hour delay in that sector.

As part of the defences of Liège, and covering crossings over the Albert Canal, was the fortress of Eban Emael. It was dug into a limestone ridge, was largely underground and equipped with steel and concrete gun emplacements protected by machine-gun posts, anti-aircraft guns and a garrison of 1,200 men. Despite its medieval appearance, Eban Emael was a formidable obstacle, and although it could eventually be reduced by land forces, this would slow down the advance and would not suit the German need for a quick victory. Attack by paratroopers was considered, but the time taken for them to concentrate, once dropped, and the difficulty of getting through the wire that enveloped the fort, seemed to rule them out. Then it was suggested that the fort had one major weakness: a flat, triangular roof 820 yards by 1,030 yards, on which gliders could be landed. The glider has had but a brief appearance on the military stage, and has long been superseded by the helicopter, but its great advantages were that it was cheap and easy to mass-produce, its pilots could be trained more quickly than those for powered aircraft, its approach was silent, and with a good pilot it could land exactly on target. The successful use of gliders demanded surprise, for once spotted they could be shot down like very fat and very slow ducks, but for the elimination of Eban Emael they were exactly what was needed.

At 0320 hours 10 May Belgian time, nine Junkers JU52 aircraft, each towing a glider, took off from Cologne. The gliders were released well inside Germany and began the long slow descent into Belgium. The defenders of Eban Emael were taken completely by surprise and not a single shot was fired at the gliders, which landed safely on the roof of the fortress. Eighty German soldiers sprang out, and disabled the guns with already prepared explosive charges. When the land invasion reached the canal later in the day, and pioneers came across to break into the bunkers with shaped charges, it was only a matter of time before the fortress surrendered, at a cost to the Germans of just six men killed. Now the road to Brussels was open. Meanwhile the German conventional advance had begun, with the army crossing the border into Luxembourg and Belgium, while the Luftwaffe concentrated on eliminating Allied anti-aircraft guns, attacking French and British aircraft on the ground, and supporting the army with ground-attack planes, particularly the infamous Stuka.

The Stuka was obsolescent by the time the war began, and by late 1940 the RAF had shot down so many of them that they were withdrawn from the Western Front. It had a top speed of only 255 mph and it lacked manoeuvrability, but in the spring of 1940 it terrified young French conscripts and British Territorials alike. Although the Germans could only ever deploy a limited number of them at any one time, attacks on ground troops by almost any aircraft were invariably reported as being by Stukas. Its ability to dive at an angle of eighty degrees, and place its bomb with great accuracy, combined with the siren that the Germans had deliberately fitted as a psychological weapon, made the Stuka a very useful adjunct to the German advance.

Although information indicating that the Germans were at last about to move had been reaching Allied intelligence since about 0100 hours on 10 May, there had been so many false alarms that it was not until about 0630 hrs, two hours after the invasion had begun, that General Gamelin could confirm that this was the real thing, and order the implementation of Plan D, the advance by the Franco-British armies into Belgium and Holland.

The kingdom of the Netherlands was established in 1815 as the successor to the pre French revolutionary Dutch republic. The republic had been warlike and not short of aggression, while the kingdom had never been to war with anyone, and encouraged by the success of its neutrality in the Great War, hoped to rely on it again in this. A strong pacifist movement contributed to the weaknesses of the Dutch armed forces, which had no tanks and only obsolete artillery pieces. The defence of the Netherlands depended on flooding (pre-war the Prime Minister claimed that he could stop an invasion by the push of a button) and there were three indifferently fortified defence lines, after which the armed forces would withdraw to 'Fortress Holland', north of the River Meuse, and sit it out behind the floods. Unfortunately this took no account of modern means of transport, nor of attack from the air. Prior to September 1939 the Dutch government had resolutely refused to enter into contingency talks with anyone, not even their neighbours the Belgians, and it was only when it became inescapably apparent that neutrality would not save them now, that they agreed the Breda variant to the Allied Plan D.

The German Eighteenth Army overran the first two lines of Dutch defence by the evening of the first day, but, as planned, General Giraud's French Seventh Army moved into Holland and on 11 May reached Breda. Unfortunately, the German 7 Air Division had seized the crossings over the Meuse estuary at Moerdijk, and Holland was now effectively cut in two. The Dutch army withdrew northward, towards Rotterdam, The Hague and Amsterdam, into Fortress Holland. This meant that they could not link up with the French and the Breda variant could not be implemented. On the afternoon of 12 May Giraud was ordered to pull back and deploy nearer Antwerp, from where the Scheldt estuary could still be denied to the Germans (the point of the Breda variant) but which could not prevent the Germans from similarly denying it to the Allies. The Dutch were now on their own, and on 13 May German troops supported by armour out-flanked the third Dutch defence line. That same day Queen Wilhelmina and an official whose signature was essential to make any newly enacted Dutch law legal, were embarked on a British destroyer. When it became apparent that Dutch resistance could not be carried on from Zeeland, in the south of the Netherlands bordering on Belgium, the queen was removed to England.

Eighteenth Army now ordered the reduction of Rotterdam as soon as possible and an air strike by Kampfgeswader 54 was ordered for 14 May. By then the Dutch military command in the city had decided to treat for peace, but the order to cancel the bombing mission arrived too late to stop the first Gruppen and an unnecessary air raid took place. The Dutch announced that 30,000 people had been killed, and considerable damage inflicted. In fact the true death toll was around 900, but it was the first major air raid of the war in the west, and reinforced the view that 'the bomber will always get through'. Next day, 15 May, the Dutch Commander-in-Chief, General Winkleman, surrendered all Dutch forces, and except for a few isolated units in the Scheldt estuary, resistance ceased.

The German 9 Armoured Division and the SS Leibstandarte Adolf Hitler Regiment held a victory parade in Amsterdam.

Although the Germans regarded the Dutch as being fellow Aryans (Dutch is but a variant of Deutsche and the language is close to German), the inhabitants of the Netherlands were shocked and offended by the violation of their neutrality. There was little active resistance to German occupation, but precious little collaboration either. A great many Dutch were Bible-reading non-conformists who regarded ethical behaviour and adherence to the law as sacrosanct. They had little sympathy for Germany's aims or approval for the flamboyance of her NSDAP government, and thought many of the tenets of National Socialism to be unchristian. The Dutch National Socialist party (strongly associated with Flemish nationalism and a wish to absorb Flemish Belgium) grew from a pre-war figure of 30,000 to around 50,000; some 5,000 Dutchmen joined the Waffen SS and about 54,000 belonged to various party organisations, but in a population of nine million this was little enough.[4] Unlike the French, the Dutch did not cooperate in the deportation of their Jews, and the University of Leyden was closed down when the non-Jewish staff refused to accept the dismissal of Jewish professors and lecturers.

With the capture of Fort Eban Emael on the first day, the Belgian army could no longer hold along the Albert Canal, and began to fall back to the River Dyle. This was not what had been intended by Plan D, which envisaged the Belgians holding along the canal long enough for the Allies to move up and prepare their positions for defence. Worse was to come, as when General Prioux, commanding the cavalry and light motorised advanced elements of General Blanchard's French First Army, moved into the Gembloux Gap he found, contrary to rumour, promise and expectation, that the so-called fortification of the gap was very rudimentary indeed and unlikely to cause the Germans more than the briefest of pauses. Prioux moved on to Hannut, forward of Gembloux, and deployed his forces to try to hold off the approaching Germans. At the same time he recommended that Plan D be abandoned in favour of Plan E, which involved a much shorter advance into Belgium. As by this time Giraud was well on his way to Breda, and Blanchard and the BEF were on the move up to the Dyle, Prioux's plea was rejected, but Blanchard was told to be in position on the Dyle by 14 May, rather than a day later as laid down in Plan D.

The BEF was able to advance the eighty or so miles to its battle area on the Dyle with little trouble – the Luftwaffe was fully engaged in Holland. Back in London General Ironside, the CIGS, had rather more trouble in getting to the War Office after an 0700 hours meeting at the Admiralty on 10 May. When the meeting ended the night watchmen had gone home and the day men had not yet come on duty. All doors were locked and barred, and the professional head of the British army had to climb out through a window into Whitehall! In Belgium the French Seventh Army pulled back from Breda; on its right the Belgian army, having withdrawn from the Albert Canal, was moving into position; then came the BEF, whose advance elements were on the Dyle on 11 May. South of the BEF was the French First Army covering the weak Gembloux Gap, then came the French Ninth Army, and then the French Second Army, linking with the Maginot Line.

The BEF deployed with two corps forward, II Corps (Brooke) with 3 Division in the line and 4 Division in reserve, and I Corps (Barker vice Dill, who had been ordered back to the UK to fill the newly created post of Vice Chief of the Imperial General Staff) on the right with 1 and 2 Divisions in the line and 48 Division in reserve. Fifty miles back was Adam's III Corps with 42 and 44 Divisions along the River Escaut, while 5 and 50 Divisions were in general reserve under the Commander-in-Chief, Lord Gort, and the three Territorial Army divisions sent out for labouring duties were labouring. On 13 May British reconnaissance elements were in contact with the Germans, and from the evening of 14 May the British line came under attack. The BEF was on the planned advance route of General von Bock's Army Group B, but the major blow was to fall south of the BEF, on the French Ninth and Second Armies.

The German Schwerpunkt, or main thrust, was entrusted to Colonel General Ewald von Kleist's Panzer Group von Kleist. Effectively a tank army, there had never been such a formation as a panzer group before. Its establishment was experimental, but it contained the bulk of the German armour. The mission given Panzer Group von Kleist was:

> ...as lead echelon of Army Group A to advance in front of Twelfth and
> Sixteenth Armies to attack in deep echelon through Luxembourg–southern
> Belgium. Employing surprise and a rapid movement, the Panzer Group... is
> to secure the west bank of the River Meuse between the River Semois and
> Sedan. Subsequently Panzer Group von Kleist is to continue its attack to
> Abbeville and the Channel coast.[5]

The group consisted of two panzer corps, XLI and XIX, XIV Motorised
Infantry Corps and 1 Flak [anti-aircraft artillery] Corps. General of Panzer
Troops Georg-Hans Reinhardt commanded XLI Corps which had two
panzer divisions (6 and 8), and 2 Motorised Infantry Division. Each of
these panzer divisions had a regiment of three battalions, with a total of
210 tanks, and a motorised infantry regiment of three battalions. Lieutenant General Heinz Guderian's XIX Corps had three panzer divisions (1,
2 and 10). Each of his divisions had a panzer brigade of two regiments,
each regiment of two battalions, and a total of 300 tanks per division.
XIV Motorised Corps, commanded by Lieutenant General Gustav von
Weitersheim, consisted of two infantry divisions (13 and 29) each of two
regiments of three battalions each. Each division, whether panzer or
motorised infantry, had its own integral artillery, engineers, reconnaissance and logistic units, while each corps and the group HQ had further
artillery and engineers. As the Germans expected a rather more vigorous
aerial response than they actually met, there was a very large number of
anti-aircraft units – twenty-seven battalions altogether – with a total of
around 600 anti-aircraft guns of various types. The 1,320 tanks allocated
to the group were a mixture of Mks I, III and IV, but each panzer battalion
(eighteen in total) had one medium company of sixteen Mk IV.

As the panzer group would have to move through the two armies of
Army Group A and then advance ahead of them, both army commanders – General List of Twelfth Army and General Busch of Sixteenth Army
– thought that one of them should take command of the group. Von
Kleist disagreed: he felt that this would unnecessarily slow him down and
that he should be directly under command of the army group, and in this
he was supported by von Rundstedt, commanding Army Group A.

To require Panzer Group von Kleist to move its 134,000 men and

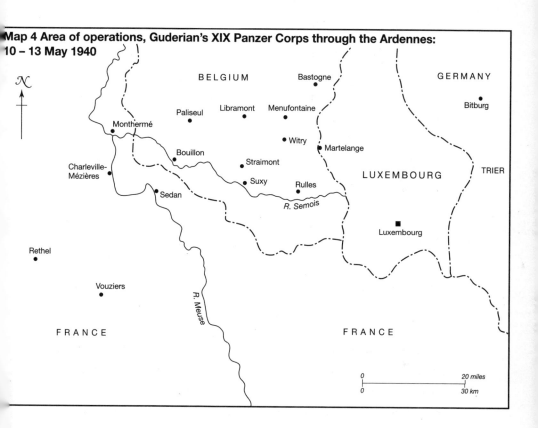

Map 4 Area of operations, Guderian's XIX Panzer Corps through the Ardennes: 10 – 13 May 1940

$\mathcal{N}$

BELGIUM

Bastogne

GERMANY

Bitburg

Paliseul

Libramont

Menufontaine

Monthermé

Witry

Martelange

LUXEMBOURG

TRIER

Charleville-
Mézières

Bouillon

Straimont

Suxy

Rulles

Sedan

R. Semois

Rethel

Luxembourg

Vouziers

R. Meuse

FRANCE

FRANCE

0   20 miles

0   30 km

42,682 vehicles, (wheeled and tracked and about a third more than the entire BEF), from its jump-off positions on the German border a distance of sixty miles as the crow flies (but as soldiers and their vehicles do not) through the Ardennes with its hills, woods and narrow roads to the Meuse at Sedan was to demand incredibly high standards of staff work and discipline, to say nothing of a huge measure of luck. It could only be an exercise in traffic control, rather than a tactical move, and if it did not achieve surprise then the whole group would be horribly vulnerable.

Defending the Ardennes across a frontage of about forty miles were the two divisions of Belgian Chasseurs Ardennais, partly motorised light infantry with some limited armoured support, whose mission was to delay. Behind them was French horsed cavalry and some light tanks (the 'petrol and oats' solution) of General Huntziger's Second Army. If the panzer group had been required to move along a single route, the distance from the leading to the last vehicle would have been 960 miles, or twice the distance from Inverness to Dover in a straight line. As it was, the group was allocated four tactical movement routes for the movement of combat units, and one main supply route for administrative and logistic vehicles. Even allowing for the use of minor roads and tracks parallel to the main routes, each route would still have a column of vehicles 190 miles long, with the first vehicles arriving at the Meuse long before the last ones left Germany.

The movement order for the group was drawn up by von Kleist's chief of staff, Colonel (later Colonel General and Chief of the General Staff of the army) Kurt Zeitzler, and was a model of what such an instruction should be. While von Kleist would have preferred to move with the two panzer corps abreast, this was not allowed by Army Group A and the group would move in three echelons, one behind the other. In the lead would be XIX Panzer Corps and 1 Flak Corps, followed by XLI Corps, with XIV Motorised Corps bringing up the rear. Just short of the Meuse XLI Panzer Corps would swing north to put it on XIX Corps' right for the crossing of the Meuse. All routes were thoroughly reconnoitred, or studied on air photographs, and rigid march timetables drawn up. Routes were one-way west, with only communications, medical and fire-fighting vehicles allowed to move east. Recovery units were placed at regular intervals, all vehicles were marked with a white 'K' on front and rear bumpers and strict speed limits were laid down: 16 mph by day and 9 mph by night for wheeled vehicles, and 12 and 9 respectively for tracks. Although the routes were exclusive to the group, other infantry formations on the way to their objectives would have to cross them, and were instructed to do so in small numbers in the gaps between vehicles. Two military police battalions were nominated to control the movement, and progress was to be regularly reported to Panzer Group HQ by observers in Fiesler Storch light aircraft.

Surprise was important not only to avoid being attacked on the line of march, which might be disastrous, but also to ensure that the Belgians and the French would not demolish bridges and man choke-points along the routes. In case security did break down it was decided to seize some of the more important bridges and pieces of vital ground in Belgium and France in advance of the panzer group. Ideally these tasks would have been given to parachute and glider troops, but as all these were earmarked for use in Holland, a battalion of the Grossdeutschland Regiment – originally a public duties ceremonial regiment based in Berlin but by now an elite motorised infantry unit – was hastily trained in the air–portable role and would be landed on their objectives by one hundred Fiesler Storch aircraft, short take-off and landing machines that could carry two passengers along with the pilot. While the citizens of Luxembourg, who had no army but an armed paramilitary police force around a hundred strong, were not expected to be able to put up any meaningful resistance to the German transit of their statelet, there was concern that the roads might be blocked by the shutting of existing steel gates and that warning might be sent to the French and the Belgians of what was on the way. To ensure that this did not happen members of the nearest thing Germany had to the SAS, the Brandenburg Battalion, would send small groups of men in civilian clothes across the border into Luxembourg the night before the advance was to begin, to capture road gates, bridges, telephone exchanges and gendarmerie posts.

The lead elements of Panzer Group von Kleist crossed into Luxembourg at 0535 hours 10 May. Preceded by motorcycle reconnaissance teams, the three panzer divisions of XIX Panzer Corps moved on three parallel axes on a frontage of thirty-five miles. In the north 2 Panzer Division faced narrow winding roads, hairpin bends and steep gorges; elsewhere there were rivers to cross and uncaptured steel gates to deal with. The Brandenburgers had done well, but had not taken all the potential obstacles. By having engineers well forward, however, the Germans bridged the rivers and either demolished the gates or, where this was not possible, simply built ramps over them. At Martelange, on the Luxembourg-Belgian border, 1 Panzer Division, the centre division of XIX Corps, found that the Belgians had blown the only bridge. Swiftly the engineer recce party identified a crossing point and a bridging company built a bridge. The reconnaissance and infantry vehicles began to drive over, to the consternation of watching Belgian prisoners, who announced that they had placed a minefield exactly on the approach to the newly constructed crossing. It transpired that the mines had been buried too deeply and the compacted earth on top could hold the weight of light vehicles without detonating the mines. The minefield was rapidly cleared by German engineers before the tanks were sent across. By early after-noon the lead units were through Luxembourg and into Belgium, where they found the Chasseurs Ardennais retreating in front of them cratering roads and blowing bridges as they went.

By nightfall on that first day Guderian's XIX Panzer Corps had advanced a near incredible thirty-five miles from the German border, and were established along the line Menufontaine–Witry–Rulles. By last light on 11 May, Whit Sunday, although XIX Corps had not reached the Meuse, as its commander had hoped it would, it had pushed forward another twelve miles to the line Paliseul–Bouillon–Straimont–Suxy, and the three panzer divisions were beginning to swing south-west in the direction of the Meuse and the French border. Now they were meeting not only the Chasseurs Ardennais, but French cavalry too. French aircraft had also picked up movement through the Ardennes, but everyone still believed that the main German thrust was in the north, a rerun of Schlieffen, and that was where the bulk of the Allied armour and the best infantry divisions were. Whatever might be poking through the Ardennes could not be more than a subsidiary thrust. By the evening of the third day, 12 May, Guderian's three armoured divisions were either side of Sedan, and the panzer group's second echelon, Reinhardt's XLI Panzer Corps, had moved to Guderian's north and was approaching the Meuse at Monthermé, sixteen miles north-west of Sedan.

The Allies had less excuse for failing to appreciate what was happening in the northern sector of Army Group A. Here, north of the Ardennes, Colonel General Guenther von Kluge's Fourth Army was pushing XV Panzer Corps, consisting of 5 and 7 Panzer Divisions, through Belgium towards the Meuse at Dinant. The defending Belgians were swept aside and withdrew to the north, and by the evening of 12 May those armoured divisions were also poised on the east side of the river. That day General Georges, the French Commander-in-Chief North-East Front (and immediate superior of the Commander-in-Chief BEF) came to the conclusion that something was up east of the Meuse, and ordered the priority for Allied bombing to be switched from the French First Army front between Louvain and Namur in Belgium, to that of the Second Army on the Meuse. Unfortunately, Georges' subordinate, General Billotte, commanding the French First Army Group, thought the order was ridiculous and largely ignored it. In the early hours of 13 May it became apparent to General Gamelin that there were now sizeable German forces on the east bank of the Meuse, but on the assumption that German tactical thinking was similar to that of the French, he considered that at least five days would be needed before the Germans could concentrate sufficiently to attempt a crossing, and that assessment was agreed by the British. The German army did not think like that.

On the morning of 13 May more than 1,500 aircraft of the Luftwaffe struck at Corap's Ninth and Huntziger's Second French armies between Dinant and Sedan. Mostly second-rate troops anyway, the experience of being dive-bombed and strafed from the air was terrifying. There was a shortage of anti-aircraft weapons and many French artillerymen abandoned their guns and searched for cover, while the infantry went to ground in their bunkers or in any ditch they could find. By mid morning the infantry of XV Panzer Corps had forced a crossing north of Dinant, and were holding the bridgehead against Belgian and French counter-attacks. In the afternoon XIX Corps had got across the Meuse at Sedan and XLI Corps at Monthermé while the rest of Panzer Group von

Kleist was closing up, the rearmost units having not yet left Germany.

Despite the failure of the French Second and Ninth Armies to prevent the crossing of the Meuse, all need not yet have been lost. The German bridgeheads were tiny, and they had not yet got any tanks across. An immediate counter-attack could well have eliminated the German hold on the west bank, and the huge traffic jam on the east bank could have been mauled by determined use of bombers, despite the large numbers of German anti-aircraft guns. Troops for a counter-attack were available, for the commander of the French 55 Infantry Division opposite Sedan had been allocated a counter-attack force of two regiments of infantry and two battalions of light tanks, which arrived at about 1900 hours on 13 May. Had these been pushed forward straight away it is difficult to see how the Germans at Sedan could have held their bridgehead: there would have been enough daylight remaining for the one at Monthermé to have been dealt with as well, with the crossing farther north at Dinant left to the following morning.

As it was, the French divisional commander, General Lafontaine, brought up in the French school of methodical, orderly battle management, where all elements must be ready and briefed before making a move, did not order the counter-attack until first light the following day, 14 May. He was not helped by roads choked with refugees and faulty communications, but by then the Germans had got a bridge over the river and were moving tanks across. Most of the French tanks were destroyed, 55 Division collapsed and panic spread to the neighbouring 71 Division. That division's commander, General Baudet, had put his headquarters in a well-constructed and perfectly protected concrete emplacement but which was so far back that he was unable to communicate with his units and could do nothing to prevent his soldiers from running away, as most of them now did. A belated attempt by the French air force and the RAF to demolish the German bridges on 14 May (the RAF were having a day's stand-down on 13 May) failed, with the loss of thirty of the seventy-one British bombers, mostly obsolete Fairey Battles, involved.

That same day another attempt at a counter-attack by a French corps of one armoured division and a motorised infantry division, sent up from Châlons, failed when, instead of immediately attacking Guderian's almost open left flank, arguments between the corps and divisional commanders, lack of radios, a need to refuel and general unreadiness led to the tanks being dispersed into defensive positions along a twelve-mile front. On 15 and 16 May French tanks did wreak considerable damage on 10 Panzer Division at Stonne, but the French were never able to concentrate their previously dispersed tanks and make use of their shock effect to stop Guderian. It was the last chance they would get, and by 15 May Guderian's leading troops of 2 Panzer Division were at Rethel on the Aisne, twenty-five miles west of Sedan, XLI Corps' 6 Panzer was at Montcornet, thirty miles into France, and XV Panzer Corps' 7 Panzer Division (commanded by Major General Erwin Rommel), having crossed the Meuse at Houx, was twenty miles in at Sivry.

The situation of the French was not made easier by Guderian's thrust at Sedan being made at the junction of the two French armies, Ninth to the north and Second to the south. The Second Army was pushed to the south-west, while General Corap found his Ninth Army pressed by Guderian on its right flank and by General Hoth's XV Panzer Corps, spearheaded by Rommel, on his left. The Ninth Army began to fall back, its corps losing touch with each other and with Army HQ, and Corap himself seems to have suffered some form of mental breakdown. In the afternoon of 15 May General Georges told Corap that he was to hand over command of the Ninth Army to General Giraud, who had led the Seventh Army tasked with the abortive Breda variant in Holland. Giraud duly arrived in Corap's headquarters at Vervins, and attempted to take command. Unfortunately the Ninth Army had by now largely disintegrated. There was very little for Giraud to take over, and the Germans were already behind him. Georges was worried that the Germans were now intending to turn south and roll up the Maginot Line, still failing to realise that the Germans were not in the slightest bit interested in the Line. They were heading straight for the Channel coast, and there was very little to stop them.

While the Germans were breaching the Meuse, creating a break-through and beginning to exploit westward, the BEF was still firm on the Dyle line. To the south of the British the French First Army had moved into position across the Gembloux Gap, thanks to General Prioux and his two light motorised divisions; they were able to hold off the two divisions (3 and 4 Panzer) of General Hoepner's XVI Panzer Corps along the line Thirlemont–Hannut–Huy, ten miles east of the gap, until 14 May before withdrawing behind the First Army, when, fatally, it was split up and its tanks doled out in ones and twos along the front. In the first-ever battle between armoured formations, the French armour, particularly the Somua tanks, performed well. The French lost 105 tanks, while the German bill was 165, but as the Germans were advancing they could recover and repair their tanks, whereas the French ones were lost forever. On 15 May the Germans attacked the Dyle line, but both the BEF and Blanchard's units stood firm. By now, however, what happened in the north hardly mattered – the Battle of France was being decided to the south.

On the evening of 15 May, with the Belgians in retreat to the left of the BEF and the First Army's right flank exposed by the collapse of the Ninth Army, Blanchard was ordered by General Billotte to withdraw over two nights back to the line of the River Escaut. Although Billotte had been delegated a coordinating role over the BEF and the Belgian army by General Georges, he said nothing either to Gort or to King Leopold of Belgium. Not until the following morning were liaison officers from both British and Belgian armies able to persuade Billotte that they too must now withdraw, and some sort of coordination was restored. To the dismay of the phlegmatic English, for whom an officer displaying emotion in public was and is very bad form indeed, a number of French officers were observed to break down and weep, and Gort's chief of staff, General Pownall, deplored being 'allied to such a temperamental race'![6]

That same day Churchill visited France, and on asking Gamelin where was the Masse de Manoeuvre (strategic reserve), was told that there wasn't one. The only army with the training and equipment to be used as such had already been committed to the Breda variant and was now under attack north of Antwerp, despite its erstwhile commander, Giraud, having been diverted to the Meuse.*

---

* The whole point of having a Masse de Manoeuvre is so that when an enemy breaks through defences there is something held back that can be moved to counter it. If all available forces are put into the line in a defensive posture, as the Allies had done, then there is nothing immediately available to deal with an enemy breakthrough.

Churchill had gone to France to try to put some backbone into the French, whose Prime Minister, Reynaud, declared that the war was lost and the road to Paris open. The French had still not realised that the German tanks were not making for Paris. Churchill's visit may have had some effect, for next day, 17 May, Reynaud appointed the 84-year-old Marshal Pétain, the hero of Verdun in 1916 and until recently French ambassador to Franco's Spain, as Deputy Prime Minister, and summoned Gamelin to Paris to sack him. On the same day the British CIGS advised the Admiralty to begin contingency planning in case it became necessary to evacuate the BEF. This was not defeatism by General Ironside – very much a fighting general – but doing what all senior commanders have to do: hoping for the best but planning for the worst. So far the British had not been seriously involved, with a mere total of 313 all-ranks killed since the opening of the battle on 10 May. That would soon change.

NOTES

1. Research Institute for Military History, Germany, (tr McMurry & Osers), *Germany and the Second World War, Vol. II,* Clarendon Press, Oxford, 2000.

2. Ibid.

3. It is surprisingly difficult to get exact relative strengths, as sources differ as to the exact number of divisions. I have taken the average of *Germany and the Second World War,* op. cit., *The World War II Data Book,* op. cit., *Grand Strategy,* op. cit., Julian Jackson, *The Fall of France,* OUP, Oxford, 2003 and Colonel A. Goutard,*The Battle of France 1940,* Frederick Muller, London, 1958.

4. I. C. B Dear and M. R. D. Foot, *The Oxford Companion to World War II,* OUP Oxford, 2001.

5. Florian K. Rothbrust, *Guderian's XIXth Panzer Corps and the Battle of France,* Praeger, New York, 1990.

6. Brian Bond (ed), *Chief of Staff: The Diaries of Lieutenant General Sir Henry Pownall, Vol. I,* Leo Cooper, London, 1972.

8

Scuttle from Europe

SO FAR CASE YELLOW was working exactly as the Germans had planned, although not without doubts both at the front and in Berlin. There were arguments between von Kleist, who thought the advance was too fast for safety, and Guderian, who thought the important thing was to crack on and not worry about the flanks, only resolved when Guderian threatened to resign and Kleist caved in. Commander Army Group B, Colonel General von Bock, was peeved when his army group received what he considered to be insufficient recognition in army orders, and even Hitler temporarily lost his nerve and was convinced that there was a threat to the left flank of the thrust to the coast. The Chief of the General Staff, Halder, saw no such threat, but both he and the Commander-in-Chief of the army, von Brauchitsch, had a hard time persuading the Führer to allow the armoured drive to continue.

Up to the withdrawal from the Dyle line the British army's casualties had been negligible, but this was not the case for the RAF. The commander of the British Air Forces in France (BAFF) – the air component of the BEF and the advanced air striking force – was Air Marshal Sir Arthur Barratt, responsible to General Lord Gort as commander of the air component, and to Bomber Command in London for the AASF. By putting one officer in command of all RAF assets in France the Air Staff hoped that the available aircraft would be used in as efficient a manner as possible, and also that Barratt would be able to mitigate what the Air Staff saw as the more unreasonable demands of the army. In the inter-war years the RAF had waged a long defensive battle against the acquisitive ambitions of the Royal Navy and, particularly, the army and one of the planks on which they fought for their continuing independence as a separate service was the Trenchard doctrine of the indivisibility of air power. Forced, like the army, into a sudden U-turn in 1939 and finding that there was, after all, to be an expeditionary force, the RAF still held to the theory that what really mattered was strategic bombing, with anything else a mere sideshow. The army, on the other hand, wanted liaison aircraft, reconnaissance aircraft, artillery spotter aircraft and ground-attack aircraft on the model of the German Stuka that they had observed and been impressed by in the Spanish Civil War.

Logical though it seemed from the RAF's point of view to have one officer commanding all aircraft in France, it meant that response to the BEF's requests for air support took longer than necessary. As the Air Staff considered the AASF to be more important than the air component of the BEF, Barratt's headquarters was co-located with that of the French Air Force General d'Astier de la Vigerie, commanding the Northern Zone of Aerial Operations, rather than with Gort at Arras or, later, at Wahagnies. It would have been better for Barratt to have been Commander RAF Europe, with an RAF officer commanding the BEF's air component co-located with and operationally under the command of Gort, with a channel to Barratt for single-service matters such as repairs, provision of spares and personnel administration. A separate commander of the AASF should have been co-located with the French.

By the opening of the battle on 10 May two of the BAFF's ten squadrons of Fairey Battles had been replaced by Blenheims, and three squadrons of Hurricane fighters had arrived. The BEF air component had four squadrons of Blenheims for long-range reconnaissance, five squadrons of Lysanders for tactical reconnaissance and four squadrons of Hurricane fighters, these latter for escort and air defence rather than for ground support. The move forward to the Dyle brought the BAFF as well as the BEF into an unbalanced position, exactly where the Germans hoped they would be. While the Germans were able to put up hundreds of aircraft as an air umbrella for their advance, the RAF on 10 May could only send four waves, each of eight slow-moving Battles, to attack the German columns. Of the thirty-two despatched, thirteen were shot down and all the rest damaged in some way. The RAF had failed to appreciate the accuracy of German anti-aircraft defences, which included not just the 88mm and 20mm guns of the Flak battalions, but also the ability of even lowly motorcyclists to shoot back with machine guns mounted on sidecars. Initially BAFF aircraft were employed in Holland and Belgium only. On 10 May the RAF lost forty-two aircraft; on 11 May forty-four and when forty-eight were lost on 12 May Air Marshal Barratt was coming under pressure from London to conserve aircraft for what the Air Staff saw as the real battle – which they considered had not yet begun. By 13 May the AASF that had started with 135 aircraft on 10 May was down to seventy-two.

When, on 12 May, the French air force decided that something very nasty indeed was coming through the Ardennes, but were denied permission to do much about it by the French army, they asked the RAF to help. Once again the Battle was shown as not being up to the requirements of modern warfare. Barratt was now desperate for reinforcement, but on 13 May, although there were the agreed number of squadrons of Hurricanes in France – ten – two more squadrons'-worth had to be despatched to replace aircraft destroyed. In London, Fighter Command's dilemma was that if, in the worst case, the Battle of France was lost and a further battle became necessary over Britain, then fighters had to be preserved for that. It was a difficult position for Air Chief Marshal Dowding to hold, but hold it he did. Dowding was of course absolutely right. Had he acceded to the requests for more and more aircraft from the French and the Belgians, from the BEF and even from his own RAF officers in France, then the aircraft and pilots that (just) won the Battle of Britain would not have been there. We know that now, but in May and June 1940 many resented Fighter Command's parsimony. The only Allied aircraft that could take on the Luftwaffe on equal terms was the Hurricane, but these had to be preserved too, and Dowding never allowed his nineteen Spitfire squadrons, superior to most German aircraft, to pass out of his control.

The German breakout from the Ardennes and the crossing of the Meuse on 13 May was as much a triumph for the Luftwaffe as it was for the army, for it was the air umbrella of hundreds of fighters and dive-bombers that prevented any effective action being taken by the few French aircraft available to attack the panzers. For the RAF, concentrating on Holland and Belgium, 13 May was a relatively quiet day, but they still lost fourteen aircraft, although seven were from Fighter Command, caught by the Luftwaffe over the Dutch coast, rather than from BAFF. On 15 May Air Marshal Barratt was forced to decide that from now on, except in circumstances of extreme urgency, the AASF could no longer take part in daylight operations. As it was also moving to airfields farther back, and as the bombers' navigational equipment was such as to make the chances of finding a point target at night remote, the AASF was now virtually out of the battle. By 16 May the BEF's air component was under extreme strain. To defend against waves of German bombers, which enjoyed plentiful fighter escort, the RAF sent up flights of only four or five aircraft, with individual pilots having to fly four or five sorties a day.

Withdrawing in conformity with the French, once Gort could persuade Billotte to include him, the BEF pulled back fifteen miles from the Dyle to the line of the River Senne on the night of 16/17 May. The Senne runs roughly south to north through Brussels, and GHQ decided to send 1 Army Tank Brigade (4 and 7 RTR) to Brussels by train to be under command of I Corps to beef up the defence. Brigadier Vyvian Pope, Director Armoured Fighting Vehicles at GHQ, was supposedly the BEF's chief adviser on all matters pertaining to armour. He was disadvantaged by being junior in rank to all the other senior arms representatives, who were major generals, and when he pointed out that if on arrival at Brussels the railways then became unusable, the Mark VI Light and the Marks I and II Matildas were not mechanically capable of long marches on tracks alone, Pope was quietly ignored, and off went the tank brigade. The brigade, under Brigadier Douglas Pratt, arrived in the forest of Soignies, south of Brussels, on the night of 15 May, and next day was told to withdraw to Tournai, the wheeled vehicles by road and the tracks by train. Sure enough, the railhead at Enghein was unusable, due to German air attacks and the French train drivers having, not unreasonably, decamped with their engines. The tanks started off by road, but, on arrival at Ath, twelve miles away, on the morning of 17 May, a written order arrived for each battalion (without a copy to Brigade HQ) from I Corps telling them to retrace their steps to Enghein, where the corps was under threat from a German panzer division that had broken through at Halle. The tanks returned to Enghein, to find that the troops there were perfectly happy and had seen no signs of German armour.

At this point Brigadier Pope, who distrusted GHQ's ability to deploy armour, and was tired of sitting around in GHQ (rear) at Arras, where there was precious little to advise about, arrived. He was just in time, as the tank brigade was about to be given wholly unrealistic tasks more suited to cruiser tanks (of which so far there were none); so he ordered the brigade forty miles back into BEF reserve at Orchies, west of the River Scarpe, where they arrived on 18 May. As no functioning trains could be found and as the British army then had no tank transporters (flat-bed vehicles on to which a tank could be loaded and then transported by road), the journey had to be made on tracks, with the brigade workshops' three Scammels (recovery vehicles) having to tow some thirty broken down vehicles at various times. About a quarter of the tanks were lost, either broken down (largely from thrown tracks) or out of fuel. Pope was too much of a gentleman to say, 'I told you so'.

On 17 May the Germans crossed the River Sambre at Mauberge, about forty miles south of Brussels. The next night the BEF withdrew again, twenty miles back to the line of the River Dendre, and next morning German troops of Army Group B crossed the Senne behind them, while farther south Army Group A had got to the line Cambrai/St Quentin. The third stage of the withdrawal took place on the night of 18/19 May, another fifteen miles to the River Escaut, where the three corps of the BEF took up position with all seven divisions (1, 2, 48, 3, 4, 42 and 44) in the line between Oudenarde (scene of Marlborough's victory in 1708) on the left and Maulde on the right. As it was now apparent that Army Group A was driving deep into France, and that there were virtually no French troops between them and the sea, the British had perforce to reorganise their lines of communication, which ran back to Calais, Boulogne and Le Havre. A garrison of Arras (which not only housed GHQ (rear) but was also an important railhead and supply depot) was formed from one infantry battalion (1 Welsh Guards) and assorted logistic troops, supported by a regiment's-worth of field guns and an ad hoc squadron of various armoured vehicles from workshops and supply depots, the whole under command of the General Officer Commanding 12 Division, Major General Petre, and to be known as Petreforce.

To watch the right rear of the BEF, and to prevent the Germans getting over the River Scarpe, where there were some units of the French First Army, Major General Mason-Macfarlane, normally the BEF's Director of Intelligence, was placed in command of one brigade detached from 42 Division, two field regiments Royal Artillery and various 'odds and sods' – as the army in its delightful way calls those whose occupations involve the spanner or the pen rather than the gun or the bayonet – and, on its arrival at Orchies, 1 Army Tank Brigade, the whole to be known as Macforce. All Royal Engineers not actually engineering, and all military policemen not controlling traffic or investigating twisted bootlaces were formed into scratch battalions and added to the GHQ reserve, which consisted of 5 and 50 Divisions, the former moved to Seclin, south of Lille, on 19 May and the latter to Vimy Ridge that night. Of the under-equipped and under-trained labouring divisions, 12 Division had one brigade each at Amiens, Doullens and Abbeville, 23 Division had its two brigades on the Canal du Nord, one at Arleux east of Arras and one about ten miles north of Peronne, both placed under command Petreforce as they would be critical in the defence of Arras. Finally, joining 5 Division at Seclin, was 46 Division. The BEF now had its three corps facing Army Group B, and its rather more scattered reserves and labouring divisions facing Army Group A.

That the French had no strategic reserve, as finally admitted when Churchill asked where it was on 16 May, came as a genuine surprise to the British. It is axiomatic today that when operating as part of a coalition each partner must know the exact order of battle of the others. There was no reason for the French not to tell the British what formations they had and where they were, but they were remarkably reluctant to do so. A subaltern of the 12th Lancers, instructed to reconnoitre possible defence lines on the Belgian border in December 1939, observed that the French guns were well sited in rear but found that the French would not tell him how many there were, nor would they allow him to inspect the forward positions, which he had to assess surreptitiously from the nearest road.[1] The British land contribution was of course minuscule compared to that of the French (one very small army with very few tanks compared to eight armies with quite a lot of tanks), and some British officers did not feel able to pressure the French too closely on matters not directly concerning the BEF, nor did the somewhat tortuous French chain of command make it easy to find out what reserves existed and where they were deployed. Yet there was no excuse for not being fully aware of the true state of the French army, and that the British were not so aware can only bring into question the competence of the various liaison officers and of the British intelligence services.

The speed of the German advance once across the Meuse surprised everybody (including quite a few Germans). Churchill commented that the 'tortoise has put its head dangerously far out of its shell'; conventional wisdom held that such a thrust would run out of momentum and must slow down or halt as it outran its logistic tail; that is what happened in 1914 and despite improved transportation was what should happen now. That it did not is a tribute to German military management, whereby engineers were well forward to bridge rivers and demolish obstacles quickly, routes were cleared for refuelling columns, or vehicles simply helped themselves from French filling stations, and where routes were impassable others were swiftly opened. German commanders travelled close up behind the leading units, with stripped-down tactical headquarters, where they could assess the situation for themselves, and the excellent communications systems (every tank had a radio) and the use of light aircraft both for reconnaissance and as airborne command posts, all contributed to the maintenance of momentum. By the time the French reacted with such local reserves as were available, it was always too late; the situation had changed and the battle had moved on. The one French counter-attack which was pressed with determination, that by Colonel Charles de Gaulle's 4th DCR (armoured division) on 19 May from Laon north against German positions on the River Serre, failed due to lack of artillery and infantry.

On 19 May the French Prime Minister, Reynaud, sacked Gamelin as Commander-in-Chief of the French army, replacing him with General Maxime Weygand, who had been commanding French forces in the eastern Mediterranean. Gamelin's last act before departure had been to hand General Georges his latest battle plan. His call for a massive pincer attack on the German corridor was correct in theory but utterly unrealistic in practice: there were no more mobile forces to deploy, no air superiority to be maintained, and a time frame of 'within hours' was simply impossible. On 19 May, too, the British in London were making equally unrealistic plans. The CIGS, Ironside, wrote in his diary: 'If the worst comes to the worst the BEF must be prepared to turn south and cut itself through to the Abbeville–Amiens line and eventually to the Seine to cover Havre [Le Havre, a major port for the British].' Also on that day, 1 Armoured Division, the only British armoured division, began landing at Le Havre. In Ironside's view, 'they may be very useful for the extrication of the BEF in the last resort'.[2]

To Gort in France the last resort was looking very likely, and he ordered the two brigades on the Canal du Nord (69 and 70 Brigades of 23 Division) to fall back, 69 Brigade to the River Scarpe and 70 to Vimy Ridge. The latter was too late, caught by German armour while on the move south of Arras on 20 May, and destroyed as a fighting force. On the same day the brigade of 12 Division stationed at Doullens was badly hammered by German tanks pushing through to the coast. On the afternoon of 19 May, Gort's chief of staff, Pownall, telephoned the War Office to warn the CIGS that it might be necessary to withdraw on Dunkirk if the gap to the south of the BEF could not be closed. This caused considerable alarm in Whitehall, and after meetings of the Defence Committee and the full cabinet, Ironside was sent off to France with orders to Gort dictated by the Prime Minister. Churchill's instructions were that the BEF must move south-west to Amiens, 'attacking all enemy forces encountered' and join up with the left of the French army on the Somme. What Churchill failed to realise (and to be fair to him what his adviser Ironside also failed to realise) was that this would involve withdrawing the three corps already in contact with the Germans on the Escaut Line, turning them around ninety degrees, pushing them through fifty miles of strong German columns, and not being certain anyway where the French left flank might be. It would also leave the Belgians completely exposed and allow the Germans to get in behind the BEF, between the British and the Channel ports; and in any case the BEF was now short of ammunition. It was complete nonsense, and symptomatic of the conviction by Churchill and others that it was possible to run battles from London, and that any objections to the Great Man's ideas were born of cowardice, defeatism or incompetence.

Ironside, once he got to the front, quickly realised that the Churchill plan, which he had originally supported, was not a starter, although Gort explained that he did intend a limited attack on the German flank south of Arras on 21 May. Ironside then went off to see General Billotte, and found him with General Blanchard, Commander French First Army, at Lens, both in a state of deep depression. Ironside tried to persuade them to attack in conjunction with Gort, and when he could get no sense from Billotte, lost his temper, picked him up by his tunic and gave him a good shaking. As Ironside was six feet four inches tall, and burly with it, the diminutive Billotte, more frightened of Ironside than of the Germans, agreed to do what he could.

On the day that the BEF's Arras counter-stroke, as it came to be called, was going in, Weygand called a meeting in Ieper, Belgium, to explain his master plan, a derivation of that bequeathed by Gamelin as the latter's last act before rustication. Weygand proposed to attack the German panzer corridor from north to south at its narrowest point, twenty miles between Arras and the Somme, where there were only two lateral roads that the Germans could use. Blanchard's First Army would attack from the north, helped by the BEF, and the new Seventh Army, in the course of being formed south of the Somme, would assist in the south. The attack would take place on 26 May, in five days' time, which, as the Germans had their lead units at Noyelles-sur-Mer at the mouth of the Somme on 20 May, was ludicrous. The meeting was vague and inconclusive, and because the BEF main HQ had just moved Gort was late hearing of the meeting and did not arrive until Weygand had left. Worse still, General Billotte was killed in a motor accident on his way from the meeting, and it took three days for Blanchard to take over as commander of First Army Group.

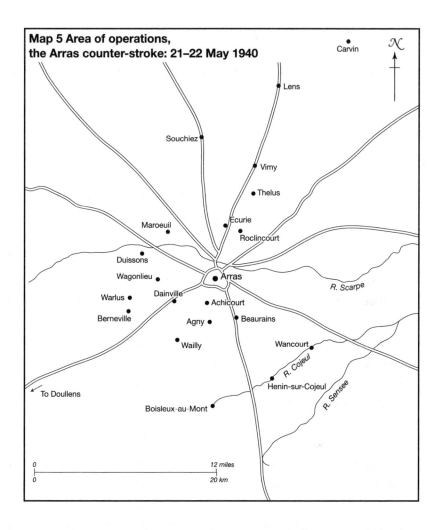

Map 5 Area of operations, the Arras counter-stroke: 21–22 May 1940

Carvin

Lens

Souchiez

Vimy

Thelus

Maroeuil

Ecurie

Roclincourt

Duissons

Wagonlieu

Arras

Warlus

Dainville

R. Scarpe

Berneville

Achicourt

Agny

Beaurains

Wailly

Wancourt

R. Cojeul

To Doullens

Henin-sur-Cojeul

R. Sensee

Boisleux-au-Mont

| 0 | 12 miles |
| 0 | 20 km |

Because the so-called Arras counter-stroke was one of the very few examples of the British taking the tactical initiative and actually going on the offensive during the Battle of France, it has been held up by some historians (particularly by Liddell Hart) to be much more than it actually was. It was not intended to cut through the panzer corridor, although at this stage that corridor was very vulnerable, but an attempt to relieve the garrison of Arras, establish some 'elbow room', as Gort called it, around and south of Arras, and block the roads in order to interfere with or stop German communications along the northern part of their corridor. It was a limited operation that might develop into something more if the French could act from the south, but neither Gort, nor most of the French generals, had any real confidence in that possibility.

To carry out this thrust south of Arras Gort formed yet another ad hoc formation, under Major General H. E. Franklyn, General Officer Commanding 5 Division. Known as Frankforce, it was, on the face of it, a powerful body. It consisted of Franklyn's own (regular) 5 Division, 50 Division (first-line Territorial Army), 1 Army Tank Brigade, and two field and two anti-tank batteries Royal Artillery. Reconnaissance would be provided by 50 Division's motorcycle recce regiment, 4 Royal Northumberland Fusiliers. On closer inspection the grouping was not as formidable as it first appeared. With the need to keep troops on the Scarpe, reinforce the garrison of Arras and provide reserves, far from two divisions there was only one brigade, 151 Brigade of 50 Division, available, and the men of its three battalions (6, 7 and 8 Durham Light Infantry) having been separated from their transport and thus having had to march all the way from Belgium, were very tired. The Tank Brigade still had fifty-eight Matilda Mark I tanks, from the seventy-seven with which they had started the war, but these were armed only with machine guns, and the brigade could field only sixteen of their original twenty-three Mark IIs, with their 2-pounder guns. Of the field batteries only one was equipped with the excellent 25-pounder, while the other had the pre First War 18-pounder, albeit now towed by a motor vehicle rather than horses, and had pneumatic tyres.

The counter-stroke had been conceived on 19 May, but much that might have affected the orders given to Frankforce happened the following day. Hoth's Panzer Corps' 7 Panzer Division had got to Beaurains on the outskirts of Arras, while 8 Panzer, with the SS Totenkopf Motorised Infantry Division following up, had reached Hesdin, twenty-five miles west of Arras and less than twenty miles from the coast, and 70 Brigade had been destroyed south of Arras. Situations alter cases, and that the situation existing when Franklyn was initially briefed had changed dramatically should have led to some alteration in his orders. To call it a raid on the German corridor might have made sense, but to pretend that the force was to block German communications from the east no longer did. As it was, Franklyn's instructions stood and he was led to believe that only weak German forces would be faced. He decided that the operation would be commanded by Major General G. Le Q. Martel, Commander 50 Division, and should be conducted in two phases. Phase one would be an advance to the River Cojeul, four miles south-south-west of Arras, and phase two would be to push on to the River Sensee, a further two and a half miles away. One artillery battery would support each column, and the AASF had been asked to target likely German positions between Arras and the coast, while the BEF Air Component would provide air reconnaissance. The assembly area (where all the troops would meet up prior to the advance) was to be Vimy Ridge, four miles north of Arras, and where British troops already were, while the start line was to be the road that ran south-west to north-east, from Doullens to Arras. [*]

Martel decided to carry out the advance in two columns. The western column, based on 7 RTR and 8 DLI, would move round well to the west of Arras through Maroeuil, Warlus and Wailly to Boisleux-au-Mont on the Cojeul, while the eastern column, based on 4 RTR and 6 DLI would skirt Arras through Écurie, Achicourt and Beaurains to Henin-sur-Cojeul, about three miles upstream of the western column. In reserve would be 9 DLI and 4 RNF, less those elements used for recce by the two columns. After declining a French suggestion that the British should attack towards

---

[*] The assembly area is where all units involved in an operation marry up and where final orders are given. It should be reasonably secure and protected from (at least) direct enemy fire. The start line (now the line of final departure, to conform with NATO nomenclature) is the line (a genuine feature on the ground such as a road or a stream, or a line on the map) from which the operation proper begins. All troops are to be in correct formation and ready for battle before that line is crossed. The time that the lead units cross the start line is H-Hour, and all timed artillery fire missions are plus or minus of H-Hour.

Peronne (twenty-five miles to the south and on the southern edge of the panzer corridor), Martel was assured by General Prioux – he whose 3rd DLM (Division Légère Mécanique, light armoured division) had done well at the Gembloux Gap earlier in the month, and who was one of the few French generals to come out of 1940 with his reputation enhanced – that his tanks would protect the British right (west) flank.

Now everything started to go wrong, in ways reminiscent of the Norway fiasco. Ad hoc formations suffer from not having their own proper headquarters, and from not having worked and trained together. For a start there were far too many chiefs and not enough Indians; Franklyn (a major general) was commanding Martel (substantive colonel, temporary brigadier, local major general) who was in charge of two brigadiers (Churchill of 151 Brigade and Pratt of 1 Army Tank Brigade) who between them boasted two infantry battalions and two weak tank battalions. Normally a force of this size would be commanded by one brigadier at most. The infantry were already in the assembly area, but the tanks had to get there from Orchies, about thirty miles away, and the last tank did not reach Vimy until 0500 hours on 21 May. The commanders then began to argue about the time of H Hour, when the attack would start. Franklyn had wanted it to be at 0500, and when this was shown to be out of the question he urged that it should be as soon as possible, whereas Pratt argued that 1500 hours was the earliest feasible time. Eventually Martell was pressurised into agreeing 1400 hours, despite Pratt's insistence that neither infantry nor artillery could be ready in time. There was doubt as to who was actually in command on the ground. Brigadier Churchill gave out his orders to his commanding officers on the morning of 21 May and there was no representative of the armour present. At least one of the infantry commanding officers was unsure which tank regiment he was to work with. The infantry thought they were in command with the tanks in support, while the RTR commanding officers thought they were supposed to command with the infantry in support[*].

---

[*] In view of the plethora of small villages and woods, which would restrict the ability of the tanks to identify targets and to deploy off roads, each column should have been commanded by the infantry CO. On the other hand the fact that the infantry COs were of the Territorial Army, whereas the RTR COs were regulars, would argue for the armoured CO being in command. But then all four COs had seen action in the First War! Whoever was to command, it should have been clearly laid down, and was not.

The infantry had carried out no training in infantry tank cooperation; there was a shortage of maps; there was no means for the infantry to communicate with the tanks; and the artillery FOOs[*] had not reported by the time the columns moved off from Vimy at 1100 hours.

It got worse. The tanks had netted in their radios (checked that they worked) at Orchies but had maintained radio silence since. When they broke silence on crossing the start line many of the radios did not work. Air recce reported no sign of German armour anywhere near Arras but did spot infantry on the roads to the south. The infantry battalions had a march of between seven and five miles (depending on the column they were in) before reaching the start line, each man carrying around 60 lbs weight in very hot weather, and inevitably they lost touch with their tanks out in front. By the time they approached the start line the inner column had only its motorcycle infantry with it, and when they met German infantry in a village just short of the start line, and quite rightly used their infantry to clear the village and go firm in it, 4 RTR had to press on unsupported. The column, or what was left of it, did get as far as Beaurains, when they were told to go no farther as the western column was having problems. The infantry hit by 4 RTR were caught on the line of march and utterly surprised by the British tanks bearing down on them. A good number of soft-skinned vehicles were knocked out and prisoners taken. It was not until Beaurains came under air attack, including Stukas, and from 7 Panzer's field artillery regiment with their 105mm and some 88mm guns deployed, that the British tanks were halted and the commanding officer 4 RTR killed. The British artillery was little help as radios to the gun were not working and target information was being sent to the gun-line by messenger, leaving the guns trying to fire at points off the map, with corrections coming too late to be effective.

The right-hand column's motorcycle infantry had not turned up; the tank's infantry liaison officer in a scout car could not communicate with

* Forward Observation Officers. Artillery guns cannot (except very rarely, in which case they are generally in deep trouble) see what they are firing at. The FOO accompanies the infantry or armoured units, can see the target and directs artillery fire by radio. The advent of a portable radio meant that in this war, fire plans (artillery tasks) could be 'on call' (that is, could take on opportunity targets) instead of running to a rigid timetable as had perforce been the case in the First War.

either infantry or tanks, and 7 RTR soon lost contact with 8 DLI which had no transport save its carrier platoon. Possibly due to a shortage of maps, 7 RTR got lost, ran into the rear of 4 RTR, never reached the start line and failed to catch a column of 150 German Mk IIIs and IVs of Rommel's tank regiment. This was probably just as well, for although they would have been vulnerable to 7 RTR's Matilda IIs, there were now only nine of these (seven having been lent to 4 RTR), and the odds would have been just too great. This column's artillery battery never came into action at all, as no form of communication was ever established with it, but after a brief scuffle with French tanks to their west 7 RTR did initially put the wind up the Germans, sending infantry fleeing and forcing some gun crews to abandon their guns. The German tank and anti-tank guns simply could not penetrate the massive frontal armour of the Matildas, and the British 2-pounder on the Matilda IIs was, just, a match for the German tanks. It was not until Rommel, Commander 7 Panzer, got a grip and organised a gun-line on a hill west of Warlus that artillery guns, including 88s, started to knock out 7 RTR's tanks. Rommel's ADC was killed beside his general, but when both the commanding officer and the adjutant of 7 RTR were killed, the column had no option but to withdraw. The infantry put up what delaying action they could, and eventually the remnants of Frankforce began to reorganise back whence they came. By first light 22 May all those who were coming back had reported into Écurie or Vimy.[3] The human casualties were trifling: six killed in the reconnaissance regiment, and a total of thirty-three in the three infantry battalions. The two RTR battalions had twelve killed between them, but much more seriously, after beating off German probing attacks north of Arras on 23 May, and withdrawing to Carvin, twelve miles to the northeast that night, the tank brigade was reduced to a total of eighteen Matildas Mk I, and two Mark IIs, with seven light tanks for reconnaissance. The two regiments were formed into one composite regiment, 4/7 RTR, on 25 May. On 26 May what was left of the brigade was ordered to move towards the coast and Dunkirk, for the situation had become much worse.

It has been said that such was the ferocity of the British attack south of Arras that Rommel and the German high command believed that rather

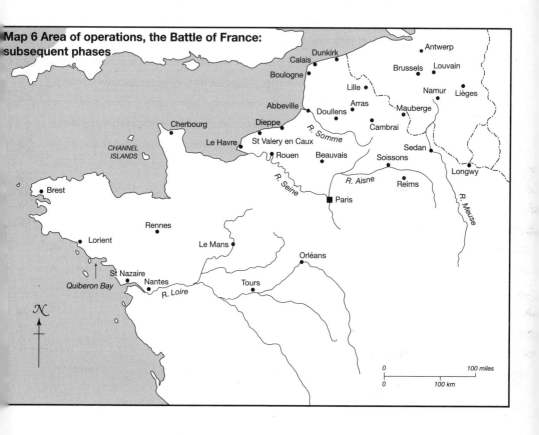

Map 6 Area of operations, the Battle of France: subsequent phases

Antwerp
Dunkirk
Calais
Brussels
Louvain
Boulogne
Lille
Namur
Lièges
Abbeville
Arras
Doullens
Mauberge
Dieppe
Cambrai
Cherbourg
St Valery en Caux
CHANNEL ISLANDS
Le Havre
Sedan
Rouen
Beauvais
Soissons
Longwy
R. Somme
R. Aisne
Reims
R. Seine
R. Meuse
Brest
Paris
Rennes
Lorient
Le Mans
Orléans
St Nazaire
Nantes
Quiberon Bay
R. Loire
Tours

N

0   100 miles
0   100 km

than being attacked by two-thirds of one tank brigade, the assault on the panzer corridor was by five divisions. It has to be doubted whether the German army, with its experience in Poland and far more combined arms training than either the British or the French, could really interpret the very limited actions of seventy-four British tanks, plus some French Somuas off to the flank, as being ten times that number. It may be that this impression by some British historians is due to a simple clerical error in Rommel's headquarters. His situation map of 1600 hours 21 May shows an enemy frontage north of Arras of about four miles across, in which is written '5 Divisionen'.[*] The German for the English word division is the same, the plural is 'divisionen'. German intelligence would have worked out fairly quickly that Franklyn, overall commander of the attack, was GOC 5 Division. The soldier marking up the map could quite possibly have written 5 Divisionen instead of 5 Division. Moreover, the Germans knew perfectly well that if there really had been five divisions'-worth of tanks they would have advanced over a much wider frontage than four miles. Frankforce's efforts may have slowed the Germans up a little, and von Kleist was worried that Arras in British hands posed a threat to his northern flank, but it made no difference to the outcome of the battle. At best it may have been a salutary example to British commanders of how not to do it.

While Franklyn's troops were reorganising back at Vimy Ridge much was happening elsewhere. The French counter-attack promised by the shaken (and now dead) Billotte emerged as one division probing south in the direction of Cambrai and quickly brought to a halt by the Germans. The Germans crossed the River Scarpe despite what was described by the British as 'fierce resistance' by 4 Green Howards (one officer and eight other ranks dead) and 2 Wiltshires (twenty other ranks dead). Churchill paid another visit to Paris and yet again issued an instruction that was crassly idiotic and impossible of achievement. Sent to Gort by telegram, it said that the Belgian army would withdraw to the River Yser, open the locks and stand on the defensive behind the flood barrier so caused.[*] The telegram went on:

---

[*] That is what they had done in 1914, and it had allowed them to preserve a tiny sliver of Belgium from German occupation.

> The British Army and the French first Army should attack south-west
> towards Bapaume and Cambrai at the earliest moment, certainly tomorrow,
> with about eight divisions, and with the Belgian Cavalry Corps on the right
> of the British... the new French Army Group which is advancing upon
> Amiens and forming a line along the Somme should strike northwards and
> join hands with the British divisions who are attacking southwards in the
> general direction of Bapaume.[5]

The only part of this message that made any sense at all was the fact that
the Belgian army was indeed withdrawing to the Yser. The suggestion
that their cavalry could attack on the British right was nonsense; the BEF
was already being attacked along the Escaut line and could not disengage;
the two divisions near Arras (5 and 50) were in no condition to do any
attacking, much less in the direction of Bapaume; the so-called French
army group was in fact only an army, and even that was having great difficulty doing anything. The Germans were already on the Somme and
Army Group A's armour was not only at the Channel coast but pressing
north as well, while its infantry was closing up rapidly. Even if the idea
had been sound – and a week earlier it might have been – to expect several
hundred thousand men and thousands of vehicles to be pulled out of
position, briefed, supplied and prepared for a major operation in a new
direction within a matter of hours showed complete ignorance of what
was possible and what was fantasy.

The reaction at the headquarters of the BEF when Churchill's message
arrived was unequivocal. 'The man's mad,' wrote Chief of Staff Pownall
in his diary: 'I suppose these figments of the imagination are telegraphed
without consulting his military advisers.'[6] In fact Churchill did discuss his
ideas with his military advisers, but only accepted their advice if it
concurred with his gut instincts. Ironside, in England, certainly thought
that the only chance left for the BEF was for it to abandon the Belgians
on its left and march south-west, with the intention of cutting the German
panzer corridor and preserving Calais and Boulogne; but this would have
allowed Army Group B to get in behind the BEF and would have forced
the Belgians to capitulate even earlier than they did. Ironside was a far
better CIGS than received perception (manufactured by the Churchill

faction) of the Second World War admits, but in allowing his political master free rein in matters of which he had no understanding, Ironside failed in his duty. Major General Ismay, chief of staff to Churchill in the Prime Minister's alter ego as Minister of Defence, had grave doubts about the order, but did not prevent its being sent. Churchill was a very strong personality, often engaging and always stubborn, and it was difficult to dissuade him; but military officers who do not oppose with all their might a plan that they know to be wrong are equally culpable. Fortunately Gort simply ignored the instruction, and that night the BEF withdrew from the Escaut back to its old line along the French frontier.

Once the Germans reached the coast on 20 May, only Boulogne and Calais were left to resupply the BEF, and garrisons were despatched to defend them. To Boulogne went two battalions and two troops of anti-tank artillery of 20 Guards Brigade, arriving on 22 May. That same day 2 Panzer Division, the left-hand division of Guderian's XIX Panzer Corps, which was now pushing north and completing the sickle-cut of Case Yellow, attacked Boulogne at 1700 hours. The defenders fended them off, and were attacked again at first light 23 May. Despite fire support from three destroyers of the Royal Navy, the Guards were unable to prevent the Germans from establishing themselves on the heights around the town, and by the afternoon only the harbour area was still in British hands. Evacuation was ordered at 1730 that night, and by 0300 hours on 24 May the navy had got most of the men away. 1 Irish Guards had two officers and eleven ORs killed, and 2 Welsh Guards three officers and twenty-one ORs. Stragglers from 20 Brigade and ad hoc units of French soldiers held out until 25 May, after which Boulogne was German.

The garrison of Calais – one Territorial battalion – was also reinforced, by 30 Brigade and 3 RTR. 30 Brigade was a hastily organised formation put together only a few weeks previously to be sent to Trondheim in Norway, and consisted of two regular motorised battalions – 2nd Bn the King's Royal Rifle Corps and 1st Bn the Rifle Brigade – taken from the only British armoured division, and a Territorial motorcycle battalion, Queen Victoria's Rifles, from London District. 3 RTR was part of 1 Armoured Division and had twenty-six light tanks (Mk VIB), fifteen heavy cruisers (A13) and eight close-support cruisers (A10). The cruisers characteristics were:

TYPE	WEIGHT	FRONTAL ARMOUR	MAIN ARMAMENT	SPEED	RANGE
A 13	14 tons	.55-inch	2-pdr (40mm) gun	30 mph	90 miles
A 10	13.75 tons	1.18-inch	92mm (3.62-inch) howitzer	16 mph	99 miles

The original idea was that 3 RTR and 30 Brigade should operate as a mobile striking force but it became obvious almost as soon as they arrived in Calais – the tanks on the afternoon of 22 May and the infantry the next day – that they would be lucky to do much more than hold their own. On the evening of 22 May 3 RTR were ordered by a staff officer to move to St Omer to protect GHQ. As the tanks were still being unloaded and then had to be cleaned of the deep preservation grease considered necessary for the sea move, only a few light tanks could be sent, but when they got to St Omer nobody was there! On the morning of 23 May another patrol was sent to St Omer, and nothing more was heard of it – Guderian's armour had got there first. Having heard nothing from its patrol, the entire battalion set off for St Omer at about 1400 hours. Threading its way through columns of French marching troops and refugees fleeing for Calais, the battalion ran into German armour at Guines, six miles from Calais, lost twelve of its A13 tanks and fell back to the high ground south-west of Calais – fortunately, as it turned out, for most of Guderian's panzer corps were moving through the area that the battalion would have had to cross.

After a failed attempt by infantry supported by 3 RTR to break out to the east with 350,000 rations for the BEF on 24 May – leaving 3 RTR with but twelve light tanks and nine cruisers – it was clear to Brigadier Nicholson, commanding 30 Brigade and the Calais garrison, that the port was now completely cut off from the interior and was of no use whatsoever to the Allies, whether for embarkation or for resupply and reinforcement. This assessment was accepted by the War Office in London and the Admiralty agreed that the Royal Navy would provide ships for evacuation. There then occurred yet another interference with the proper conduct of military affairs that should never have been tolerated by British commanders. The French General Fagalde, who was nominally in charge of the defence of the Channel ports, ordered that Calais was not to be evacuated, and the War Office agreed, despite admitting in a signal to

Nicholson on the evening of 24 May that the harbour was of no importance to the BEF.[7] Now Churchill took a hand, and a signal full of empty
rhetoric and high-sounding phrases about Allied solidarity and the eyes of
the Empire being upon Calais, drafted by the Prime Minister personally,
informed Nicholson that there would be no evacuation and that he was to
fight to the last. Young men accept that old men will often send them to
die – that is the nature of soldiering – but they would prefer that their
deaths were to some purpose. It was utterly pointless to throw away two
regular battalions and one of the better Territorial battalions in the defence
of Calais, considered by the Germans to be of little importance and which
could not affect by one jot what was happening elsewhere.

When the Germans attacked Calais in earnest, Nicholson and his men
did their best, and refused an offer to surrender on the grounds that 'it
is the duty of the British Army to fight, as well as it is the Germans''.
Naval gunfire support was very limited as there were no ground liaison
officers to direct the fire, and by 26 May the garrison, broken up into
small pockets of resistance, attacked from the air, shelled by German
artillery, and with German armour and infantry in the town in overwhelming strength, had no alternative but to surrender. That did not stop
Churchill sending a personal signal to Gort at 0430 hours 27 May saying:
'A column directed upon Calais while it is still holding out might have a
good chance.' The survivors of Calais marched off into five years in
prisoner-of-war camps; it would have been much better to evacuate them
and bring them back to England to fight another day, or to take them off
and land them at Dunkirk, farther along the coast.

Elsewhere Gort had decided to evacuate the garrison of Arras, now
dangerously exposed, which gave the French generals an excuse to avoid
attacking south. In London Churchill was buoyed up by French reports
that their new Seventh Army Group had captured Peronne, Albert and
Amiens (it had not) and was putting in attacks all along the Somme (it
was not), and wanted to know why the British were not doing likewise. In
fact it was already clear to Lord Gort that the situation was hopeless. On
the night 21–22 May his staff had worked out that if the worst happened,
the only solution would be in the withdrawal of the BEF to the coast –
the stretch between Dunkirk and Ostend seemed best – and evacuation to

England. Commanders have to plan for the worst, but on the morning of 25 May Gort still intended to take part in the planned Allied attack of 26 May, using 5 and 50 Divisions now removed from Arras. The situation on 24 May was that four divisions of the BEF held the line Maulde to Menin, where it joined with the Belgian army, which had taken up position along the River Lys up to Ghent and then north to the Scheldt estuary. On the BEF's right flank and protecting against a German advance from the south-west, were 2 and 48 Divisions, responsible for the thirty-five-mile La Bassée–St Omer–north to the coast stretch of the La Bassée and Aa Canals. Augmented by all sorts of scratch detachments formed from men of logistic units transformed into infantry, often supported by only a single gun, this was still a desperately thin line and there were only a few French units between it and the Germans. The BEF was under threat from Army Group B to the west and from Army Group A to the south and east. Already the Germans were getting across the La Bassée and Aa Canals, only twelve miles from Dunkirk – and then the German armour halted!

Much has been written and said about the German Haltbefehl or Halt Order of 24 May. Liddell Hart attributed it to the Arras counter-stroke on 21 May, while von Rundstedt in his post-war memoirs said that it was because Hitler did not want to inflict a humiliating defeat on the British, with whom he still wished to come to terms. In fact the order was given by Rundstedt, and only confirmed by Hitler at OKW the next day, and was given for very sound military reasons. Since leaving their jump-off positions in Germany on 10 May the German armour had travelled 250 miles on tracks with little time for maintenance, repairs or rest. German tank losses had been considerable, from French and British tanks and anti-tank guns, but also from breakdowns, overheating and fire. Tracks were loose and worn, and men were tired. In any case Flanders, with its low-lying marshy ground and numerous waterways, was not good tank country. The Allies were now cut in two, with the smaller portion in the north. The Belgians could not go on for much longer, the French were doing nothing and the British could easily be dealt with. Rather than Army Group B being the hammer that would crush the BEF, the French First Army and the Belgians against the anvil of Army Group A, the roles would now be reversed. In any event, with the battle in the north almost won, the real battle would be against the remaining forty French divisions in the south, as catered for in the Manstein version of Case Yellow, and the armour must be husbanded for that. The Luftwaffe and the infantry could take care of the north. Generals von Kluge and von Kleist approved of the order; Guderian was furious and so was the Commander-in-Chief of the army, von Brauchitsch, and his Chief of the General Staff Halder, but the order stood.

While the British knew about the order to halt – the Germans sent it by radio in clear – they did not yet appreciate its significance. From about 0700 hours on the morning of 25 May reports were coming in to GHQ, now at Premesques, south-east of Armentières, that the Belgians were under heavy attack between Menin and Courtrai, not far from where their line joined that of the British. It soon became clear that the Belgians could not hold, and that a gap was opening up that would have to be plugged. The Belgians had no reserve: if the gap was to be filled it would have to be done by the British. Gort was now faced with a dilemma. His agreement with Weygand was for him to attack southward with two divisions on the morrow; his own government, his Prime Minister and even the CIGS were urging him to do just that. On the other hand, if he did nothing about the gap at Courtrai, the Germans would pour through, and cut the BEF off from the coast. Gort's only available troops were the two divisions promised to Weygand. Contrary to all instructions from his government and urgings from the French, Gort decided to plug the gap in the Belgian line, and by that decision he saved the BEF.

Gort had been planning for an evacuation for some time. He had already shipped the perhaps surprising total of 27,936 non-essential soldiers back to the UK. Reluctantly, and after more discussions with the French, the British cabinet now agreed that evacuation was the only answer and on 26 May Gort was told that his priority now was to get as many men and as much equipment back to England as he could. Weygand, however, would not yet order French troops to evacuate – which was to sour relations between the two Allies when the French assumed (not without cause) that the British were deserting them. Gort's plan was for a bridgehead between Nieuport and just west of Dunkirk, and an 'escape corridor' leading back to it. The flanks of the corridor would be held until all troops had withdrawn through it to the bridge-head. The perimeter of the bridgehead was about twenty-five miles around and up to eight miles deep, following as far as possible natural obstacles, mainly streams and canals. It was held by the British from Nieuport Bains through Veurne to Bergues, and from there to Mardyk, about four miles west of Dunkirk, by units of the French First Army. The corridor to it stretched for thirty-five miles, from as far away as La Bassée and Lille, and running north-west and north to the coast. The defences of this corridor were desperately thin, but the German halt order helped, for by the time it was lifted on 26 May – by when even those German generals originally in favour of it had changed their minds and were vociferously demanding that it be rescinded – the Allies had pulled back sufficient troops through the corridor to augment the defences on its flanks.

The order for Operation Dynamo – the evacuation of the BEF – to begin was issued at 1857 hours on 26 May, but already ships were arriving off Dunkirk. The officer nominated to run Dynamo was the 57-year-old Vice Admiral (later Admiral Sir) Bertram Ramsay, who had retired in 1938 but was recalled on the outbreak of war and appointed Flag Officer Dover. It was from his eyrie cut into the white cliffs of Dover that he commanded the operation. The first ship to arrive at Dunkirk was the former Isle of Man steam packet, now an armed boarding vessel, *Mona's Close*, which arrived in the afternoon of 26 May, picked up 1,400 troops and left in the early hours of 27 May. Shelled from the shore by German artillery and attacked from the air by the Luftwaffe, she arrived back in England with twenty-three men killed and sixty wounded. The perimeter was initially held by anyone whom Brigadier Lawson, the officer charged with commanding the defence of the perimeter, and his French equivalent, could grab from units flooding into the bridgehead. Three Corps areas were designated, and as units approached the perimeter all vehicles except artillery prime movers, headquarters transport needed for communication and any armoured fighting vehicles, were rendered unusable and abandoned. There was no room inside for vehicles or heavy equipment that were not essential to the defence.

Troops not required for the defence of the perimeter then moved on to the seafront to be embarked. The navy had designated three routes from Dunkirk to England, routes X, Y and Z. Route Z was the shortest – forty-five miles – but also the most dangerous, for it ran directly to Dover and for nearly half the journey ships were in range of shore-based artillery as they sailed parallel to the French coast. Route X was sixty-three miles long and went due north away from the coast for seven and a half miles before turning north-west and heading for the North Goodwin lightship and then west of the Goodwin Sands to Dover. Route Y was the longest, but also the safest once it had been swept for mines, and ran north-east and then due west for the North Goodwin lightship. Troops could be picked up from Dunkirk harbour itself, until that was so damaged by shelling that only the mole could be used; and when that, too, became unusable, from the beaches.

Because warships were designed to carry weapons and the men to serve them, rather than passengers, they were not ideal for rescuing troops. The only place to put soldiers picked up by a fighting ship at action stations was on deck, which was not only cramped but also made the vessel top heavy and affected its manoeuvrability. The best ships for moving passengers were those designed for just that purpose – cross-Channel ferries – and the Royal Navy commandeered a number, placed Royal Navy officers in command, and used them in the absence of their normal business of moving tourists back and forth. Other commercial ships of various types were also pressed into service, but apart from those that could get in and out of the harbour at Dunkirk, none could come close enough inshore to allow the soldiers to board; hence the 'little ships'. A myth of the Dunkirk evacuation is that hundreds of little ships – yachts, canal boats, pleasure boats, dinghies, lifeboats, wherries, cockle boats, pinnaces, anything that could float – were pressed into service to go over to France, pick up a few soldiers and bring them back to England. That was not, of course, the purpose of the little ships, nor were they by any means all owned and operated by patriotic civilians. The Royal Navy already had a small boats pool and to it was added the fifty Schuyts, 200-ton motor boats brought over to England from Holland before that country's surrender, and while civilian boats were also pressed into service it was not for some days that they could be used. The purpose of the little ships was not to bring men back to England – only the Schuyts could carry enough men to make that a worthwhile exercise – but principally to pick men up from the beaches and ferry them out to the transport ships. Of the 848 small boats used, 203 were privately owned, although not all were privately crewed. Seven small boats were lost to enemy action and 135 by other causes (collision, sinking, swamping and running aground).[8]

The evacuation got off to a slow start. On 27 May 7,699 men were taken off, and on that same day the British and the French discovered that the Belgians were asking for an armistice. In the early hours of 28 May King Leopold announced the capitulation of the Belgian army. This caused considerable anger, particularly to the French. Prime Minister Reynaud said that the surrender was 'a deed without precedent in history, without warning to French or British troops who had come to the aid of his country in response to his agonised appeal'. This was less than fair to the Belgians. While Gort had succeeded in temporarily bolstering up the Belgian line on 26 May, the subsequent British withdrawal towards the coast and increased German pressure had created a gap between the British and the Belgians which was widening by the hour and which neither could close. By 27 May the Belgians were entirely on their own, defeated, with no tanks and hardly any ammunition. The British had not told them of the withdrawal to the coast, and in any case cared little for them. When Pownall was asked by the head of the British Military Mission to Belgium whether some Belgian troops might be evacuated along with the BEF he replied, 'We don't give a bugger about the Belgians.'[9] There was little the Belgians could do except run up the white flag, but they did not do so until the British had already been evacuating their own men for more than twenty-four hours.

The tempo of the evacuation increased. As more ships became available, so more men could be lifted, and the total for 28 May was 17,804, of whom the majority had been embarked in Dunkirk harbour. The escape corridor was now shortening, and on that same day the 12th Lancers imposed a considerable delay on the Germans at Dixmuide, only seven miles from the bridgehead, when they caught a German lorry-borne infantry column driving along the main street towards the only bridge over the Ijzer Canal, and having inflicted considerable casualties, persuaded a roving subaltern of the Royal Engineers to blow the bridge. GHQ now withdrew to La Panne, on the coast and eight miles east of Dunkirk.

On 29 May there was a general withdrawal to the bridgehead: the corridor could not be held open any longer, most of the troops that could pull out had done so, and in any case the German armour was now starting to roll again. The garrison of Cassel, one of the strongpoints along the corridor where two infantry battalions and a yeomanry regiment had held out against increasingly ferocious German attacks since 25 May, began to withdraw to the bridgehead. They should have moved earlier, but having obeyed orders and destroyed their codes and ciphers they were unable to read the (encoded) order to do so. They began to pull back at 2130 hours that night, but very few managed to break through the German encirclement. The 4th Battalion Oxfordshire and Buckinghamshire Light Infantry had ninety-six men killed between 25 and 30 May and the 2nd Battalion The Gloucestershire Regiment seventy-seven. Many of the rest went into captivity. That day 47,310 men were evacuated, but with German air attacks and shelling of the harbour, movement of shipping in and out was getting more difficult.

On 30 May the last two corps commanders, Brooke of II Corps and Adam of III Corps were taken off. Commander I Corps, Barker, had already left. British officers do not put their own safety ahead of that of their men, but whereas you can train a private soldier in a few weeks, you have to grow generals, and Britain simply could not afford to lose experienced senior officers. They did not want to go, but their orders for home brooked no discussion. That day 58,823 men were evacuated.

On 31 May Churchill was again in Paris, and boasted proudly that the BEF had already evacuated 165,000 men to fight another day. When General Weygand enquired how many of those were French, Churchill, after a hasty consultation with his staff, had to admit to only 15,000. In fact it was Weygand himself who refused to authorise any French evacuation until 29 May, but in any case Gort's view was that his priority was towards the BEF, and that every Frenchman saved was one British soldier who was not. Nevertheless, for obvious reasons of Allied solidarity, the government now ordered that henceforth 50 per cent of all evacuees

Top **MK VI LIGHT TANK (BRITISH)** Brought into service in 1936 as a reconnaissance tank, it was armed with machine guns only and was lightly armoured. Used in France, Greece, Crete and in North Africa MK VIs were often used, wrongly, in place of medium tanks and thus suffered heavy losses. This one, on exercise on Salisbury Plain, belongs to the 2nd Royal Gloucestershire Hussars (Territorial Army). (© IWM H5934)

Below **CARDEN-LOYD BREN CARRIER (BRITISH)** One of the few really good pieces of equipment obtained by the British infantry between the wars, it was soon modified for use by other arms and, becoming the Universal Carrier, saw action in nearly every theatre. These, in North Africa, are somewhat optimistically armed with the Boys anti-tank rifle. (© IWM E11701)

CHURCHILL TANK (BRITISH) Originally designed as an infantry tank, the British Churchill was rushed into production and first saw action in the Dieppe raid in August 1942, when twenty-eight of them were lost or abandoned. Its slow speed and initial mechanical unreliability almost saw its withdrawal from front line units, until the Tunisian campaign showed that it was better at going up hills than any other tank. It was well protected and its four inches of frontal armour meant that it could take a lot of punishment. The Churchill was the basis for the series of 'funnies' – bridgelayer, flamethrower, mine clearance and track laying tanks – that supported the Normandy invasion in June 1944, and also came in AVRE (Armoured Vehicle Royal Engineers) and recovery variants.

GRANT TANK (AMERICAN) Called the Lee in its US specification and the Grant when built for the British, the American M3 was the first tank to go into volume production in the USA. Although it was not what the British ideally wanted, it did meet their immediate need for a reliable tank in North Africa. With 57mm (2.24 ins) of frontal armour it could take a lot of punishment, although its high silhouette (over 10 feet) made it difficult to conceal, and its main armament, a 75mm canon, was mounted on a sponson on the right side of the hull, giving only a limited traverse. First used at Gazala in May 1942 it outgunned most German tanks – although superior German tactics won the battle.

SHERMAN TANK (AMERICAN) By the time of the Normandy invasion in June 1944 the American M4 (Sherman to the British) had become the standard main battle tank of all the Allies. It was far from ideal, inferior to the German Mk V Panther and Mk VI Tiger and arguably only just a match for the German Mk IV, but it was manoeuvrable and mechanically reliable, and had the great merit of being able to be produced on assembly lines in huge quantities. Called the Tommy Cooker by the Germans because of its propensity to go on fire, its faults were noted by the British when it was first deployed in North Africa in 1942, but had still not been corrected by the end of the war, after which the Sherman stayed in service with numerous armies all over the world.

SHERMAN DD TANK (ALLIED) The need for a tank that could arrive on the beaches with the infantry in an amphibious assault was identified as one of the lessons of the Dieppe raid, and the result was the Sherman DD (Duplex Drive). While tanks have the natural flotation properties of a brick, a rubberised canvas screen allowed an adapted Sherman to float, while the drive was diverted to two propellers in rear. On arrival on the beach the screen was dropped, the drive switched to the tracks and the DD became a normal tank. Heavy seas caused the US First Division to lose nearly all of its DD tanks on launching off Omaha Beach, which contributed to that beach being the most difficult on D-Day.

FIREFLY TANK (BRITISH) The standard Allied Sherman had a 75mm gun, firing a round that would simply bounce off a German Tiger. The British Firefly was a Sherman armed with an adaptation of the 17pdr anti-tank gun, achieved by adding a box-shaped extension to the rear of the turret, to accommodate the breech and recoil of the much larger gun. The round fired would penetrate five inches of armour at 1000 metres, and was the only British tank that could take on a Panther or Tiger. There was one Firefly in each troop of four tanks.

SOMUA TANK (FRENCH) In production from 1936, the 19 ton French SOMUA with 40mm (1.57 ins) of frontal armour was well protected for its time. It had a cast hull and turret, a good 47mm gun as its main armament, a coaxial machine gun, and a V8 petrol engine that gave it a road speed of 25 mph and a range of 143 miles. Although there were problems with access to the engine compartment, and the small turret meant that the commander had to be his own gun aimer and radio operator, it was a better tank than most of those opposed to it in 1940. Unfortunately for the French there were not enough of them (only just over 400 had been produced) and French doctrine tended to spread their armour over the whole front, rather than concentrating it and using its shock effect.

CHAR B1–bis TANK (FRENCH) Potentially an excellent French heavy tank, well protected, with a good 75mm gun in the turret and a 47mm one in the hull, it had to be painstakingly built by craftsmen, so that when war came there were not nearly enough of them, and like most French tanks the turret would only hold one man, who usually found coping with the roles of gunner, commander and radio operator too much. Even with that handicap, and the fact that the hull gun had no traverse, the Char B might have been a lot more effective had the numbers available been concentrated, rather than being dispersed in small numbers over a wide area.

MK I TANK (GERMAN) Originally intended to be a training vehicle and armed only with machine guns, the PzKpfw I light tank was used in large numbers by the German army in 1939 and 1940, mainly as a reconnaissance tank but also to make up numbers in armoured formations. Withdrawn from front line service as a tank in 1941, many were modified as self-propelled anti-tank and field guns, command vehicles and carriers. (© IWM MH 8875)

MK III TANK (GERMAN) A highly versatile design, the PzKpfw III remained in service in various modifications throughout the war. Although not many were available for the Battle of France in 1940, they spearheaded the German invasion of Russia in 1941. Despite its small size, compared to later tanks, it had a crew of five (commander, gunner, loader, radio operator and driver). Early versions had a 37mm gun and just over an inch of frontal armour, but as the war went on heavier guns were added and armour thickened. This picture shows Mk IIIs parading through Tripoli in Libya, on 27 March 1941, shortly after Rommel's DAK had arrived in theatre.

Opposite top **MK IV TANK (GERMAN)** Although officially replaced as the standard German army tank by the Mk V Panther in 1943, the PzKpfw IV remained in service until the end of the war and was still regarded with considerable respect by Allied soldiers. A remarkably versatile vehicle, continually improved and up-gunned, even as late as 1944 the year's production total grew to 3225. With a crew of five and a good 75mm gun in its final models it was at least a match for the Sherman. As well as a battle tank there were command vehicle, ammunition carrier, self-propelled gun and tank-destroyer variants.

Opposite below **PANTHER TANK (GERMAN)** The PzKpfw Mk V, or Panther, replaced the Mk IV as the German army's standard main battle tank in 1943, although large numbers of the latter remained in service. Designed to counter the Russian T34, the Panther was rushed into production and initially suffered from being over-engineered and too complex to maintain or repair easily in the field. Once these faults had been rectified, however, the Panther with its sloping armour, powerful 75mm gun and wide tracks was probably the best medium tank of the period. Fortunately for the Allies, the Germans could not produce enough of them to influence the result of the war.

Top **TIGER TANK (GERMAN)** On its first appearance in 1942 the PzKpfw VI, at 56 tons, was the heaviest tank in the world – as heavy as a modern main battle tank. Its main armament was the superb 88mm, developed from the anti-aircraft gun, and the tank was so well armoured that even up to the end of the war there was no Allied tank that could take it on singly. It did have weaknesses – a slow turret traverse and a limited range of 121 miles – but it so put the wind up the Allies that in Normandy virtually any German tank was reported as a Tiger. This picture is a rare example of a Tiger that has been abandoned by its crew just short of the British First Army front line in Tunisia in April 1943. There were only twenty-five Tigers in North Africa, and as there is no obvious battle damage the tank may well have simply run out of fuel. (© IWM NA 2351)

Below **88MM ANTI TANK GUN (GERMAN)** Operated by the Luftwaffe in its anti-aircraft role and by the army as an anti-tank gun, in the latter variant the 88 fired a round that could penetrate 110mm (4½ inches) of armour at a range of 2000 yards. As no British or American tank had that amount of frontal armour, the 88 was a very serious proposition indeed. Its high silhouette made it difficult to conceal unless dug in, but its range and accuracy were such that it was only really at risk from the air. (© Getty Images) were to be French. That day, despite unfavourable seas, 68,014 men were evacuated, 45,000 from the harbour, the largest number of any day of Operation Dynamo. Most of the remaining divisional commanders left that day, as did General Lord Gort, having been ordered to do so by a personal telephone call from the Prime Minister. The senior British officer in the bridgehead was now Major General the Hon. Harold Alexander,[*] who exercised joint command with the French Admiral Abrial, a command that was getting geographically smaller, as with Nieuport now untenable the perimeter was forced in to La Panne.

So far, despite Göring's claim that the Luftwaffe could finish off the BEF, the weather had mainly favoured the British, being cloudy and overcast. Even when it was not, the pall of smoke that emanated from the burning oil-storage tanks in Dunkirk made precise dive-bombing difficult. Another of the myths of Operation Dynamo is that the RAF was ineffective. Army veterans of the evacuation are often shown or quoted as claiming that 'we never saw the RAF'. Of course they never (or rarely) saw the RAF, for if they had then the RAF would not have been doing its job, and that was to keep the Luftwaffe away from the beaches and the ships in the Channel so that the embarkation could continue. This meant meeting the German aircraft inland over France, or well out to sea. While the Luftwaffe did attack the beaches and attack ships in the Channel, they would have been far more effective, and could have halted the evacuation entirely, had not the RAF devoted much of their scarce resources to providing air cover for Dynamo. On 27 May alone the RAF flew 300 sorties in support of the BEF. On 1 June, the worst day for air attacks on the BEF, the RAF mounted eight fighter sweeps, each of three or four squadrons,[**] and destroyed twenty-nine German aircraft, for a loss of thirty-one of their own. Coastal Command aircraft also patrolled, and Bomber Command directed their heavy (for the time) aircraft against road junctions and bridges and advancing German columns.

---

[*] Who, on his promotion to that rank in 1937, at the age of forty-six, was the youngest general in the British Army. Today a major general who had not reached that rank well before that age would be regarded as having missed the career bus.

[**] A squadron had anything from twelve to twenty-four aircraft.

Increasingly, men were being picked up from the beaches rather than the harbour. Soldiers formed queues from the beach out into the water where they were loaded into small boats and taken out to the transport ships for the journey to England. Typical was the cross-Channel ferry *Royal Sovereign* which berthed at the east mole in Dunkirk at 0445 hours on 29 May, loaded its passengers and sailed at 0545 hours, reached Margate at 1215 hours, unloaded its soldiers and was back off the beach at La Panne by 1730 hours. Despite the efforts of the RAF and the Royal Navy itself, there were horror stories. On the same day that *Royal Sovereign* was ploughing backwards and forwards across the Channel, the destroyers HMS *Wakeful* and HMS *Grafton* took on men from the beach at Bray Dunes, and just after midnight joined a minesweeper and a minelayer to sail for England by Route Y (the long one). *Wakeful* was zigzagging at twenty knots when she was torpedoed off a light buoy twenty miles north-east of the coast, where the route turned to head for Goodwin. The ship broke in two and sank in seconds. HMS *Grafton*, the minesweeper HMS *Lydd* and the minelayer HMS *Comfort* began to pick up survivors (of which there were not many) when another torpedo hit *Grafton*. The sinking *Grafton* and the *Lydd* thought *Comfort* was a German E-boat* and opened fire on her, killing most of her crew and the survivors she had picked up. *Lydd* then rammed *Comfort* and sank her.

Inevitably there were soldiers and units that misbehaved. Small boats ferrying troops to the transports were rushed and swamped, some men tried to bribe civilian or merchant navy crews for a place, some men bullied weaker ones for a place in the queue, but in general discipline held, and, as always happens, it was the regiments that were well led and well disciplined in peace that proved to be so in war. Some may have laughed when Guards regiments marched at attention down to the beach with rifles at the slope; but it was the Guards that got all their men aboard ship with their weapons and personal kit in an orderly fashion, when battalions that had been reduced to a rabble (and there were some) did not. One of the more alarming aspects of the evacuation was that only 75 per cent of the troops returned with their personal weapons (rifles and Bren guns).[10]

---

* Called by the British E-boats – E for enemy – and by the Germans Schnellbooten, these were fast motorboats armed with torpedoes, depth charges and guns. The British equivalents were the MTBs and MGBs.

No soldier ever willingly parts with his personal weapon unless there is no alternative short of death, and that up to 50,000 men lost or threw away their rifles in the rush to the beaches is a damning indictment of the state to which British defences had been allowed to deteriorate, leading to a far too rapid expansion of the army in the run-up to war.

In the withdrawal down the corridor there were atrocities. Probably the best known is the shooting of perhaps as many as eighty men of the 2nd Royal Warwicks, Cheshires and Royal Artillery taken prisoner by the Waffen SS on 28 May; but there were others, by both sides. In general the German army, like the British, obeyed the laws of war strictly to the letter, but the SS, a newer organisation not greatly influenced by notions of gentlemanly behaviour, were less punctilious. One British veteran, now dead, told this author that any Germans taken prisoner in ones and twos during the retreat (there were not many) were liable to be shot, as there were insufficient men to make it worthwhile detailing a sentry for only a few prisoners; and there were instances of downed German aircrew being shot as they tried to surrender. These cases, German and British, were not institutionalised, and were carried out at a very low level by NCOs or, occasionally, tolerated by junior officers too frightened or too inexperienced to intervene.

On 1 June General Alexander and Admiral Abrial agreed that daylight evacuation was now getting too dangerous, and that with the Germans getting nearer a final last-ditch perimeter should be formed with all anti-aircraft and anti-tank artillery around the town of Dunkirk. From first light on Sunday 2 June evacuation would be by night only. Ships' crews were now getting very tired, and in many cases merchant navy crews had been replaced by men of the Royal Navy, but on 1 June and up to dawn on 2 June, 64,429 men were evacuated. Alexander had hoped that he could get the last of the British troops off behind a thin French rearguard that night, but it soon became apparent that not all could be taken off before first light. On the night of 2 June another 26,256 were embarked, and on 3 June 26,746, mainly French. A final foray on 4 June took another 26,000 French but many had to be left behind when German shelling increased from about 0330 hours and the operation had to stop. There is debate as to the last ship to leave Dunkirk. It was either the Isle of Man ferry

Tynwald, or the destroyer HMS *Shikari*, or MTB 107, commanded by Lieutenant John Cameron, a future Scottish law lord. The Germans were one and a half miles from the beaches.

NOTES

1. TNA Kew, WO 197/10, 12 L Recce Report French Defences on Belgian French border 14 December 1939.

2. Roderick McLeod & Denis Kelly (eds), *Time Unguarded: The Ironside Diaries 1937–1940*, David McKay, New York, 1962.

3. For the best succinct account of the Arras counter-stroke see Richard Holmes, *Army Battlefield Guide, Belgium and Northern France*, HMSO, London, 1995.

4. Reproduced in Holmes, ibid.

5. Roderick McLeod & Denis Kelly (eds), op. cit.

6. Brian Bond (ed), *Chief of Staff: The Diaries of Lieutenant General Sir Henry Pownall*, Vol. I, Leo Cooper, London, 1972.

7. Quoted in Walter Lord, *The Miracle of Dunkirk*, Allen Lane, London, 1983.

8. Stephen W. Roskill, *The War at Sea 1939–1945*, Vol. I, HMSO, London, 1954.

9. Quoted in Julian Jackson, *The Fall of France*, OUP, Oxford, 2003.

10. Roderick McLeod & Denis Kelly (eds), op. cit.

9

Alone at Last

INCLUDING THE TROOPS evacuated from Dunkirk before the operation proper began, Dynamo brought back to England 366,162 troops, of which all save fewer than 30,000 were carried in British ships.[*] This was an enormous improvement on the 45,000 that Ironside and, initially, Gort thought might be got away, and although nearly all the vehicles and heavy equipment, including guns, light tanks and armoured cars, had to be left behind,[**] a quarter of a million British soldiers and 110,000 French had been taken out of the trap. It was not, however, as is so often and irritatingly alleged, a miracle, nor was it divine deliverance, nor luck, nor due to a fluke of the weather nor because of German incompetence. Neither did it, as the Official History claims, engender 'profound relief and satisfaction', or 'national rejoicing'.[1] Nor should it have: it was an operation of war, and one that only the British could have executed. Only the British could have done it because only the British had a navy which had, as one of its traditional and primary roles, the removal of a small British army from one theatre of war in order to use it somewhere else. From Drake in the West Indies in the 1580s,

[*] The little ships brought back just over 6,000.

[**] Left behind were 2,300 artillery pieces, 7,000 tons of ammunition, 90,000 rifles, 8,000 Bren guns, 400 anti-tank rifles and 120,000 vehicles of all types. Only 310 guns and 2,292 vehicles were brought back.

through the Duke of York at Dunkirk in 1794, Moore at Corunna and Chatham at Walcheren in 1809, to Hamilton at Gallipoli in 1916, the Royal Navy had enabled the British to intervene on land where they wished and then to decamp to fight another day. In May 1943 in Tunisia, on the other hand, a quarter of a million German and Italian troops were taken prisoner. From Tunisia to Sicily is about as far as it is from Dunkirk to England, and yet only about 200 Axis soldiers got away. In 1940 the British were fortunate in that they also had an air force capable (just) of providing the air cover needed to allow the navy to fulfil its task, but the operation was not achieved without considerable cost. During the evacuation the British lost a total of seventy-two ships of all types to enemy action, including six destroyers, another 163 to other causes, and forty-five damaged, including nineteen destroyers.[2] The Royal Air Force flew 3,561 sorties from the UK and lost 145 aircraft, including forty-two Spitfires.[3] More seriously, as many as eighty pilots may have been lost.

The end of Operation Dynamo was not the end of the Battle of France, nor was it the end of Britain's involvement in Europe. Despite evacuation from Dunkirk there were still about 140,000 British troops in France, while evacuation of Norway had only just started, and would go on until 8 June. The British troops left in France south of the River Somme included large numbers of communications, administrative and logistic troops in depots, workshops, and reinforcement centres along the routes from the ports that were not yet in German hands, as well as individuals posted to units of the BEF but who had not yet reached their regiments. Also still in France were 51 (Highland) Division and 1 Armoured Division, the latter without any infantry and less 3 RTR (both squandered at Calais). The units scattered about the lines of communication had already been thinned out, and some of the men evacuated prior to the start of Dynamo. Now what was left was included in yet another ad hoc force of divisional size under Brigadier Beauman (hitherto commanding the northern portion of the lines of communication) and named Beauforce. Also still in France was the RAF less the air component of the BEF, and now consisting of six bomber and three fighter squadrons, increased to five fighter squadrons to assuage British guilty consciences, and with the promise that six more UK-based fighter squadrons would be available to support the French.

The sole British armoured division was originally intended to land at Cherbourg and then make its way to the French tank-training area at Pacy, south of the River Seine and forty miles from Paris. The last elements landed at Cherbourg on 23 May 1940, but lacking its infantry and with its artillery diverted elsewhere, its only support consisted of anti-aircraft artillery (equipped only with the 1915 vintage Lewis light machine gun) and anti-tank artillery with 2-pounders. The division had 134 light tanks and 150 cruisers, but much equipment had not been available when they embarked in England. There were very few radios, a shortage of periscopes and no armour-piercing ammunition. The initial orders given to the division were for it to move north to the Somme and protect the flank of the BEF for the projected Anglo-French attack on 26 May. As the Germans had been at the coast since 20 May, and the infantry was rapidly closing up on the panzers, 1 Armoured Division was now completely cut off from the BEF and the order was outdated and impossible. The division was next told to seize crossings over the Somme (what for, one wonders?) but found the river so strongly held that this too could not be achieved. Next the division was placed under command of the new French Tenth Army, in the process of being formed under General Altmeyer (who despite his name was French), and alerted for an attack on the German positions at Abbeville, on the Somme estuary, on 27 May, when the two brigades of the division were to lead three French mechanised light cavalry divisions. The attack began at 0430 hours 27 May and achieved nothing, largely because the French infantry were unable (or unwilling) to come up and support the tanks once the latter had gone firm. By the end of the day the British had lost sixty-five tanks. On 30 May an attack on Abbeville by de Gaulle's 4th DCR also failed. An attempt by the French corps commander to have the British tanks dispersed all along the French front was vetoed by Major General Evans, commanding 1 Armoured Division, but the British never did get the French to understand that British cruiser tanks were intended for manoeuvre, and lacked the frontal armour either to act as defensive pillboxes or to engage in frontal assaults.

51 (Highland) Division, commanded by Major General Victor Fortune, had been placed with the French on the Maginot Line in the Saarland, in order to give them some experience of operating under French command. When the first half-hearted attacks on the Maginot Line began, 51 Division assisted in repulsing them, and in the normal process of rotation was placed in reserve in the Argonne area. Once it was obvious that the north could not hold, and that the thrust from the Ardennes to the sea could not be cut, the French attempted to hold a new line – the Weygand Line – running from the coast along the course of the Somme and Aisne and then along the Maginot Line. 51 Division was moved by road and rail to the Somme, placed under command of General Altmeyer, and ordered to hold the extreme left of the line, fifteen miles from the sea running south-east to Villers-sur-Mareuil. In front of them was the River Somme and canal, and under command was placed 1 Armoured Division and Beauforce. As a result of its losses in futile attacks on the Abbeville sector, the armoured division was now reorganised, with 2 Armoured Brigade forming one composite regiment which remained to support 51 Division while 3 Armoured Brigade moved back to Rouen to refit.

On 4 June, the day when the last elements of the BEF were being taken off the beaches at Dunkirk, yet another attack was ordered against Abbeville. General Fortune was told to lead it, with two French divisions under command. At first the attack made some progress, with a number of the hamlets and hill features south of Abbeville being captured, but then, on 5 June, phase two of Case Yellow began: the German drive south. With the Somme–Aisne line held far too thinly, and with no reserves behind it, German armour, which had refitted and regrouped remarkably quickly, broke through. The British, pushed back to the line of the River Bresle, fifteen miles from the Somme, were now in grave danger of being cut off. With rather more transport than the rest of the French IX Corps, of which 51 Division was a part, the British could (and perhaps should) have looked after themselves and headed for Le Havre and embarkation. The suspicion in which the British were already held by the French, many of whom considered the Dunkirk evacuation to have been a betrayal, and a consequent wish to present himself as a dependable ally, dissuaded General Fortune from doing this, until it was too late to get to Le Havre anyway. On 8 June Beauforce and 1 Armoured Division were withdrawn south of the Seine, and on the same day 51 Division was ordered to withdraw fifty miles to that river over the next four days. By this time German tanks had entered Rouen, and any withdrawal to the Seine was impossible. Fortune decided to go for Le Havre, and sent off an advance party to protect the port and prepare it for evacuation. This was yet another ad hoc formation, consisting of his own 154 Brigade and one of Beauforce's brigades, to be called Ark Force. The force reached Le Havre but the German 5 and 7 Panzer Divisions, spearheads of Rundstedt's Army Group A, having taken Rouen, were now haring north-west for the coast, right across the proposed line of 51 Division's withdrawal.

Since Dieppe was mined and blocked (by the British), this left as the only possible port of embarkation the tiny harbour at St Valery en Caux, half way between Dieppe and Fécamp. The French IX Corps and Fortune's 51 Division began to move into St Valery on 11 June, and standing by offshore was the Royal Navy with nine destroyers and transports. Unfortunately for Fortune, it was on that same day that Rommel's tanks forced the high ground overlooking St Valery harbour. The navy did its best. Ark Force was taken off from Le Havre but at St Valery two destroyers were hit by German artillery from the clifftops while trying to take troops on board. More and more German guns came up, the Luftwaffe began targeting ships, and when thick fog came in from the sea it became impossible to carry out an evacuation of any significance that night. Fortune hoped that he might get his men away the following night, but on the morning of 12 June a forest of white flags was flying – the French had surrendered. Fortune tried to fight on but when a written order arrived from the French corps commander, General Ihler, he too surrendered. The vast majority of the division went into captivity.

Two days before 51 Division's surrender at St Valery, on 10 June, the French government left Paris and Italy entered the war on the German side, having waited until there seemed no doubt as to who would win the war. The RAF's AASF was still in France and was instructed to bomb

Italian military targets. The Allied Supreme War Council was meeting the next day, and at about 2100 hours 11 June an incandescent Air Marshal Barratt telephoned Major General Ismay, at dinner with the members of the council, to tell him that the French at Salon would not allow the RAF bombers to take off. Ismay reported this to Churchill, who tackled Reynaud and Weygand, who insisted that this was clearly a misunderstanding and would be corrected forthwith. Ismay was woken at 0400 hours by a now apoplectic Barratt who reported that the French had driven farm carts onto the runway to make absolutely sure that the bombers could not get into the air.[4] Regardless of what their Prime Minister might order, the French armed forces were too frightened of Italian retaliation to allow any bombing from French soil.*

Still Churchill harboured ideas of continuing to fight in Europe. There were only three divisions left in England, and these were not fully equipped, but two would be sent to France through Cherbourg, to where the remnants of 1 Armoured Division was withdrawing. 52 Division, a first-line Territorial Army division recruited from the Scottish Lowlands, was embarked and it was decided as well to send 1 Canadian Division, which had been in England since the end of 1939, too. There was much nonsense talked by the French about a national redoubt in Brittany, and Churchill thought that a second BEF would stiffen French morale and keep them in the war, despite all the glaring evidence to the contrary. Again, he should never have been allowed to get away with it. Ismay, his chief of staff, Dill the CIGS and Ironside, now Commander Home Forces, were all against it, but the Prime Minister would brook no opposition and insisted that Britain could not let down the French. That the French generals had now lost control over their men, the Germans had broken the Weygand Line and the Maginot Line had been outflanked made no impression. The man who would command this second BEF was Lieutenant General Sir Alan Brooke, who had commanded II Corps of the BEF. He was knighted by the King at Buckingham Palace on 11 June and left that same day for France, arriving at Cherbourg in the late evening. He met Weygand in Orléans on 14 June. Weygand told Brooke that 'the

---

* The RAF did mange to raid Genoa on the night of 15–16 June and Genoa and Milan the following night from Salon, to little effect other than to put the wind up the Italians.

French army had ceased to be able to offer organised resistance and was disintegrating into disconnected groups. That Paris had been given up and that he had no reserves whatever left...'

Brooke was well aware that what he had been asked to do was no more than a futile political gesture, and what he had seen and heard in his few days back in France confirmed that opinion. He telephoned the CIGS and found that his views were fully agreed and that Dill had already ordered the embarkation of troops for Cherbourg to stop. Churchill took a bit more persuasion, but Brooke was able to order all British troops in France (and there were still around 100,000 of the original BEF, mostly administrators and logisticians) to fall back on ports not yet in German hands. Between 15 and 18 June, in Operation Ariel – the second evacuation from France – the Royal Navy lifted 30,630 men from Cherbourg, 21,474 from St Malo, 28,145 British and 4,439 Allied (Poles and Czechs who did not consider themselves bound to remain under French orders) from Brest, 54,471 British and 2,764 Allied from St Nazaire and Nantes, and 2,303 British and 2,000 Poles from La Pallice, while the RAF provided air cover. 1 Armoured Division, reduced to just fourteen A13 cruisers and twelve light tanks, embarked on the last ships to leave Cherbourg on 18 June, just before Rommel's panzers, which had covered 150 miles in one day through enemy territory, stormed into the port.

Apart from the loss of 3,000 men drowned on 17 June when the *Lancastria* was hit by a German air attack in Quiberon Bay, caught fire and sank, and the accidental ramming of the Canadian destroyer *Fraser* by HMS *Calcutta*, Operation Ariel produced remarkably few casualties. Even then the rescue efforts did not stop, for until the French surrender the navy continued to lift isolated groups of soldiers, RAF ground crew and British civilians and consular and diplomatic staff from ports all the way down to the Spanish border, and that was followed by the removal of all men of military age from the Channel Islands, over 22,000 in all. In a mere twenty-eight days the Royal Navy, with the Royal Air Force flying fighter cover, had lifted well over half a million men from a coastline 1,200 miles long, against the efforts of a determined German air force and the best army in the world, and they had delivered the overwhelming majority of them safe and sound in England.

On 14 June the German army entered Paris, and the French government headed for Bordeaux. On 15 June the RAF's AASF left France. On 16 June Reynaud resigned as Prime Minister in favour of Pétain and Churchill made his offer of an indissoluble Anglo-French union. This being declined, on 17 June Pétain asked for an armistice, and on 22 June France surrendered.

If Norway had shown up British unpreparedness and incompetence, then the Battle of France underlined it, but in a less obvious way. The British contribution to the land battle – the BEF – was derisory in numerical strength and was at no stage able to direct the course of events. All it could do was act as an appendage to the French army and fall in with whatever strategy the senior partner tried to implement. The British lost 9,524 men killed between 10 May and 18 June 1940, the French ten times more. In addition, by the time of the surrender, two million Frenchmen were prisoners of war. To understand why the Battle of France was such an overwhelming German victory in such a short time one must look at German successes and their corollaries, French failures. The Germans knew that they had to win quickly, and once Case Yellow had been amended by Manstein (and, to be fair, Hitler) they had the plan to do it. They had a plan in 1914 too, but this time they also had the means – ground support aircraft, armoured and motorised divisions, excellent communications. Above all, the Germans, despite the unprecedented expansion of their armed forces between 1933 and 1940, had instilled into their officers the need for 'hot planning' and a flexibility that enabled them to regroup and find a way round, over or through whatever obstacles were placed in their way. German commanders were well forward, engineers up with the leading echelons, and the momentum was never allowed to slacken. Contrary to Allied propaganda, Germans were not mere automatons slavishly following orders, but encouraged, indeed required, to use their own discretion when the situation changed.

The French had entirely failed to appreciate the tempo of modern warfare. Far too many of their generals, raised in the reflected glory of Foch and Pétain, still thought that war could only be fought when the entire orchestra had been assembled and tuned up; they saw little difference between spring 1918, when the great German offensive had at last run out of steam, and 1940, when it would surely do the same. They had utterly failed to appreciate that advances in the air, and the advent of reliable mechanical transport and portable battlefield radio, had made everything happen far more quickly than it had in the First War. Now that the initiative was constantly with the attacker, they could only react, and by the time they were ready to do so, it was far too late and the battle had moved on. The French had many tanks and some of them were very good, but while the Germans had understood the need to concentrate armour and use it to punch through the defensive shell, the French, despite the number of their armoured divisions, far too often spread their tanks out to bolster up a defence line, diluting and rendering useless their shock effect. The French never believed that a major attack would be developed through the Ardennes, thinking it would take much too long, and when it did erupt across the Meuse on 13 May they were too slow, too bemused and too inflexible to stop it, and were never able to coordinate their forces effectively to cut off the panzer corridor once it developed.

French units varied enormously in quality. General René Prioux's mechanised cavalry corps fought well, as did de Gaulle's 4th DCR armoured division, but one division could do little unless supported, which his was not. Some of the reserve divisions, particularly the older Territorials, were ill-equipped, badly led and of low morale. When things began to turn against them they disintegrated. On the other hand, during the second phase of Yellow, when the Germans headed south, some French units fought with great determination, but were simply bypassed and cut off by German thrusts through less stubborn divisions on their flanks. The Maginot Line was not quite the white elephant that has been portrayed; when it was attacked from the east it generally held out, but it could only have been a fully effective means of defence if it had continued through Belgium, or around Belgium to the sea. As it was, once the Germans attacked from the north, the Line was outflanked and of no further use.

There was never anything that the BEF could have done to prevent the collapse. The French did not want British soldiers, except as a statement of British intent; they wanted British aircraft and those they could not have, or not in the quantities they would have liked. The British were never in a position, with their meagre three corps and a very late arriving armoured division, to influence the campaign. Even if the Arras counter-stroke had been competently conducted – which it was not – it could never have been more than an irritating flea-bite on the German flank; and the attacks on the Somme by 1 Armoured Division were much too late and in too little strength to achieve anything. That division should either have been sent across a month earlier (which was impossible as it was only then in the process of formation) or not at all, and the notion of a second BEF was complete Churchillian pie in the sky that should have been stopped dead in its tracks by the CIGS. The only occasion when Lord Gort did use his discretion (or to be accurate, disobey orders) was when he decided to send two divisions to plug the gap between the BEF and the Belgians, on the British left flank, rather than send those same divisions south on a French frolic that would have wasted them to no avail. By doing what he did, Gort ensured that the men of the BEF got back to the coast to be taken off by the navy, and he deserved more credit for it than he ever received.

The removal of British forces from France exacerbated French suspicions. Most Frenchmen saw it as a betrayal, and German propaganda played on the animosity and bitterness evident during the evacuation. At one stage General Fagalde (who had ordered that there must be no evacuation from Calais) threatened to use French troops to stop the British embarking.[6] Before the evacuation had even started the view of the new CIGS, Dill, was that the failure of the French army had cost the loss of the BEF. The Battle of France was indeed lost by the French, not the British, but the shortage of British equipment – particularly radios – the lack of combined arms training, the lack of tanks in quantity, the inability to provide close air support in time, the refusal by Churchill to allow the garrison of Calais to embark, and Fortune's misplaced loyalty to a defeated ally in not removing his division to the coast and home when it was possible, all lead to the inescapable conclusion that the little the BEF did do was not done well. Even British generals had little experience of handling anything larger than a brigade in the field, and at regimental level the pre-war army was so short of men that companies were often no bigger than platoons. Politicians did not realise that it is one thing to expand an army by finding more manpower, and quite another to equip it. Even given the equipment, it is necessary for it to train, and the BEF had been too busy building pillboxes along the Belgian frontier to carry out much realistic training.

It has been suggested that British commanders were too old and too set in their ways to cope with modern warfare. In a small professional army promotion is inevitably slow, and it is true that British generals were older than their equivalents today, when the retirement age is younger than it was then. The two officers who held the appointment of CIGS during the period, Ironside at sixty and Dill at fifty-nine, were getting on a bit, but their German equivalent, von Brauchitsch, was fifty-nine too. The Commander-in-Chief of the BEF, Gort, was fifty-four, but German army commanders List, at sixty, and Kluge at fifty-eight, were older. Brooke as a corps commander was fifty-seven, but von Kleist was fifty-nine. The oldest British divisional commanders were Herbert (23 Division) at sixty, followed by Ransome (46 Division) and Fortune (51 Division), who were both fifty-seven, while the youngest were Holmes (42 Division) at forty-eight and Alexander (1 Division), Lloyd (2 Division) and Roberts (48 Division) who were all forty-nine. Of the German divisional commanders Kirchner (1 Panzer) was fifty-five, Schaal (10 Panzer) fifty-one and Rommel (7 Panzer) was forty-nine. It would seem that age was irrelevant; what mattered was mental agility.

The surrender of France posed two immediate problems for the British: the presence of around 120,000 French troops evacuated during Dynamo and Ariel, and the French fleet. International law required that soldiers of a warring nation that ceased to be at war had to be repatriated if they so wished. The British rather hoped that most of the French troops now in England would volunteer to stay on and fight the Germans in a Free French Army under British direction and commanded by General de Gaulle, who had been in England since 18 June and who had already been allowed the use of the BBC to broadcast to France. Unfortunately the vast majority of the French troops removed to England by the Royal Navy (and a few by the French navy too) had not the slightest interest in carrying on the war, and elected to be returned to France. Only around 4,000 opted for de Gaulle, and 1,500 for the Free French navy, under Admiral Muselier, while all the rest were repatriated (with their personal possessions but without their military equipment) in French merchant ships. While one may have some sympathy with French conscripts who had witnessed their nation's utter defeat and who wanted to see their families again, it is hard to argue with those members of the Royal Navy who wondered why they had risked life, limb and ship to take them away from France in the first place.

The French navy in 1940 was a powerful force, and although it had played little part in the Battle of France it could, if used against the British, tip the naval balance in Germany's favour. At or before the surrender many French warships in home ports had sailed; some to England, some to British ports abroad and many to ports in French colonial North Africa. By the terms of the armistice with Germany, all French warships then at sea or in ports outside France were to sail to German or Italian ports. Apart from those ships needed to defend French colonies, and for minesweeping along the coast of France, the French navy was to be demobilised and ships manned by reduced crews. The Germans and Italians undertook not to make use of those ships in the prosecution of the war. To the British there were two risks; first, the Germans might not keep their promise, or would find some breach of the armistice conditions by the French that would allow them to claim that it was no longer valid; and second, that France, whose government was now established at Vichy under Marshal Pétain with the Anglophobe Pierre Laval as Deputy Prime Minister, might re-enter the war on the German side. Furthermore, with Italy now in the war and France out of it, the balance of naval power in the Mediterranean had already shifted, and must be restored to Britain's advantage.

Before anything could be done about the French fleet, British naval mastery of the western Mediterranean had to be re-established, and on 28 June Force H, based on Gibraltar, came into being. It consisted of the aircraft carrier *Ark Royal*, the battleships *Valiant* and *Resolution*, the battlecruiser *Hood*, one light cruiser and four destroyers, under the command of Vice Admiral Sir James Somerville, who flew his flag in the *Hood*. Although Somerville's base was to be Gibraltar, headquarters of the Flag Officer North Atlantic, a full admiral, Somerville did not come under the command of that officer but reported directly to the Admiralty. The existence of Force H, while it did not entirely redress the imbalance of the removal of the French fleet and the addition of the Italian quantitatively, did a great deal qualitatively, and whilst the Royal Navy would suffer many losses in men and ships in the Mediterranean in the years ahead, it never lost control of the Straits of Gibraltar, nor a strong, if not always overwhelming, presence in the western Mediterranean.

Now something could be done about the French fleet. In UK ports at the surrender were two French battleships, five destroyers, seven torpedo boats and a number of smaller craft, and in Alexandria, headquarters of the British Mediterranean Fleet, were the French battleship *Lorraine*, four cruisers and a number of escort and support ships. The rest of the French navy was outside British control. Two brand-new French battleships, *Jean Bart* at Casablanca in Morocco, and *Richelieu* at Dakar in Senegal, could by themselves alter the whole course of the war in the Atlantic, quite apart from the risk posed by those French bases should they fall into the hands of the Germans, when they could cut the British route to the Middle East round the Cape. In the Mediterranean there were two modern battlecruisers, *Dunkerque* and *Strasbourg*, two old battleships including the *Provence*, a seaplane carrier and six destroyers at Mers-el-Kebir in Algeria; next door in Oran were seven destroyers and four submarines. In Algiers were six cruisers, while in the French port of Toulon lay another four cruisers. Both Pétain and Admiral Darlan, Commander-in-Chief of his navy, had several times assured the British that no French warship would be allowed to pass into German or Italian hands. Not unnaturally, the British placed little reliance on the good faith of either man, and in any case the Germans had already showed their ability to mount lightning *coups de main* to seize what they wanted. Even if the British had known of Darlan's instructions to the captains of French ships that in the event of an attempted take-over by Germans or Italians they were to sail to American ports or in the last resort scuttle, it would have made little difference. The British can be a ruthless people *in extremis*, and neither the government nor the chiefs of staff shrunk from what they were now prepared to do: sink the French fleet.

On 29 June the Admiralty (actually Churchill, whose poodle A. V. Alexander, the First Lord of the Admiralty, was) informed Commander-in-Chief Mediterranean Fleet, Admiral Sir Andrew Cunningham, Flag Officer North Atlantic, Admiral Sir Dudley North and Commander Force H that the French in Mediterranean and North African ports were to be given four options followed by one alternative. They could either:

> Throw in their lot with the British and continue the war with them, either as part of the Royal Navy or the Free French Navy,
>
> or
>
> Sail their ships to British ports with reduced crews,
>
> or
>
> Sail to French West Indian ports with reduced crews,
>
> or
>
> Scuttle their ships.

If none of the options offered was acceptable to the French they could be offered the last chance alternative of 'demilitarising' their ships, that is of making the guns incapable of being fired and of discharging fuel, in their present berths, provided that such action was completed to British satisfaction within six hours, and that it rendered the ships incapable of being repaired in under a year. Should the French still refuse to cooperate then the British were to sink them.

In 1801 and again in 1807 the British had presented the same stark choices to Denmark, a small neutral nation that was inherently pro-British. The Danes refused to comply and the British government ordered their fleet destroyed to prevent it falling into the hands of the French. On those occasions both Admiral Parker (1801) and Admiral Gambier (1807) protested that what they were being asked to do infringed professional naval honour. In 1807, too, Major General Sir Arthur Wellesley (later the First Duke of Wellington) thought the whole thing distasteful. In the end orders are orders and on both occasions the Danish ships were sunk, burned to the waterline, or boarded and taken back to England. In 1940, too, the three admirals expressed their disapproval, although only

Admiral North actually sent a letter of protest after the event, and his career suffered for it.

In Alexandria patient and diplomatic discussions between Admiral Cunningham and the French Admiral Godfroy eventually resulted in the French ships being rendered unusable, without bloodshed. On 3 July Force H sailed for Mers-el-Kebir, and ahead of it went a destroyer carrying Captain C. S. Holland RN with the ultimatum for the French. At first the French Admiral Gensoul refused to see Holland, but when he did he asked for time to consider. Gensoul signalled the Vichy Admiralty to the effect that he had been given six hours to sink his ships or the British would use force. Presented like that, Vichy could hardly do otherwise than tell Gensoul to refuse, although it is difficult to see how, even if Gensoul had signalled the full terms of the British ultimatum, once Vichy had been asked for instructions, the French government could do other than order resistance. Force H mined the entrance to the harbour and, having extended the time limit for French compliance, Admiral Somerville opened fire at 1745 hours. The *Bretagne* blew up, the *Dunkerque* ran aground and the *Provence* and a number of smaller ships were seriously damaged. *Strasbourg* and five destroyers got out of the harbour and back to Toulon, despite the best efforts of the Swordfish torpedo bombers from *Ark Royal*. In all forty-seven French officers and 1,250 sailors were killed, and another 351 wounded. Somerville called it 'a filthy job', and Cunningham a 'ghastly error'.[7] On 7 July the *Richelieu* was immobilised in Dakar by attacks from British carrier aircraft and motor torpedo boats, at the cost of another 154 dead Frenchmen, but she was not sunk nor her guns rendered useless. French ships in British ports were boarded and seized without loss of life, and French warships in the West Indies made no attempt to return to France. On 12 July the British announced that they would take no further action against French ships.

All three British admirals involved were convinced to their dying day that force was unnecessary, and that negotiation could have brought the French navy over to the Allied cause, or at least persuaded it to immobilise its ships. The Vichy government ordered an air raid against Gibraltar – which had little effect – and broke off diplomatic relations, but stopped short of a declaration of war. The French navy have never forgiven Britain for what they consider to have been an act of the basest treachery, and de Gaulle in his memoirs accused the British public and parliament of glorying in it – which was at least partly true. The Germans, eager to capitalise on yet another demonstration of Albion's perfidy, suspended the clause in the armistice requiring French naval demobilisation, and released French naval prisoners of war.

The sinking of the French fleet at Mers-el-Kebir may or may not have been necessary, but it was at least efficiently done, which was not the case in the next naval encounter with the Vichy French – Operation Menace – when Churchill allowed himself to be persuaded by General de Gaulle that a landing in Dakar would deliver Senegal into the hands of the Allies. On 29 August 1940 two British battleships, the *Barham* and the *Resolution*, the aircraft carrier *Ark Royal*, three cruisers, ten destroyers and three sloops of the Free French navy, escorting six transports in which were embarked 4,200 British and 2,700 Free French soldiers and marines, set off from Scapa Flow, the Clyde and Liverpool, the whole jointly commanded by Vice Admiral J. H. D. Cunningham (no relation to Sir Andrew Cunningham, Commander-in-Chief Mediterranean Fleet) and Major General M. N. S. Irwin and including de Gaulle in person. They arrived at Freetown in Sierra Leone, 500 miles south of Dakar, and were reinforced from Force H at Gibraltar.

There was, however, a snag. The Vichy French, concerned lest Chad's opting for de Gaulle would trigger wholesale defections by the French African colonies, had obtained permission from the German–Italian Armistice Commission to send ships from Toulon to stiffen the resolve of the Vichy authorities overseas. This fleet, of three cruisers and three destroyers, sailed through the Straits of Gibraltar on 11 September, and was noted and reported by the Royal Navy but not intercepted. The French docked first in Casablanca, and by the time that the British had obtained agreement from the Admiralty to blockade them there, they had slipped out. One was persuaded to return to Casablanca but two docked in Dakar. This now put a different complexion on the whole affair, and on 16 September orders came to cancel the operation. Cunningham and Irwin, however, egged on by de Gaulle, protested that the landing could still take place, and after some debate at home the two commanders were told that they should do 'what they thought best to give effect to the original purpose of the expedition'.[8]

On the morning of 23 September, in thick mist, the expedition arrived off Dakar. The plan was for Free French intermediaries to be landed on the airfield, and others to be put ashore to try to convince the Vichy officials that they should declare for de Gaulle. The landing at the airfield was prevented and the landed emissaries had also to beat a hasty retreat. The French would defend Dakar. Hostilities opened mid morning when the mist cleared slightly and one of the French forts opened fire on a Royal Navy destroyer, followed by all the shore batteries opening up on the ships. Cunningham replied with a short bombardment, but no doubt mindful of the historic difficulties ships have always had in duelling with shore-based guns, soon ceased fire, with one of his cruisers and two destroyers hit. It was now decided, in view of the antagonism of the French and the lack of visibility for artillery spotting and aircraft reconnaissance, to postpone the landing at Dakar but to land the Free French ten miles east of the port instead. At this stage communications between Cunningham and de Gaulle broke down, the transports carrying the Free French could not be found in the mist and when eventually at around 1700 hours a mini-landing took place it was stoutly repelled with some Allied casualties.

Eventually, at around 2345 hours, an ultimatum to the Dakar officials was broadcast demanding surrender of the port to the Allies by 0600 hours the following morning. At 0400 hours the governor of Dakar radioed an unqualified refusal, and the British ships prepared to bombard. A French submarine was sunk but again the mist prevented either effective bombardment or attack by carrier aircraft, while not affecting the capability of the French ships, including the *Richelieu* – attacked but not disarmed in July – to hit British ships, the situation being made worse by the French laying down a smokescreen across the harbour. The fleet withdrew, to resume the bombardment in the afternoon but with little success. The two commanders now agreed with de Gaulle that the next day, 25 September, the fleet would try to put the French ships in the harbour out of action and land the British troops. Once again the bombardment had little effect, while the French were scoring hits on Royal

Navy ships. It was clear that there was not the slightest chance of the port being given up, and this concentration of British ships could not stay in the area for much longer – they were needed to return to other duties. Cunningham, Irwin and de Gaulle agreed to abandon the operation and send the troops back to England. Operation Menace had been a total failure. Not only had British intelligence overestimated the level of support for de Gaulle in Dakar, but the Free French in England were a security nightmare. Nothing told them was ever safe from the Germans for long, not because the Free French contained German agents but because they could not keep their mouths shut. Careless talk, or letters home via neutral countries, might give away anything they were entrusted with, and as time went on the Free French were told less and less, to de Gaulle's increasing irritation. When the fleet for Menace left England in August there was a very good chance that they could take Dakar. By late September Vichy was well aware what was up and the chance had passed. The chief casualty was Admiral Sir Dudley North, Flag Officer Gibraltar, who was sacked for failing to prevent the French fleet from passing through the Straits.[*]

In Britain, with France fallen and the BEF bustled out of Europe, the hunt for the guilty began. Gort was appointed Inspector General of Training for the Home Guard (a non-job), and Ironside promoted to Field Marshal and told to retire, to be replaced by Brooke as Commander-in-Chief Home Forces. The First Sea Lord, Pound, who had disappointed his fellow admirals by not standing up to Churchill, remained in post for that very reason – although, in fairness, he was probably already suffering from the brain tumour that was to kill him three years later. As the Battle of France had to be painted to the British public as 'an unbeaten army brought back to fight again', the errors and the lessons could not be publicly admitted, but the army, in particular, knew where some of the faults lay, and began to try to put them right, ranging from the method of officer selection to the establishment of radio sets.

* Despite the fact that Britain was not at war with Vichy France and that North's instructions from the Admiralty were vague and contradictory. His previous protest about the Mers-el-Kebir caper did not help his chances, and he was refused an official inquiry into his removal. Most naval officers at the time, and naval historians since, thought he was unfairly treated.

Despite the polemic of the time, which portrayed plucky Britain as the only country standing up to the German and Italian bullies, Britain was not, of course, alone. She had the resources of a very considerable Empire, and the friendship of the President of the United States. The only part of the Empire that had an army of any size was India, an all-volunteer professional force very like the British but without the latter's pre-war recruiting difficulties, and which would remain all-volunteer throughout the war. Indian animal transport units of the Royal Indian Army Service Corps had fought in the Battle of France, there because the hard winter of 1939–40 made it difficult for the all-mechanised British army to supply some of its units along narrow, muddy or frozen tracks, and mules had to be employed instead. An Indian division was already in Egypt and another was on the way. The pre-war armed forces of Canada, Australia, New Zealand and South Africa were tiny, but once war was realised to be inevitable they had begun to expand. A Canadian division had been in England since the end of 1939, a second started to arrive in May 1940, and that same month the Canadian government began to form a third division and mobilised the infantry of a fourth. An Australian division and the leading elements of a New Zealand one had arrived in Egypt in February 1940; in March the Australian government agreed to form a second for overseas service, and in May a third.

Britain had also acquired the Norwegian and Dutch merchant navies, and the assets of those French colonies that had adhered to de Gaulle. It was intended to establish a Polish division and Dutch, Belgian and Norwegian brigades in the UK. All these were, in due time, formed, but another of Churchill's wheezes, the formation of a British Foreign Legion of anti-Nazi Germans, never came to fruition, largely because there were very few anti-Nazi Germans, and those that did exist were either too old or too unfit to become soldiers. The few that were capable of military service were put in the Auxiliary Pioneer Corps, where they undertook labouring duties well away from danger. This was probably just as well, as had they been captured by the Germans they would, perfectly lawfully, have been tried for treason and executed.

President Roosevelt wanted the British to win; or rather, he did not want the Germans to. He bent the laws of neutrality as far as he possibly could to assist the British, despite the advice of his Secretary of State Cordell Hull, who wanted the British to be persuaded to move their fleet to America to prevent it falling into German hands when Britain was forced to make peace. Neither did he heed the US ambassador to Britain, Joseph Kennedy (father of J. F. Kennedy), who was anti-British, hoped for a German victory and continually gave it as his opinion that Britain would lose; nor the American ambassador to France, William C. Bullet, who was convinced that Britain's refusal to send more aircraft to Europe was because she was conserving her navy and air force as bargaining chips in eventual peace negotiations with Germany. Roosevelt helped the British not for any love of them, nor, despite what Churchill felt and hoped, because there was any 'special relationship' between the English-speaking peoples, but simply because he recognised that it was not in the American interest for Germany to dominate Europe, for if she did there would come an inevitable confrontation with the United States. Defence spending in America was tiny and the majority of the President's countrymen did not share his views. Until they did, Roosevelt was limited in what he could do, and ensured that the British paid a high price for what they received, but until America herself came into the war, Britain and Canada absorbed half of all American arms production.

In Germany the overwhelming success of Case Yellow, and the speed at which victory in the Battle of France had been achieved, surprised government and armed forces alike. German casualties were light; 27,000 soldiers and 453 sailors killed, although the figure of 2,668 dead airmen, nearly all of them aircrew, was more serious. The terms of the armistice with France were deliberately mild, in order to detach France from Britain and dissuade her from carrying on the war from French overseas possessions. France was to remain as a state with its own government and institutions, only the north-west and the coastal strip was to be occupied, the French armed forces would demobilise but their ships and aircraft would remain French. Certain frontier adjustments would be made – such as Alsace-Lorraine, which had once been German anyway – but the French colonies would not be annexed.

In the aftermath of the French surrender, it was intended to reduce

Map 7 German Expansion in Europe

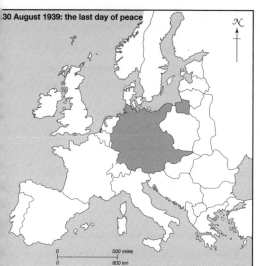

30 August 1939: the last day of peace

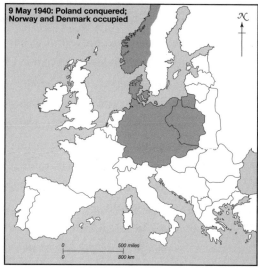

9 May 1940: Poland conquered; Norway and Denmark occupied

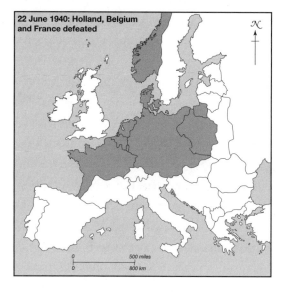

22 June 1940: Holland, Belgium and France defeated

the German war-strength army from the existing 160 divisions to 120 divisions, including twenty armoured and ten motorised, with a large increase in artillery units. Staff work also began on a peacetime army of sixty-two divisions, twenty-six to be infantry, twenty armoured, ten motorised and six mountain. At the same time, priority for production was ordered to be switched from the army to the navy and the air force. As the instructions to double the number of armoured divisions in the army from ten to twenty and to give priority to the other two services were contradictory, Hitler next ordered that the three priorities should be the Junkers 88 programme (a twin-engine bomber for the Luftwaffe), submarine construction and the equipping of mobile troops.

There was still, of course, the matter of Britain. The options for the elimination of Britain were persuasion, invasion, or starvation. For a while Hitler still hoped for persuasion; the German press was instructed not to be too stridently anti-British, and to peddle the line that all Germany wanted was for Britain not to interfere in continental Europe. By August, however, it had become increasingly apparent that Britain was not going to accept a compromise peace, and Hitler, with an eye now to the east as well, cancelled his instructions for a reduction of the army and demanded that it should be increased to 180 divisions. Persuasion having failed, next came invasion. The Army high command had been toying with the idea since late May, and Halder mused about fog in the Channel; cliffs at Beachy Head, Dungeness and Dover; the possibility of concentrating 1,500 motor boats; the use of Rhine barges; railway ferries to carry tanks, and airborne landings in support. The Army Ordnance Office reported that they could modify 100 Mk III and twenty Mk IV tanks to make them amphibious, and the operations branch thought that the first wave of any invasion should be six picked divisions supported by four armoured battalions.

At this stage talk of invasion was theoretical discussion only; Hitler did not want it except as a last resort, the army was dubious, the navy worried and even the Luftwaffe, keener than the other two services, had doubts. On 30 June Major General Alfred Jodl, head of the operations branch at OKW, submitted a paper in which he proposed that the defeat of Britain should be undertaken by the German navy and air force.

Between them they would destroy the RAF, mount terror raids on civilian targets, strangle the British economy and cut off her seaborne trade. In addition, peripheral attacks on the Empire would be mounted by appealing to those who had most to gain by its dissolution. Spain would be encouraged to attack Gibraltar, and Italy the Suez Canal. Hitler rejected the plan. He did not want terror raids at this stage because he still hoped that a wedge might be driven between the British people and their government, and he thought that the instability created by the destruction of the British Empire would not be in Germany's long-term interests. Finally he realised that, for the present at least, naval resources were insufficient for a campaign against British seaborne trade to produce results in the immediate future.

Even when the armed forces were instructed by Hitler on 16 July to prepare a plan for an invasion of England – Operation Sea Lion – Hitler emphasised that it was a last resort. The army could provide the men, and the amphibious tanks, and the air force the parachute and glider borne troops, but the main difficulty lay with the navy, which had not yet come up with suitable transport for the leading wave of troops, and which was very concerned about the air threat. All were agreed that a sine qua non for a successful invasion was air superiority over the Channel. OKW's first plan for Sea Lion envisaged the invasion fleet sailing from ports between Ostend and Cherbourg, and landing between Margate and Weymouth, later amended to between Folkestone and Worthing. Given the difficulties in reconciling the differing requirements of the three services, the date for Sea Lion was tentatively fixed for mid August, and then, after objections by the navy, which thought it could not be attempted until May 1941 at the earliest, to mid September. After that the weather would render any attempt at a Channel crossing too risky. In the meantime, the Luftwaffe must obtain air superiority.

In the Führer Directive for the Conduct of the War 16, amplified by Directive 17 dated 1 August 1940, the Luftwaffe was instructed to target as its prime objectives RAF flying units, ground installations and supply organisations; and the British aircraft industry, including those plants manufacturing anti-aircraft weapons and equipment. Initially targets would be RAF Fighter Command units and installations within the range of the German Messerschmitt 110 fighter, which meant southern England, after which bombers could attack airfields used by the RAF to bomb German industry, which they had been doing since the night of 15–16 May. Ports and ships could also be attacked, but harbours in the south and south-east were to be left alone – they would be needed for landing the German army. The Luftwaffe could drop mines, but again not along the south coast; London was out of bounds and, at least for the time being, there were to be no night attacks and civilian losses were to be avoided if at all possible. The Luftwaffe (and the RAF) correctly realised that RAF Fighter Command would have to be dealt with first, for only if the British fighter threat could be eliminated could German bombers attack major targets on the ground. What is surprising is that little emphasis was placed on knocking out the British Radio Direction Finding stations along the south coast – Chain Home, or radar.[*] The Germans certainly knew about them, as Göring, Commander-in-Chief of the Luftwaffe and newly promoted to Reichsmarschall,[**] mentioned them as targets in a telephone call to his air fleet commanders in early August, but the full significance of these stations does not seem to have been appreciated.

To carry out the destruction of the RAF and obtain air superiority over the Channel and southern England to facilitate a landing, the Luftwaffe could deploy two air fleets (Luftflotte) in France and one in Norway. In France, and facing the south and south-east coasts of England were Luftflotte 2 commanded by Field Marshal Albrecht Kesselring, and Luftflotte 3 under Field Marshal Hugo Sperrle, both promoted to that rank in July. Between them and available for operations they disposed of 227 twin-engine fighters and fighter-bombers, 703 single-engine fighters, 316 dive-bombers and 875 long-range bombers. In Norway General Hans-Jurgen Stumpf's Luftflotte 5 had thirty-four twin-engine fighters and 123 long-range bombers.

---

[*] Until the middle of the war it was known as Radio Direction Finding, and then Radio Direction and Ranging (RADAR).

[**] A tri-service rank, one above *Generalfeldtmarschall*, or Field Marshal, for which there is no British equivalent. There had only been one previous holder of the rank, Prince Eugen of Savoy, Marlborough's partner in the War of the Spanish Succession against the French in the early 18th Century. Eugen had earned it.

To confront the German air assault RAF Fighter Command could field fifty-two squadrons: nineteen of Spitfires, twenty-five of Hurricanes, two of Defiants and six of Blenheims. The establishment of fighters was 800, of which 600 were actually available; and of pilots 1,456, of whom 1,259 were available. As the aircraft that actually mattered in the forthcoming contest were the fighters, the German Messerschmitt 109 and 110, and the British Hurricane and Spitfire, a comparison may be useful:

TYPE	DATE FIRST IN SERVICE	MAX SPEED	CEILING	RATE OF CLIMB	RANGE	WEAPONS	NUMBER AVAILABLE
Me 109 single engine	1938	350 mph	34,450 ft	2,981 ft per minute	410 miles	3 x 20mm cannon 2 x 7.9mm machine guns	703
Me 110 twin engine	1939	325 mph	32,800 ft	2,150 ft per minute	680 miles	2 x 20mm cannon 5 x 7.9mm machine guns	261
Hurricane single engine	1938	310 mph	33,400 ft	2,353 ft per minute	525 miles	8 x .303 machine guns	288
Spitfire single engine	1938	360 mph	31,900 ft	2,500 ft per minute	395 miles	8 x .303 machine guns	219

On the face of it, 964 modern fighters versus 507 seems very far from a fair fight, but the bare figures do not tell the full story. The German Me 110 was not a match for either the Hurricane or the Spitfire; though its speed, ceiling and rate of climb were broadly comparable, it could not turn as quickly and was not as nimble as either. The Me 109 could take on both British fighters, but with its limited range it could only remain over England for a short time. In 1939 Colonel General (Field Marshal from July 1940) Erhard Milch, Inspector General of the Luftwaffe, had ordered production of drop-tanks to increase the range of the Me 109, but there were other priorities and these had only just become available. As the pilots had not had a chance to train with them, they tended to distrust them and at this stage of the war rarely used them. The Germans did not realise until far too late that the British fighters were controlled from the ground by radar, which vectored them on to their targets. British pilots shot down landed in their own country and if uninjured would be quickly back in action; similarly RAF aircraft that crash-landed might be repairable, whereas German pilots and aircraft shot down were either captured by the British or landed in the sea. The German air-sea rescue service – the Seenotflugkommandos – used transport aircraft to drop liferafts and buoys to downed aircrew in the Channel, and seaplanes to pick them up. These aircraft, designated air ambulances by the Germans, were marked with the Red Cross but this protection was not recognised by the British, who shot them down. Churchill's view was that he was not going to have aircrew rescued so that they could bomb Britain again – understandable, but a dubious interpretation of the laws of armed conflict.

To the British the Battle of Britain began on 10 July, whereas to the Germans Adler Tag, or Eagle Day, was 13 August, and everything before that was mere fencing. Prior to Eagle Day itself the Luftwaffe tried to tempt the RAF into giving battle by sending fighters over England. When the RAF failed to take the bait, the Germans sent a few bombers heavily escorted by fighters, but these were little more than nuisance raids and did not succeed in luring up large numbers of the RAF. Attacks on shipping in the Channel, in the hope that the British would then provide fighter escorts for the ships, sank 30,000 tons in June, July and August up to Eagle Day, but that was nothing compared to the one million tons of shipping passing unmolested through the Channel every week.

The British air defence system – the only aspect of the British ability to make war that had received any serious attention at all in the inter-war years – depended on the meshing together of radar, the Observer Corps, anti-aircraft units and the RAF's own fighters. Control was vital and the whole system depended on communications. In theory, German aircraft forming up for an attack around, say, Cap Gris Nez, would be detected by one of the twenty-one fixed Chain Home stations around the English coast. These radars could detect aircraft at a range of about 150 miles provided they were at an altitude of at least 15,000 feet. They could accurately calculate speed and direction, although they could only give an approximation of numbers of aircraft and altitude. This infor-mation would be telephoned to Fighter Command Headquarters at

Stanmore, just north of London, which would order the relevant RAF fighter group to intercept. Group would order one or more squadrons to take off and head on an interception course. Once the German aircraft got near the English coast they would be picked up by one of the Chain Home Low tracking stations, which had a much shorter range but could accurately detect number of aircraft and altitude. To back up the Chain Home Low network was the Observer Corps, formed between the wars from civilian volunteers, and which manned observation posts around the coast to report the height, direction and numbers of any hostile aircraft, particularly useful in the case of raids that were not picked up by Chain Home.

This system meant that the British did not have to keep fighters in the air at all times – there was no necessity for a patrol system – but need only scramble them when an incoming threat was detected. This of course meant that the RAF had far more time over target than the Germans, whose fighters rarely had more than fifteen or twenty minutes before they had to return to their home airfields. It did not, however, leave much time for the passing on of information. Flying time for the Germans from Cap Gris Nez to targets in the south-east was only six or seven minutes, and for a Spitfire to climb to a height where it could intercept – say 25,000 feet – took ten minutes. It was therefore essential that the radar operators identified a potential threat when the German aircraft were still forming up and got that information through to Fighter Command without delay, and that Fighter Command scrambled the necessary fighters. Once those fighters were in the air, detailed information from Chain Home Low and the Observer Corps as to course, altitude and speed of the Germans was radioed to them, and they could be guided by radar. There was little margin for error, and although to begin with information was often late in being passed on, speed of transmission rapidly improved.

The fighter defence of the UK was based on four fighter groups, each commanded by an Air Vice Marshal. It was on 11 Group, commanded by Air Vice Marshal Sir Keith Park, responsible for the south-east and the approaches to London that most of the burden fell, but Sir Trafford Leigh-Mallory's Number 12 Group, covering the midlands, was also heavily committed and frequently required to defend 11 Group's airfields while that group's aircraft were deployed against German attackers elsewhere. Park and Leigh-Mallory disagreed on tactics: Park went for deploying individual squadrons of aircraft, whereas Leigh-Mallory was an advocate of the 'Big Wing' of five or more squadrons. The matter was never resolved, and it is not within the scope of this book to debate the merits of the opposing schools of thought; suffice to say that there were advantages and disadvantages to both.

Anti-aircraft guns and their associated barrage balloons, searchlights and radars were the responsibility of Anti-Aircraft Command, formed in April 1939 and commanded by Lieutenant General Sir Frederick Pile, and it was essential that this command and Fighter Command were in close touch. If RAF fighters were dealing with raiders then the guns could not be allowed to fire, and if guns were firing the fighters had to be directed away from the danger area.[*] The whole system was orchestrated from Bentley Priory at Stanmore, an underground command post with its own telephone and teleprinter network, where were to be found the Commander-in-Chief Fighter Command, Dowding, General Pile and the Commandant of the Observer Corps, or their representatives, with liaison officers from Bomber and Coastal Commands, the Royal Navy, the War Office and the Home Office.

With the end of the preliminary phase, which failed to entice the RAF into a fighter versus fighter battle, Adler Day was launched more with a whimper than a bang. Weather for the first few days was against the Luftwaffe but as the skies cleared, raids built up from those on coastal installations to fighter battles, attacks on airfields and on those factories that were within reach of the German fighter escorts. The worst phase for the RAF was the period 23 August to 6 September when 295 British fighters were destroyed and 171 badly damaged. More serious, because they took longer to replace than the aircraft, was the loss of pilots: 103 killed or missing, 128 wounded. In the same period the Germans lost 214 fighters and 138 bombers.

---

*According to this author's mother-in-law, who served in an anti-aircraft artillery unit in the Wirral, an aircraft was shot down one night and was duly claimed by every gun in the area. When it was then discovered that the aircraft in question belonged to the RAF, every gun reported that it had been mistaken!

On 5 September Hitler authorised attacks on cities, hitherto banned, and on 7 September 300 bombers targeted the east London docks, followed up by 250 more that night. This was not the first raid on London, but it was the first as part of a deliberate policy, and on this occasion Fighter Command was caught unprepared – it had been expecting more attacks on airfields. Thereafter, when the Luftwaffe abandoned diversionary attacks to put everything into attacks on London, British radar was able to identify the attackers and a Big Wing from 12 Group was directed south to defend the capital. The RAF celebrates the Battle of Britain on 15 September, for it was on that day in 1940 that the British claimed 174 enemy aircraft destroyed by the RAF and another eleven shot down by anti-aircraft guns, for a loss of twenty-six British planes. In fact the true total of German losses was much less – around sixty – but it was then the British realised that they were not going to lose air supremacy over the United Kingdom, and that by diverting their effort to raiding cities the Germans had unwittingly lost the chance to deal the RAF a blow from which it would have been difficult to recover. The British, whose radio and newspapers were under less state control than those of Germany, generally admitted their losses eventually, whereas the Germans tended to understate them. The number of German aircraft claimed shot down by the RAF during the sixteen-week period, admitted by the Germans, and actually verified were:[9]

PERIOD	CLAIMED BY RAF	ADMITTED BY GERMANY	ACTUAL
10 Jul–7 Aug	188	63	192
8 Aug–23 Aug	755	213	403
24 Aug–6 Sep	643	243	378
7 Sep–30 Sep	846	243	435
1 Oct–31 Oct	260	134	325

It was in September that photo-reconnaissance aircraft of the RAF began to report the massing of Rhine barges (which could carry troops) in ports from Ostend to Le Havre, and there were several invasion scares and a number of false alarms. By the end of September the numbers of barges were steadily being reduced, and by October the British cabinet could be told that while the risk of invasion had not entirely gone, the weather would make it increasingly unlikely. At the end of October the Battle of Britain became the Blitz, in which the Luftwaffe attacked centres of industry and population in an attempt to destroy the British economy and morale. Although not apparent at the time, this was far less dangerous to Britain's ability to stay in the war than determined continuation of attacks on Fighter Command and Chain Home would have been.

The Luftwaffe had been designed for, and so far had been used as, a tactical arm to operate in support of the other two services, particularly the army. It had not previously been asked to do anything on its own, and in the event was not up to the task. The Luftwaffe had no plan to deal with Britain after the fall of France – and neither had Hitler, OKW or OKH. It was not at all sure what its immediate objectives should be, and it did not have the aircraft capable of achieving what it eventually thought it wanted. The heavy fighter, the Me 110, was not capable of escorting the bombers, and had to be itself escorted by Me 109s; the bombers could not carry a sufficient bombload to obliterate a target and render it incapable of being repaired; and the pilots insisted on the fighters providing close escort, rather than flying top cover well above, where they could far better deal with the defending RAF fighters. Instead of concentrating on airfields and radar stations, the Luftwaffe allowed itself to be distracted by other targets, which while useful were not critical to the aim of the campaign – the elimination of Fighter Command. Between the middle of July and the end of October Fighter Command lost about 788 aircraft to 1,294 German. Both sides continually overestimated their enemy's losses, but German intelligence was doubly at fault. The Luftwaffe had estimated British fighter aircraft production at a maximum of 225 in June, 380 in July, and 280 in each of August and September.[10] This, coupled with overestimation of RAF losses, led the Germans on several occasions to believe that Fighter Command must be near to breaking point. In fact, British fighter production was 446 in June, 496 in July, 476 in August and 467 in September, while German fighter (Me 109) production for the same four months was 164, 220, 173 and 218.[11] The German air force had originally been designed to conform to the German doctrine of quick victory. It was a tactical air force, and when it was asked to act strategically, it failed.

In that Fighter Command retained control of the skies above the UK, the RAF won the Battle of Britain, and Churchill was right when he coined that memorable tribute about owing so much to so few. They were, indeed, few. Altogether there were only 2,945 aircrew involved in the Battle of Britain, of whom 580 were Empire or Allied. They were, of course, supported by many times that number of ground crew, but the price paid by those fewer than three thousand men was high: 507 (110 Empire or Allied), or 17 per cent, killed and about the same number wounded. [12]

Contrary to accepted myth, not all were young and carefree public schoolboys going to their deaths with a smile on their lips. Just over 40 per cent of the aircrew who fought in the Battle of Britain were sergeants or flight sergeants. Not all the other rank aircrew were pilots. The Beau fighters, Blenheims and Defiants (withdrawn in August) were two-seaters and had an observer or gunner as well as a pilot, but these squadrons were a minority (nine out of sixty-nine squadrons by the end of the battle), and as the majority of the fighters involved were single-seat Spitfires and Hurricanes, most of the sergeants were pilots. In deciding whether a man should be commissioned or not the RAF had to take into account not the man's ability to fly – that was ascertained by objective testing – but his future employability, which meant that those with a public or grammar school education were more likely to be commissioned than those without. Whereas the officer pilot, if he survived, would go on to become a flight, squadron and station commander, the sergeant, if not commissioned, would go on flying, his operational tours interspersed with postings as an instructor. The sergeants thus often became much more talented and experienced pilots than the officers, who would go on to be promoted, and with advancing seniority would fly less and less. The sergeant pilots do not seem to have minded that some of those doing exactly the same job in the air lived in better quarters and received more pay: the sergeant would not expect to have any extraneous responsibilities once on the ground, whereas the officer would be nominated as station sports officer, press officer, mess secretary, welfare officer or some other extramural task, devoid of excitement and glory, but none the less important to the smooth running of the organisation. One should not forget, however, that for every young gentleman who affected a handlebar moustache and a silk scarf, and pretended to find the whole thing a bit of a bore – the Hollywood image of the RAF fighter pilot – there were almost as many working-class lads with provincial accents who also risked their necks way up there in the clouds.

It has to be asked whether Germany ever had a serious intention to invade Britain. The Luftwaffe high command certainly thought the whole thing was a bluff, the navy was set against it and Hitler frequently emphasised that it would be a last resort. Most generals thought it could only happen against a Great Britain already close to collapse from air attacks and strangulation of trade – although Halder likened it to a large-scale river crossing, something at which the German army were rather good.[*] The Germans had no landing craft capable of carrying the number of troops that they would need, and Rhine barges, with their very low freeboard, are all very well for carrying cargo up a river, but would hardly have survived a crossing of the notoriously stormy Channel. Göring believed that if he had four airborne divisions to throw at England immediately after Dunkirk he could have done it, but he only had one such division. There is no doubt that had the German army been able to get to England and been supported by follow-up troops in the spring or summer of 1940, it would have defeated the disorganised and unequipped British units that would have opposed it. The Home Guard, stout patriotic souls though they undoubtedly were, would have been brushed aside and, despite recent attempts to laud their capabilities, a few old men hiding in underground bunkers in woods would have had little effect on inevitable German victory. The point is that the German army could not get to England, and even if by some quirk of fate the German navy had managed to bounce a Channel crossing and get, say, six divisions ashore, with another division air-landed or dropped, it is inconceivable that the Royal Navy would not have sacrificed most of the entire Home Fleet, if necessary, to prevent any follow-up or reinforcement, leaving what had been got ashore to wither on the vine. Operation Sea Lion was a chimera, and always had been.

---

* He rather lost interest when he discovered that the navy wanted ten days to get the first wave across the Channel, and that his staff estimated a need for sixty thousand horses in the first two waves (Halder, *Diaries*).

NOTES

1. J. R. M. Butler, *Grand Strategy, Vol. II*, HMSO, London, 1957.

2. Captain S. W. Roskill, RN, *The War at Sea, Vol. I*, HMSO, London, 1954.

3. B. Collier, *The Defence of the United Kingdom*, Weidenfeld & Nicolson, London, 1957.

4. General the Lord Ismay, *The Memoirs of General the Lord Ismay*, Heinemann, London, 1960.

5. Alex Danchev and Dan Todman (eds), *War Diaries 1939–1945: Field Marshal Lord Alanbrooke*, Weidenfeld & Nicolson, London, 2001.

6. Professor Brian Bond and Michael Taylor, *The Battle for France and Flanders, Sixty Years On*, Leo Cooper, Barnsley, 2001.

7. Stephen Roskill, *Churchill and the Admirals*, Collins, London, 1977.

8. Captain S. W. Roskill, RN, op. cit.

9. Derek Wood and Derek Dempster, *The Narrow Margin*, Arrow, London, 1969.

10. Research Institute for Military History, Germany (tr McMurry & Osers), *Germany and the Second World War, Vol. II*, Clarendon Press, Oxford, 2000.

11. John Ellis, *Brute Force, Allied Strategy and Tactics in the Second World War*, André Deutsch, London, 1990.

12. Wood and Dempster, op. cit.

10

Survival

BRITAIN HAD SURVIVED the efforts of the Luftwaffe to dominate the skies over England, and the threat of invasion, if it ever really existed, had receded. To the Germans Operation Sea Lion remained as a possible plan on their books, but very much at the back of the filing cabinet and only for resurrection when all other outstanding matters had been settled. Persuasion and invasion having failed, starvation could be tried and the German navy could get on with commerce raiding and the sinking of ships carrying essential materials and foodstuffs. This would take longer than an invasion, but was much more likely to yield results. In any case, if the German army could not get at the British, then neither could the British army, or what was left of it, get at the Germans. The German eye was now very much on the Russian ball; Britain was a nuisance, but if her last hope – and what was making her hang on in the war– was the possibility that Russia would turn on Germany, then by eliminating Russia, Britain too could be brought to her knees.

For the next four years the bulk of the British army would concentrate on rebuilding itself and preparing to return to Europe; anything else it did might be good for its own morale, annoy the Germans and give cheer to the occupied countries, but could do little towards the defeat of the main enemy. The RAF, on the other hand, could hit back at

Germany; indeed it was the only way by which Britain could attack the German homeland. First, however, it had to deal with the Blitz.

The Battle of Britain developed almost inadvertently into the Blitz on 25 August when at 1000 hours a hundred German bombers attacked London. Whether this was an accident, a Luftwaffe commander on a private jaunt or a reprisal – the RAF had bombed the suburbs of Stuttgart the night before (probably accidentally) and killed four civilians[1] – is not known; the nearest the Germans have to an Official History says that the records have been lost.[2] As at this stage the Germans were still trying to eliminate Fighter Command, it certainly made sense to go for the one target that would draw up maximum RAF aircraft in its defence, but Hitler had not yet lifted his ban on attacks on London, and would not do so until 5 September. This raid precipitated the first attack by the RAF on Berlin, on the orders of the war cabinet, and that night fifty bombers, a mix of Wellingtons and Hampdens, set off for the German capital. Thick cloud over Berlin meant that most of the bombs fell in the country-side to the south, although two civilians were wounded when a bomb hit a gardeners' hut. Six aircraft were lost on the way home. The raid did, however, allow the Germans to claim that the British had started the bombing of cities, and a leaflet dropped over England bore the well-known photograph of Churchill holding a Thompson sub-machine gun with 'Wanted for Murder' inscribed upon it.

The Germans make no distinction between the Battle of Britain and the Blitz; to them it was all one air campaign that started on Adler Tag, 13 August 1940, and ended in mid May 1941, after which date German air force units began to be withdrawn from operations against Britain to prepare for adventures in the east. To the British there is a distinction – and a reasonable one – between the attempt to obtain air superiority in preparation for an invasion, and what the British claimed were terror attacks on the population, and the Germans claimed was war on the economy. Birmingham was also attacked on the night of 25–26 August, and Liverpool several times between 28 and 31 August. So far these attacks were all on military targets – docks and factories – but the bombing of London on 7 September, in which 460 Londoners were killed, was not obviously aimed at military targets and so is regarded by the British as the start of the Blitz. Hitler had authorised raids on London and other major cities by day and night two days previously, and Luftflotte 2 assumed the role of daylight bombing while Luftflotte 3 took over at night.

Initially there were all sorts of problems for the British. There were less than a hundred anti-aircraft guns defending the capital and very few were radar-controlled; the searchlights were of little use over 12,000 feet, whereas the 4.7-inch anti-aircraft guns they supported could fire up to 30,000 feet; fire-control arrangements between the guns and the fighters were bad (unlike farther south, where practice during the Battle of Britain had made them superb). The Germans had difficulties too, however. Kesselring, commanding the daylight-raiding Luftflotte 2, was well aware that:

> The obvious thing would have been to choose our targets according to their
> importance, raze them to the ground by incessant attack, and then watch for
> any signs of reconstruction, so as to harass the workers and destroy their work,
> but if priority plans for the economic war were there, the means to carry them
> out were lacking.[3]

The Luftwaffe had no effective long-range fighters to escort the bombers deep into British territory, and the bombers themselves were really only converted transport aircraft. What was needed was a four-engine bomber with range, speed and load-carrying capacity, but the Luftwaffe, with its origins as a tactical air force operating in support of the army and navy, did not have such an aircraft, and development of one had been cancelled by Göring in February 1937: 'The Führer does not ask how big my bombers are, but how many I have.'[4] German bombers were further hampered by the British weather, and often follow-up raids could not be mounted because of cloud or rain.

For convenience the Blitz can be divided into three phases. Phase one lasted until the middle of November 1940, during which the Luftwaffe concentrated on London; phase two, until mid February 1941, saw them attack provincial cities and ports, although London remained as a target. The final phase continued until mid May 1941 when the Germans went mainly for ports in the south and south-west.

Increasingly, as Anti-Aircraft Command defences improved, the Germans shifted their campaign to night bombing. Here they were aided by their own developments in radar technology, which had concentrated on navigational aids, rather than the British approach of developing long-range warning systems. The most difficult aspect of night bombing in 1940 was navigation. Unless bombs could be dropped exactly on target they were of little use, and at night and in bad weather navigation could only be approximate. The Germans had developed what they called the Knickebein system, whereby two radio beams were transmitted from two different places in Europe, intersecting over the target area. A specially trained pathfinder aircraft flew along one of the beams and when it picked up the second it could drop its bombs, with the following aircraft using the resultant explosions as aiming marks. The beams were accurate only to within about a mile, however, and as a 500-kilogram bomb (the largest in the German armoury at this time) dropped a mile away from a railway marshalling yard will do no harm at all to the railway, this system could only guarantee to hit the town or city and not the specific target. To improve accuracy of bombing the X-Gerät system was introduced. By using three beams instead of two, and a simple timing device to measure the time taken to fly from one beam intersection to the next, the navigator was able to ascertain the exact ground speed of his aircraft, regardless of wind or his own map-reading errors. This was said to allow bombing to within twenty yards of a target.

To begin with, the British were almost defenceless against the night bombers; there were hardly any night fighters and not enough anti-aircraft guns. But as General Pile increased the number of guns around cities – which although they rarely shot a bomber down could force it to increase height, drop its load early, or go off course – and as more guns were linked to radar and could thus engage an unseen target, and as effective night fighters came on stream equipped with radar that allowed the pilot to track his target in darkness, raids became more dangerous for the Luftwaffe.

In terms of deaths caused and damage done, the Luftwaffe won the Blitz. By the middle of November, when the first phase ended, they had dropped over 16,000 tons of high explosive on London alone, and more than one million incendiaries. By the end of the Blitz 43,000 British civilians had been killed, and around 140,000 more wounded. Historic buildings had been destroyed, and much of the nation's housing stock, particularly in London, had been lost. German losses (from 1 August 1940 to 31 March 1941) were at most 4,278 aircrew killed, captured and missing, and 1,142 bombers and 1,132 fighters lost, or about 3 per cent of sorties flown.[5] But – and this is the point – the Blitz did not succeed in halting, or even severely disrupting, British aircraft production, which remained steady at a maximum of 1,730 of all types for March 1941 and a minimum of 1,198 in January 1941, while Luftwaffe intelligence was predicting half that. Nor did the Blitz succeed in destroying, or even severely damaging, the economy. Destroyed or severely damaged housing was certainly a problem, but its rebuilding provided employment and much of it, particularly in the East End and around the docks, would have had to be replaced before long anyway. By attacking the industrial areas of London, Liverpool, Birmingham, Manchester, Sheffield, Newcastle, Bristol and Belfast, where working-class families tended to live, the Germans in fact carried out a partial slum-clearance programme, although the residents would hardly have seen it in quite that light at the time. Most of all, and contrary to all the pre-war theories, the raids did not succeed in provoking the civilian population into demanding an end to the war – although it is difficult to see what the civilian population could have done even if they did want an end to the war, as long as the government controlled the armed forces and but the organs of state.

The German air force generals thought that the Blitz failed because they did not have a bomber capable of delivering a heavy enough load; because targets were constantly changed for political reasons, and because the British very quickly developed the best night air defence anywhere. While no doubt terrifying at the time, the amount of explosive dropped was not great by later standards. During the heaviest raid on London, on 19 April 1941, 1,026 tons of high explosive were dropped. This compares with between 3,000 and 4,000 tons per raid dropped by the RAF when its bombing campaign got into its stride later on. Many German airmen thought that if they had been able to deliver a bigger bombload and could have concentrated on targets until they were destroyed, the result of the Blitz would have been different, but the later experiences of RAF Bomber Command do not bear them out, as we shall see.

For most of her recorded history as a nation, Britain had relied on the navy. Without an army the British could not intervene abroad, but without a navy they could not exist. In the Napoleonic wars and in the Great War the navy's greatest contribution to victory was not Trafalgar, or Jutland, important though those victories were, but blockade, the gradual but inexorable starvation of the enemy population and the denial of raw materials for enemy industries. Now, with France out of the war, the enemy coast to be blockaded ran for nine thousand miles from the north of Norway to the Strait of Gibraltar, along the north coast of the Mediterranean, past the Italian colony of Libya as far as French North Africa. Worse, the Molotov–Ribbentrop Pact had given the Germans a back door that was not available to Napoleonic France or, except for the last year of the war, to Hohenzollern Germany. In the Second World War the Royal Navy adopted a policy of blockade at source, that is the prevention of cargoes destined for Germany and Italy leaving their home waters, but the prevention of the shipment of raw materials such as rubber to ports in the Russian Far East (such as Vladivostok) was rendered almost impossible by British weakness in the Far East, and a wish – a need even – to avoid upsetting Japan. Even in the Mediterranean, as long as Turkey was neutral Britain could not send ships into the Black Sea (by international law the Dardanelles was closed to the warships of belligerents, unless Turkey herself entered the war). In this war the blockade was no longer the most effective weapon in the Royal Navy's armoury.

For Germany, the two-pronged policy of starvation of Britain as an alternative to persuasion and invasion had failed as far as the air prong – the Battle of Britain and the Blitz – was concerned, but a naval strangulation of trade and the denial of food from abroad was still an option. In the Great War the German navy had come close to doing what their army could not, and in 1917 the First Sea Lord, Admiral Jellicoe, alarmed the war cabinet by telling them that shipping losses to German submarines were such that Britain would be unable to continue the war into 1918. He was unnecessarily pessimistic, but the threat was great, and only countered when the navy adopted the system it had used in many previous wars, that of making merchant shipping sail in convoy escorted by warships. In the Second World War methods of detecting submarines were very much better and the convoy system was introduced almost from the outset, but for a country that even at the height of the war still had to import almost a quarter of her food, the threat posed by German (and Italian) submarines was serious. Fortunately, in keeping with the German doctrine of short wars, the submarine-building programme had not been given a high priority before the war, and only fourteen U-boats were at sea when war was declared. Initially the German submarines were instructed to adhere to the laws of war on the high seas, which allowed a U-boat to sink an enemy merchant ship, but had first to stop it on the surface, inspect the cargo and give the crew time to take to their lifeboats, unless it was sailing in a convoy escorted by warships, in which case even a neutral could be sunk on sight. Passenger ships not carrying any warlike materials could be stopped and searched but not sunk. On 3 September 1939 the German submarine *U 30* took the passenger liner *Athenia* for an auxiliary cruiser, and sank her. Of the 1,400 passengers, 112 died, including twenty-eight Americans, and the British, wrongly assuming that the Germans had begun unrestricted submarine warfare, instituted the convoy system and began to form submarine-hunting groups.

Between the outbreak of war and the withdrawal of British forces from Europe in June 1940, German submarines sunk 300 ships – British, Allied or neutral heading for British ports – totalling 1,136,926 tons, and in the same period the German navy lost twenty-four submarines: fourteen sunk by surface ships of the Royal Navy, four to mines, two to submarines of the Royal Navy, one by combined action of RAF aircraft and surface vessels, one to the RAF alone, one rammed accidentally by a German surface ship and one to unknown causes. While the sinkings by submarines made the headlines, in the same period the Allies lost only very slightly less tonnage, and rather more ships (396) to enemy aircraft, mines, surface raiders, E-boats and the natural perils of the sea. The real successes of the German submarine arm at the time were the exploits of *U 29*, which sank the aircraft carrier HMS *Courageous* on 17 September 1939 in the Western Approaches, and *U 47*, which managed to get into the heavily defended base of the Home Fleet at Scapa Flow on 14 October 1939 and sink the battleship HMS *Royal Oak*.

It was from the late summer of 1940 to the spring of 1941 that was referred to by the German U-boat crews as 'the happy time', when on average each of the twelve or so U-boats actually at sea was sinking five or six ships a month. After that the number of operational U-boats increased dramatically, but the tonnage that they sank did not, as this table shows:[6]

PERIOD	U-BOATS OPERATIONAL (ROUGHLY 50% AT SEA AT ANY ONE TIME)	ALLIED MERCHANT SHIPS SUNK BY U-BOATS	ALLIED TONNAGE SUNK BY U-BOATS	U-BOATS SUNK
Jul, Aug, Sept 1940	28	153	758,778	5
Oct, Nov, Dec 1940	27	132	711,610	3
Jan, Feb, Mar 1941	22	191	566,585	5
Apr, May, Jun 1941	32	162	885,010	7
Jul, Aug, Sept 1941	65	99	377,339	6
Oct, Nov, Dec 1941	80	52	255,490	17

The reason for an increased number of submarines achieving fewer sinkings is attributable to the Royal Navy and the RAF getting much better at detecting and dealing with submarines; fewer ships trying to travel away from convoys (this category had accounted for many of those sunk in the early period of the war); the increased sophistication of British radio interception and codebreaking; and the removal from the equation (by reason of their having been killed) of some of the best U-boat captains and their experienced crews.

Whereas the ending of the Battle of Britain and the Blitz did not mean the end of air attacks on Great Britain, which continued until the end of the war – albeit with far less determination until the V weapons programme began to bear fruit in late 1944 – so the ending of the U-boat 'happy time' did not leave the sea lanes safe for Allied shipping. Improvements in submarine design by the Germans and improvements in detection by the British and, later, the Americans, jockeyed for pre-eminence, and there were times when the U-boats seemed to be getting the upper hand, particularly on the route to Russia and in the Atlantic when the Germans instituted the wolf pack system. By this latter, submarines were spread out across the likely route of a convoy from America to Britain. When a submarine detected the approach of the convoy it radioed the course and speed to U-boat headquarters in Paris, which then directed all other U-boats in the vicinity to a rendezvous where they could intercept the convoy. Initially this system worked, but Allied radio intercept and improved sonar and radar detection made the wolf pack itself a target that even the idlest escort corvette, dumping depth charges at random, could hardly miss.

Italy's entry into the war created a new threat for Britain in the Middle East. Italy should never have joined hostilities – she was neither militarily nor economically capable of engaging in modern war – but it is not true to allege, as many do, that her soldiers were cowards and her officers poltroons. The Italian peasant is a tough, loyal fighter, as he proved in the Great War with 600,000 dead from a population of 38,000,000, pro-portionately rather more than the British, despite Italy not joining the war until May 1915. In the Second World War, when they could be properly administered and supported, Italian troops often fought well, and some Italian naval units showed outstanding bravery. It was the Italians' misfortune that they often lacked the wherewithal to maintain their armies in the field, and that their chief ally despised them, poking fun at some of their outlandish uniforms and affecting to disparage an army that needed to issue cappuccino machines and had on its establishment a mobile brothel – although envy may have played a part in regard to the latter item. The Italians were defeated because of incompetence on the part of their government and their high command, whose capabilities could not match their ambitions, and by a logistic inability to keep their troops in the field, rather than by a lack of fighting spirit.

Egypt housed three British commanders-in-chief. Admiral Sir Andrew Cunningham, flying his flag in the battleship *Warspite*, commanded the Mediterranean Fleet, based in Alexandria; General Sir Archibald Wavell commanded the land forces as Commander-in-Chief Middle East, and the Air Officer Commanding-in-Chief Middle East was Air Marshal Sir Arthur Longmore. Wavell's responsibilities were more diverse than those of any other commander-in-chief at that time. He was responsible not only for Egypt but for the Sudan, Palestine, Aden, Transjordan, Iraq, Cyprus, East Africa (Kenya, Tanganyika and Uganda) and British Soma-liland. The importance of this area rested on two essentials to the survival of Britain as a great power: oil and communications to India. If the British were evicted from the Middle East they would lose a supply of oil that they controlled, and could thereafter buy it only from the United States,

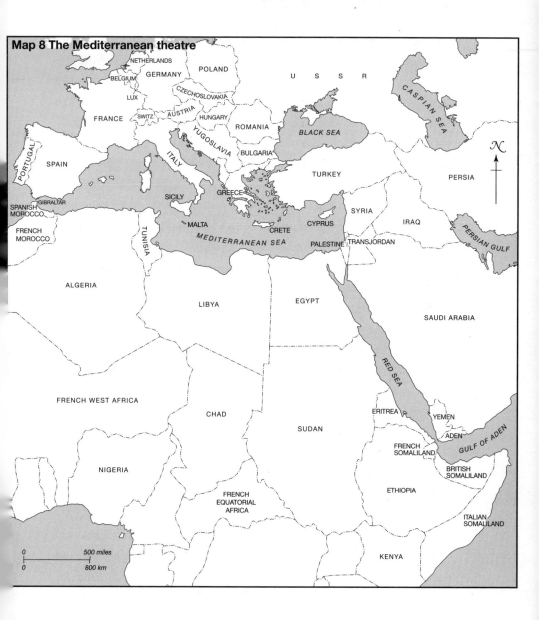

Map 8 The Mediterranean theatre

or from South American countries not necessarily well disposed towards her. The Middle East was the western flank of the defence of India. An enemy established there could not only threaten India itself, but force the substitution of the direct route through the Mediterranean and the Suez Canal for the much longer trip round the Cape of Good Hope.

The immediate threat to the British in the Middle East came from Italy. To the west of Egypt was the Italian colony of Libya, taken from a decaying Ottoman Empire in 1911 during a campaign in which the Italian army was noted more for the atrocities it committed than for its military prowess, and where there were now around 70,000 troops of General Gariboldi's Italian Tenth Army in Cyrenaica. To the south-east, in the recently conquered Ethiopia and in Italian Somaliland, were another 250,000 Italians under the Duke of Aosta. To counter this Wavell had a modest garrison in Egypt itself; a British brigade and the British-officered Sudan Defence Force in the Sudan; two brigades of the King's African Rifles (also British-officered) in Kenya; two Indian, one Rhodesian, two King's African Rifles and one British infantry battalions in British Somaliland; and a garrison in Palestine occupied in trying to deal with Arab and Jewish terrorism.

Before the war the only mechanised force the British had outside the United Kingdom was The Mobile Division in Egypt, renamed The Armoured Division (Egypt) on the outbreak of war, and becoming 7 Armoured Division in February 1940. The division's two brigades had also gone through several changes of title. The Heavy Armoured Brigade (Egypt) became 4 Heavy Armoured Brigade in February 1940 and 4 Armoured Brigade in April. Similarly, the Light Armoured Brigade (Egypt) became 7 Light Armoured Brigade (Egypt) before settling down as 7 Armoured Brigade. Between them the two brigades originally mustered two mechanised cavalry regiments (7th and 8th Hussars), and two battalions of the Royal Tank Regiment (1 and 6). Divisional troops included two battalions of motorised infantry (1st Battalion the King's Royal Rifle Corps and 2nd Battalion the Rifle Brigade), a reconnaissance regiment (11th Hussars plus two independent squadrons), an anti-tank, a field and an anti-aircraft regiment of artillery. In the armoured brigades each regiment had fifty-two tanks; half cruisers and half light tanks for the

RTR, and in the case of the cavalry forty-three light tanks and nine cruisers. The reconnaissance units were equipped with armoured cars.

As soon as Italy entered the war Wavell ordered his armoured division to move up to the border between Egypt and Libya (marked by a wire fence twelve feet thick and five feet high, built by the Italians and running for four hundred miles south from the sea) and cause as much trouble as possible. Using mainly light tanks, armoured cars and infantry, and supported by RAF bombers, the units of 7 Armoured mounted a series of pinprick raids which alarmed the numerically far stronger Italians, captured their border posts and even chased them out of Forts Maddalena and Capuzzo, the major Italian defensive positions above the Halfaya Pass, which marked the frontier.* The Royal Navy bombarded their ports and British patrols penetrated up to one hundred miles into Libya, with the Italians locking themselves up in their forts and surrendering the desert to the British. Mussolini's plan for the conquest of Egypt was to mount a pincer movement from Libya on the one hand and Italian Somaliland on the other. The difficulty was that Marshal Graziani, the Italian Commander-in-Chief in Libya, was more of a realist than the ex-journalist Duce in Rome. Graziani had been in post since the end of June 1940, when his predecessor's aircraft was shot down by his own anti-aircraft gunners, and had a reputation as the 'Lion of the Desert' for his putting down of a rebellion in the 1930s. Butchering unsophisticated Senussi tribesmen was not quite the same thing as taking on the British, however, a fact of which Graziani was well aware, and which persuaded him to send a stream of excuses back to Rome explaining why he could not invade Egypt just yet.

The British war cabinet was well aware of the significance of the Middle East, and in August General Wavell was summoned to London, to discuss with the Chiefs of Staff and the Prime Minister what might be done. Wavell met Churchill on 8 and 15 August, and the Prime Minister was not impressed. The two personalities were so different that it is unlikely that they could ever have been close. Churchill had grown up in

---

* This author found nothing left of Capuzzo, save a few stones – like Marble Arch, the Italian triumphal monument in Libya, it has been razed to the ground by the Gadaffi regime. Much of the wire fence is still there, however.

the political arena, where vituperation, invective and personal abuse, followed by dinner afterwards, were all part of the game. Wavell, a soldier brought up to behave like a gentleman, found Churchill's criticisms of apparent military inactivity offensive and unnecessary, particularly from someone who had no real understanding of modern war but thought he had. In trying to explain why troops recently arrived in Kenya could not be instantly deployed against the Italians, Wavell found that Churchill thought:

> ...that because a comparatively small number of mounted Boers had held up a British division in 1899 or 1900 it was unnecessary for the South African Brigade to have much more equipment than rifles before taking the field in 1940... Winston's tactical ideas had to some extent crystallised at the South African War.[7]

Wavell was everything that Churchill disliked in a general, or rather he lacked everything that Churchill liked. He was not demonstrative, romantic, ebullient, aggressive; he did not engage with Churchill, he was not combative in discussion, and above all he was what Churchill saw as 'bookish'. Wavell had been educated at Winchester, and Wykehamists, then as now, are noted for being on a higher intellectual plane than the rest of us. He was thoughtful, read poetry and judged poetry competitions, peppered his operation orders with classical allusions, was an acknowledged military historian and had given the Lees Knowles series of lectures at Cambridge University in 1939. Wavell was more intelligent than most of his peers, but he did have a curious inability to articulate his thoughts verbally to people whom he saw as being unsympathetic to his views, or as being intellectually incapable of understanding them. With such an audience he was infuriatingly taciturn, and would simply sit in silence. Churchill may not have consciously compared his relationship with Wavell with that between his political idol Lloyd George and Haig in the Great War, but it was a not dissimilar situation, and it was one that increasingly fed Churchill's dislike and distrust of Wavell.

As a result of Wavell's discussions in London it was agreed that 5 Indian Division, heading for Basra, should be diverted to Egypt to join 4 Indian Division already there, and that the Australian and New Zealand brigades should be removed from Palestine and allotted to Egypt. Churchill then took a brave decision, and that was to reinforce Egypt with scarce weapons and tanks at a time when England, while not perhaps in reality under the threat of invasion, was certainly believed by many to be so. There is, of course, the possibility that Churchill never for one moment believed in invasion, but used the fear of it as a way to cement the country together. It is difficult to see how, if he considered invasion a serious possibility, he could ever have agreed to send so much weaponry out of the country. Whatever Churchill believed, off went two convoys with the 3rd Hussars (fifty-two light tanks), 2 RTR (fifty-two tanks, mainly A13 cruisers, but with some A9s and A10s), 7 RTR (fifty-two Matilda infantry tanks), a regiment each of anti-tank, anti-aircraft and field artillery – the latter with 25-pounders – 500 Bren guns and 250 Boys anti-tank rifles, with as much ammunition as could be scraped together for them all.

Now Churchill entered into another row, this time with the navy, supported by the army. The Admiralty considered that to send the convoys – which contained about half the total number of tanks and heavy weapons held by the army in the UK – through the Mediterranean was too dangerous, and that they should be sent the long way, around the Cape. Churchill, anxious to see action at the earliest possible moment, wanted them sent to Egypt by the shortest and most direct route. In the end the professionals won, but the argument merely reinforced Churchill's view that the soldiers and sailors were far too cautious. The two convoys, one carrying the men and the other the tanks and heavy equipment, went via Capetown, arriving in Egypt at the end of September.

If Italy's generals were reluctant to put their necks into what might turn out to be an Egyptian noose, British Somaliland was a different matter, and on 3 August 1940 twenty-six battalions of Italian infantry, supported by light tanks and aircraft, invaded the British colony. The garrison of five British and colonial battalions, commanded by Major General Godwin-Austin – who had been flown in only a few days before – let the Italians push deep into British territory, stopped them on a line of hills fifty miles from the sea of the Gulf of Aden, and then withdrew in good order and embarked at the port of Berbera. The British had some 250 casualties, the Italians 2,000. The Italians could have British Somaliland, at least for the moment. It could only have been held by the British if massively reinforced; there were no reinforcements and in any case the colony was not essential to the British war effort. The Italian propagandists made much of their great military triumph along the road to a new Roman Empire, and Churchill, with the unthinking unfairness of which he was increasingly capable, demanded the dismissal of Godwin-Austin. Wavell, who had only just returned from his meetings in London, refused, adding in his telegram that the few British casualties in the operation did not indicate a lack of tactical competence in the troops – quite the reverse. Churchill, seeing that he had been caught out as an advocate of mere pounding, was furious, and his relationship with Wavell deteriorated even further. Wavell was absolutely right to back Godwin-Austin, whose decision to recommend evacuation was the right one, and apart from Major General Ismay, who was Churchill's poodle, the generals, including the CIGS, agreed.

At last Graziani in Libya was told by Mussolini to stop prevaricating and get on with the invasion of Egypt. On 13 September five Italian divisions started to move across the Egyptian border, down the Halfaya Pass, heading for the (then as now) unprepossessing fishing village of Sollum, from where the British garrison (one platoon of the Coldstream Guards) wisely withdrew. Italian intelligence had grossly overestimated the strength of the British forces in Egypt and, preceded by massive artillery bombardments of empty desert, Graziani's men moved slowly along the coast, harassed by the RAF, mines and the Royal Artillery, until they came to Sidi Barrani, a town of no strategic significance whatsoever, fifty miles into Egypt and 400 miles from Cairo, where they stopped, dug in and wondered what to do next. That, in fact, would be decided by Wavell, who was preparing plans for aggressive action against the Italian squatters, while trying to avoid the more fanciful suggestions sent to him by Churchill who, despite having never been anywhere near the Middle East for over forty years, was trying to direct the movements of single battalions from his study in London.

Wavell's deliberations were not aided by Churchill's next great gesture. Mussolini, in a mixture of imperial ambition in the Balkans, and annoyance that Hitler had not told him in advance of German plans to occupy Romania,* had invaded Greece from Albania with eight divisions on 28 October. Churchill immediately offered British assistance to Greece, but although the British, with the French, had given a territorial guarantee to Greece (among others) after the German dismemberment of Czechoslovakia in 1939, the situation had changed and in no sense could Britain be said to be still under that obligation. As previously with Poland, any commitment Britain might have made to Greece would be fulfilled in the long term only by winning the war, and the offer of troops to Greece, which could only come from the Middle East, made that possibility rather less likely. Nevertheless, soldiers were found and delivered to Crete by the navy, and aircraft were flown to Greece, while the Royal Navy tried to tempt the Italian navy out of its ports and into battle.

The garrison of Egypt contained, as any great headquarters does, a large number of administrative troops, but the combat element, once reinforcements from England, India and Palestine had arrived, as they had by late October, packed a lot of punch for its size. Titled the Western Desert Force, later to become XIII Corps and later still Eighth Army, it had as its fighting formations 7 Armoured Division, 4 Indian Division, of two brigades with a third (16 British Brigade) attached, and yet another ad hoc formation, Selby Force (effectively the garrison of Mersah Matruh, about a third of the way from the Libyan border to Alexandria), of one infantry battalion, a machine-gun company, three infantry companies from different battalions, a troop of the 7th Hussars in armoured cars, and a light anti-aircraft battery Royal Horse Artillery. As part of 'corps troops', in the hand of the commander, was 7 RTR with its Matilda tanks. The Western Desert Force was commanded by Lieutenant General Richard O'Connor, an intelligent and far-sighted officer who had long been an advocate of flexible tactics enhanced by mobility. O'Connor's immediate superior was Lieutenant General 'Jumbo' Wilson, General Officer Commanding Egypt, who in turned reported to the Commander-in-Chief, Wavell.

Wavell's plan, outlined by him, refined by Wilson and turned into detail by O'Connor, was to cut off the Italian forces in Egypt from their

---

* Romania was part of the Berlin-dominated Axis, although not yet at war with anyone. On 7 October 1940 German troops entered the country, ostensibly to train the Romanian army but in reality to secure the Romanian oil fields in preparation for the invasion of the Soviet Union.

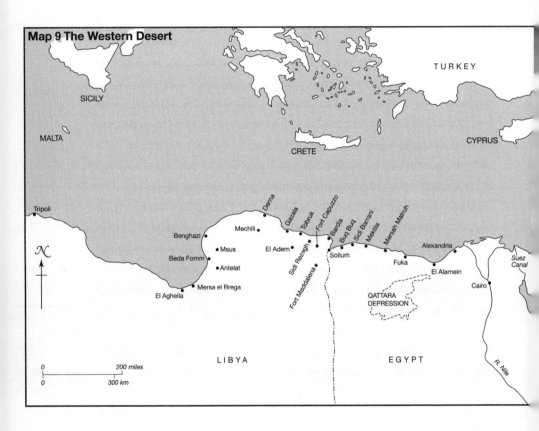

Map 9 The Western Desert

TURKEY

SICILY

MALTA

CRETE

CYPRUS

Tripoli

Derna

Gazala

Tobruk

Fort Capuzzo

Mechili

Benghazi

Msus

Beda Fomm

Antelat

El Adem

Sidi Rezegh

Fort Maddalena

Bardia

Buq Buq

Sidi Barrani

Mektila

Marsah Matruh

Sollum

Fuka

Alexandria

El Alamein

Cairo

Suez Canal

Mersa el Brega

El Agheila

QATTARA DEPRESSION

N

LIBYA

EGYPT

R. Nile

0 — 200 miles
0 — 300 km

base in Libya and destroy them. At this stage the Italian deployment consisted of a front line of forts (dug-in and wired defensive positions) running from the sea at Mektila, about fifteen miles east of Sidi Barrani, south-west for about fifty miles. These forts were garrisoned by three divisions of native Libyan troops commanded by Italian officers and NCOs, backed up by tanks, which were spread out along the front in support. Behind this front line at Sidi Barrani was the Italian headquarters, with one Italian division and part of another, while farther back still were five Italian divisions between Buq Buq and the Libyan border. Having thrown a sop to Mussolini by entering Egypt, Marshal Graziani now saw his priorities as being to consolidate his present position and then improve roads and tracks, for despite his troops being supposedly motorised there was such a shortage of vehicles and the roads were so bad that his men could only move along the one coast road, and that slowly.

The Italians outnumbered the British by more than two to one in manpower, and by about two to one in artillery. The Italian artillery was probably the best trained and most skilful part of their army, but that was largely negated by the standard Italian field gun being the 75mm, which fired a shell weighing 14 lbs to a range of 11,000 yards, compared to the British 25-pounder that fired a shell weighing 25 lbs out to 13,400 yards.

Italian tanks were a mix of the L3, M11/39 and M13/40. They compared with the Western Desert Force's tanks as shown:

TYPE	WEIGHT	FRONTAL ARMOUR	MAIN ARMAMENT	SPEED	RANGE
British cruiser A9	12 tons	0.55-inch	2-pdr gun	25 mph	150 miles
British cruiser A10	14 tons	1.18-inch	2-pdr gun	16 mph	100 miles
British cruiser A13	14 tons	0.55-inch	2-pdr gun	30 mph	90 miles
British cruiser A13 Mk II	15 tons	1.18-inch	2-pdr gun	30 mph	90 miles
British Matilda Mk II	27 tons	3.07-inch	2-pdr gun (1.57-inch)	15 mph	160 miles
British Mk VI light tank	5 tons	0.65-inch	0.5-inch machine gun	35 mph	125 miles
Italian L3 light tank	3 tons	0.56-inch	2 x 8mm machine guns	26 mph	78 miles
Italian M11/39 medium tank	11 tons	1.18-inch	37mm gun (1.46-inch)	21 mph	124 miles
Italian M13/40 medium tank	14 tons	1.65-inch	47mm gun (1.85-inch)	20 mph	124 miles

Apart from the L3, which was utterly useless, the Italian tanks should, on the face of it, have been able to give a reasonable account of themselves, but there were only a very few of the quite acceptable M13/40, and in any case neither it nor the M11/39 had turrets that could traverse, so that the whole tank had to swivel to bring the gun to bear. Lack of spare parts, shortage of transport to move fuel and ammunition, a lack of technical know-how among the soldiers, and the inclination of Italian commanders to spread their tanks out rather than to concentrate them, all put the Italians at a disadvantage against British armour, quite apart from the fact that the British had, for once, considerably more tanks than their opponents.

Wavell was well aware that Cairo leaked like a sieve, with Italian and German agents at every turn, and strict security was enforced in the planning of what would be named Operation Compass. Only Wavell, Wilson, O'Connor and key staff officers knew anything about the attack, and Wavell did not tell London anything – thus reinforcing Churchill's conviction that the only British army in the field was doing nothing – until Anthony Eden, now Secretary of State for War, arrived in the Middle East to see what could be removed from there to go to Greece. Wavell then had to tell Eden, who told Churchill. The Prime Minister was delighted that something was being done, but then tried to tell Wavell how to do it. The immediate aims of the two men were in any case divergent. Wavell wanted to expel the Italians from Africa, including their troops in Abyssinia and Italian and British Somaliland, and saw Compass as lasting no more than five days. It would be a smart blow to set the Italians in Egypt reeling back, thus allowing him to detach a division (4 Indian) south to deal with the Duke of Aosta in the horn of Africa. Churchill, on the other hand, saw Wavell's operation as a precursor for shifting the centre of gravity of the war from the Middle East to the Balkans, with the main effort against Italy being from Greece rather than in Africa.

Rehearsals for Compass began in earnest, but with no indication that what was going on was anything more than training. The final exercise, in the last week of November, was mounted against camps constructed to resemble as nearly as possible the actual Italian forts. As a result of lessons learned on the exercise, the plans were given their final tweaking. O'Connor intended to send Selby Force along the coast road to attack the Italian positions frontally, from the east. While all eyes were on this, 7 Armoured and 4 Indian Divisions would swing far to the south and get into the rear of the Italian positions through the gap between the two southernmost forts. The Indian infantry would then attack the forts from behind, supported by the Matilda tanks of 7 RTR, while 7 Armoured would drive on and cut off the Italian line of retreat. The main task of the RAF was to keep the Italian air force from spotting the flanking move south, while also bombing dumps and rear areas. Ships of the Royal Navy, safe in their recently restored supremacy in the Mediterranean, would bombard Italian positions near the coast.

Command of the sea had only recently swung back towards the British, thanks to one of those quite extraordinary escapades that the Royal Navy seems able to pull off every now and then against all common sense, and for which only a half-witted bookmaker would offer anything but the very longest odds against. Their coat-trailing around Italian ports having failed to entice the Italian navy out to sea, Admiral Cunningham decided to try what had never been done before – an attack on an enemy fleet using carrier-borne aircraft alone. On the evening of 11 November 1940 two waves of Swordfish aircraft took off from HMS *Illustrious*, flew 180 miles across the ocean and attacked the Italian fleet lying at anchor in Taranto Bay. The harbour was well defended with barrage balloons, anti-aircraft guns, machine guns and searchlights, but the Fleet Air Arm raiders got in, dropped their torpedoes – from a height of thirty feet – and sank three battleships, including the brand new *Littorio*. Despite being detected as they approached, and coming under fire from 4-inch guns and several hundred machine guns, all the aircraft save two returned to the mother ship, and of those two the crew of one survived. Had this action been undertaken by modern aircraft it would still have been highly creditable, but the Swordfish, known as the stringbag, was obsolete before the war began. It was a biplane of 1934 vintage that could barely get up enough speed to stay airborne once it left the carrier's deck. The crew of pilot and observer sat in open cockpits, with a high explosive torpedo weighing 1,500lbs beneath them, and with a top speed of only

128 mph had to hope they could complete their tasks without meeting any land-based fighters, against which they would have had no chance whatsoever. This outstanding success, which reduced the firepower of the Italian navy by half, was noted with interest by navies around the world, not least by that of Japan.

Operation Compass, too, was a resounding success. On 7 December 1940 the attacking units moved out of their camps near Mersah Matruh and began the seventy-mile approach march to their assembly areas. The RAF ensured that no Italian aircraft got anywhere near the route, and also attacked Italian airstrips, destroying thirty-nine aircraft on the ground on that and the following nights. On the night of 8 December the Royal Navy shelled Mektila and Sidi Barrani, while 7 Armoured and 4 Indian Divisions, supported by 7 RTR, passed undetected into the Italian rear area. Shortly after first light on 9 December, following a short but intense artillery bombardment, Indian and British infantry of 4 Indian Division,[*] supported by the Matildas, attacked the Italian forts. This division had carried out considerable infantry tank cooperation training and both infantry and armour trusted each other and knew what to do. By nightfall they had taken out three large Italian forts. 7 Armoured had by this time driven to the coast between Sidi Barrani and Buq Buq, cutting the telegraph wires and the oil and water pipelines and also blocking what was not only the Italians' main supply route, but the only route by which they could retreat. Selby Force, meanwhile, had retained the attentions of the garrison of Mektila to such effect that as soon as night fell they withdrew back to Sidi Barrani, being shelled by the Royal Navy in both locations. The following day, 10 December, an attack by 4 Indian Division supported by tanks of 7 Armoured, delivered in a sandstorm, took Sidi Barrani, capturing over a hundred artillery pieces and, much more useful, large quantities of Italian wine and cheeses.

Next morning O'Connor ordered 7 Armoured Division, which had spent the hours of darkness repairing and refuelling its tanks, to cut off the Italian retreat. Pushing north-west, they caught the Italians in a long column of vehicles and took forty-eight guns and 14,000 prisoners. One British officer commented:

* Indian army brigades had two Indian or Gurkha battalions and one British.

No defeated army has ever cooperated with its opponents to the extent that the Italians did on this day. They assembled their own lorries. Refuelled them with their own fuel, and drove them full of their own prisoners to Mektila, and then came back for more, all without escort of any kind.[8]

It was quite clear that a stunning victory had been achieved, and that if followed up it could lead to even greater things. O'Connor, naturally enough, wanted to crack on, chase the Italians, give them no time to rest or regroup and destroy them utterly. Wavell was not necessarily opposed to that, but he had always intended to push 4 Indian Division – the only fully trained infantry he had – south to the Sudan. Orders for the redeployment of the division reached O'Connor on 11 December and he was dismayed, being of the view that the unexpected success of Compass should have altered the wider plan, and intending to use the division to back up his armour in a race to cut off the retreating Italians who had escaped earlier. Wavell promised the 6th Australian Division, just arriving in theatre, to the Western Desert Force, but O'Connor well knew that their standards could not be those of the regulars of the Indian army – they had done no infantry tank training for a start – and that he was to retain the British brigade attached to 4 Indian was little comfort. O'Connor also had to cope with Imperial politics; there was a New Zealand brigade already in Egypt, but the New Zealand government had been adamant that its troops would only fight as part of a New Zealand formation. The units to make up that formation – the New Zealand Division – were on their way, but until they arrived the commander of New Zealand's troops in Egypt, Major General Bernard Freyberg, who had won the Victoria Cross at the Somme in 1916 commanding a battalion of the Royal Naval Division, was not prepared to deviate from his government's instructions.

In hindsight Wavell might have been better to have left 4 Indian Division where it was. Despite Mussolini's grandiose plans, the Duke of Aosta's army was quite incapable of mounting an attack on Egypt, even if the administrative machinery to move it a thousand miles across inhospitable country with the Royal Navy controlling the Red Sea had existed, which it did not.

On 12 December 7 Armoured Division had reached Buq Buq; on 17

December Sollum, on the Egyptian side of the border, was reoccupied and on Christmas Eve Bardia, just inside Libya, was cut off and invested. On New Year's Day the Western Desert Force became XIII Corps, and between 3 and 5 January 1941 6 Australian Division were blooded in the capture of Bardia, which despite the bombast of its commander, General 'Electric Beard' Bergonzoli (who managed to slip away) could not withstand the attention of Australian infantrymen determined to do well in this, the first Australian battle of the war. Still O'Connor did not stop; by 21 January he was closing up on Tobruk, and on 22 January, supported by the entire British corps artillery (182 field and forty-two 5.5-inch medium guns),[*] Royal Naval shore bombardment, the RAF and Matilda tanks, the Australians added that town to their battle honours. More captured prisoners, guns, tanks and vehicles compounded the administrative difficulties of looking after them, and more welcome was the capture of two months'-worth of rations for the garrison.

On 5 January, the day the Australians captured Bardia, Wavell had already instructed the joint planning staff to consider operations against Benghazi once Tobruk was taken. Benghazi was another five hundred miles along the coast from Tobruk. It had a good harbour and could be developed into an air and naval base to support operations to the west with supplies brought in by sea. Then, on 6 January, orders came from the Prime Minister asking for four or five squadrons of aircraft to be sent to Greece. Air Marshal Longmore actually sent two squadrons, but on 10 January another telegram from Churchill informed Wavell that decoded German radio traffic suggested an invasion of Greece was imminent and that reinforcements intended for him would be diverted. Once Tobruk was taken the priority was to be Greece.

Wavell and Longmore flew to Athens for discussions and found that the Greek view was that the somewhat paltry forces that Britain could provide were insufficient to deter a German invasion and would only provoke one. As the Greeks had administered a severe bloody nose to the Italians trying to get through the mountains from Albania, where Italians were now dying of hypothermia, they were perfectly capable of

---

[*] Which could project a shell weighing 80 lbs out to a range of 17,800 yards.

defending their country from that particular enemy. Once again British priorities changed, and on 21 January Wavell was informed that Benghazi was, after all, now the goal.

After Tobruk, the Italians tried to hold along a line from Derna to Mechile, about one hundred miles west of Tobruk, but they abandoned this on 28 January. On 6 February 6 Australian Division took Benghazi, while on 5 February 7 Armoured Division, by a prodigious flanking movement of 150 miles by way of Mechili, Msus and Antelat, over going that was murderous for vehicles, had already established a blocking position at Beda Fomm, eighty miles south of Benghazi, in order to catch the Italians as they tried to retreat. The Battle of Beda Fomm was the Italian Tenth Army's last gasp. Marshal Graziani had now decided to evacuate Cyrenaica completely, and to pull back as far as Tripoli. Caught on the march by 7 Armoured, the Italians fought hard to escape the trap, but despite outnumbering the British they were unable to break through. By nightfall white flags began to flutter, and the Italian Tenth Army surrendered.

Operation Compass had originally been intended as a five-day raid. It had lasted sixty-eight days, covered seven hundred miles, and captured 110,000 prisoners including twenty-two generals and one admiral, 380 tanks of various types, 845 guns, vast numbers of soft-skinned vehicles and, so it was said, the mobile brothel. The butcher's bill for XIII Corps was just 500 dead (of whom only twenty-four were British army) and 1,400 wounded and missing. The RAF lost eleven fighters and four bombers, at a cost to the Italians of 1,249 aircraft shot down in combat, damaged or captured on the ground.

At the other end of Wavell's command, in Italian East Africa, matters were progressing equally well. There the plan was for Lieutenant General Platt with 4 and 5 Indian Divisions (with one of the brigades of the latter commanded by Brigadier W. J. Slim), supported by B Squadron 4 RTR with Matilda infantry tanks, to advance eastward into Eritrea from the Sudan; Lieutenant General A. G. Cunningham (brother of Admiral Sir Andrew) with 1 South African Division and a brigade from each of Southern Rhodesia (now Zimbabwe), Kenya and the Gold Coast (now Ghana) would attack the coast of Italian Somaliland from Kenya while

Abyssinia would be invaded from the west by local guerrillas under the command of British officers including Major Orde Wingate. The RAF would provide air support from Aden, Kenya and the Sudan, and once ports on the coast were captured, the Royal Navy could land supplies.

In a brilliant campaign, made the more difficult by inhospitable terrain and the need to coordinate three forces many miles apart, the capital of Italian Somaliland, Mogadishu, was captured on 25 February, Asmara, capital of Eritrea, on 1 April, and Addis Ababa, capital of Ethiopia/ Abyssinia between 6 and 9 April. On 5 May the exiled emperor, Haile Selaisse, was back on his throne and on 19 May the Duke of Aosta surrendered all Italian forces in East Africa. The campaign had cost Italy 230,000 killed, wounded and taken prisoner. Platt's troops had covered over one thousand miles; the tanks of 4 RTR had come eight hundred miles on tracks alone, and had lost only two tanks due to mechanical breakdown.

With the conclusion of Compass and its accompanying campaign in East Africa, it began to look as if the British had learned from their mistakes in Norway and France. It was a false dawn. Wavell's operations had worked because British tanks, guns and aircraft were technically superior to those of the Italians and because the British infantry and the armour had trained together, trusted each other and had worked out standard operating procedures that would give each element a drill to work to in any given tactical situation. Even when the experienced Indian infantry were replaced by the inexperienced Australians, simpler, but still effective, drills were quickly worked out. The armoured division had been put together and trained initially by the great Percy Hobart (and if the Royal Tank Regiment practised ancestor worship then it would be to him they would pray), and while he had been removed from command in 1939 for disagreeing with his superiors, it was his ideas and methods that still drove the division.* The co-location of army and air headquarters

---

* He was sacked because he could not get on with Wilson, GOC Egypt. Wilson's request for his removal was agreed by Wavell, and there are those who hold this against Wavell. In the latter's defence, when the GOC says he has no confidence in one of his divisional commanders, there is little that the Commander-in-Chief can do other than support his GOC – unless, of course, he sacks the GOC, which does happen, but not very often.

is often thought of as being Montgomery's idea, (a view propagated by Montgomery), but for Compass O'Connor and his RAF commander had their headquarters next door to each other; matters that caused friction, delays or misunderstandings in Norway or France here were rapidly resolved by the commanders talking to each other directly. Another – and vital – factor was the British ability to supply and administer their troops. It was done with great difficulty, but done it was, while the Italians often could not. Finally, Richard O'Connor was one of few really good British generals of this war who was given a chance to show what he could do. Had he not been taken prisoner on 6 April 1941 the story of the North African and Italian campaigns might have been very different.

The difficulties of administering an army in the conditions of North and East Africa were frequently not appreciated in London, particularly by the Prime Minister:

> I feel I have a right to ask you to make sure that the rearward services do not
> trench too largely on the fighting strength, that you have less fat and more
> muscle, that you have a smaller tail and larger teeth. You have well over 350,000
> troops on your ration strength and the number of units which are fighting or
> capable of fighting appears to me disproportionately small. It is distressing to
> see convoys sent by the heart's blood of the nation's effort consisting so largely
> of rearward services of all kinds.[9]

Once again the Prime Minister could not understand – or did not want to understand – that modern war requires many men behind for every one in front, that troops need to be transported, fed and equipped; that armoured units are useless without workshops, fitters, fuel convoys; that artillery cannot function without ammunition columns, and that troops cannot be put in the field until they have received at least the minimum rudimentary training for the theatre in which they are to operate.

With the success of Compass, O'Connor was convinced that now was the time to drive on and expel the Italians from North Africa completely. He had a plan for an advance along the coast supported by the Mediterranean Fleet which would have had him in Tripoli by the end of February, and it might – just – have worked. Wavell sympathised, but the situation had changed again. By order of the Defence Committee of the Cabinet the advance along the North African coast was to be halted at Benghazi; military efforts were to be limited to providing a secure bastion against attack on Egypt from the west, and everything else that could be spared was to go to Greece. Once more eyes in London and in Cairo were looking towards Greece, but eyes in Berlin were looking towards North Africa.

NOTES

1. Martin Middlebrook and Chris Everitt (eds), *The Bomber Command War Diaries*, Midland, Leicester, 2000.

2. Research Institute for Military History, Germany, (tr McMurry & Osers) *Germany and the Second World War, Vol. II,* Clarendon Press, Oxford, 2000.

3. Field Marshal Albrecht Kesselring (tr Wm Kimber Ltd), *The Memoirs of Field Marshal Kesselring*, Greenhill, London, 1988.

4. David Irving, *Göring: A Biography*, Macmillan, London, 1989.

5. Research Institute for Military History, Germany op. cit. Figures for aircraft include those lost to accidents in landing, usually caused by bad weather, and aircraft that got back to base or were recovered, but were severely damaged.

6. Stephen Roskill, *The War At Sea*, HMSO, London, 1956.

7. John Connell, *Wavell, Soldier and Scholar*, Collins, London, 1964.

8. Capt B. H. Liddell Hart, *The Tanks: The History of the Royal Tank Regiment*, Vol. II, Cassell, London, 1959.

9. J. R. M. Butler, *Grand Strategy*, Vol. II, HMSO, London, 1957.

11

More Disaster

1940 HAD BEEN A good year for the German armed forces, and they were rewarded accordingly. On 19 July those who had been instrumental in conquering all of western Europe were promoted. Colonel Generals Keitel (Chief of OKW), and von Brauchitsch (Commander-in-Chief of the Army) both became field marshals, as did army group commanders von Rundstedt, von Leeb and von Bock, army commanders List, von Kluge, von Witzleben and von Reichenau. General of Artillery Halder (Chief of the General Staff) became a colonel general and Major General Jodl (head of the operations branch at OKW) got two promotions to General of Infantry. In the Luftwaffe Colonel General Milch (Commander Luftflotte 5 for Norway and then inspector general of the air force) and Generals of Flyers Sperrle (Commander Luftflotte 3) and Kesselring (Commander Luftflotte 2) became field marshals. This did not just mean a rise in pay and status; field marshals never left the active list and were entitled to a personal staff (generally a driver, an orderly and a groom) for the rest of their lives, as well as a monetary award and an estate.[*]

Now that Hitler had decided not, after all, to reduce the size of the

---

[*] This had long been the case in the British army too (Marlborough – Blenheim; Wellington – Stratfield Saye; Haig – Bemersyde) and only stopped when the generals at the end of the Second World War said that they did not want money or estates (presumably because they knew that a Labour government would not grant them).

army but to increase it, there was yet another expansion, carried out by the tried and trusted method of breaking up existing divisions and forming new ones on the bits. Over the winter of 1940–41 the German army raised eighty-four new divisions, and by June 1941 had a total of 205 divisions, of which twenty were panzer divisions. The jump from ten to twenty armoured divisions did not, however, mean a doubling of the number of tanks, as the organisation of a panzer division was changed from two panzer regiments each of two tank battalions, to one regiment of two battalions, a drop from 280 tanks to 140, although a few divisions retained a single three-battalion regiment. The infantry in the division was increased from one regiment of two battalions to two regiments, each of two battalions. Of the motorised infantry divisions, two were converted to panzer divisions but the total was increased from four to ten by converting eight infantry divisions, reduced from three to two motorised infantry regiments each. Despite the numerical increase in divisions, the 205-division German army was not very much stronger than the 140 divisions that had embarked on the Battle of France. German industry was unable to keep pace with army expansion; five panzer divisions still had captured Czech equipment, there was almost no increase in artillery, and while each new division had a leavening of trained and experienced men, they were filled out by recruits from the depots. In June 1941, immediately before the attack on the Soviet Union, there were just thirty-eight infantry divisions in the west, all undermanned and lacking in equipment, and seven of them static. There was not a tank, nor a single motorised infantryman. As there was no threat from the west, this did not matter a jot.

Italy's entry into the war did not necessarily please all Germans. The Italian offensive against France through the Alps directed against Lyon did not start until 23 June 1940, by which time the Franco-German armistice talks had begun. It immediately ran into fierce resistance from the outraged French, and came to a halt in the mountains. Anxious to grab at least a bit of France to give them bargaining power at the peace conference, the Italians asked the Germans if Italian troops could be flown to Munich and inserted behind the German lines, in order to justify claims to a zone of occupation. General Halder was outraged:

The whole thing is the cheapest kind of fraud. I have made it plain that I will not have my name connected with that kind of trickery. In the end the whole thing turns out to be a plan hatched by Roatta [General M. Roatta, Italian army chief of the general staff] and disapproved by Marshal Badoglio [Italian chief of army staff and Roatta's superior]… a scheme proposed by a subordinate, which the responsible Italian Marshal (who seems to be the only respectable soldier in the lot) has rejected as dishonourable.[1]

The relationship between Germany and Italy was always ambiguous. Mussolini was a Fascist dictator long before Hitler, and the NSDAP had copied much of the Italian Fascists' doctrine and methods, including their salute. Hitler retained an astonishing loyalty to Mussolini personally, long after it was no longer in Germany's interest so to do. Germany was well aware that Italy lacked the economic strength to be of much help in the war, but as it would be a short one that did not matter too much. Militarily too Italy's weaknesses were fully recognised in Berlin, which assessed only 26 per cent of the Italian army divisions as being complete in manpower, equipment and transport.[2] It was, of course, essential from the German point of view that Italy did not do as she had in the First War and declare for Britain, which would have given the British complete control of the Mediterranean and airfields much closer to greater Germany than those in England. While Germany quickly became a far more influential player on the world stage than Italy, she did not, until well into the war, succeed in establishing common war aims and a common strategy, and when she did it was only because Italy was too weak to do other than be at the German beck and call.

Traditionally Italy had leaned towards the British orbit, rather than the European. While not quite a British creation in the way that Belgium was, Italy's existence as an independent state in modern times since 1861 owed much to British support, and as long as the Mediterranean was a British lake it paid to be polite. Besides, Italy had territorial claims on Austria, not all of which had been resolved as a result of Italy's participation in the Great War on the Allied side, and while the majority of the Italian population was strongly anti-Communist, it was anti-German too. Italy had not been pleased with the Anschluss, and had moved troops to the Brenner Pass, nor had she approved of Germany's treatment of Czechoslovakia. At the same time, it was Britain who had objected most strongly at the League of Nations when she invaded Ethiopia, and who had criticised her for sending troops to the Spanish Civil War. In the last analysis Fascist Italy would go to war for political and ideological reasons: she hankered, or Mussolini hankered, for great power status; she resented British control of the seas around her; she wanted influence in the Balkans and an overseas empire, and she was strongly anti-Communist. All these aims were more likely to be achieved by alliance with Germany than with Britain – assuming, of course, that Germany won the war, which at the time of Italy's entry seemed but a mere formality.

Despite his sympathies with Germany, Mussolini nevertheless conducted what he called a 'parallel war' for as long as he could. He did not tell Germany of his intention to invade Albania, Greece or Egypt, and then found himself having to be baled out by the Germans, much to their annoyance. It was the Italians' misfortune that their ambitions rarely coincided with the realities of power. As Operation Compass progressed it became clear to the Germans that if they did nothing, their ally would be evicted from Africa altogether. Twenty-eight per cent of Italy's entire army was in Libya and East Africa, and as O'Connor advanced through Libya, and Platt and Cunningham through East Africa, it began to look as if all or most of it would end up under the sand or in British prison camps. Although Germany did send some Stukas to Sicily, which made life difficult for British ships trying to enter Tobruk, the situation did not initially concern the Germans overmuch. Germany's future lay in Europe, not in colonies overseas, but the risk of the British controlling the entire southern Mediterranean coast, the possibility that Italy, if driven out of Africa completely, might leave the war, enabling the British troops in Africa to be used elsewhere, and the chance that French North Africa might break away from Vichy, forced a change in German perception. By now most German staff work and planning was directed towards the coming campaign in the east, and North Africa did not take up much time at OKW or OKH, but on 19 December 1940 Major General von Rintelen, the German military attaché in Rome, reported that unless a panzer division and enough equipment to supply ten Italian divisions was despatched, the Libyan front would collapse.

At this stage Hitler would not sanction the despatch of a panzer division, nor any equipment for the Italians, but he did agree to send 5 Light Division, an ad hoc formation of one infantry regiment of two battalions, one reconnaissance battalion, two anti-tank battalions, two machine-gun battalions and one field and one army anti-aircraft artillery battalions. In support would be a Luftwaffe reconnaissance gruppe (about forty aircraft) and an air force anti-aircraft artillery battalion. The entire force was to number 8,000 men with 1,300 vehicles and was to be commanded by Major General Freiherr von Funk, who left for Africa on 9 January to assess the situation before the arrival of his troops. Funk was back on 1 February with a pessimistic report. The situation continued to deteriorate and the need for armour was urgent. OKW agreed, and OKH ordered that a panzer regiment should be added to 5 Light Division, now to be commanded by Lieutenant General Streich (Hitler thought that Funk was far too gloomy and insisted on his replacement), and that 15 Panzer Division should also be sent. As this increased the size of the force to that of a corps, Major General Erwin Rommel, lately commander 7 Panzer in the Battle of France, was promoted to lieutenant general and appointed to command what was to be known as the Deutsches Afrika Korps, or DAK. Rommel flew to Tripoli on 12 February, to be met by a somewhat disheartened group of Italian generals, whose morale cannot have been improved when they discovered that Rommel's Pour le Mérite, worn as a neck decoration, had been won against the Italians.[*] Two days later the advance party of German troops began to arrive in Tripoli harbour.

From the British perspective Greece was what mattered now, and Wavell scraped together anything he could send there. The troops in East Africa could not be moved just yet, but from Egypt the New Zealanders, now a division, could go, as could the Australian 6 Division, and one of the brigades of 2 Armoured Division, formed from the men and vehicles sent out from England. There were changes in the command arrangements too. To demonstrate Britain's commitment to Greece the Prime

---

[*] In the aftermath of the disastrous Battle of Caporetto in November 1917.

Minister insisted that a well-known senior commander should be appointed there, and as the only general anywhere near Greece of whom anyone had heard, apart from Wavell himself, was Wilson, then off Wilson went. O'Connor replaced him as GOC Egypt, XIII Corps ceased to exist and in its place was formed Cyrenaica Command, under Lieutenant General Philip Neame who arrived from Palestine. Neame was a Royal Engineer who had won a Victoria Cross as a lieutenant on the Western Front in December 1914, had commanded 4 Indian Division and was a close friend of O'Connor's. Unfortunately for Neame, the troops in his command were not the XIII Corps that had done so well in Operation Compass. The reasonably experienced 6 Australian Division had been replaced by the untried 9 Australian, of which two brigades were actually from 7 Australian Division and were understrength, short of transport and untrained; 7 Armoured Division was now in Cairo with what was left of its tanks in workshops undergoing repair; the one brigade of 2 Armoured – 3 Armoured Brigade – had 156 tanks, but eighty-six of them were captured Italian M13/40 which had no radios, and of the fifty-two British cruisers half were already in workshops and the others prone to frequent breakdowns. The only remnants of the once victorious XIII Corps that remained were the King's Dragoon Guards with their Mormon-Harrington armoured cars.

Although the British knew from radio intercepts that Rommel and German reinforcements were on the way, they reasoned that by the time the Germans had arrived, got acclimatised, done some training and dumped stores forward, it would be May at least and probably June before they could pose a threat. By then Neame would have got his motley force sorted out and trained; at least one of the Indian divisions would be back from East Africa and 7 Armoured's tanks would be in running order. The British main defence line at this stage ran south from El Agheila, and while Wavell, when he visited it on 16 March was not happy and ordered Neame to make certain adjustments, he still thought that time was on his side.

German officers were trained to think and operate in a less stately manner. Already the Luftwaffe was bombing Benghazi from Sicily, at Rommel's urgings and against the wishes of the Italians who protested that many senior officers and party officials owned property there. By 4 March, long before all his troops had arrived, instead of accepting the Italian front line as a laager around Tripoli, he had pushed men of his reconnaissance and anti-tank battalions forward to Mugtaa, four hundred miles east of Tripoli and only twelve miles from the British, and had established a twenty-mile strip of mines and armoured cars running from the coast inland. He had personally reconnoitred the British line (and was not impressed by what he saw) and had ordered 5 Light Division, whose panzer regiment with its tanks, half of them Mk III or Mk IV, was still arriving, to be ready for an attack on El Agheila. Then he was off to Berlin to expound on grandiose plans for the reconquest of Libya, the capture of Egypt and the taking back of East Africa.

Berlin had little time for North Africa, Rommel, or his plans. OKH were furiously beavering away at the plans for Barbarossa – the invasion of the Soviet Union – as well as for the invasion of Greece, and while Rommel could not be told about either, he was informed that there were no more troops for him. After all, with a panzer regiment and a panzer division on the way, he already had two panzer divisions'-worth of tanks, and unlike the troops earmarked for Greece, his would not be available for Russia. He was to go back to Africa, initiate limited operations to take the British forward defence line if possible, advance no farther than Benghazi, and prepare for a possible attack on Tobruk in the autumn. Disobeying orders is not necessarily the mark of a good commander, but knowing when to disobey and get away with it is, and that is exactly what Rommel intended to do.

Rommel arrived back in Africa on 24 March 1940, and the next day the reconnaissance battalion of 5 Light attacked El Agheila. The small garrison of the airstrip and fort – a few Australian infantrymen and a troop of the KDG – pulled out to Mersa el Brega, about thirty miles back along the coast. On 31 March 5 Light attacked that too, and the British withdrew. On 2 April 5 Light were into Agadabia, fifty miles east, and again the British withdrew. Disregarding the orders of his nominal superior, the Italian General Gariboldi, to proceed no farther, Rommel split his forces into three groups. The reconnaissance battalion was to head straight for Benghazi up the coast road while two task forces, one led by the commander 5 Light (Streich) and the other by Lieutenant Colonel von Schwerin, cut across the peninsula through the desert towards El Mechili and Derna to try to intercept the retreating British. The Germans entered Benghazi at 2200 hours on 3 April, and reported that they were welcomed by crowds of cheering Italians who complained that the British had looted the town before departing. After a move of more than two hundred miles with maps that were little more than fictional representations, along tracks strewn with mines by the Italians when they had retreated, constantly chivvied by Rommel who flew around the desert in a Fiesler Storch light aircraft, regularly losing his temper and threatening to sack commanders whose vehicles, through no fault of their crews, had run out of fuel, broken down or had got lost, Streich's and Schwerin's task forces were closing up on Mechili, stubbornly defended by the regular soldiers of 3 Indian Motor Brigade, albeit with no heavy weapons.

For the British between Benghazi and Mechili there was, quite simply, chaos. Communications were breaking down, if they existed at all, commanders were taking their own decisions regardless of what Neame's headquarters was trying to get them to do, and units, bits of units and individuals were straggling back as fast as they could towards Mechili. To Wavell in Cairo Rommel's move had all the ingredients of a disaster. On 2 April, when Reconnaissance Battalion 3 was being briefed for the dash to Benghazi, Wavell flew up to Barce, sixty miles short of Benghazi. What he saw confirmed his low opinion of Neame and he signalled O'Connor to come up from Cairo and take over. O'Connor arrived next morning, and persuaded Wavell not to supersede Neame in the middle of a battle, but to allow O'Connor to stay as his adviser. The British army does not have political commissars, nor does it have 'advisers', and one can only assume that this extraordinary arrangement was born out of O'Connor's reluctance to see an old friend sacked, and a very natural disinclination to take over a battle that was probably already lost. Wavell flew back to Cairo, stopped the embarkation of troops for Greece and looked to see what reinforcement he might send west.

Neame and O'Connor moved the headquarters fifty miles east to Maraua and tried, without much success, to impose some order on a rapidly deteriorating situation. There was confusion and delay, numerous cases of firing on friendly troops, the destruction of the main fuel depot at Msus because the defenders thought an approaching patrol of the recently formed Long Range Desert Group (LRDG) were German tanks, and instances of troops surrendering when attacked by a huge German-initiated dust cloud. The Australians, despite their inexperience, performed well under a resolute commander, Major General Morshead, while (depending upon which source one consults) the one armoured brigade of Major General Gambier-Parry's 2 Armoured Division either behaved disgracefully by abandoning their tanks and jumping on board passing lorries to save themselves,[3] were guilty of 'complete disobedience of orders',[4] 'had little fighting capacity left as a coherent formation',[5] were the victims of confusing orders and lack of fuel (as the Germans thought),[6] or were extremely unlucky and suffered massively from mechanical and radio breakdowns.[7] The truth is probably a mixture of all, though it would have been out of character for the men to have deliberately abandoned their tanks, unless no fuel was available or they had suffered a breakdown that could not be repaired. Certainly their tanks, both captured Italian and British, left a very great deal to be desired, and matters were not helped by the brigade commander, Brigadier Rimmington, being captured on 6 April, but it is not good enough to blame lack of desert training for the brigade's failure to achieve more: Rommel's men were landed at Tripoli and sent straight into the desert with no more training than the British, and in many cases less.

On 6 April, the day the Germans invaded Greece, Neame and O'Connor, in Neame's staff car and with Neame driving to allow his driver a rest, were retreating along with everyone else when they took a wrong turning, found themselves behind the advancing Germans and were captured. The loss of Neame probably did not make much differ-ence to the outcome of that particular battle – he was out of contact with most of his units, and it is difficult to see how any general could have done much more with the raw troops that he had – but the removal of O'Connor was a severe blow to the British cause. Speculation may be pointless, but it is great fun nevertheless, and O'Connor, having made his name with successful command of a corps in battle at a time when

Montgomery (two years older) had only commanded a division, and that in a defeat, would surely have commanded the Eighth Army rather than Montgomery. O'Connor was at least as good a military technician as Montgomery, far better at getting on with allies, and eschewed the cheap showmanship of Montgomery, which might have fooled most of the soldiers but was seen for what it was by many of the officers. He was far less ponderous than Montgomery and might well have made a much better job of the North African and Italian campaigns, and perhaps Normandy and north-west Europe too. 'Might' and 'perhaps', because O'Connor was a man of stern principle and would have been quite capable of resigning if Churchill pestered him the way he pestered every other commander. Nevertheless, Rommel versus O'Connor would have been an interesting contest.[*]

On the afternoon of 8 April those of the garrison of Mechili who were unable to break out in the morning were ordered to surrender by Gambier-Parry, Commander 2 Armoured Division, who assumed (wrongly) that the smoke and dust raised by his attackers indicated an overwhelming force coming against him. By 10 April Rommel's troops were at Tobruk, found it held by the Australian 9 Division and flowed on towards the border. On 28 April the Germans captured Bardia and Fort Capuzzo above, and Sollum below, the Halfaya Pass. The whole thing had been a complete disaster for the British, the only saving grace being that successive attacks on Tobruk were resisted, the besieged garrison being supplied by the Royal Navy despite constant air attack. Rommel's success, however, was not entirely appreciated at home. There North Africa was an irritating sideshow while far greater things in Greece, Yugoslavia and, soon, Russia were afoot. Halder's diary displays considerable tetchiness towards Rommel and his incessant demands for more troops, more aircraft and more tanks. On 3 April, 'Reminder not to be reckless' and 'further advance only when British armoured elements have been taken out of area'; on 14 April, 'Our prime objective is building up a front of ample width in the Sollum area... apart from this, only raids'; on 15 April, 'Now at last he [Rommel] is constrained to state that his forces are not sufficiently

---

[*] Wavell tried to persuade Whitehall to offer to exchange O'Connor for any six captured Italian generals. Whitehall refused on the grounds that exceptions could not be made for generals!

strong to allow him to take full advantage of the "unique opportunities" offered by the overall situation. That is the impression we have had for quite some time over here'; and on 24 April, the day that Halder decided he must send a senior representative to see exactly what was going on:

> Rommel has not sent us a single clear cut report all these days, but I have a feeling things are in a mess... Rommel is in no way up to his operational task. All day long he rushes about between the widely scattered units and stages reconnaissance raids in which he fritters away his forces... air transport cannot meet Rommel's senseless demands.

To observe and report, and with the authority of OKH to rein in Rommel, Halder sent his deputy, Lieutenant General Friedrich Paulus, who 'has good personal relations with Rommel from way back when they served together and he is perhaps the only man with enough personal influence to head off this soldier gone stark mad'.[8]

Paulus's reports informed his chief that the DAK was overextended, tactically unbalanced, at the end of a tenuous logistic chain and with tanks badly in need of major repair and maintenance. He had instructed Rommel that the best the DAK could hope for now, even if Tobruk fell, would be to hold Cyrenaica no farther forward than Sollum, and that if Tobruk held out then the DAK should defend farther back, and await an opportunity later. These reports were being intercepted by the British, and decoded at Bletchley Park. The impression they gave – that Rommel was in no position to advance and might easily be forced to retreat – encouraged Churchill, who had been surprisingly understanding about the British disasters so far, to demand aggressive action.

Wavell had a huge amount on his plate; not only did he have to worry about Libya and Egypt, but Greece had turned very bad indeed, there had been a pro-German revolution in Iraq, and German influence in Vichy Syria was believed (wrongly, as it transpired) to have increased to the stage where it was necessary for the British to invade. Wavell launched Operation Brevity, an attempt to recapture the Halfaya Pass and Capuzzo on 15 May, with the regular 22 Guards Brigade (3 Coldstream and 2 Scots Guards and 1 Durham Light Infantry) supported by fourteen Matildas of 4 RTR, 2 Rifle Brigade (motorised infantry belonging to 7 Armoured

Division) and a grouping of the rest of 7 Armoured's infantry plus twenty-nine cruiser tanks, the whole commanded by Brigadier 'Strafer' Gott. The British took Sollum and the pass and attacked Capuzzo, but had to pull back to the pass by the morning of 17 May. On 27 May the Germans counter-attacked and retook both Sollum and the pass. Brevity had achieved the British nothing save the loss of more men and more tanks. Although lack of fuel prevented Rommel from advancing any farther, he had put the Italians back where they were before Compass, and there was considerable propaganda value in what he had done, even if the German high command in Berlin were unhappy. For the moment, both sides were at a standstill.

In Greece too the battle was lost. In January 1940 original offers of British assistance after Italy's invasion of Greece had been turned down by President of the Council (prime minister) Metaxas, on the grounds that Greece could handle Italy alone and the proposed British contribution would be too small to guard against a German invasion and might only provoke it. Metaxas died on 29 January, to be replaced by Koryziz, whose view was somewhat different from that of his predecessor. While Greek forces had pushed the Italians back into Albania, the Greek army was having problems itself in the mountains and was almost out of ammunition. If something was not done quickly, the front might even collapse. Koryziz would be glad of any assistance the British might offer, although transport and warm clothing would be particularly welcome. At this, all the British ambitions for a Balkan front were rekindled.

In principle there was nothing wrong in wanting to establish a Balkan front; it would enable the British to interfere with German and Italian oil shipments from the Black Sea to the Aegean, to bomb Italy and the Romanian oil fields and force the Germans into fighting on another front, which for them would be at the end of a long logistic chain. Among the disadvantages were that the entire British strategic reserve in the Middle East (if that is not too grand a description of what was available) would have to be committed; the shipping required to maintain it would be prodigious, and there was no end in sight – no exit strategy. Discussions between Dill, Wavell, Longmore and the Greek generals resulted in an agreement that the defence of Greece would be based on what was known as the Aliakmon Line, which ran from the Aegean Sea north of Katerini, seventy miles north-west through Verria (where it crossed the River Aliakmon) and Edessa to the Yugoslav border. This meant giving up the Salonika peninsula, but was felt to be acceptable given the as yet uncertain position of Yugoslavia. The Greek Commander-in-Chief, General Papagos, agreed that he would begin to withdraw Greek troops from Albania and Macedonia (which covered Salonika) immediately, and would begin to develop the defences of the Aliakmon Line, into which British troops, when they arrived, would go. This position would enable a stout defence against German inroads from Bulgaria, and allow a fighting retreat if that became necessary. On 1 March Bulgaria openly adhered to the Axis, and troops of the German Twelfth Army began to move into that country. On 4 March Operation Lustre, the insertion of British troops into Greece, began.

Throughout February and March the CIGS, Dill, and the Foreign Secretary, Eden, had been trying to cobble together their Balkan front. As this made little sense in the context of Greece alone, the British tried very hard to persuade the Turks and the Yugoslavs to join them in a coalition which might deter German aggression. Yugoslavia was vital to British plans because if she was on the side of the Allies she could attack in flank German forces assaulting Greece from Bulgaria, and do the same to Italians coming from Albania. On the other hand, if Yugoslavia declared for Germany, then the Greek defences could be outflanked. The Yugoslavs refused to see either Eden or Dill, while Turkey made sympathetic noises, asked for huge quantities of arms and equipment that the British could not possibly provide, but stopped short at any form of military alliance.

Then, on 25 March, the Yugoslav government signed the tripartite pact adhering to the Axis cause. This caused outrage in the country, where the Croats were not opposed to Germany but disliked being dragged into the war, and where the Serbs, who disliked everybody, recalled that they had fought against Germany in the First War. On 27 March a *coup d'état* overthrew the pro-German regime and installed General Simovitch as prime minister. Despite the involvement of British agents in the staging of the coup, it was not to resound to the British advantage. Simovitch was anti-German but at the same time had no wish to involve his country in a war. He would see Dill, but not Eden, and while he expressed sympathy with the Allied cause, he would not embark on any form of collective defence.

Despite the agreement that the British generals thought they had with the Greeks, on arrival they found that Greek troops had not been pulled back from Salonika or from the Albanian border. It was now politically impossible to withdraw, said Papagos, and even if it could be done his troops would be caught on the line of march. In any event, he claimed, he had only agreed to do so if the Yugoslavs mounted a serious resistance to the Germans, which they had not done. It was a foretaste of the difficulty of trying to work with the Greeks, a difficulty which carried on long after the war had ended. British units nevertheless began to move into the Aliakmon Line, and Papagos, reluctantly, started to move some Greek troops there as well.

The only forces that the British were able to send to Greece were the 6th Australian and the New Zealand Divisions, supported by 1 Armoured Brigade and its 166 A10 cruiser tanks. Wavell hoped that it might be possible later to augment this by another Australian division and a Polish Brigade, but while the armour, the artillery, the engineers and the supporting arms were mainly British, the fact that the infantry battalions, who would do most of the fighting, were entirely Dominion was an embarrassment. It was not lost on the Dominion governments either, who agreed to their troops being sent to Greece not because Anthony Eden or General Wilson had come to an agreement with the Greeks without reference to Australia or New Zealand, but because they considered it morally right to support Greece and because Dill, Wavell, Blamey* (the Australian commander) and Freyberg had assured them that there was a realistic chance of being able to do so.

General Wilson deployed what was now known as W Force on the Aliakmon Line with the New Zealand Division on the right, next to them a Greek regiment in the mountains, then one brigade of 6 Australian in the Verria Gap, and on the extreme left (north) was the balance of the Greek forces allotted to him, two divisions less the regiment already

* Blamey later claimed he had been railroaded into agreeing – he probably had.

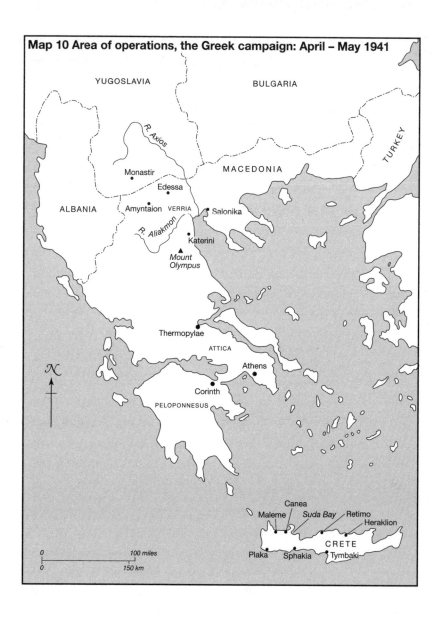

Map 10 Area of operations, the Greek campaign: April – May 1941

YUGOSLAVIA

BULGARIA

R. Axíos

Monastir

MACEDONIA

Edessa

TURKEY

ALBANIA

Amyntaion   VERRIA

Salonika

R. Aliakmon

Katerini

▲
*Mount
Olympus*

Thermopylae

ATTICA

Athens

𝒩

Corinth

PELOPONNESUS

Canea

Maleme   *Suda Bay*   Retimo

Heraklion

CRETE

0   100 miles

0   150 km

Plaka   Sphakia   Tymbaki

deployed. As a screen out in front in the direction of Salonika was the armoured brigade, less one regiment in reserve behind the left of the main position at Amyntaion, and there was a second sizeable reserve in the centre rear, consisting of the remaining two Australian brigades.

On 6 April German forces invaded Yugoslavia and Greece, and the Greek prime minister committed suicide. The Germans made short work of Yugoslavia, whose enormous army was riven by dissent, politics, corruption and general incompetence. On 12 April the Germans took Belgrade after bombing it and on 17 April Yugoslavia surrendered, but the preceding lack of resistance allowed the German XXXX (Motorised) Corps to approach the Greek border.

By 8 April the German XVIII Mountain Corps, supported by 2 Panzer Division, was driving south from Bulgaria towards Salonika, and there was very little to stop it. The Greek commander, General Bakopoulus, considered evacuating his troops by sea, but the antiquated Greek navy could do nothing and the British navy had quite enough to worry about elsewhere, so the Greek supreme command in Athens ordered all Greek units east of the River Axios (that is, all in the Salonika peninsula) to surrender. On 9 April 60,000 Greek soldiers laid down their arms. General Wilson had always doubted the Greek ability to hold Salonika – indeed the British had always considered that it should not be defended at all – and he withdrew the armoured brigade back to Amyntaion. Wilson's concern at this stage was the German XXXX Corps moving down through Yugoslavia; once they advanced beyond Monastir they could easily outflank the Aliakmon Line. Well briefed by London as to German intentions,* Wilson ordered a withdrawal on the night of 11–12 April, to a line running west from Mount Olympus, W Force to hold the right and Greek units from the Army of Epirus (who had been facing the Italians in Albania) the left. On 14 April Wilson ordered a further withdrawal to a position around Thermopylae, which he hoped to hold with British troops

---

* ULTRA, the British codebreaking and deciphering organisation, was one of the most closely guarded secrets of the war, and only admitted to many years after the war was over. The Official History, published in 1957, makes no mention of it. Very few field commanders were even told of its existence, and Wilson was one of the handful who was informed that the intelligence predictions he was getting were taken from intercepted German signals. Even he, however, was not told of how extensive the system was.

alone, the Greeks having become ever more difficult to communicate with, and increasingly unwilling or unable to conform to Wilson's orders. By the time 1 Armoured Brigade reached Thermopylae most of its tanks had been lost, more due to mechanical breakdown or tracks wearing out than to the attention of the Germans, and 3 RTR had none at all. With the Luftwaffe now giving its full attention to Greece, the RAF was out-numbered by about twelve to one (eight squadrons of some ten opera-tional aircraft each opposed to 1,200 aircraft),[9] and W Force, withdrawing along bad roads and over difficult terrain, was constantly harried by ground-attack fighters and fighter-bombers. Worse, supply columns trying to come up were attacked, and even if less damage was done than the Germans hoped and the British feared, the not unnatural reaction of an inexperienced vehicle driver (and most were) to bale out at the sound of any approaching aircraft and take cover in a ditch slowed everything up and made traffic control a nightmare, not helped by Greek refugees and disorganised Greek units clogging the roads.

By now it was obvious to most British and Greek commanders that the cause was lost, and even Papagos, the Greek Commander-in-Chief, recommended that the British withdraw. On 19 April Wavell flew to Athens, and the withdrawal was agreed. On 21 April the Greek army in Epiros mutinied, deposed its commanders and surrendered to the Germans – they refused to surrender to the Italians on the (not unreasonable) grounds that they had not been beaten by them. W Force withdrew south through Attica to Peloponnesus, effectively a huge island separated from the mainland by the Corinth Canal, over which was one bridge. The Royal Navy would once again fulfil one of its traditional roles and remove a British army from an inhospitable mainland. When the Germans dropped two parachute battalions on the canal they failed to seize the bridge, which was blown in time, but no more withdrawing troops could enter Pelo-ponnesus and the navy now had to pick up soldiers from all over Attica as well. The British had sent 62,000 soldiers and airmen to Greece. The evacuation began on the night of 24/25 April, and in a week the Royal Navy embarked around 50,000 of them, losing two destroyers and four transports in the process. As in Norway and as in France, most of the guns, vehicles and heavy equipment had to be abandoned.

The Balkan front had collapsed, but in truth it had never really existed. Only if Turkey, Yugoslavia and Greece had been locked into a realistic coalition with Britain could it ever have worked, and the Turks and the Yugoslavs were well aware that whatever their sympathies might be, Britain was in no state to provide meaningful military support. Even without the Turks and the Yugoslavs, the defence of Greece might have made some sense politically and morally if there had been sufficient troops and sufficient aircraft to make a difference, and if the main Greek armies had been pulled out of Salonika and Albania in early March and concentrated on the Olympus Line – the Aliakmon Line was never going to be able to defend Greece once the Germans had overrun Yugoslavia. As it was, even if the Greeks had done exactly as the British wanted, a stiffening of two Dominion divisions, one armoured brigade and a few aircraft which would have been far better employed elsewhere, was nothing like enough, and was simply a disaster waiting to happen – as, of course, it did.

One can understand Churchill's emotional reaction to a threat against Greece, the cradle of civilisation, and another state, like Belgium and Italy, whose very existence as an independent entity in modern times owed much to British benevolence. His wish to help the Greeks was supported by the Foreign Secretary, Eden, and the British ambassador in Athens, Sir Michael Palairet, but there can be no excuse for the generals agreeing with it. Dill, initially opposed, came round to approving the sending of troops to Greece, as did Wavell. Neither of these generals were fools, nor were they mere lackeys of the Prime Minister, and one can only conclude that their judgement was at fault – as Churchill later admitted his was too. The British had been given a golden opportunity to get themselves off the Greek hook by the refusal of Prime Minister Metaxas to accept the help offered in January, and they should have taken it. Certainly the Balkan campaign, initiated by the Germans solely to rescue the Italians from a mess of their own making, delayed the onset of the Russian campaign by a few weeks, but this would have been so whether or not British troops were involved – their presence imposed little if any delay.

Large numbers of the men evacuated from the ports, harbours and

inlets of Peloponnesus and Attica were offloaded on Crete, so as to allow
for a fast turnaround of ships. Crete had been occupied by the British on
6 November 1940, as a reaction to the Italian attack on Greece, and 14
Infantry Brigade, a regular formation consisting of 2 York and Lancaster
Regiment, 2 Black Watch and 1 Welch, engineers, field and anti-aircraft
artillery, a signals company and supporting services were delivered there,
along with a squadron of fighters. The occupation made sense, as Crete
dominated the eastern Mediterranean, commanded the Aegean Sea, and
was well within bomber range of the Romanian oil fields and southern
Italy. Conversely it would be very useful to the Germans and Italians if
occupied by them. Crete is 160 miles from east to west and thirty-six miles
from north to south. It had three airports on its north coast, but only the
western one, Maleme, fifteen miles west of the capital, Canea, was a
proper airport, the others – Retimo and Heraklion – being basic airstrips.
The ports were mere fishing harbours and there were no facilities to take
ships of any size, although there was a reasonable anchorage at Suda Bay,
to the east of Canea. The few roads that did exist were narrow. By late
April, when troops evacuated from Greece were arriving, very little had
been done to improve the defences of the island. There were no hard
shelters for the aircraft, not much road improvement had been done, and
there had been little attempt to prepare airfield defences. While plant
was certainly in short supply, the Royal Engineers could have acheived
more, and in nearly six months three battalions of infantry with picks
and shovels should have done a great deal more than they did.

It was now obvious that the Germans would follow up their successes
in Yugoslavia and Greece with an assault on Crete. The men transported
to Crete from Greece could not all be got away to Egypt and would have
to help in the defence, short of kit though many were. Major General
Freyberg, commanding the New Zealand Division, was appointed as the
overall commander, and to defend the island he had around 43,000 men,
of whom some 10,000 were Greeks of the existing garrison or evacuated
from the mainland. Of the 33,000 British, Australian and New Zealanders, however, many were not combat troops and of those who were,
numbers lacked equipment or did not belong to complete units. The
fighting troops available to Freyberg, besides 14 Brigade, were two

brigades (4 and 5) of his own division, one weak brigade (19) from 6 Australian Division, and some Greek infantry who would have to be armed by the British. Additionally from Egypt came a few light tanks and six Matildas – almost worn out but better than nothing. From the soldiery who had been separated from their units and from spare men from the coastal gun and anti-aircraft artillery teams, and Greek infantrymen, Freyberg created a brigade-sized formation, stiffened by one battalion from 14 Brigade, known as the Composite Force. Additionally he formed New Zealand soldiers whose units were not present or were not complete into the ad hoc 10 Brigade, made up by the addition of Greek infantry. By the end of April Ultra intercepts had told him that he had three weeks to organise the defence. Those men who were either not needed or who could not be armed and equipped were evacuated to Egypt.

Freyberg based his defence of Crete on the airfields. To the west, covering Maleme and the area between it and Canea, he placed 5 and 10 NZ Brigades, with 4 NZ Brigade to the rear in reserve. In the Canea and Suda Bay area was the Composite Force, commanded by Major General Weston, Royal Marines,* while Retimo was the responsibility of the Aus-tralian 19 Brigade, and 14 Brigade, less one battalion, looked after Heraklion. There were only sixty-eight anti-aircraft guns, of various calibres, on the whole island. Freyberg knew that communications would be difficult. There were insufficient radios and many did not work; there was only one road linking all the positions and it could easily be cratered by bombing – in any case there was little transport to move along it. It was unlikely that a reserve held centrally would be able to get to any threatened point, so Freyberg did not attempt to form one. Instead he briefed each commander that he would have to hold his position without reinforcement, and shared out the few tanks among them. Freyberg's deployment meant that there were no troops to cover a German landing anywhere other than on the western half of the north coast, but the British had absolute and detailed knowledge of the German plan.

The attack on Crete, Operation Merkur, was entrusted to General

---

* There were a number of Royal Marines, from ships' landing parties, and also some of the newly raised commandos (then army rather than Royal Marines) in Crete. The commandos had originally been sent out on a hare-brained Churchillian scheme to capture Pantellaria, which was, fortunately, cancelled.

Kurt Student's IX Airborne Corps (Fleigerkorps) which would operate from Greece. The plan was to saturate the island with bombing from the air, using 430 bombers and 230 fighters, and then assault all three airfields simultaneously with paratroopers and gliderborne infantry, in the hope that at least one would be captured. Through that would come the first reinforcements, six infantry battalions landed in transport aircraft, after which would come the sea-tail with more infantry and elements of 5 Panzer Division. This plan was known to the British in intimate detail, down to the landing zones for individual companies of parachute infantry, thanks to Ultra, but there were two major snags to the possession of this knowledge. First, a nine-stone weakling in a cul de sac at midnight is not necessarily advantaged by being given warning that he will shortly be mugged by a sixteen-stone giant; and second, any deployment that might make the Germans suspect their radio traffic was being read had to be avoided. Freyberg knew that he could afford to ignore the south coast, and the east of the island, but he could not place his troops to conform too closely to German intentions or they would realise what was happening and redesign their Enigma machine, which up to now they considered unbreakable. Ultra's ability to decipher Enigma codes was one of the most important weapons of the war for the British and they would, now and in future, sacrifice men, ships and aircraft to protect it. Prior knowledge of what an enemy is up to is only of use if you can act on it.

The Luftwaffe attacks on Crete began on 14 May, and went on for six days. On 19 May the last six serviceable aircraft of the RAF fighter squadron left for Egypt, before they too were shot down or destroyed on the ground. At first light on the morning of 20 May there was a particularly heavy raid that destroyed anti-aircraft guns in their positions, raised huge clouds of dust and added even more craters to the coast road. Then, at 0800 hours, Operation Merkur began, as gliders and transport aircraft appeared over Maleme, Retimo and Heraklion, and eight battalions (it should have been nine but one flight of aircraft were unable to take off) parachuted in and began to land by glider. There were no RAF aircraft to shoot down the lumbering transports and the slow gliders, nor were there ships of the Royal Navy to drench them with anti-aircraft fire – the

Luftwaffe's complete air superiority had seen to that – but casualties to the attacker were heavy nevertheless. The German parachute was very simple – almost primitive – and the inability to turn it into the wind meant that accidents on landing, leading to broken ankles at best or broken backs at worst, were common.* In some cases the men's weapon containers – dropped separately – fell where their owners could not reach them, and some gliders landed in the sea or were shot down before landing. The tactic was for the gliders, which could be positioned accurately, to land as close to the objective – gun position, bridge, building – as possible, while the paratroopers landed elsewhere, well away from the enemy, sorted themselves out and then went on to support the glider infantry. While Freyberg was not permitted to put men on every parachute-dropping zone, for fear of giving Ultra away, a large number of Germans did land in the middle of defensive positions and many gliders came down within the fields of fire of the defenders.

At first, the defenders more than held their own; fighting in some areas was savage, often hand to hand (far less common than is often supposed), but then misunderstanding and confusion led to a precipitate withdrawal from Maleme, and the Germans captured that airfield at dawn on 21 May. The British were unable to recapture it by counterattack, and the battle for Crete was lost; it would just take a few more days before the British realised it. Once they had an airfield the Germans pushed more and more transport aircraft in; the runway was under fire and over eighty transports crash-landed or were destroyed on the tarmac, but more and more mountain infantry were disgorged, and when Student put in his last parachute battalion on 21 May there was no possibility of the British recovering Maleme. That night the Royal Navy routed the German sea-tail, but in the hours of daylight (and the nights are short in the Cretan spring) the Luftwaffe was able to roam at will, giving close and accurate support to the German infantry. On 22 May the Royal Navy removed the King of Greece and the British minister from Crete; on 26 May Freyberg

* The British parachute had four lift webs, two attached to each shoulder, which gave the soldier some steerage and allowed him to turn under control, avoid obstacles, face into the wind and land with minimum lateral movement. The German parachute had one strap at the small of the man's back which then connected with the rigging lines of the parachute. The German parachutist was entirely at the mercy of the wind and severe oscillation could mean his hitting the ground at considerable speed.

told Wavell that he could not hold much longer, and on 27 May Wavell ordered evacuation.

Once more the navy was called upon to come to the rescue of an out-classed army. Operating under far more difficult conditions than from Norway or from Dunkirk, or even from Peloponnesus, the navy now had to operate from Alexandria, over four hundred miles away, with hardly any air cover and from an island where the only reasonable anchorage was on the north coast. The navy had already been slipping what rein-forcements and supplies for the army it could into inlets and Suda Bay by night, with Churchill constantly demanding more and even counter-manding Admiral Cunningham's orders to individual ships. At Heraklion, 14 Brigade, still holding on, were taken off on the night of 28 May, but the Australian brigade at Retimo could not be rescued and had to surrender. The rest of the garrison that was capable of doing so, led by Freyberg himself, went south and were evacuated from Sphakia, Plaka and Tymbaki on the south coast. Evacuation continued until 1 June, and the navy got 18,600 men away. Another 12,000 were taken prisoner. The losses to the navy were high: three cruisers and six destroyers were sunk; an aircraft carrier, two battleships, six cruisers and seven destroyers were damaged, and 1,800 officers and ratings were killed, compared to about the same number of army deaths, of which 612 were British as opposed to Empire. Once again most of the vehicles and heavy equipment had to be left behind. It was while the evacuation from Crete was in full swing that Admiral Cunningham, asked whether the losses in ships were worth it, said 'It takes the Navy three years to build a ship, but three hundred years to build a reputation. We must not let them down.'[10]

The defence of Crete achieved nothing, and as the island then played little part in the rest of the war it was perhaps less important than either the British or the Germans thought. It did, however, have more chance of being held than did Greece, and if its potential significance had been recognised in, say, November 1940, and preparations for its defence put in hand at that time, then perhaps, with aircraft in bomb-proof shelters, more armoured cars, some engineering work on the roads and rather more anti-aircraft guns in concreted-in emplacements, the air assault might have been defeated. Whether Crete would then have been much use, with Greece in German hands, is another matter. Comparisons with Malta are not relevant – Malta had been a British military base for a very long time, and had a splendid harbour. As it was, yet another British defeat stoked Dominion suspicions of British competence, with Dominion generals anxious to avoid responsibility for agreeing to go to Greece, and then Crete, in the first place.

It is always easy for Dominion governments and military commanders to blame the British for their setbacks, the implication being that splendid Dominion manpower has been wasted by stupid British generals. There is some truth in the 'splendid' bit: the Dominions had a far smaller proportion of their manpower in the services or involved in war industries than did the British, so could afford to be more selective with troops that they sent abroad. Dominion units, however, were very largely militia, or the equivalent of the Territorial Army; but whereas Territorial Army divisions had regular commanders at brigade and above level, and regular staff officers, this was not the case with the Dominions, whose regular armies were tiny. Inevitably, at this stage of the war, at anything above division, or occasionally, corps level the command had to be British because no Dominion officer had the experience to fill the appointment. Dominion criticism of British competence was often unfair, but if Dominion troops alone, or a majority of Dominion troops, were employed on what subsequently turned out to be a shambles, then such criticism could only be expected.

For the victorious Germans the lesson was clear: the casualties and the risks in an operation relying solely or mainly on air-landed, air-portable or parachute troops were too great. German deaths in the battle for Crete were 4,000, mostly from the 11,000 airborne soldiers, and these were some of the best troops Germany had. Never again would Germany mount an airborne operation of this magnitude. In Greece the Germans had disarmed the Greek soldiers and then sent them home, but not here. Surprised, and impressed, by the performance of the Greeks, they held them as prisoners. Student considered that Cretan civilians had helped the Allies and that some had committed what he called atrocities. He ordered that the units affected were to return to the villages where the incidents had occurred and 'exterminate the male population, and demolish or burn down all the houses'.[11] If the civilians had taken part in the fighting and were not in uniform, then the Germans were entitled to take stern punitive action, but not to the extent of executing the whole male population. German sources do not report whether these orders were ever carried out, or if they were, how many Cretans were executed. While the Luftwaffe as a service was more politicised and less 'correct' than the army, it may be that these words were said in the heat of the moment and not actually acted on. Whatever the truth of the allegations of atrocities made against the Germans, there is no doubt that their behaviour did provoke fierce anti-German sentiments among the Cretans, sentiments that even today have not entirely disappeared. Student did appear in front of a British war crimes court in 1946 which sentenced him to a term of imprisonment, but this was not subsequently confirmed.

As if retreat to the Egyptian border, withdrawal from Greece and defeat in Crete were not enough, Wavell also had to deal with the problem of Iraq. A nominally independent country since 1932, it was ruled by a regent with a pro-British prime minister. The British retained a major interest in the oil fields at Mosul and Kirkuk, the right to move troops through the country, and RAF bases at Basra and at Habbaniya, forty miles from Baghdad. Originally the responsibility of Middle East Command, Iraq had been passed to India in March 1940, much to Wavell's relief. On 3 April 1941 a pro-Axis *coup d'état* installed Rashid Ali as prime minister, and Iraqi troops began to invest Habbaniya, supported by German aircraft and with some *matériel* supplied by the Vichy French in Syria.

Despite the responsibility now being India's, Whitehall changed its mind and demanded action by Wavell, who pointed out that there was rather a lot going on elsewhere, and that he could spare no troops from Palestine. He particularly enraged Churchill by suggesting that negotiations through a third party – the USA or Persia – might be a better way of resolving the situation. Ordered to intervene militarily, Wavell sent a column from the 1st Cavalry Division in Palestine, still converting from horses to wheels. Again the lack of an instantly available mobile column attracted Churchill's ire, despite his knowing full well that equipment to mechanise the division had not been made available, either before or during the war. Cobbling together what it could, a more-or-less mobile column known as Habforce set off in the direction of Baghdad, joined by 1,500 men of the Arab Legion from Transjordan (now Jordan). Meanwhile two brigades of 10 Indian Division arrived at Basra by sea, and when the defenders of Habbaniya, despite the loss of five of their rather antiquated aircraft and seventeen deaths from Iraqi shelling, proved more than a match for the Iraqi conscript army, Rashid Ali and his supporters, believing that they were about to be descended upon by massive numbers of British tanks (there were actually only a few light tanks) and savage Hindus with a blood lust for killing Muslims (Hindus were, in fact, in the minority)* fled to Persia on 28 May. An armistice was agreed, the regent and his pro-British administration returned, and in January of the following year Iraq declared war on the Axis.

The difficulties of simultaneous evacuation of Crete and the action in Iraq were compounded by what the British government thought might be happening in Syria and Lebanon. Both were French mandates, governed by the Vichy French and with a French garrison, and could, if occupied by the Germans, pose a serious threat to Egypt. Some German aircraft had already landed there to support Rashid Ali in Iraq. For some time the government had wanted action to neutralise Syria, but Wavell rightly pointed out that with North Africa, Greece, Crete and then Iraq on his plate, he lacked the resources to do anything. When the Defence Committee in London noted that there were six Free French battalions in the Middle East, under General Catroux, it was thought that something might be done by them. Catroux claimed to have intelligence as to exactly what was going on inside Syria and Lebanon, and was sure that he could persuade the French troops there to declare for him. A Free French operation was attractive to the Defence Committee and at first they were inclined to let Catroux get on with it. But Wavell distrusted Catroux, thought his plans for an invasion of Syria were unsound (as indeed they

---

* Of the nine infantry battalions in 10 Indian Division, three were British (and presumably Christian), two were Gurkha, one was Muslim, one was mixed Hindu/Sikh/Muslim and two (battalions of the Royal Garhwal Rifles and the Mahratta Light Infantry) were Hindu. See *Official History of The Indian Armed Forces in World War II*, (ten volumes), Combined Services Historical Section India & Pakistan, Calcutta, 1960.

were), and had no intention of allowing the Free French to dictate strategy in the Middle East. He told the Defence Committee that the operation could only go ahead if British troops were to lead, and that if the government would not accept the advice of the commander on the spot, himself, then they had better relieve him of his command. He got a dusty answer, telling him to get on with invading Syria, with or without British troops, '…and should you feel yourself unwilling to give effect to it, arrangements will be made to meet any wish you may express to be relieved of your command'.[12] One detects the pen of Churchill, who, of course, chaired the Defence Committee.

Operation Exporter, the invasion of Syria and Lebanon, began on 8 June. The forces available were two brigades of 7 Australian Division; 5 Indian Brigade from Eritrea; a Commando battalion from Cyprus; part of 1 Cavalry Division with some light, but no cruiser or infantry, tanks, and one regiment on horses, and Catroux's Free French contingent. In support were four squadrons of the RAF, bomber, fighter and army cooperation, and two Royal Navy cruisers with some destroyers to watch the left flank. Contrary to the insistence of the Free French, the garrison, of eighteen battalions of infantry and ninety tanks, including some medium, put up a stout resistance. Prisoners insisted that there were no Germans in Syria, and it was clear that they were entirely loyal to Pétain and disliked the Germans almost as much as they disliked the British. Only the political need to reconcile the different French factions after the war prevented the British from putting a number of French officers on trial for their appalling treatment of British and Indian prisoners in Syria.

It took the British until 21 June to get to Damascus, compared with the one day that the planners had envisaged, and even then the French fought on. Not until 10 Indian Division, commanded by Major General W. J. Slim, and Habforce arrived from Iraq did the French ask for terms on 11 July. An operation that was expected to last for a few days, a week at most, had dragged on for a month.

The terms dictated by the British caused a serious and open rift with de Gaulle and the Free French. Anxious that Syria and Lebanon give them no further trouble, and well aware that French rule was unpopular, the British promised independence after the war. De Gaulle, more concerned with his own position after the war than in winning it, and deeply suspicious of British motives, wanted the French mandate restored. The British would not budge – France had surrendered, the Free French were welcome but strategy would be decided by the British, whose forces in the Middle East far outnumbered those of the Free French. Another bone of serious contention was the disposal of the surrendered French soldiers. De Gaulle wanted them to be given the option of joining his Free French or of being imprisoned. The British gave them the option of joining the Free French or of being repatriated to France in Vichy ships. To de Gaulle's chagrin, 6,000 opted to join him, and 37,500 went home.

While Wavell was juggling with more calls on his slender resources than any British commander in modern times, he was also examining what might be done to improve the position in North Africa. He wanted to wait until he could build up a superiority of tanks and, especially, aircraft, and then train the troops in all-arms cooperation, before attacking, which might take three or four months. This was quite unacceptable to the Prime Minister, who was constantly demanding action now, wanted a victory to compensate for the loss of Crete, and could not understand why the tanks sent to Egypt in the 'Tiger convoy'[*] could not be used immediately. Eventually, and against his better judgement and that of the CIGS, Wavell launched Operation Battleaxe on 15 June, while fighting in Syria was still going on. It was intended to be a three-phase operation: phase one the recapture of Sollum, the Halfaya Pass and Capuzzo; phase two the lifting of the siege of Tobruk; and phase three subsequent exploitation. To carry it out he had the partially reconstituted XIII Corps, now commanded by Lieutenant General Sir Noel Beresford Pierse (previously Commander 4 Indian Division), and consisting of 7 Armoured Division and 4 Indian Division. The armoured division had two regiments of Matildas, one of cruisers and one of the newly arrived Crusader,[**] a support group of two infantry battalions and four regiments of artillery, as well as a reconnaissance regiment in armoured cars, a field squadron

---

[*] Tiger was a fast convoy sent through the Mediterranean to Egypt. It left England on 26 April, and despite losing one ship to a mine, arrived in Egypt on 12 May with forty-three Hurricane fighters and 238 tanks.

[**]The Crusader was the Mark VI cruiser, or A15. Speedy but under-armoured it suffered from frequent mechanical problems.

and a field-park squadron Royal Engineers. 4 Indian Division had one Indian brigade and 22 Guards Brigade, an armoured-car regiment, two field regiments of artillery and four field companies, and a field-park company Sappers and Miners (the Indian equivalent of engineers). In support were ninety-eight fighters and 105 bombers of the RAF.

Battleaxe failed. It failed for the same reasons that nearly every British action so far in this war had failed: it was launched far too soon; there was insufficient logistic support; the tanks were too few, of the wrong sort and mechanically unreliable; there were insufficient aircraft; and the troops lacked training, particularly in infantry-tank cooperation. It was the end for Wavell.

NOTES

1. Charles Burdick and Hans-Adolf Jacobsen, (eds), *The Halder War Diary 1939–1942*, Greenhill, London, 1988.

2. Research Institute for Military History, Germany, (tr McMurry, Osers & Willmot), *Germany and the Second World War*: Vol. III, Clarendon Press, Oxford, 1995.

3. Barrie Pitt, *The Crucible of War: Wavell's Command*, Cassell, London, 2001.

4. O'Connor, quoted in Pitt, op. cit.

5. David Fraser, *And We Shall Shock Them*, Hodder & Stoughton, London, 1983.

6. Research Institute for Military History, Germany, op. cit.

7. Capt B. H. Liddell Hart, *The Tanks*, Vol. II, Cassell, London 1959.

8. Burdick and Jacobsen, op. cit.

9. Research Institute for Military History, Germany, op. cit.

10. T. A. Heathcote, *The British Admirals of the Fleet 1734–1995*, Leo Cooper, Barnsley, 2002.

11. Research Institute for Military History, Germany, op. cit.

12. J. R. M. Butler, *Grand Strategy*, Vol. II, HMSO, London, 1957.

12

Dismissals and Defeats

FIVE DAYS AFTER WAVELL halted Operation Battleaxe, Prime Minister Churchill decided that there must be a change of command in the Middle East. There was never a meeting of minds between Churchill and Wavell, and the enormous problems of trying to deal with three major theatres of operations simultaneously, with resources barely sufficient for one, had never been appreciated by the Prime Minister. Churchill had come to power in a wave of public and parliamentary anger at the utter incompetence evident in the Norway debacle – for which he had, unknown to the public, been at least partly to blame – and yet his first year of office had been marked by even more spectacular defeats. He needed a victory, and if Wavell, through no fault of his own, could not give him one, then Wavell must go.

Wavell could not, however, just be sacked. He might, suggested the CIGS, consider that he had been unfairly blamed for the mistakes of the government, and he might say so openly. He had many friends and supporters in England who would spring to his defence. It would be better if Wavell were not brought back to England at all, and as the officer whom Churchill wanted to replace him with was currently Commander-in-Chief India, and as Wavell had served in India, perhaps the two could simply exchange posts. Wavell was not, it was true, an officer of the Indian army, but it was not unusual for that appointment to be held by an officer of the British service. The current Commander-in-Chief India was General Sir Claude Auchinleck, who had attracted the resentment of some British officers by having been given command of a British corps, a post that they felt ought to have been reserved for them, and then by making (entirely justified) criticisms of British troops employed in the Norwegian campaign. After Norway he had been Commander V Corps in England, and then General Officer Commanding Southern Command, arousing yet more jealousy, not least in Montgomery, who succeeded him at V Corps (and later at Southern Command) and who proceeded to reverse almost all of Auchinleck's policies. Auchinleck was appointed Commander-in-Chief India at the end of January 1941, and began a much-needed reorganisation of the Indian army, which had been starved of funds in the inter-war years to an even greater extent than the British army.

On the very day that Wavell was told he was to be superseded as Commander-in-Chief Middle East, without any home leave between postings, Germany made the first of the two major decisions that would lose her the war. At 0300 hours on 22 June three army groups, supported by nearly 3,000 aircraft, attacked the Soviet Union in Operation Barbarossa. It was the largest military force ever assembled for offensive operations: seventeen armoured divisions, thirteen motorised divisions, ninety-five infantry divisions, four mountain divisions and a cavalry division that were all considered capable of any offensive action, backed up by a further seventy-three divisions whose quality ranged from 'reduced offensive strength' to 'security tasks and limited local operations only'. Additionally, and with varying military capabilities but useful as auxiliaries none the less, were allied contingents: eighteen Finnish divisions, four divisions and four brigades from Romania, and promises of troops from Hungary and Slovakia. Altogether Germany attacked the USSR with 3,050,000 men, 625,000 horses, 600,000 wheeled vehicles, 3,350 armoured fighting vehicles and 7,146 artillery pieces of various calibres.[1]

Looking back at this point to hostilities so far, it was twenty-two months since Britain had declared war against Germany. In that time the Royal Navy had rescued the army from Norway, from north-west Europe, from Greece and from Crete, while the RAF had made the evacuation from Dunkirk possible and had prevented the Luftwaffe from obtaining air superiority over the UK and the Channel. But the army had been defeated in Norway, France, Greece, Crete and recently in North Africa. The only victories had been against 'second-class' enemies – Italy in East and North Africa, and the Vichy French in Syria – and even the latter was achieved only with difficulty. As soon as a 'first class' enemy – the Germans – appeared, the British army had not prevailed.

Going to war was a much more difficult prospect for the army than it was for the other two services. In terms of manpower the Royal Navy increased from a peacetime strength of 180,000 officers and ratings to 395,000 by June 1941, an increase of 119 per cent. In the same period the RAF grew from 193,000 to 662,000, an increase of 243 per cent. The army, from a peacetime strength of 207,000 all ranks was 897,000 strong by the outbreak of war by the addition of the Regular Army Reserve, the Supplementary Reserve (mainly tradesmen and specialists) the (recently doubled) Territorial Army and the first intake of conscripts.[2] By June 1941 it was 2,221,000 strong and had increased by 1010 per cent! It was not, however, the size of the increase alone that made the army's task more difficult. The Royal Navy did not man a ship entirely with recruits. The men called back from the Royal Naval Reserve[*] and the Royal Naval Volunteer Reserve, and those conscripted into the navy, were not all posted together; every vessel had a good share of experienced men and the novice or the rusty were easily assimilated. In the RAF there were many inexperienced pilots when the Battle of Britain began (although not many at the end of it) but there were enough experienced men to act as flight and squadron commanders and to advise and train the newcomers. In any case, both the Royal Navy and the RAF needed men with a higher technical awareness than did the army, and therefore tended to get the better educated recruits, while the army took

---

* Apart from officers and ratings who had served in the Royal Navy and still retained a reserve liability, the RNR consisted of members of the merchant service who became combatants in time of national emergency. The RNVR (the wavy navy) was the nearest the navy got to a territorial force and was largely composed of enthusiastic amateur yachtsmen. As RN officers remarked, the RNR was a body of sailors trying to be gentlemen, while the RNVR was a body of gentlemen trying to be sailors. Both have now been amalgamated into the Royal Naval Reserve.

anybody who could pass the (not very stringent) medical examination.

Apart from the period 1916–18, the British had avoided conscription, and would have regarded the European system of universal military service in time of peace as dangerous and oppressive. Now, they accepted the necessity of conscription but were still suspicious of it. The army was not a mindless, uncaring sausage machine, but many people thought it was; and the inter-war disillusionment with all things military meant that the press were ever ready to champion the cause of what they saw as fairness and the rights of the little man against the state. The citizen-soldiers of this generation were more suspicious, less trusting, more questioning, less deferential than their fathers of 1914 had been. There is a huge difference between a regular army and a wartime citizen army. Soldiers of the regular army were there because they wanted to be, or because they could find nothing else. The army was their home and their life and they looked to it to provide employment, a career and, eventually, a pension. They regarded themselves and the organisation that they served in a very different light from those summoned to the colours for the war. The pre-war Territorial other ranks considered they were a cut above the regulars (as socially and educationally they often were), while their officers saw themselves as patriotic gentlemen prepared to come to the aid of the nation when the trumpets sounded. If in reality many Territorial soldiers were there because it was a jolly good drinking club, or an opportunity to get away from nagging wives, and some officers wanted the social cachet of a rank without having to do the work that went with it, and it was understrength and starved of modern equipment, it was still the only reserve army that Britain had, and while inexperienced it had received at least a rudimentary military training. Conscripts – who would make up by far the largest part of the army, and would outnumber the regulars in the other two services – accepted the necessity to fight, but were completely uninterested in anything beyond the immediate objective of winning the war, or at least in not losing it. This caused inevitable strains between the regulars, who thought many of the newcomers were far too questioning of accepted military virtues, and the conscripts, who saw the regulars as being stick-in-the-muds entrammeled by history and tradition to the detriment of modern methods. There was some truth in both viewpoints.

One of the lessons of the First War was that there was no point in having the men if there were no uniforms or equipment to give them, and when war broke out in 1939 the British began a phased programme of calling up only that number of men who could be kitted out properly and given meaningful training. After the defeat in France in 1940, however, Churchill wanted to make it appear that the British were doing something, and the rate of call-up was increased – an utterly pointless exercise as there was no equipment to give them, and they could do little but close-order drill.

Before the war a potential officer applied for a place at either the Royal Military College Sandhurst (if he wanted to join the cavalry or the infantry), or the Royal Military Academy Woolwich for those arms that required some technical training: the Royal Artillery, Royal Engineers, Royal Signals, Royal Tank Corps and Royal Army Ordnance Corps. Entry to both establishments was by competitive examination, the standard roughly equivalent to a good 'A' Level now, and fees were charged according to the parents' ability to pay. Over the years the length of the course varied between one year and two (two by 1939) and on successful completion of the course a Gentleman Cadet was awarded a regular commission. Apart from the examination and cursory interview, there was no selection process as such, but as those who do not consider themselves to be leaders, or who do not wish to be leaders, do not generally aspire to be leaders, there was (almost) a sufficiency of young men of the right type. What was the right type was the subject of debate within and without the army throughout the inter-war years. There was no rule that an aspiring officer must come from a certain social stratum, but the vast majority came from the upper middle (although not necessarily moneyed) class. There was no bar on boys from state schools, but most were the product of the independent sector. That army officers were in many ways a self-perpetuating oligarchy, where the most common profession of Gentlemen Cadets' fathers was army officer, did not matter very much – the army needed only around 700 newly commissioned officers a year, and a combination of the examination and the rigours of the two-year course usually weeded out the unsuitable.

Reformers outside the army (and some inside it) often agitated for a broadening of the pool from which officers were drawn. The problem was that the army was underpaid and, depending upon the regiment, expensive. Many families with no military tradition would much rather their sons became doctors, lawyers, accountants or businessmen than impecunious subalterns whose activities seemed to provide no tangible return for the public money spent on them. During the First War many officers at regimental level had started the war as other ranks, subsequently being commissioned. The system had worked perfectly well, so why could it not have been continued after 1919, when instead the army rapidly reverted to its pre-war social exclusivity? The reason was that commissioned NCOs could certainly lead platoons and companies, and in some cases even battalions, in battle but either lacked the education to deal with all the administrative and planning matters essential in peacetime, or were too old on commissioning to attend all the various steps in training needed to achieve a full career. There was, and still is, a huge difference between the role of a sergeant and that of a captain. Both are essential, but they are not interchangeable.

Regular officers were promoted by qualification in promotion examinations, time in the rank and recommendation. Territorial officers had very little professional training, and while they sat promotion examinations, and some attended short courses at the Royal Military College, probably the greatest weakness was in the commanding officers of infantry battalions and yeomanry regiments, themselves Territorial officers and often holding the appointment because they were notable figures in the county rather than as a result of any military competence.[*] Because Territorial Army training was restricted to drill nights and a few weekends, with an annual camp once a year, it was rare for the commanding officer to be able to get all the components of his command together and train with them. The result was that far too many of them were, through no fault of their own, incapable of commanding a major unit.

On the outbreak of war in 1939 Gentlemen Cadets at Sandhurst and

---

[*] By tradition the Commanding Officer of the Northamptonshire Yeomanry (a Territorial Army regiment converted from horses to tanks) was also the Master of the Pytchley Hunt. I have been unable to discover which appointment came first.

Woolwich, who by a quirk of military law were technically civilians, were all enrolled into the Territorial Army. The cadets in the senior intake were then commissioned into their respective regiments (the last to be granted regular commissions until after the war), and the junior intake was transferred to Officer Cadet Training Units (OCTUs) all over the country. The competitive examination was shelved, and fees were abolished. It was decided that all potential officers must spend some time in the ranks, a politically motivated regulation designed to break down what were seen by some parliamentarians as class divisions. In fact it merely wasted time that might have been used to train the candidate in being an officer, rather than a private. The responsibility was now thrust upon commanding officers to pick out suitable candidates and put them in front of a local selection board, which had a regular officer as its permanent president and other members co-opted from units stationed nearby.

Pre-war there were around 13,000 regular army officers. By the outbreak of war the army had 53,000 officers, and the traditional sources – the universities and public schools for regulars, the professional classes and landowners for the Territorials – were drying up. A few weeks could produce an infantry private, a few months a gunner or a tank driver, but officers and NCOs took far longer. By 1 January 1941 the army was short of 18,000 officers and only 12,000 were under training. Commanding officers were constantly being chivvied to submit suitable candidates but there were not enough, and many who were commissioned were not up to the job. The report of an investigation into the supply of officers, carried out for the Vice Chief of the General Staff, Lieutenant General Sir Archibald Nye, said that there was 'growing discontent, both among officers and other ranks concerning present selection for commissions...'[3] Too many of those being commissioned were regarded as 'uncouth', which offended both the other subalterns who had to live with them, and the soldiers, who failed to see why someone so like them should be placed in authority over them – 'Most serious is the lack of respect for these officers.' The case of the officer commanding a company of the Pioneer Corps (at that time a military labour corps) was cited. He had been told to report the number of warrant officers and NCOs in his unit fit for commissioning. He submitted a nil return, pointing out that 'most of the men are of recent intakes and little experience, and much more important they are men of the labouring type wholly unsuited by education, upbringing or experience to hold a commission or command troops.' The result was that he was ordered to nominate candidates nevertheless. One can only pity the wretched men placed under them.

One obvious source of officers was that body of men who had held commissions in the last war. If they had joined in 1914 aged nineteen (the minimum age for service overseas) they would be forty-five in 1941; getting on a bit for running around as platoon commanders, but easily capable of commanding companies or training units. Not everyone agreed, and one un-named commanding officer in the Middle East was quoted as addressing a newly arrived batch of officers who had seen service in the last war:

> I don't care a — for your — medal ribbons or your — former service, you
> are useless to me unless you can unlearn all that you think you know about
> active service. If you are prepared to consider yourselves as ordinary young
> tykes of subalterns, quite ignorant on every subject, and are prepared to
> sweat your — guts out to learn again, we shall get on all right. If you are not
> and if you think because you are a bit older and have these — ribbons on
> your chests you know something, I'll — well soon see that you get your —
> bowler hats and clear off back to civilian life.

This was a quite extraordinary way to behave, and while we do not know what the excised words were, we can guess. Although troopers may well swear, expletives from officers were and are regarded as very bad form. As the officer who reported this speech had himself been a major in the Great War and was now a captain, he may have egged the pudding somewhat.

The report commented on the views of some commanding officers who felt that officers from the last war newly commissioned for this one would be ignorant of the lessons of modern warfare, and went on to ask what the lessons of modern warfare actually were:

> Seven or eight months trench digging, a few weeks of haphazard flap,
> frenzied rearguard fighting largely lacking in tactical or strategical [sic]

science, devoted mainly towards rushing back as rapidly as possible to the coast. Are these few weeks of little coordinated frenzy – during which few other than veteran military policemen ever thought of waiting to destroy dumps or supplies etc – to be compared with a two, three or four years experience of active service in 1914–18?… some authorities think that any NCO or man evacuated at Dunkirk is *ipso facto* an infinitely more worthy subject for commissioned rank than one who was demobbed in 1919 after four years commissioned active service in France or some other theatre…

Even where commanding officers welcomed veterans of the First War – and to be fair, most did – the thought of a return to the colours and the officers' mess was not necessarily attractive to all. Ex-officers had to start again, as second lieutenants. The pay, of eighteen shillings a day, was barely enough to live on for a 20-year-old with no responsibilities, but for a mature man with a family it was derisory.* One former officer who was in a reserve occupation and exempt from conscription, but who could volunteer, objected that those over him would be less experienced than he, 'I'd be telling them what to do — why should I?' A recommendation was that men with previous service as officers should be commissioned as full lieutenants with promotion to captain after one year.

If the system of officer selection was at fault, so too was the training. There was a large number of OCTUs set up all over the country (Sandhurst became the largest one for the Royal Armoured Corps), and the report quoted comments from one young officer who had recently graduated. He felt that the sergeant instructors treated the cadets as if they were peacetime recruits – 'unwilling, stupid, requiring to be driven'. He objected that there had been no explanation of the 'issues' of the war, and nothing in the syllabus about the enemy. None of the instructors had any active service experience of the present war, all being veterans of the Great War or earlier; there was too much drill, too much polishing of buttons and equipment, and too much emphasis on teaching adminis-tration, while the staff complained about not having enough time for training.

* Eighteen shillings is ninety pence. When this author was commissioned in 1962 the pay was twenty-nine shillings a day (£1.45), an increase of 60 per cent in twenty-three years, which either says quite a lot about inflation over the period, or even more about the parsimony of British governments.

Most of these criticisms can be dismissed – a young civilian could not be expected to understand the importance of drill in promoting team bonding, and wheras administration may be boring it is essential to successful command of troops. It is doubtful whether experience of the present war (largely failure) among the instructors would have been any better than experience of the last. He may have been right about the 'issues'. Regular soldiers had no interest in issues, and nor should they; their task was to go to war with whomsoever they were told. Hostilities-only conscripts, however, officers and other ranks, did need to be told what they were fighting for, and this would eventually be included as part of basic training.

Much more valid were the criticisms of the syllabus. The respondent said that his course had received only one live firing lesson on the LMG (light machine gun, probably the Bren); that they had neither seen nor thrown hand grenades; they had not seen 3-inch mortars, Tommy guns,[*] or carriers. They had received but one lesson on the Lysander[**] and no training with tanks, artillery or medium machine guns. That there was, even in early 1941, barely enough hardware to give to the fighting units, or those that might have to fight, never mind the training units, was no consolation to students or instructors. At this time selection boards were failing 30 per cent of those candidates appearing before them, and OCTUs a further 25–30 per cent, so that around 50 per cent of all candidates, who had been recommended by their commanding officers as suitable for commissioning, were in fact unsuitable. Clearly the selection procedure was getting it badly wrong. The VCGS was, not surprisingly, concerned as to the contents of the report. He noted that in some cases commissioned officers dismissed for incompetence returned to civilian life and were then conscripted as private soldiers, something that ought to be avoided. He also preferred a direct entry for officers, rather than an insistence that they could only be selected for officer training after service in the ranks, but felt that it would be politically difficult to move away from what appeared to politicians and journalists as an egalitarian selection process. At the end of the day, thought the VCGS, commanding officers

---

* The Thompson sub-machine gun, bought from America and shortly to be replaced by the British Sten gun.
** The Lysander was an army cooperation aircraft, now obsolete.

must be responsible for putting forward the right type of man, but he accepted that the selection system had to be improved.

Very sensibly, the British looked to where the officer selection system obviously did work, and considered how the German army selected its leaders. There, rather than relying on examination and interview, potential officers were subjected to psychological testing to discover whether they had the temperament and strength of character to be officers. Could they operate as part of a team; were they able to command respect; could they perform without an immediate superior to tell them what to do; could they think on their feet and make sensible decisions under stress; would they put their men and the task before themselves? The British now adopted most of this system, and so the War Office Selection Board, or WOSB, was born. Instead of one permanent president and temporarily co-opted members looking at candidates for an hour or two, the WOSB was composed of a permanent team of officers with a psychologist, and candidates spent several days undergoing a series of mental and physical tests designed to identify officer qualities, or the lack of them. Although the failure rate at the selection stage went up, there was a noticeable improvement at OCTUs, where the failure rate dropped considerably, and there was much less complaining by commanding officers about the standard of newly commissioned subalterns. In time the WOSB became the Regular Commissions Board, which to this day selects officers, and whose methods have changed little since their adoption in 1941.

The training system improved slowly, but never to the standard of German officer training, which aimed to produce an officer who could command a battalion if need be. The British concentrated on producing platoon and equivalent commanders, and had in any rate a higher officer to other rank ratio than did the Germans. The German army had never seen the necessity of having an officer to command a platoon of thirty or forty men. Command at that level was not a cerebral occupation, and could perfectly well be exercised by a senior NCO, leaving the expensively trained officer to carry out those responsibilities that his education and training fitted him for. The British knew this perfectly well, but considered that command of a platoon was important as part of the training of a young officer – it gave him experience of minor tactics, and in an army where there was still, and would continue to be, a social difference between the leaders and the led, it allowed the newly appointed subaltern an opportunity to get to know the characteristics of the men he would command, without being able to do too much damage. In any case, as everyone except the young officer knew, it was the platoon sergeant who really commanded.

Finding enough officers to command platoons was not difficult in the small pre-war regular army, but with the huge expansion alternatives were looked at. One was the creation of a new rank – that of Warrant Officer Class 3, or Platoon Sergeant Major.* This innovation should have worked, but was an abject failure. The British simply were not ready for such a step, and there were tensions between the Company Sergeant Major and the Platoon Sergeant Major, the latter being junior to the former, whereas the other (officer) platoon commanders were, at least in theory, senior. There were also problems with some platoon commanders being in the sergeants' mess, while the others were in the officers' mess. The scheme was soon discontinued.

Another disadvantage that the British army laboured under, and which was entirely of its own making, was a lack of a common doctrine – indeed the British army had no doctrine at all, operational methods being cobbled together as required. While the British had established a school of artillery between the wars, there was still no school of infantry. In a pre-war army scattered all over the world this did not matter very much, but when divisions, corps and armies were being formed it did matter, because formations and units were unable to work with each other until they had decided what their operational procedures should be, and had then practised them together. While there were some excellent single-arm training pamphlets, dealing with the operation of weapons and the tactics

---

* In combatant regiments and battalions a Warrant Officer Class I (WO1) was the Regimental Sergeant Major, the senior other rank, and there was only one. A WO2 was the Company or Squadron Sergeant Major (CSM or SSM) and was the senior OR in the squadron or company. In simple terms the RSM or SSM/CSM were responsible for discipline and duties, and often for ammunition resupply in the field, but their role was much more important than that: they were the advisers to the CO or OC, and at company level the company commander and the CSM between them ran the company, regardless of the other four officers (a company second-in-command and three platoon commanders). It was (and is) a very British system and incomprehensible to soldiers of any other nation.

to be followed by that particular arm, there were no army-wide standing operating procedures (SOPs); rather each battalion and regiment had its own, and each brigade, divisional, corps and army commander had to create his own when his particular formation came into being. Partly this was because of the considerable latitude that the British army allowed to individual regiments, a hangover from the days when they were the property of the colonel, whose prerogatives could not be trampled on, and partly a factor of the British cult of the amateur, where attempts to standardise were regarded as suspiciously militaristic. This was not the case in the German army, where everyone was trained in the same way and in conformation with the same army-wide SOPs. A German armoured division, infantry division, artillery regiment and engineer regiment that had never met before, could be put together and could instantly operate together. In the British army, apart from there being little or no experience of combined arms training, units could not operate jointly until they had spent a lengthy period of training together, so that major British operations took far longer to prepare than German ones.[*]

THE GERMAN INVASION OF the Soviet Union on 22 June 1941 meant that OKW would take even less interest than before in Erwin Rommel and his North African adventures. To General Auchinleck, who formally assumed the appointment of Commander-in-Chief Middle East on 4 July 1941, the likelihood that Rommel would not be reinforced, and was therefore unlikely to go on the offensive in the near future, meant that there would be time to build up the British and Empire forces and train them before mounting an attack. To Churchill, however, the same assumptions meant that now was the time to attack, without any delay. After telling the Prime Minister to keep his nose out of matters which did not concern him, when he tried to get involved in the details of garrisoning Cyprus, Auchinleck was summoned to England to explain to the Prime Minister personally why an immediate attack would not be a good idea. The general's grasp of the facts and figures of the situation convinced the Chiefs of Staff that he was right, but not Churchill, and Auchinleck returned to Cairo committed to mounting an offensive – Operation Crusader – in November.

[*] There was no formal British defence doctrine until 1996, and even then hardly anyone bothered to read it.

Auchinleck was a thoroughly experienced, intelligent and level-headed officer, but he suffered from a number of disadvantages. First, he was an officer of the Indian army and not known by, nor did he know, many senior British commanders. Second, he upset the staff of GHQ in Cairo by ordering the headquarters to move from the fleshpots of the city into a tented encampment in the desert. When it became apparent that this was impossible (for reasons of communication and administration) he moved himself and his personal staff, thus creating yet another, albeit small, headquarters, without impressing the fighting soldiers to whom the move was intended to appeal. 'Any fool can be uncomfortable' was a remark often heard. Third, Auchinleck fell out with his deputy commander, the Australian Lieutenant General Sir Thomas Blamey, the commander of the Australian Imperial Force, who went over Auchinleck's head to the Australian government when Auchinleck would not replace the Australians in Tobruk by British troops.[*] Between August and October the Royal Navy removed most of the Australians and replaced them with British and Free Polish troops, losing three ships sunk and four badly damaged in the process. Blamey, the son of a cattle drover and one of the few Australians with regular army experience, complained that Auchinleck regarded the Australian army in the same way as he regarded the Indian army. As Auchinleck loved the Indians one wonders what Blamey was objecting to.

At least men and equipment were now becoming more plentiful. The American lend-lease scheme had circumvented the neutrality acts and British industry was gearing up for total war. The shortages and the scrimping and saving that Wavell and O'Connor had to contend with would weigh less heavily on Auchinleck, who was now overseeing the evolution of the Western Desert Force, otherwise known as XIII Corps, into the Eighth Army. To command that army Auchinleck chose the younger brother of the Admiral Commander-in-Chief Mediterranean, Lieutenant General Sir Alan Cunningham, who had made his name in the East African campaign, where he had shown himself to be a forceful,

---

[*] As Chief Commissioner of Police for the state of Victoria, he had been forced to resign as an alternative to dismissal, after several instances of abuse of authority. In 1950 he was promoted field marshal in the Australian Military Forces.

intuitive commander with a flair for mobile operations. Cunningham should have been just the man for the Eighth Army, but he had no experience of armoured warfare, nor of the desert, which was quite different from the scrubby hills of Italian Somaliland and Abyssinia, and he had little time to accustom himself to it before launching his still-forming Eighth Army across it.

The years of bitter debate between the protagonists of the tank and those who opposed it – made even more acrimonious when it became clear that because of British financial stringency the provision of more tanks meant something else having to be scrapped – had led to hardening of positions on either side. The armoured lobby, including men such as Hobart, who should have known better, had moved towards an extreme position which maintained that tanks alone could win a battle, and that infantry would be needed only to hold bases and clear up afterwards. Cunningham, an artillery officer who had commanded an infantry division, perforce accepted the advice of armoured commanders in theatre, who were mostly of that view, and Auchinleck, equally without armoured experience, was not in a position to overrule him. Accepting that tanks could achieve great things alone, Cunningham created two corps, one armoured, XXX Corps, and one infantry, based on and retaining the title of XIII Corps. XXX Corps, commanded by Lieutenant General Norrie, consisted of 7 Armoured Division, 1 South African Division less one brigade, and 22 Guards Brigade, while XIII Corps under Lieutenant General Godwin-Austin (whose promotion and appointment drew Churchill's ire) had 2 New Zealand Division, 4 Indian Division and 1 Army Tank Brigade.

This was the best-equipped army Britain had yet fielded in the war, and on the face of it should have been able to sweep the floor with the DAK and Rommel's Italian allies. 7 Armoured Division had three armoured brigades, 4th with 166 Honeys, 7th with a mix of Crusaders and A13 and A10 cruisers, 129 in all, and 22nd with 158 A15 cruisers. In 1 Army Tank Brigade were 135 tanks, two of the three regiments with Matildas, and one with Valentines. The Honey, later renamed the Stuart, was the first example of an American-made tank provided under lend-lease, while the Valentine was an infantry tank originally designed in 1938 as a private venture by Vickers, but finally accepted by the army. Characteristics of these two tanks were:

TYPE	FRONTAL ARMOUR	MAIN ARMAMENT	MAX SPEED	WEIGHT
Honey	2-inch	37mm gun	36 mph	13 tons
Valentine	2.56-inch	2-pounder gun	15 mph	17 tons

With 32 Army Tank Brigade (1 and 4 RTR and a squadron of 7 RTR) inside Tobruk, with 120 Matilda tanks, the Eighth Army could field 708 tanks. Despite all this, however, there were dark clouds on the horizon.

Churchill could never understand why a tank delivered to Port Said or Suez could not simply be moved into the desert and go straight into action. That the tanks arrived in deep preservation after their long journey round the Cape and had to be thoroughly cleaned, batteries fitted, engine filters modified for desert conditions, guns calibrated and radios fitted and netted in, and that all this took time, was a mystery to him; nor could he understand why tank crews sent out from England could not go straight into the fray.

It was not only the army that had to put up with Churchill's constant meddling and demands for action, but the RAF too. Since early June the Air Officer Commanding in Chief Middle East was Air Marshal Sir Arthur Tedder, who had only just got to know (and respect) Wavell and now had to adjust to the new Commander-in-Chief, Auchinleck, with whom he would establish an excellent relationship. Churchill's particular objection to Tedder (whom in any case he considered as a mere technician) centred on the manpower needed by the RAF in the Middle East. Churchill would divide the number of RAF officers and men in the theatre by the number of aircraft, subtract the aircrew, arrive at the conclusion that the number of ground crew was absurdly large and unilaterally reduce the number of RAF men due to go to Egypt. It was, of course, ridiculous, and took no account of the fact that not all the RAF personnel in the Middle East were connected directly with aircraft. Airmen, too, needed to be fed, housed, clothed, transported, disciplined, paid and cared for when ill or wounded, and in any case aircraft are highly complex pieces of machinery that need expert care if they are to be kept serviceable. Inevitably, Churchill soon wanted to sack Tedder, and was only dissuaded from doing so when the officer earmarked by Churchill as his replacement, and the Chief of Air Staff himself, Portal, threatened to resign if he was. Perhaps if the other two Chiefs of Staff had been more robust, the damage inflicted on the war effort by Churchill might have been less.

General Norrie had commanded 1 Armoured Division in England, but now he was to command more tanks than the British had ever tried to operate in one formation before. The Germans, with their experience in the Battle of France, had found that an armoured division of four panzer battalions with a total of 280 tanks was too big and too unwieldy to be commanded by a single headquarters, and had reduced the armour in the panzer divisions to two battalions with a total of 140 tanks. Norrie was now having to control 453 tanks, over three times the number of his German counterpart. The men of 1 Army Tank Brigade had arrived in theatre in mid June, while their tanks, sent out in the Tiger convoy, had been used by other units for Operation Battleaxe, and were now in workshops being repaired. Crews and tanks would not be united until mid September. 22 Armoured Brigade, which had been part of 1 Armoured Division in England, had arrived even later, in October, and they, too, had little time to adapt to desert war and to train with other arms before Crusader was due to begin. Perhaps one of the most telling factors of which the British appear to have been completely ignorant was that their most effective weapon was not tanks, or the 2-pounder anti-tank gun, but their field artillery which, although without an armour-piercing round, could hit tanks with high explosive to great destructive effect. The Germans had realised this very early on and hoped that the British would not.

The aim of Crusader was ambitious: to destroy the enemy in Cyrenaica, relieve Tobruk, occupy Tripolitania and then, having advanced one thousand miles, exploit westward. The plan, drawn up by Cunningham from alternatives given him by Auchinleck, was for XIII Corps to mask* the Axis frontier defences, then surround and eliminate them. The armour of XXX Corps, meanwhile, would drive across the frontier at Fort Maddalena, fifty miles to the south, head north-west and destroy

---

* To mask, a technical military term, is to deploy in such a way as to prevent a position or a formation from being able to react to something happening elsewhere.

the Axis armour at Gabr Saleh before linking up with the garrison of Tobruk, who would break out, and then swing west along the coast. Simple though this appeared to be, it did not find favour with all the commanders. Godwin-Austin was concerned that his infantry was insufficiently protected by armour, and it was agreed that the right-hand brigade of 7 Armoured Division, 4 Armoured Brigade, would guard the left flank of XIII Corps, without being under command of that corps. It was an unhappy compromise. Major General Brink, the commander of 1 South African Division, was unhappy about the state of his division, severely weakened by the fighting in Eritrea and brought up to strength by hastily trained recruits, and he was not convinced that they were up to the tasks given them. While he was allowed to commit only two, rather than three, brigades, he was told to shut up and get on with it. Norrie, who had only been in command of XXX Corps for six weeks, questioned the assumption that the DAK would obediently advance to give battle, and wanted to strike directly for Sidi Rezegh and Tobruk. Cunningham, however, was convinced that Rommel would have to give battle at Gabr Saleh to prevent Tobruk being relieved and to safeguard his own movement north and south.

Berlin's instructions to the Axis forces were to remain on the defensive, but to take Tobruk, which was not only an irritating impediment to movement up and down the coast, but was also denied to the Italian navy as a port for resupply. Contrary to popular belief Rommel was not, of course, the Commander-in-Chief of Axis forces in North Africa; that post was held by the Italian General Etore Bastico, but as the representative of the senior partner in the alliance, and now promoted to General of Panzer Troops, Rommel's views carried considerable weight and Italian commanders generally deferred to him. Prior to the opening of Crusader, Rommel's Panzer Group Africa had under command the DAK, commanded by Lieutenant General Crüwell, and the Italian XXI Corps commanded by Lieutenant General Navarrini. The DAK now had two armoured divisions, 15 and 21 (the latter a reorganised 5 Light) and 90 Light Division, while XXI Corps had five partially motorised divisions of infantry supported by tanks. Additionally, and not under Rommel's command but having agreed to cooperate with him, was General

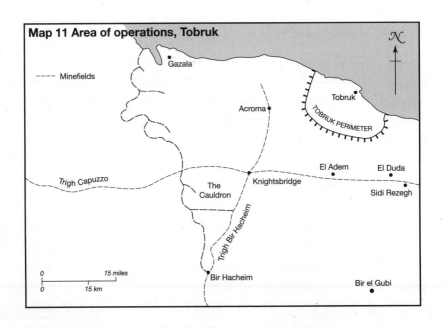

Map 11 Area of operations, Tobruk

Minefields

Gazala

Tobruk

Acroma

TOBRUK PERIMETER

El Adem

El Duda

Trigh Capuzzo

The
Cauldron

Knightsbridge

Sidi Rezegh

Trigh Bir Hacheim

0   15 miles
0   15 km

Bir Hacheim

Bir el Gubi

Top **SWORDFISH TORPEDO BOMBER (BRITISH)** Obsolete before the war began, with a crew of two in open cockpits and a top speed of 128 mph with the wind behind it, these aircraft of the Royal Navy (shown here testing rocket-assisted take-off) reduced the firepower of the Italian navy by half in a daring raid on Taranto Bay in November 1940. Not only did it give the British a much needed success, but it was the first time that carrier-launched aircraft had alone carried out a major operation of war. (© IWM A27683)

Below **HMS ARK ROYAL** Most thinking sailors (but not Churchill) had concluded long before 1939 that the aircraft carrier would replace the battleship as the capital ship of the Royal Navy, and Britain had intended to build a number between the wars. Lack of funding meant that only two got built, one being *Ark Royal*. Launched in 1937, she is seen under attack from Italian aircraft in November 1940, a year before she was torpedoed and sunk by a German submarine in the Mediterranean. (© IWM A2298).

FAIREY BATTLE BOMBER (BRITISH) Introduced into service in 1937 it was obsolescent by 1939, but in the absence of anything better was used by the RAF in the Battle of France, before being withdrawn from operational service in 1940. The RAF's first VCs of the war were won posthumously by the crew of a Battle shot down on 12 May 1940. (© IWM C604)

Opposite top **LANCASTER BOMBER (BRITISH)** From 1940 the only way the British could hit at Germany directly was to bomb her cities, and from 1942 the Avro Lancaster was the weapon used to do it. With a crew of seven and able to carry a bigger bomb load than any other Allied bomber, over 7,000 of them were built, employing over a million workers. The average Lancaster completed twenty-one missions before being lost through enemy action or accident. (© IWM 13453)

Opposite below **THE OBSERVER CORPS** Later the Royal Observer Corps, this all-volunteer civilian organisation was formed between the wars and became part of the anti-aircraft defence of the UK, supplementing the Radar screen by noting and reporting the numbers, direction, height and type of hostile aircraft crossing the coast. At its height in 1942 the Corps had 34,000 members, mostly unpaid and working in pairs from observation posts like this one. (© IWM FLM1466)

NEVILLE CHAMBERLAIN (1869–1940) The British Prime Minister from 1937 until replaced by Churchill in 1940, Chamberlain was the first politician in office to advocate rearmament. Far from being soft on Fascism he was well aware that Britain had neither the military strength, the will, nor the support of the Empire to go to war in 1938, and that appeasement was the only possible way to buy time for a measure of preparation. Depicted as a silly little man with an umbrella he was a far better figure of a man than his successor, and has been unjustly blamed for all the ills that beset the UK at the outbreak of war. Here he is inspecting a French guard of honour in Amiens during a visit to the front in 1939. (© IWM O2147)

WINSTON CHURCHILL (**1874–1965**) Prime Minister as a result of the Norway debacle, for which he bears at least some of the blame, he was a charismatic leader and an inspirational orator, but his interference in matters of which he had little understanding gravely hindered the conduct of the war. His attitude to military matters was likened to that of a small boy who has a new toy, of which he then becomes tired and abandons it before moving on to another. He liked uniforms and here inspects naval ratings (who do not appear to be overjoyed at the visitation) at Rosyth dressed as an elder brother of Trinity House. As the first author to have a history of the war on the bookshelves, it is the Churchill version of the war that has become accepted in British mythology. (© IWM A1479)

FIELD MARSHAL SIR CLAUDE AUCHINLECK (1884–1981) Seen here in discussions with
Norwegian officers before he recommended a withdrawal from that theatre in 1940, Auchinleck
was one of the brightest stars of the Indian Army, and suffered resentment from his British colleagues as a result. He was General Officer Commanding–in-Chief Southern Command, where
one of his corps commanders was a thoroughly disloyal Montgomery, before returning to India as
Commander-in-Chief of the Indian Army. Taking over from Wavell in North Africa, he won the
First Battle of Alamein and planned the Second, although Montgomery was to reap the credit. A
genuinely great and decent man, his reputation has suffered from having been treated unfairly by
Churchill and denigrated by Montgomery. (© IWM H5927)

Opposite top **GÉNERAL DE DIVISION CHARLES DE GAULLE (1890–1970)** Major General
Spears, Liaison Officer to the Free French, and (self promoted) Géneral de Division Charles de
Gaulle on board the troop transport SS *Westernland* on their way to the abortive raid on Dakar in
Senegal in September 1940. De Gaulle was a most difficult ally but probably the only Frenchman
who could garner the support of at least a working majority of his countrymen. Among the many
things about him that irritated the British was his use of the Cross of Lorraine, last used by a
mentally deranged anorexic teenager who had proved a considerable nuisance to the English
during the Hundred Years War. (© IWM A1475)

Opposite below **FIELD MARSHALS VISCOUNT ALANBROOKE AND VISCOUNT MONTGOMERY**
Montgomery when General Officer Commanding-in-Chief South Eastern Command and Brooke
as Commander-in-Chief Home Forces in early 1942. Montgomery would be a psychiatrist's delight
were he alive today: an extraordinary mixture of insecurity and bombast, of meticulous preparation
and cautious execution, his reputation as Britain's greatest general was largely manufactured by
himself. Brooke was an uninspiring leader but a highly competent administrator with a sound
grasp of strategy and of what was possible. As Churchill's appointee he did manage to control
some of the PM's wilder flights of fancy, but acquiesced far too often in his meddling in matters
that should not have concerned him. (© IWM H5930)

GENERAL MONTGOMERY AND GENERAL RITTER VON THOMA In the greater scheme of things the North African campaign was a sideshow, and to the Germans a minor sideshow. For the British, other than Burma, it was the only front where they were engaged, and so it assumed great significance. Having won the Second Battle of Alamein, using Auchinleck's plan, Montgomery then began to move cautiously along the North African coast while the outnumbered and starved of logistic support Axis handed him off and withdrew to Tunisia. In November 1942 General Ritter von Thoma, now commanding the DAK, was captured by the British and brought to Montgomery's tactical headquarters. (© IWM E19129)

Gambara's Italian XX Corps, with one armoured and one motorised division. On the Sollum front an Italian division supported by elements of the German 90 Light had constructed a defensive line running from Sollum thirty miles south to Sidi Umar, while the rest of the Panzer Group was in the Tobruk area or between there and the frontier.

There were huge supply problems for the Axis. In August the Royal Navy and the RAF between them had sunk or destroyed half of all the stores and supplies sent to Rommel, and by October that had risen to two-thirds. The DAK had received only forty-four Panzer Mk III and sixteen Mk IV as replacements; it was short of artillery and the supply of fuel and spares was a constant concern. Prior to Operation Crusader the German ration strength[*] in North Africa was 48,500, of whom 11,066 were sick.[4] Rommel had 249 German tanks, of which seventy were Mk II armed only with a 20mm cannon, and 137 Italian M13/40. He could call on 430 serviceable aircraft (seventy-six German and 290 Italian) compared to the RAF's 550, and while the Luftwaffe in Greece could help, this was offset by the RAF operating from Malta. The biggest difference in the air was that the RAF had plentiful fuel and spares, whereas the Axis had not.

From 14 October to 17 November the Desert Air Force kept up an unceasing bombardment of German positions, routes, supply dumps and ports, flying up to eighty sorties a day. By the time the army was ready to deploy, the RAF had achieved complete air superiority over Cyrenaica. On 16 and 17 November the Eighth Army began to move into position, Churchill still considering that it was 'intolerable' that the British had done nothing in the five months since Battleaxe. Each infantry brigade needed a thousand wheeled vehicles to move men and stores (including a reduced ration of a gallon of water per man per day),[**] and at a standard distance between vehicles of 200 yards (necessary as a precaution against air attack and to reduce dust), each brigade column was over a hundred

* The total number of men in a theatre is the ration strength, whereas the combat strength is the (much smaller) number available in fighting units.

** This author recalls serving in the Libyan Desert in the days before the Gadaffi regime expelled Good King Idris and the British. The availability of water was such that one first boiled one's egg in a mess tin over a hexamine Tommy Cooker, washed and shaved in the same water, filtered that water through a face flannel and then made tea with it. We remained remarkably healthy.

miles long, and at 10 mph (and some columns moved more slowly) took over ten hours to pass a point. Many of the drivers were untrained in desert driving, and a sudden sandstorm accompanied by violent electric storms and heavy sleet and rain flooded wadis (dry stream beds) and turned normally firm patches of sand into quagmires. Groups got lost; vehicles turned over and in many columns chaos reigned. Fortunately the weather was equally inclement for the Germans and Italians.

Rommel had intended to launch his attack on Tobruk in mid September, but supply problems forced him to postpone until mid November, and when XXX Corps crossed into Libya on 18 November, he assumed that it was merely a diversion to distract him from Tobruk. Here appeared the first flaw in the British thinking. The German and Italian armour did not conform to the plan and by last light on 18 November XXX Corps had penetrated forty miles and had seen nothing but reconnaissance units withdrawing. Next day XXX Corps continued in the direction of Tobruk, the gap between it and the infantry of XIII Corps gradually widening until 4 Armoured Brigade was effectively detached from 7 Armoured Division. When 22 Armoured Brigade ran into tanks of the Italian Ariete armoured division at Bir el Gubi, off to the left of the British advance, instead of masking them, which might have been done by one regiment, and carrying on towards Tobruk, the whole brigade, with the concurrence of the divisional commander Major General 'Strafer' Gott, became involved in an attempt to destroy the Ariete. The brigade's A15 cruisers were fast – excellent suspension allowed them to exceed their theoretical maximum of 27 mph – but only lightly armoured, and when the inexperienced Territorial Army crewmen lined up their tanks and simply charged the Ariete as if at the first fence in a hunter chase, it looked initially as if they would succeed. When the objective reached turned out to be but an outpost line, the balance swung and well dug-in Italian tanks began to take a severe toll. Control was lost as radio communications broke down, all three regiments of the brigade, 3 and 4 County of London Yeomanry and the Royal Gloucestershire Hussars, were roughly handled and by last light had lost half their tanks, while the Italians still held Bir el Gubi.

That same day 7 Armoured Brigade reached Sidi Rezegh. Now, instead of the British armour being concentrated, as had been intended, the division had its three brigades spread out with 4 Brigade at Gabr Saleh, 22 at Bir el Gubi twenty miles to the west, and 7 at Sidi Rezegh another twenty miles to the north. Rommel still refused to believe that the British advance was anything but a diversion, but eventually yielded to Crüwell's pleas and allowed the DAK to send a battle group (a panzer regiment with some anti-tank guns) from 21 Panzer to Gabr Saleh, where the British got the worse of the encounter. From now on the fighting became very confused, both to those taking part and to later historians attempting to piece together what happened. Rommel, still determined to attack Tobruk on 21 November, ordered the DAK to concentrate between the British and the Egyptian frontier, to cut this inconvenient intrusion off from its supplies; the British responded by moving 22 Armoured Brigade east to join 4 Brigade and the two became involved in a tank battle with 15 Panzer, while 21 Panzer ran out of fuel. The British managed to concentrate their two brigades and hold their ground. Gott ordered his support group (two lorried infantry battalions and field, anti-tank and anti-aircraft artillery) forward to Sidi Rezegh and Norrie sent 1 South African Division of XXX Corps forward to mask the Italian armour at Bir el Gubi, while Cunningham ordered the Tobruk garrison to break out on the morning of 21 November. Rommel, finally accepting that there was a major British thrust towards Tobruk, now ordered the DAK to about-turn and head for Sidi Rezegh.

On the morning of 21 November 7 Armoured Brigade began to move towards Tobruk, to link up with 70 Division trying to break out. Progress was slow, thanks to well-sited German anti-tank guns, and the situation was made much worse by the capture of the east end of Sidi Rezegh ridge by the DAK. On 22 November XIII Corps began to attack Axis positions around Bardia and Capuzzo. Despite the thick armour on the Matildas, losses in 1 Army Tank Brigade were high, due once again to anti-tank guns well sited behind a minefield, but even so XIII Corps made reasonable progress, so that 1 New Zealand Division could be sent along the Capuzzo escarpment in the direction of Sidi Rezegh. They would be sorely needed, for that same day the DAK extended its lodgement on Sidi Rezegh, 6 RTR losing almost all its tanks in an attempt to stop them. By nightfall the whole ridge was in German hands. Rommel now attempted to encircle the British armour, using the DAK and the Ariete Division, and in moving to the south-west of Sidi Rezegh 15 Panzer overwhelmed a brigade of 1 South African Division on the way. There was now, 23 November, an untidy tank battle south of Sidi Rezegh, in which both sides took heavy losses in tanks, but the British the worse. Both Rommel and Cunningham now came to conclusions which, in hindsight, were mistaken. Rommel got away with it, just, while for Cunningham it was the end of his career.

At Eighth Army headquarters east of Fort Maddalena on the evening of 22 November, and during the following day, reports and returns began to come in. They made a depressing picture, the more so because up to now the British had thought they were winning, with the press in Cairo claiming that the Germans were in full retreat and reporting figures of Axis tank losses considerably greater than the total Rommel actually possessed. It was now becoming clear to Cunningham that 7 Armoured Brigade had not a single tank that was serviceable and 22 Brigade was down to thirty. Nobody had any idea where 4 Brigade was as its HQ, although not its regiments, had been overrun by the DAK. The New Zealanders had, by an extraordinary combination of good luck and bad map-reading, stumbled upon and captured the DAK's main HQ, although General Crüwell and his chief of staff, von Bayerlein, were not there. This one ray of sunshine could not hide the fact that what Cunningham had believed and hoped was potentially a major victory, was already becoming a disaster.

Generals do not usually suffer from stress. By training, experience and application they are accustomed to long periods without sleep, difficult decisions and incomplete information. They have to possess a certain streak of ruthlessness and be able to subsume personal feelings and emotions in the interests of the task in hand. The ability of soldiers (and sailors and airmen) to distance themselves from the death or maiming of their friends or those for whom they are responsible is not due to their having been brutalised by service, but a defence mechanism, necessary to allow them to get on with what they are paid and trained to do. In war it is not the dead who matter to commanders, but those who are still

alive. Cunningham was under great pressure. He had fought a successful, but wearing, campaign in East Africa, and had then been translated to
a theatre of which he knew nothing, to fight a war the type of which he
had no experience, with subordinate commanders who thought they
knew more than he did. He had been pushed into launching Crusader
earlier than he would have wished by Auchinleck, himself under unbear-
able pressure from Churchill. By 23 November he had had no rest for
months, and now to have all his hopes dashed was too much. He had
been a heavy smoker and had only just given up, which may have been
part of the problem, but he does seem to have suffered if not a nervous
breakdown, at least a temporary attack of the jitters. He was now seriously
considering breaking off the operation, and sent an urgent message to
Auchinleck, asking him to come forward for consultation. That even the
loyalty of Cunningham's staff was uncertain is evinced by his chief of
staff, Galloway, telephoning the chief of staff at Middle East HQ, Dorman-
Smith, to tell him that 'another influence was required at Eighth Army
HQ if the battle was not to get out of hand'.[5]

Rommel's conclusion, from the same facts, was that the best way of
dealing with the British offensive was to make a lightning strike against
Egypt, which would force the British to pull back to deal with it, and
might give the DAK an opportunity of catching them on the line of march
and destroying them. That the DAK logistic chain was not up to such a
manoeuvre bothered Rommel not a jot: his units could replenish from
British dumps in Egypt, and in any event he had never cared very much for
logistics – one of the reasons why, while undoubtedly a great leader, he
was never a great general. In what would have been, had it worked, a
classic example of the modern concept of manoeuvre warfare, Rommel
took 15 and 21 Panzer and the Ariete Divisions on what became known as
'the dash for the wire', aiming to use the positions at Bardia and Halfaya
Pass,[*] still held by the Axis, as springboards to roll up XIII Corps and force
a retreat by XXX Corps. It did not work, for three reasons: Auchinleck
arrived at the front, the British artillery stopped Rommel's tanks, and the
DAK ran out of fuel.

Auchinleck arrived at Maddalena by aircraft that afternoon, 23

* Halfaya was held by 1st Battalion Rifle Regiment 104, commanded by Major The Reverend Wilhelm Bach.

November, and his presence alone imposed a calm upon that very jumpy headquarters. Having listened to the views of Galloway and the two corps commanders, Auchinleck decreed that while he accepted that Eighth Army might lose all its tanks, the possibilities of relieving Tobruk and writing down the Axis armour made the risk worth it, and directed that the attack would continue, prodding Cunningham into sending the New Zealanders towards Tobruk with XXX Corps' armour protecting their left flank. The next day was one of movement and confusion to both sides. Parties of New Zealanders moving west and Germans moving east ran into each other, narrowly avoided each other, or mistook each other for friends. On 25 November the New Zealanders, supported by tanks of 1 Army Tank Brigade, were approaching El Duda, thirty miles from Tobruk. On 26 November they and the advanced elements of 70 Division from Tobruk met, and on 27 November 1 New Zealand Division recaptured the Sidi Rezegh ridge.

In Headquarters Panzer Group Africa, at El Adem twenty-five miles south of Tobruk, there was mounting anxiety. Nothing had been heard from Rommel for over twenty-four hours, nor was there any communication with Crüwell. The only radio link open was that to Headquarters 21 Panzer, whose commander, Lieutenant General von Ravenstein, also had no idea where Rommel was, and aircraft sent out to find the commander Panzer Group Africa had either failed to find him or been shot down by the RAF. On arrival at the frontier the DAK, seriously short of fuel and water, had run into British artillery and suffered accordingly. They did manage to fight their way into Bardia, and replenish there, but by 26 November it was obvious to Rommel that his counter-stroke had failed and that while his dash had scattered headquarters to right and left, and sent logistic units flying, the British combatant units had not moved. Reluctantly he ordered his divisions to leave Bardia and move west, along the Trigh Capuzzo, the escarpment running parallel to the coast.

On that same day Auchinleck reluctantly relieved Cunningham of his command, putting in his place Major General (local lieutenant general) Neil Ritchie, lately deputy chief of the general staff at HQ Middle East Command. To remove a commander in the middle of a battle is a very serious matter: it is bad for the morale of your own troops and a boost for those of the enemy; it is bad public relations and will be made maximum use of by ill-disposed propagandists. Auchinleck knew all that, but felt that Cunningham was under such strain and had begun to think in such a defensive manner that there was no alternative. There can be little doubt that by this time Cunningham had lost the confidence of his subordinate commanders, particularly Galloway, Godwin-Austin and Gott, and Auchinleck was right to remove him, painful though it must have been. The change was not announced until 11 December, by which time the battle was over.

The next day, on their way west, the DAK ran into British tanks of 4 and 22 Armoured Brigades (7 Brigade had been withdrawn) south of Sidi Rezegh. Here was an opportunity for the British, but with the approach of darkness they broke off the action earlier than they need, or should, have done, and next day the three Axis armoured divisions attacked El Duda, cutting the New Zealand Division in two and damaging the 70 Division salient poking out from Tobruk. The British armoured division had now insufficient tanks to do very much, but the Germans and Italians were exhausted too. On 1 December the New Zealand Division was withdrawn, and shortly afterwards 4 and 22 Armoured Brigades were amalgamated into one brigade. Serious though the British losses had been, however, they were receiving resupply and reinforcements, whereas the Germans and Italians were not. Despite the meeting at El Duda Tobruk had not been relieved by the British, but Rommel, with the DAK down to only seventeen Mk IIs (from seventy-three), thirty-one Mk III (from 144) and nine Mk IV (from thirty-eight), and with a supply line from Italy to Africa so tenuous that everything from petrol and ammunition to radio batteries to boots and socks was running short, decided that the town could no longer be held. On 6 December Panzer Group Africa slipped away, abandoning their garrisons at the frontier, and headed west, twenty-five miles to Gazala.[*]

The British, after a half-hearted attempt to outflank the Gazala Line was beaten back, decided to attack it with 7 Armoured Division's one brigade, commanded by Brigadier Gatehouse who, after the capture of

---

[*] The frontier positions were eventually taken, the gallant Rev. Bach holding out until 17 January 1942, when, out of ammunition, food and water he eventually surrendered.

his 4 Brigade headquarters (but not of him), had for a while commanded his brigade from an armchair strapped to the top of a squadron tank. This was to happen on 19 December, but on the night of 16–17 December, Rommel slipped away again, 270 miles west to El Agheila. On 24 December the British entered Benghazi for the second time, to the not altogether unalloyed delight of the inhabitants, who had not appreciated being bombed by the RAF for the past two months. Operation Crusader was over.

In that Crusader had ultimately seen the Germans abandon Cyrenaica, albeit on their own terms rather than being driven out by the British, and that Tobruk was relieved, it could be said to be a partial success, but it hardly compared with Blenheim and Waterloo, as the Prime Minister had predicted it would,[6] and it came at a heavy cost. Although from a total strength of 118,000 British Empire forces only 2,900 were killed (of whom fifty-eight were British), compared to 1,100 Germans out of 65,000 and 1,200 Italians out of 54,000, the loss of tanks and the damage to morale was very much greater. While tanks could be, and were, replaced, the men of the Eighth Army began to feel that German equipment was better than theirs (not entirely true) and that German troops were better than themselves. Brevity, Battleaxe and now Crusader had shown that years of neglect and underfunding could not be redressed in a mere two years. There were faults in British tanks, among them the lack of a cap for the 2-pounder shell, which could not therefore punch through all German armour; the various types of tank had cross-country speeds so different that they could not move and fight together, and they had inferior optics and gun sights. Despite this, British tanks were not, at this stage, markedly inferior to the German; indeed some were better, and the British had more of them, but in their anti-tank guns and in the way that they used them, the Germans had a decided advantage.

In keeping with their doctrine of all-arms cooperation and short wars, the Germans had paid considerable attention to ground-support aircraft and anti-aircraft defence. Their concentration on developing armoured tactics included anti-tank defence, and German specifications demanded that every artillery piece, whether field or anti-aircraft, should have an anti-tank capability. Pre-war, all German guns had been tested in the anti-tank role, and the most effective had proved to be the 88mm Kwk 36 anti-aircraft gun, which from the beginning of the war the Germans used in both roles. With a muzzle velocity (at this early stage) of 2,660 feet per second, or two and a half times the speed of sound, the 88's anti-tank round could penetrate four inches of armour at a range of 1,000 yards. The British 2-pounder anti-tank and tank gun was extremely unlikely to hit anything at that range, but if it did could penetrate only just over one and a half inches of armour. At 2,000 yards the 88 could still penetrate nearly three and a half inches, whereas the 2-pounder would simply bounce off, even in the unlikely event of it hitting the target. The 88 had a high silhouette, but its very long effective range meant that it could deal with any threat on the ground long before it was itself in danger, and while vulnerable from the air, it could be dug in to provide some protection. Fortunately for the British, Rommel only had sixteen 88s at the time of Crusader. The standard German anti-tank gun at the start of the war was a 37mm weapon, with a maximum range of 500 yards, but this had now been almost entirely replaced in North Africa by the Long 50mm Kwk 39 gun, that could punch through two inches of armour at 1,000 yards range.

Not only were these guns better than those of the British, but the Germans saw their guns, rather than their tanks, as the chief tank-killing weapon. A standard tactic was to put out a line of anti-tank guns, well concealed behind a fold in the ground or dug in, and allow the British to advance on to them. The guns would then start to take out British tanks at maximum range, to which the British tank guns could not reply, and when the British had been sufficiently damaged and disorganised, the German armour would move in from a flank and finish the job.

It was not, however, equipment but method and training that made the difference. The British still clung to the idea that tanks could operate independently, and sought a tank-against-tank battle. The Germans believed that the tank engine was as important as its gun and saw the tank not as a mobile gun platform, but as a way of delivering shock in the flanks, or in the rear. They believed in mixed groups of all-arms and although their tanks were of widely varying quality, they could all work together and move at the same speed. German soldiers could arrive in

Libya and go into action straight away – they had all been trained in the same way. British troops could not, and needed a long work-up before they could cooperate with other arms and become accustomed to the desert.

It says little for the state to which the British army had been reduced that for its major effort in 1941 it could field only six divisions, in a theatre regarded by the Germans as an unimportant sideshow, and that even then the overwhelming majority of the infantry were not British. But it was not only on land that 1941 was another bad year for the British, and it would get worse before it got better.

NOTES

1. Statistics from Research Institute for Military History, Germany, *Germany and the Second World War, Vol. IV*, Clarendon Press, Oxford, 1996.

2. Figures taken from Peter Howlett, *Fighting with Figures: A Statistical Digest of the Second World War*, HMSO, London, 1995.

3. TNA Kew, WO 216/61, report on the supply of officers for the army, dated January 1941.

4. Research Institute for Military History, Germany, op. cit.

5. Quoted in Barrie Pitt, *The Crucible of War: Auchinleck's Command*, Cassell, London 2001.

6. Nigel Nicolson, (ed), *Harold Nicolson, The War Years: Diaries and Letters 1939–1945*, Atheneum, New York 1967.

13

The Pendulum War

FOR THE BRITISH THE year 1941 was one of almost unmitigated disaster, and not only for the army. At sea the Royal Navy was facing what was probably the greatest challenge in its long history – for the Spanish had only one armada, and Napoleon no submarines. Now the navy had to maintain the blockade of Germany all the way from Brest to the Baltic, keep the sea-lanes open for foodstuffs and supplies coming into Britain and for troops and equipment going out, and have available sufficient force to contain and destroy any attempt by the German navy to break out into the Atlantic and embark on commerce raiding. At any one time there might be eight convoys in the North Atlantic alone, and when Mediterranean traffic and shipping to Russia are added the convoy escort burden was considerable. Because of the dual threat from German submarines and surface raiders, these escorts had to carry considerable punch. As an example, convoy WS 5B, which sailed from England on 12 January 1941 with 40,000 troops for the Middle East, was escorted by the battleship HMS *Ramillies* with the cruisers *Naiad*, *Australia* and *Phoebe*, and twelve destroyers.

The Royal Navy and Coastal Command of the Royal Air Force kept a constant watch on German and German-occupied ports, and when the brand new battleship *Bismarck* and the cruiser *Prinz Eugen* sailed from

Gdynia in the Baltic on 18 May the RAF identified them refuelling in a Norwegian fjord south of Bergen on 21 May, before sailing north. On 22 May the Home Fleet sailed from Scapa Flow, and despite bad weather and worse visibility, on 23 May the cruisers *Norfolk* and *Suffolk* spotted the two German ships sailing south-west through the Denmark Strait, between Iceland and Greenland. The battleship HMS *Prince of Wales* and the battlecruiser HMS *Hood* closed to intercept. Although the *Hood* was twenty years old, she was armed with eight 15-inch guns, while the *Prince of Wales* was Britain's newest battleship. Commissioned in January 1941, she carried ten 14-inch guns and this was her first operational sortie. In firepower alone, the two British ships outgunned the eight 15-inch guns on *Bismarck* and the eight 8-inch guns on *Prinz Eugen*. What happened next appalled the nation, for when fire was opened at a range of 26,500 yards at 0553 hours on 24 May, it took a mere seven minutes for the *Hood* to catch fire, blow up and sink. There were just three survivors, a midshipman and two ratings, from a crew of 1,419 all ranks. With the *Hood* gone, the German ships could concentrate on the *Prince of Wales*, which sustained a number of hits and so much damage that at 0613 hours her captain broke off the action and turned away.

There were all sorts of excuses: the *Hood* had never been modernised and her deck armour was incapable of withstanding heavy shells; the *Prince of Wales* had not yet had time to properly work up, there were mechanical problems with her gun turrets and a number of civilian shipyard workers were still on board attempting to right them; Admiral Holland, commanding from his flagship *Hood*, may have misjudged the angle of approach, so that not all his guns could be brought to bear – he went down with his ship so could not offer an explanation; there were problems with the radar, still relatively new on board ship, and with the rangefinders which, like those on tanks, were markedly inferior to those used by the Germans, and communications between Holland and the two cruisers was confused. Whatever the causes, the disaster shocked the navy, and the damage inflicted by the *Prince of Wales* which led to the sinking of the *Bismarck* by a combination of shadowing RAF Catalinas, the battleships *Rodney* and *King George V*, torpedo bombers from the carriers *Victorious* and *Ark Royal*, and the Fourth Destroyer Flotilla, as she tried to run for St Nazaire on 27 May, was only a partial consolation. *Prinz Eugen*, which had separated from the *Bismarck* on 24 May, managed to get into Brest on 1 June.

The despatch of twenty-five German submarines to the Mediterranean meant that the *Hood* was not the only capital ship to be lost in 1941; the battleship HMS *Barham* was sunk by *U 331* in the Mediterranean on 24 November, and while not technically a capital ship, or at least not yet, the aircraft carrier HMS *Ark Royal*, regularly claimed as sunk by William Joyce (Lord Haw Haw) in his broadcasts from Berlin, was finally bagged on 14 November, when she sank under tow to Gibraltar having been torpedoed the previous day by *U 81* and *U 205*. On 19 December three Italian two-man human torpedoes managed to enter Alexandria harbour unobserved. With great courage the crews attached explosives to the undersides of the battleships HMS *Queen Elizabeth* and HMS *Valiant*, causing considerable damage that took many months to repair. Admiral Cunningham was now without a single capital ship, and only retained control of the Mediterranean by adopting an even more aggressive posture than normal, with the maximum of his remaining cruisers and destroyers at sea. His policy worked, and the Italian navy never did attempt to challenge him in force. The *Prince of Wales* was not a lucky ship, for she and the battlecruiser HMS *Repulse* were sunk by Japanese aircraft on 10 December off Malaya, thus underlining, if underlining was needed, the inescapable fact that large ships without their own aircraft were liable to be sunk by the enemy's.

The one ray of sunshine for the British at the end of what had been a generally dreadful year was the entry of the United States of America into the war. On 7 December Japanese carrier aircraft, in what they saw as a pre-emptive strike, attacked the US Pacific Fleet at anchor in Pearl Harbor, Hawaii, sinking or putting out of action all eight battleships and a number of smaller vessels. They failed to get the heavy cruisers and the aircraft carriers, which were on exercise out at sea at the time. Simultaneously Japanese forces attacked British and Dutch possessions in the Far East, and declared war on Britain and the United States.

Four days later, on 11 December, the German government, effectively Hitler, made the second of two major errors that would lose them the war: they declared war on the United States. Hitler need not have done this: the agreement between Germany and Japan stated that if either country was attacked, the other would consult to see what help could be given. Since it was Japan that had done the attacking, without warning the Germans in advance, there was no requirement for Germany to become involved. Presumably Hitler thought that as the USA was already supporting Britain with weapons, supplies and money, and was even helping to escort convoys, in contravention of the laws of neutrality, and would come into the war herself at some stage, he might as well get it over with now. Hitler may well have been right, but by his declaration of war he ensured that the major British fear – that America would put all her efforts into the Pacific theatre – did not come to pass, and Churchill was able to persuade President Roosevelt, despite the objections of a number of American admirals, to adopt the 'Germany first' policy.

After the withdrawal from northern Europe and the disasters of Greece and Crete, the only British troops facing the Germans were those in North Africa; not many of them were British and they were not facing many Germans. The navy could of course attack German shipping wherever it was found, but what Britain really wanted to do was hit back at Germany directly. One way this could be done was by bombing. The majority of senior officers in the RAF had always believed that the real purpose of their service was strategic bombing. At the end of 1940, while the danger of invasion might not have disappeared entirely, the RAF was emerging from its purely defensive and anti-invasion roles, and looking where they might carry the war to the enemy. Fighter Command was still largely occupied with the defence of the United Kingdom against the Blitz, but Bomber Command could now revert to its *raison d'être*, the destruction from the air of the enemy's ability to make war. Even before the Battle of Britain had begun, in the early summer of 1940, Churchill had been thinking ahead to the offensive employment of Bomber Command. Writing to Lord Beaverbrook, the Minister for Aircraft Production, the Prime Minister said:

He [the Germans] will recoil eastwards, and we have nothing to stop him.
But there is one thing that will bring him down, and that is an absolutely

devastating attack by very heavy bombers from this country on the Nazi homeland. We must be able to overwhelm him by this means, without which I do not see a way through.[1]

Later Churchill said that although the Royal Navy might lose Britain the war, only the RAF could win it. In view of Churchill's later treatment of Bomber Command, it is as well to remember what his views were in 1940.

On 25 October 1940 Air Chief Marshal Sir Charles Portal took over as Chief of Air Staff from Air Chief Marshal Newall. As an ex- Commander-in-Chief Bomber Command, Portal had no doubt as to what strategic bombing might achieve:

We have the one directly offensive weapon in the whole of our armoury, the one means by which we can undermine the morale of a large part of the enemy people, shake their faith in the Nazi regime, and at the same time and with the very same bombs, dislocate the major part of their heavy industry and a good part of their oil production.[2]

That the destruction of enemy morale and destruction of enemy industry were not necessarily the same thing was not yet apparent, although it would become so, and as the Blitz continued into the winter of 1940 and the early part of 1941, demands that the RAF should hit back intensified. There were problems. Although British aircraft production was improving, even by the middle of 1941 the RAF had fewer operational aircraft than the Luftwaffe and could only muster 400 operational bombers on any one night, whereas the Germans, despite the Luftwaffe never having been considered as a strategic air force, could regularly send more than that against a single English city.

Another problem was navigation. In fine weather by day the British bombers could usually find their targets, but the German anti-aircraft guns and air-defence fighters could also find the bombers, and with no long-distance fighter escorts at this stage of the war, the RAF increasingly had to rely on night bombing, when navigation was very much an art rather than an exact science. In late 1940 Commander-in-Chief Bomber Command, Air Marshal Sir Richard Peirse, calculated that on short-range raids only one in three bombers found its target, and at long ranges only one in five. By 1941 bombing was aimed increasingly against area targets at night, and this inevitably meant blowing up civilians. While the RAF had wanted to destroy enemy morale, and accepted that destroying cities was part of that, the more squeamish had managed to convince themselves that after one or two raids the civilian population would leave the urban areas and take to the countryside, although why the continued bombing of these evacuated cities would contribute to the lowering of morale was not explained.

Initially, due to the shortage of aircraft and the increasing obsolescence of the Blenheims and the Battles, there were numerous raids by small numbers of aircraft. During the 120-day period 13 October 1940 to 10 February 1941, Bomber Command mounted 567 sorties in eighty-three operations by day, and 6,030 sorties in ninety-three operations by night, losing 126 aircraft all told. In February Bomber Command was ordered to concentrate on German synthetic oil plants, and in the thirty days to 12 March 1941 mounted twenty-one day operations of ninety-four sorties and sixteen night operations of 1,635 sorties, losing twenty-eight aircraft to the Germans and a further seventy that crashed in the UK. From 13 March to 7 July 1941 Bomber Command was instructed to concentrate on finding and attacking German commerce raiders, U-boats and naval bases, and during that 117-day period flew 106 day operations of 2,189 sorties, and eighty-seven night operations of 10,532 sorties, losing 321 aircraft.[3]

It was not until July 1941 that Bomber Command could focus on what it considered its primary role: bombing Germany. On 7 July Bomber Command was directed by the Chief of the Air Staff, himself directed by the Chiefs of Staff Committee to:

> ...direct the main effort of the bomber force, until further instructions, towards dislocating the German transportation system and to destroying the morale of the civilian population as a whole and of the industrial workers in particular.[4]

In practice, this meant attacking military and industrial targets – railway yards, factories, docks – during moonlit nights, when the bomber crews could see what they were looking for, and bombing cities on nights when there was no moon. To navigational difficulties was now added the Kammhuber Line, an air-defence system that stretched from the Atlantic coast into Germany, and used a combination of radar, searchlights, night fighters and anti-aircraft guns to identify and then deal with bombers entering German air space.[*] In the 126-day period from 7 July to 10 November, eighty-three days and ninety-two nights of operations totalling 13,558 sorties cost Bomber Command 526 aircraft, the worst night being 7–8 November when Commander-in-Chief Bomber Command insisted on sending out 392 aircraft in appalling weather. Thirty-seven bombers were lost, to little effect. Then, like a bolt from the blue, came the Butt Report.

D. M. Butt was a civil servant in the air ministry, and because of the very high losses in aircraft and crews he had been told to analyse the effectiveness of RAF bombing raids. To do this he examined 4,065 photographs taken on one hundred night raids in the summer of 1941. The photographs were taken by cameras fitted to bombers – supposedly only to aircraft flown by the better pilots – and were compared with the reports submitted by the pilots on their return from raids. Butt looked at raids where the pilots had reported that they had actually bombed their targets – only two-thirds of all raids – and his findings were catastrophic. On clear nights with moon and good visibility, only one in four bombers had been within five miles of its target, and on nights with no moon, only one in twenty. Even then, within five miles might suffice for area bombing of a city, but might as well have been fifty miles if the target was a precision one, such as a railway marshalling yard or an aircraft factory. High casualties may be sustained, at least for a time, if the officers and men can see that they are worthwhile. Now, although the Butt Report was not made public, or even circulated at squadron level, it was clear to the Air Staff and to the Chiefs of Staff that the present bombing campaign was not worth the expenditure of lives and machinery, and that doubt began to trickle down to the aircrews. On 13 November 1941 Sir Richard Peirse had an uncomfortable meeting with the Prime Minister at Chequers, when Bomber Command was ordered to halt the current

[*] General of Flyers Josef Kammhuber was Commander-in-Chief of the Luftwaffe's night fighter command.

offensive, and to scale back all operations while the future of strategic bombing was examined.

That debate was intense. On the one hand were the advocates of independent air power who insisted that despite disappointments to date, the German economy and German morale could be destroyed from the air. On the other were those who questioned whether Britain, with her resources stretched as they were, could or should maintain this expensive strategic bombing force, when its results had so far been negligible. The results, of course, had been far from negligible, but fierce argument pushes cases to the extreme and certainly the results were not what had been promised. In the end Portal and the Air Staff convinced Churchill and the war cabinet that if Bomber Command had the right aircraft and enough of them (Portal wanted 4,000), and concentrated on German cities, it could achieve momentous results. The alternative, argued the bombing school, was a long, costly and bloody land campaign on the European continent, all too reminiscent of the last war.

Three things happened that would transform Bomber Command. The first was the by now inevitable sacking of Sir Richard Peirse as Commander-in-Chief Bomber Command, and his replacement by Air Chief Marshal Sir Arthur Harris; the second was the promise of more, new and better aircraft, and the third was the introduction of improved navigational instruments. The new directive to Bomber Command, approved by the war cabinet, stated:

> The primary objective of your operations should now be focused on the morale of the enemy civil population and in particular of the industrial workers.

This was unequivocal: German cities were to be attacked, German civilians, men, women and children were to be blown up, their buildings destroyed and their homes burnt to the ground. Although Harris, who would lead Bomber Command until the end of the war, was an enthusiastic supporter of this policy, he did not initiate it. It came from the Chief of the Air Staff, Portal, with the full agreement of Churchill and the war cabinet, and Trenchard cheering it on from the wings.

Much later, the actions of Bomber Command came in for fierce

criticism, and to this day some maintain that Harris and his aircrew were war criminals in that they had deliberately targeted 'innocent civilians'.*
It is very easy for modern protesters to condemn the actions of airmen a generation ago: they did not have to endure the Blitz nor live through a war where the very existence of this nation was at stake. For four long years the only visible and continuous way that Britain could hit back at Germany was by bombing. The technology of the time did not permit the kind of precision bombing that satellites and laser markers allow today, which meant that there was little alternative to area bombing of cities. Had the RAF not bombed German cities, when the means to do so was available, then public outrage would have been uncontainable; and in any case, the Germans started it.

The premise that German morale would collapse was, however, mistaken. It did not, and it is difficult to see why the British thought it would – after all, morale at home had not collapsed during the Blitz, indeed if anything it had hardened. There was still a residue of 1930s theorising that the bomber will always get through, and also an element of wishful thinking that predicated an underlying opposition to Hitler among the German public that was just waiting for an opportunity to emerge, an opportunity that attacks on their cities might encourage. This was dangerous nonsense: the German public were overwhelmingly behind Hitler and his government and they, like the British, could take it. In the previous war the blockade, near-starvation and the influenza epidemic, on top of appalling losses at the front, had proved that the Germans were a stoical people. Yet even if British planners had realised that the destruction of German morale was pie in the sky, the bombing campaign would have gone on – public opinion would have demanded it. The price paid by Bomber Command was a heavy one. It was heavier than the army's or the navy's, and heavier than any other part of the RAF. Bomber Command comprised 7 per cent of all British military manpower during the war: it sustained 24 per cent of all British military deaths.

The arrival of better aircraft and more accurate navigational aids did improve the effectiveness of bombing raids. Coming into service with Bomber Command in 1942 were the Short Stirling (14,000lbs of bombs),

* Why are civilians and bystanders always 'innocent'?

the Handley Page Halifax (13,000lbs), the De Havilland Mosquito, an all-wood unarmed aircraft that relied on its speed (400 mph) for protection and whose two-man crew could deliver a bombload of 4,000lbs; and the Lancaster.

The Lancaster four-engined heavy bomber first came into service in March 1942, and could deliver 14,000lbs of bombs at a range of 1,000 miles, and up to 22,000lbs when modified. It carried a bigger bombload than any other Allied bomber of the war. The American B17 Flying Fortress (in service when America entered the war) carried 6,000lbs and even the B29 Super Fortress (in service from 1943) only carried 12,000lbs. The biggest load-carrying German bomber was the Heinkel H177A, in service from late 1942, which carried 13,300lbs, but this aircraft was over-engineered, suffered from constant mechanical problems and saw little service. There were three reasons why American bombers carried a smaller bombload than their British equivalents. American bombers were designed to do their bombing from America if need be, and so had to have a range twice that of British craft; American doctrine had bombers flying at an altitude above the range of anti-aircraft guns; and the United States Army Air Force (USAAF) placed great emphasis on defensive armament, both machine guns and armour plating, thus increasing the weight of the aircraft while reducing its load-carrying capacity. Although the altitude, added armament and protection on American bombers allowed them to concentrate on daylight precision bombing, compared to the RAF's area night raids, the USAAF, too, suffered heavy casualties and needed up to twice the number of aircraft to deliver the same load.

Navigation, that constant problem faced by bomber crews trying to find their targets, was greatly improved by the introduction of the Gee, a system that broadcast pulses from three different locations in the UK that when picked up by a receiver in the aircraft allowed a positional fix. This was superseded in early 1943 by OBOE, a radar directional system that guided the aircraft to the vicinity of the target. The disadvantages of both these systems were that, because they were line of sight, at a range of more than about 450 miles, or an altitude lower than 20,000 feet, the curvature of the earth blocked reception, and they could, of course, be jammed once the Germans worked out what they were.

The new Commander-in-Chief Bomber Command, Harris, was a single-minded professional, and he introduced major changes in operational procedures determined to make the new policy, or rather the up-gunned old policy, work. Instead of raids scattered all over Germany with relatively few bombers going to each, and each flight or squadron of aircraft making their own way from UK airfield to the target, which meant that any particular raid could last for hours, Harris generally attacked only one major target per night. Aircraft were assembled over England, and then crossed the Channel as one huge formation, thus often overwhelming the Kammhuber Line, and reducing the time spent over the target. Harris's tactic was to mark the target by flares, using skilled navigators and the best pilots, often in Mosquitoes, and then opening the attack with high-explosive bombs to crater roads and make it difficult for rescue and fire-fighting services to approach the target area. Realising that it was easier to burn a building down than to blow it up, phase two of a Harris raid involved dropping a mix of high-explosive (usually 4,000lb bombs) and huge numbers of 4lb incendiary bombs. The result was massive damage by both blast and fire. Despite new aircraft and improved navigation, Bomber Command in 1942 still could not deploy any more bombers than it had in 1941, nor, initially, did its casualty rate go down; but it could deliver twice the weight of bombs, and with far more accuracy.

There was another, if less visible, way that the British could hit back, and that was by sabotage, subversion and raids on occupied countries. The Special Operations Executive was established in July 1940 with the purpose of, as Churchill put it, 'setting Europe ablaze', while the Commandos, raised about the same time as a raiding force, were, in another Churchillian phrase, 'to leave a trail of German bodies behind them'. Both organisations started off in that very amateurish and rather eccentric fashion supposedly so beloved by the British. The problems faced by SOE when attempting to stir up resistance included the fact that most citizens of German-occupied Europe had no wish to have a trail of German bodies lying around, if only because of the inevitable reprisals. In France the vast majority of the population much preferred to keep their heads down and get on with their daily routine, even in the unoccupied Vichy zone, where the word of Marshal Pétain held good for most, and where in any case the British were seen to have left France in the lurch. There were the inevitable inter-departmental wrangles: MI6, the British overseas intelligence service, who wanted to promote tranquillity so that their agents could collect intelligence without attracting the attention of the security forces, clashed with SOE, who wanted to blow things up and thus invariably did attract attention.

Some of SOE's activities, although lauded as examples of great heroism, and the subject of films, plays and books, in hindsight seem of questionable value. In 1942 SOE found that the Germans had taken over a Norwegian hydroelectric plant that had been making heavy water for the pre-war Norwegian atomic research programme. Heavy water, or deuterium oxide, is used as a moderator, a substance to slow down, and thus control, a nuclear reaction. That the Germans had occupied the plant and increased its production indicated that they had an atomic programme. SOE decided that the plant must be destroyed, and in October 1942 an advance party of Norwegians trained by SOE in England was parachuted onto the Norwegian Hardanger plateau, to set up a base and wait for the main body who would carry out the attack on the plant. A month later two Halifax bombers, each towing a Horsa glider, took off from Wick in the north of Scotland. In each glider were fifteen soldiers of the Royal Engineers and two pilots. The weather on take-off was bad, and as the aircraft approached Norway it got worse. The radar on the leading Halifax went unserviceable on crossing the Norwegian coast. The aircraft flew into thick cloud, ice formed on the towrope, which froze and then snapped. The glider crashed, killing eight men outright, and injuring four. The Halifax got back to Wick, just. The second Halifax found the weather too bad to continue and tried to turn back, likewise snapping its towrope. Navigating by dead reckoning the Halifax crashed, killing all the crew, and shortly afterwards the glider crash-landed. The nineteen men who survived the crashes were captured and shot by German security police. The engineers were in uniform and should have been protected by the laws of war, but the German Commando Order of October 1942 did not recognise clandestine or raiding forces as legitimate combatants.

Had the operation succeeded, the men were supposed to escape to neutral Sweden, where they might, if very lucky, have been able to get back to England but would have been far more likely to have been interned, or even handed over to the Germans. Sweden is 130 miles from the hydroelectric plant, which was situated in a largely uninhabited area with few roads, deep snow, and a winter temperature of up to sixty degrees below freezing. The men did not speak Norwegian, did not know the area, and were not skiers. Even with the help of the Norwegian advance party, their chances of getting to neutral Sweden can only have been remote. The operation was eventually carried out successfully by Norwegians, but if the heavy water really had been as vital as the agents were told it was, the Germans could surely have set up a heavy-water plant in Germany or Poland. It is difficult to escape the conclusion that brave men's lives were thrown away by sloppy planning.

The Commandos did not get off to a good start. In June 1940 the Germans occupied the Channel Islands, the British having rightly decided that resistance was pointless and giving the population the option of being removed to England by the Royal Navy. After the occupation the Prime Minister ordered a commando raid: it would be a good test of the new organisation and would remind the Germans that they were not safe anywhere that could be reached by air or sea. On 14 July 1940 two destroyers took 140 Commandos to Guernsey. It was a complete and utter nonsense. Two of the three raiding parties landed on the wrong beaches, one even on the wrong island. When the Commandos did get ashore they could not find the German barracks, and when they did find them there were no Germans there – they had all gone to a film show. By then the tide had come in and the wind had got up, and the only way to get back to the boats was to swim. As many of the soldiers could not swim, they had to stay behind. Churchill, quite understandably, was not amused.

Things improved, however, as both SOE and the Commandos instituted proper selection methods and training and the success rate of both organisations improved. Special Forces sprang up wherever the British were. In the Western theatre alone, besides the Army Commandos, were the Special Air Service, the Special Boat Service, the Long Range Desert Group, the Small Scale Raiding Force, Popski's Private Army (officially No 1 Demolition Squadron), the Parachute Regiment and, from 1942,

Royal Marine Commandos, with both Special Forces and SOE supported by RAF special duty squadrons. As most of the raids mounted needed the assistance of either or both the RAF and the Royal Navy, a combined operations headquarters was set up under Lieutenant General Bourne of the Royal Marines. Almost immediately Bourne was replaced by an old friend of Churchill's who had last held an active appointment in 1931, had been a Conservative MP since 1934, and had been badgering Churchill for a job since the beginning of the war. Admiral of the Fleet Sir Roger Keyes was sixty-eight in 1940 and full of schemes that Churchill thought were bold and imaginative, and the Chiefs of Staff and theatre commanders thought were rash and impractical.[5]

Keyes' enthusiasm and drive were instrumental in gaining support for the Commandos, but he was senior in rank to all of the Chiefs of Staff, which made things difficult for them, nor had he been forgiven for making a speech in the House of Commons, dressed in his admiral's uniform, highly critical of the Admiralty's conduct of the Norwegian campaign. When he decamped from the Admiralty and tried to turn his headquarters into an operational directorate, rather an administrative and coordination centre, he really began to upset the system. His abrasive manner and complete lack of tact and diplomacy did nothing to assist the mounting of operations that needed the support of commanders in various theatres and from all three services. In October 1941 Keyes was replaced, and eventually given a peerage to prevent him criticising the government from the back benches. The new adviser, subsequently chief, of combined operations was Lord Louis Mountbatten,[*] until then a captain RN, promoted to commodore, and then in March 1942 to vice admiral (and the equivalent ranks of lieutenant general and air vice marshal in the other two services) with a seat on the Chiefs of Staff Committee. Mountbatten's royal connections at this stage were fairly tenuous – his mother was a granddaughter of Queen Victoria – but he milked them for all they were worth, and although some in the Royal

---

[*] The 'lord' was a courtesy title. His father was a minor German princeling – a grandson of the Grand Duke of Hesse – who had joined the Royal Navy, been quite unfairly forced to resign as First Sea Lord in October 1914, changed his name to Mountbatten and had been raised to the English peerage as the First Marquess of Milford Haven, hence his son was entitled to the 'lord'.

Navy considered him a rash and flamboyant mountebank, he appealed to Churchill, and there is no doubt that his gift for public relations and his personal charm did a great deal to advance the cause of combined operations, even if his inflated staff, peopled by personal friends, irritated more conventional officers.

Joining the Commandos, or any of the Special Forces, was attractive to many young men when the army was otherwise doing very little. Raids on the Norwegian coast made for good newspaper headlines and reminded the world that Britain was still doing something. Whether the blowing-up of fish oil factories and the sinking of a few German merchant ships on remote coastlines made any real difference to the prosecution of the war is doubtful, but the Germans did keep a quarter of a million men in Norway throughout the war – a far larger force than was necessary to keep order and which could have been used to far greater profit elsewhere – concerned lest the constant British raids were a harbinger of an invasion of Norway. More than a few officers thought that Special Forces, by taking some of the best men away from conventional units, reduced the effectiveness of the army as a whole, and the frequent setting-up and then cancelling or postponing of operations reinforced this view. While many of the operations actually carried out were either pointless or ill thought through, and many were allowed to go ahead when the planners must have realised that the chances of the raiders returning alive were minimal, on balance Commando-style operations allowed the services, and the public, to feel that they were doing something, and they had an influence over neutral opinion out of all proportion to their military value.

The most controversial raid organised by Combined Operations HQ was also the largest, on Dieppe on 19 August 1942. It happened at a time when the Russians were clamouring for action to take the pressure off them, when the Americans were pressing for a cross-Channel invasion that year, and when Churchill was, as usual, demanding aggressive action anywhere. The accepted reason for the one-day raid was that it was necessary to test German defences along the Channel coast, with subsidiary aims of destroying invasion barges kept in Dieppe harbour, examining German radar equipment, putting the nearest airfield out of action, and provoking a battle with the Luftwaffe which the RAF expected to win. Originally intended to be launched in July 1942 as Operation Rutter, the raid was jointly planned by Combined Operations HQ and Lieutenant General Montgomery's South Eastern Command. Bad weather caused it to be cancelled, only to be resurrected (after Montgomery had left for North Africa) as Operation Jubilee. As the troops for Rutter had been stood down and released from security quarantine, this decision must have raised grave security doubts, and there is no record of the revival ever having been approved by the Chiefs of Staff.

The raid involved landings on five beaches over a frontage of ten miles centred on Dieppe, and while British army Commandos would be used on the flanks and one of the floating reserves would be a Royal Marine Commando, the bulk of the troops to be used would be from 2 Canadian Division, commanded by Major General J. H. Roberts. This was not, as has been alleged, because the British were quite prepared to risk the lives of colonial troops but not their own, but because the Canadians had demanded it. Canadian troops had arrived in England very shortly after the outbreak of war, and had there been an invasion their presence would have been decisive. Once this threat had passed, Churchill wanted to send them to North Africa, but the Canadian government demurred, insisting that the primary purpose of Canadian troops was the defence of the mother country. By the time the Canadian government had relented, Churchill was embarrassed by the preponderance of Empire over British troops in North Africa and did not send the Canadians. In the Canadian parliament, by 1942, questions were being asked as to why this huge (by Canadian standards) army was doing nothing, and in England the CIGS was being badgered by Canadian generals pleading for a task for their troops. The result was Dieppe.

To carry out the raid the Royal Navy deployed eight destroyers and 229 ships and boats of various types, including landing craft. Air cover was provided by around 1,200 RAF aircraft, from sixty-seven squadrons, fifty-four of them fighter squadrons, and 100 USAAF planes from seven squadrons. Land forces included elements of 2 Canadian Division, 4,963 men in total, Numbers 3 and 4 Army Commando, twenty-nine tanks and fifty members of the United States Rangers, a body only just formed along the lines of the Royal Marines and on the raid to gain experience.

The operation was a disastrous failure. The navy considered the restricted waters of the Channel to be too dangerous to risk a battleship, so shore bombardment was limited to the guns of destroyers, and the RAF were not prepared to divert heavy bombers away from Bomber Command's main task of obliterating German cities. Had the raid been put to the Chiefs of Staff these issues would surely have been resolved. Surprise was lost when one of the convoys ran into patrolling German E-boats; intelligence had not revealed the presence of guns dug into the sides of the cliffs that enfiladed the main beach at Dieppe itself; most of the tanks, landed directly on to the beach, could not get over the sea wall, and those that could were unable to penetrate the town because the sappers could not demolish the roadblocks; and there were communication difficulties between Roberts, afloat, and his subordinate commanders on land.

By the time the troops were withdrawn on 19 August and the remnants were on their way home, the navy had lost one destroyer and thirty-three landing craft, and 106 RAF planes had been shot down or crashed. Fifty-four Canadian officers and 828 other ranks had been killed, and 119 and 1,754 taken prisoner.[6] About 200 British soldiers and marines were killed. All the tanks were lost, including one of the first Shermans to see action, along with thirteen other vehicles. Of the 305 Canadian officers and 4,658 ORs that had set out, 132 and 2,078 returned. Total German casualties were about 600, and they lost forty-eight aircraft. Many a commander had been sacked for less, but Mountbatten always maintained that Dieppe was an essential rehearsal for Overlord, the D-Day landings in Normandy in June 1944. It is difficult to give credence to that assertion. The tactical lessons of Dieppe – that very heavy fire support was essential prior to and after landing, that contemporary tanks could not cross sea walls, that sappers with demolition kit needed to be well forward, and that reliable communications were vital – could surely have been learned without the deaths and imprisonment of so many men.

There is another possible answer, which would account for the somewhat implausible aim of the raid and its revival against all the normal principles of security, and that is that the British knew the operation would fail. Only recently in the war, the Americans took a very straight-forward view of how it should be won, which was by invading German-occupied Europe as soon as possible, and defeating the German army. The British knew better. They had been involved in failed amphibious operations, they knew that the Allies had neither the manpower nor the landing craft for an invasion yet, and they feared that if they were forced into attempting one that failed the Americans might abandon the Germany First policy and concentrate their efforts on the war in the east. The Dieppe raid would show the Russians that the Allies were doing something and if (when?) it failed would prove to the Americans that a cross-Channel invasion in 1942 or 1943 was not an option. It has to be admitted that this author has been unable to unearth any evidence what-soever to support this supposition.

By this time there had been more changes in the high command in London, and Churchill had got rid of yet another general who would not tell him what he wanted to hear. General Sir John Dill as CIGS had done his best to restrain the Prime Minister's more madcap schemes, and had earned dislike and the nickname of 'Dilly Dally' because of it. Churchill sought a way to get rid of him, and invented a new rule obliging the CIGS to retire at the age of sixty, which Dill would be on Christmas Day 1941. Dill's successor was General Sir Alan Brooke, with a promotion to general backdated to May 1941, who once again profited from Churchill's propensity to sack commanders who were unable to conceal what they thought of the Prime Minister's qualities as a strategist.[*] Brooke had no doubts about the reasons for the antipathy between Churchill and Dill. In his diary entry of 20 October 1941 Brooke wrote:

> Winston had never been fond of Dill. They were entirely different types of character, and types that could never have worked harmoniously together. Dill was the essence of straightforwardness, blessed with the highest principles and an unassailable integrity of character. I do not believe that any of these characteristics appealed to Winston, on the contrary, I think he disliked them as they accentuated his own shortcomings in this respect.[7]

---

[*] He had been appointed Commander-in-Chief Home Forces when Churchill got rid of Ironside from that post in July 1940.

In fairness to Brooke, who was Churchill's creature and who managed to retain his position for the whole of the war, he liked and admired Dill and did his best to persuade Churchill to recommend a peerage for the ex-CIGS. Churchill, who could be remarkably mean spirited, refused to do so, but fortunately he did agree to the appointment of Dill, with a promotion to field marshal, as head of the British military mission in the United States, where he established an excellent and most useful relationship with American politicians, industrialists and service chiefs. When Dill died of aplastic anaemia in Washington in November 1944 he was given a state funeral and buried in Arlington Cemetery, the only foreigner ever to have been so honoured. In Brooke's first two weeks in the job he had to persuade Churchill not to order an assault on Trondheim in Norway, not to invade Sicily, and not to give two British divisions to the Russians.

In North Africa the Royal Navy's misfortunes in the Mediterranean in late 1941, combined with the Russian winter causing reduced activity on the Eastern Front, released Luftwaffe aircraft for use in Libya and allowed Rommel to receive some substantial reinforcement for the first time for many months. One convoy that arrived in Tripoli on 5 January 1942 brought him fifty-five tanks, twenty armoured cars and large quantities of fuel. With increased air cover from Italy, and without telling either Berlin or the Italian high command, he decided to go on to the offensive once again. It was unfortunate that just about then Auchinleck was writing to Churchill painting an optimistic picture of the situation of the Eighth Army, accepting that reinforcements on their way to him would now have to be diverted to the Far East, and agreeing to send an armoured brigade, a field battery, an anti-tank battery and four fighter squadrons to India.

On 21 January 1942 the newly named Panzer Army Africa attacked, and by the end of the day had advanced thirty miles. It would have been more had the tanks not run into bad going, but they captured sixteen British 25-pounder field guns, a number of soft-skinned vehicles and took around one hundred prisoners. As the RAF were too busy evacuating forward airstrips and were, unusually, short of fuel, the Luftwaffe had air superiority. Next day Rommel pushed forward another forty miles, and

Panzer Army Africa was in control of the road running from Agadabia north-east to Antelat. On 25 January the two German panzer divisions caught 1 Armoured Division, now with its second brigade and commanded by Major General Frank Messervy, and routed it. By the end of the day the British had lost thirty-eight guns, ninety-six tanks and 190 soft-skinned vehicles. There followed two days of order, counter-order, disorder and confusion. Godwin-Austin, commanding in Cyrenaica, was of the view that Benghazi could not be defended and recommended withdrawal to Mechili and Gazala. Ritchie, the army commander, supported by Auchinleck and Tedder, disagreed, and took Godwin-Austin's 4 Indian Division under his own command. Unseemly verbal brawling among the British generals over the radio was listened to with glee by the German intercept service.

Benghazi could not be defended, and by 4 February the British were all back in the Gazala area while Panzer Army Africa scoured the battlefield for anything left behind that they could usefully divert to their own purposes. This included seven million cigarettes and twelve lorry-loads of rum found in Benghazi. On 2 February Godwin-Austin asked to be relieved of his command on the grounds that he had forfeited the confidence of the army commander, Ritchie. In a decision that is difficult to understand, Auchinleck accepted the request. Ritchie had been put in as a stopgap army commander when Crusader was at its height, despite being junior to both corps commanders. As the battle was being fought by the two latter, Auchinleck no doubt thought that less disruption would be caused by putting in an army commander, than by pulling out a corps commander, but once Crusader was over it is difficult to see why one of the corps commanders could not now become the army commander, with Ritchie either taking over the resultant vacancy or reverting to deputy chief of staff. This would have entailed no loss of face to anyone. Having left Ritchie in post, however, he now had to choose between him and Godwin-Austin, and as Godwin-Austin's assessments in the retreat to Gazala had been the more realistic, Auchinleck would appear to have made the wrong choice.

In Berlin, despite the concentration on the Eastern Front, Rommel and his activities were being looked on with rather more favour than hitherto, partly because of a suggestion by the German navy that the British might be deprived of their major sources of oil in Persia and the Gulf by a two-pronged attack south from the Caucasus and east from Libya. To this end Malta was subjected to yet another series of intensive raids by the Luftwaffe throughout March and April 1942. Consequently Rommel was able to receive a major part of the supplies sent to him, and Churchill renewed his demands on Auchinleck for an offensive.

The Gazala Line was intended to be a holding position from which the next British offensive could be launched, and there was not as much attention paid to defence as there should have been. Eighth Army still consisted of XIII and XXX Corps, XIII commanded by 'Strafer' Gott and XXX by Norrie. In XIII Corps were 1 South African and 50 (Tyne Tees) Divisions, the latter a British Territorial Army formation brought over from Cyprus, while in Tobruk, thirty miles to the east of Gazala, was 2 South African Division. The corps' armoured support was provided by 1 and 32 Army Tank Brigades. XXX Corps contained 1 Armoured Division commanded by Major General Herbert Lumsden, with 2 and 22 Armoured Brigades and a lorried infantry brigade (210 Guards), and 7 Armoured Division commanded by Major General Messervy, with 4 Armoured Brigade, two lorried infantry brigades (7 and 3 Indian) and two marching infantry brigades, 29 Indian and 1 Free French. Ritchie's deployment had 1 South African Division and 50 Division holding a front of about forty miles running south from Gazala to Bir Hacheim, with the French anchoring the south in Bir Hacheim itself. Each division had its army tank brigade about ten miles back, and there was extensive mine-laying in front. From Bir Hacheim roughly east for forty miles to Bir el Gubi the line was held by 3 Indian Motorised Brigade, a battalion of 7 Motorised Brigade and 29 Indian Brigade. The two armoured divisions (totalling three armoured brigades) were held back, each brigade being in what was considered to be a defensive box; one (2 Armoured) at Knightsbridge, roughly in the centre of the position where also was 201 Guards Brigade (motorised), and the other two (22 and 4 Armoured) either side of Point 175, twelve miles south-east of Knightsbridge. XXX Corps HQ was ten miles north of Bir el Gubi, and XIII Corps HQ south of El Adem where also was the corps reserve, a battalion of 9 Indian Brigade from 2 South African Division.

In Panzer Army Africa the yet again promoted Colonel General Rommel now had the DAK commanded by Lieutenant General Walter Nehring, still with its 15 and 21 Panzer and 90 Light Divisions, the Italian XX Corps with the Ariete Armoured and Trieste Motorised Divisions, and the Gruppe Crüwell of the Italian X and XXI Corps with four infantry divisions between them under the command of the German Lieutenant General Crüwell. The Luftwaffe could field 542 aircraft to the RAF's 604, but the German total included 120 Me 109s which in the desert were at least a match for the RAF's Hurricanes.

Both sides had been improving the quality of their tanks; the Germans had been putting extra armour on theirs, and the first batch of Mk IVs with a long-barrelled 75mm gun had arrived. Fortunately for the British there were only four of these and there was as yet no ammunition for them. More serious was the arrival of the Mk III (J) Special, with two inches of frontal armour and a 50mm gun. For their part the British had now received the American-made Grant[*] medium tank in large numbers. This twenty-seven-ton tank had 2.25-inches of frontal armour, a top speed of 26 mph and a range of 120 miles, with a 75mm gun as the main armament and a subsidiary 37mm canon. A disadvantage was that the main armament was mounted in a sponson on the right-hand side of the hull, giving limited traverse and making concealment difficult. By late May the British had 850 gun-armed tanks, including 160 Grants, with an immediate reserve of 120, and another 300 in Egypt, of which 250 were Grants. The Axis had 560 tanks, including 242 Mk III, thirty-eight Mk IV and 19 Mk III (J) Specials.

At first glance the British tanks were not only numerically superior to those of the Axis, they were marginally better in quality, too. At the usual range of engagement of 1,000 yards, British tanks could pierce the frontal hull armour of German tanks as follows:

* The American designation was M3 (Lee Mk I). Robert E. Lee was a Confederate general; Ulysses S. Grant was a Union general, and later President of the USA.

TARGET TANK

FIRING TANK	MK III	MK IV	MK III (J)
Matilda	No	No	No
Crusader	No	No	No
Stuart	No	No	No
Valentine	No	No	No
Grant	Yes	Yes	Yes

The Matildas, Crusaders, Stuarts and Valentines could pierce the turret armour of all the German tanks, but this was such a small target at 1,000 yards that only a lucky shot could do it. If the above table makes British performance against German tanks look unimpressive, a look at the same capability in reverse shows:

TARGET TANK

FIRING TANK	MATILDA	CRUSADER	STUART	VALENTINE	GRANT
Mk III	No	No	No	No	No
Mk IV	No	No	No	No	No
Mk III (J)	No	Yes	Yes	No	Yes

The Grant, of which the Eighth Army had 160, could get through the frontal armour on all German tanks (and, of course, the more lightly armoured Italian ones), whereas only the Mk III (J) could do the same to three of the five types of British tank, and Rommel had only nineteen of those. It was not, however, solely a matter of the penetration of armour. British sights were not generally as good as those of the Germans, those masters of optical instruments; British ammunition was not as effective; and British tanks were more likely to burst into flames when hit. Contrary to received wisdom this was not due to their being fuelled by petrol (German tanks ran on petrol too) but because of the way their ammunition was stowed, with less protection than that of the Germans, and hence a greater likelihood of exploding if the tank took a hit. The Germans had the 88mm anti-tank gun, and Rommel now had forty-eight of them to back up his 50mm standard issue. The British 2-pounder anti-tank gun could only take on most Axis tanks from the side, and while the 6-pounder was now coming into service with the Eighth Army there had been no time to train with it. It remains a mystery to this author (admittedly but a simple infantryman) why the British did not use their excellent 3.7-inch anti-aircraft gun in the same way as the Germans used the 88mm. An anti-tank round could surely have been produced, and rare examples of gun crews in North Africa using the 3.7-inch as an anti-tank weapon *in extremis* show that it could be effective even with a high-explosive projectile.* German tanks appeared to have been more reliable and less prone to breakdown than British ones, but this may have more to do with the German ability to recover and repair their tanks more quickly than the British could, rather than with any inherent mechanical superiority.

Ever since the British withdrawal to the Gazala Line Churchill had been pressing Auchinleck to attack, and Auchinleck had protested that he needed more time to build up the Eighth Army and to train, suggesting that November would be the right time for a British offensive to drive the Axis out of North Africa for good. As far as Churchill was concerned this was quite unacceptable, and Auchinleck was told to attack in June, or face dismissal. As it was, Rommel got his blow in first, and while Ultra told the British when it was coming, it did not tell them how.

The main weakness in the British defensive layout was that it could be outflanked, always a possibility in desert terrain. Rommel's plan was to attack the infantry with Crüwell's Italian infantry divisions plus the Trieste Motorised division, and then to take the DAK plus the Ariete (armoured) round to the south of Bir Hacheim to strike north at the rear of the British, cut them off from their supplies, destroy their armour and capture Tobruk. At around 1400 hrs on 26 May 1942 the attack on XIII Corps began. It did not get very far, and Rommel's armour moving off to the south was seen and reported. Auchinleck had calculated that Rommel's options were a thrust along the coast road, a southern outflanking move with the armour (the one he actually took) or, much more likely, the use of the armour to split the Eighth Army in two by attacking the centre, north of Bir Hacheim. For that reason he advised Ritchie to have both his armoured divisions on the Trig Capuzzo, ready to deal with an armoured thrust from either the south or the west. Ritchie had come to

* I have asked numerous officers of the Royal Regiment (who despite being clever at sums are quite approachable) why the 3.7 was not used in this way, and am bombarded with technical details, including problems with the sight mechanism. And still I wonder...

the same conclusions as to Rommel's options, but thought that the southern flanking move was the more likely. Although Ritchie was right as to Rommel's intentions, he did not take Auchinleck's advice to concentrate his armour, which would prove to be an error.

By the early morning of 27 May Rommel's armour had swept round Bir Hacheim, scattered 3 Indian and 7 Motor Brigades and had overrun HQ 7 Armoured Division, capturing General Messervy and his senior staff officer.[*] Tanks from 4 Armoured Brigade then appeared, and to the consternation of the Germans the Grants began to hand out a pasting to both 15 and 21 Panzer, before being driven off. The DAK's drive to the coast had been halted, but Rommel was not despondent:

> Ritchie had thrown his armour into the battle piecemeal and had thus given us the chance of engaging them on each separate occasion with just about enough of our own tanks. This dispersal of the British armoured brigades was incomprehensible. In my view the sacrifice of the 7th armoured division south of Bir el Harmat served no purpose whatsoever... the principal aim of the British should have been to have brought all the armour they had into action at one and the same time... Mobile warfare in the desert has often been compared with a battle at sea – where it is equally wrong to attack piecemeal and leave half the fleet in port.[8]

On 28 May more tank-versus-tank duels took place, but the German panzers could not achieve their objectives; 21 Panzer was stopped at Point 209, while 15 Panzer ran out of ammunition near Knightsbridge, the Ariete was brought to a halt before Bir Hacheim and 90th Light was prevented from moving east by air and ground attacks. The lightning thrust had failed, the coast road had not been reached, the British armour had not been destroyed. On 29 May Rommel went on to the defensive, but he did it inside the British position, east of the Gazala minefields and west and south-west of Knightsbridge, supplied by a tenuous route south of Bir Hacheim, and then through a narrow corridor that the Trieste Division had managed to clear through the minefield just south of 50 Division's left flank. Now was the time for the British to concentrate all

---

[*] Messervy put on a private soldier's tunic before he was captured, and the Germans failed to realise who he was. He escaped twelve hours later and rejoined Eighth Army.

their armour and counter-attack, but they were far too slow and by the time they did react, late in the afternoon, the attacks were uncoordinated and made more difficult by a sandstorm. Nothing happened on 30 May, or on 31 May, which gave Rommel time to establish his own defences in an area known as the Cauldron, and to begin an attack himself, on one of the defensive boxes held by 150 Brigade of 50 Division, supported by a regiment from 1 Army Tank Brigade.

On 1, 2 and 3 June the British held numerous conferences, but did very little, allowing Rommel to eliminate the 150 Brigade box. At last, on 5 June, the British attacked. The command arrangements were shambolic – a sort of joint command with Major General Briggs, commanding 5 Indian Division, the Eighth Army reserve, and Major General Messervy, commanding 7 Armoured Division, sharing responsibility. Both were competent generals but command should have been entrusted to one or the other – probably to Briggs, as the majority of troops involved were his. The attack was an utter failure – and would have been anyway, regardless of the command arrangements – and the British were driven off, with the loss of 200 tanks and a large number of guns, and with Messervy and his headquarters being captured yet again.[*]

Ritchie, and most of his subordinate commanders, were still amazingly optimistic, when all the evidence contradicted them. The French made a very gallant stand at Bir Hacheim. The French general in command, Koenig, thought the fortress should be evacuated, but Ritchie could not make up his mind and the French fought on, which gave Ritchie time to swing his left flank back through ninety degrees so that it now ran through Knightsbridge and along the Trig Capuzzo, before Bir Hacheim fell on 10 June. On 11 June Rommel resumed the offensive, and on 12 June, largely due to contradictory orders by British generals trying to command the same troops, the British armour lost 260 tanks and had suffered such a hammering it was clear that the Gazala battle was lost. Panzer Army Africa was now between Knightsbridge and El Adem, and the only way east for the beleaguered British on the Gazala Line was the coast road that led back to Tobruk, and that was in danger of being cut by Rommel's armour at any time. On 13 June Knightsbridge was isolated, and that

* He escaped again.

night the garrison withdrew. Now began an acrimonious and confusing exchange of signals between Ritchie, Auchinleck and, from London, Churchill. Ritchie wanted to withdraw the Eighth Army to the Egyptian frontier; Auchinleck wanted to hold the Axis west of Tobruk, and Churchill wanted to make sure that Tobruk would not be abandoned. As the three Commanders-in-Chief Middle East had agreed in January that they could not again support a besieged Tobruk, and London had been told of this and had not protested, this put a further wild card into the pack.

Despite Auchinleck's instructions to Ritchie that the Eighth Army must hold west of Tobruk, Ritchie was already extracting his troops, in what became known as the 'Gazala Gallop'. There was in fact no chance whatsoever of holding at Gazala, or of holding anywhere west of the Egyptian frontier, and the British were lucky to extract anybody at all. As it was, had it not been for the order to hold Tobruk, most of the Eighth Army could have been extracted to Egypt. Churchill's increasingly emphatic signals and orders that Tobruk must be held led to Auchinleck obeying orders and ordering 2 South African Division with 11 Indian Infantry Brigade, the Guards Brigade, 4 RTR, and a number of British units that had found their way into Tobruk and were unable to get out, to hold the town, while the rest of the British forces retreated to Egypt. By 18 June Tobruk was surrounded, and on 20 June the attack began with the main thrust going in from the south-east against the 2nd Battalion Cameron Highlanders and 2/5th Mahratta Light Infantry. As it had not been intended to hold Tobruk again, most of the mines had been lifted and the defences had been allowed to fall into disrepair. It has to be said that Major General Klopper, commanding the garrison, was not an inspiring leader, but problems with communications, arguments with subordinates and contradictory instructions from Ritchie did not help. On 21 June Klopper surrendered. The Camerons held out for another twenty-four hours, before being granted the honours of war, and the 2/7th Gurkha Rifles saw no need to surrender at all and tried to make their way back to Egypt on foot along the coast. Almost the whole of the Italian XX Corps had to be employed in rounding them up, and the last were not caught until four days later, a hundred miles away in the Sollum area.

It was now obvious to Ritchie and to Auchinleck that the frontier defences could not be held without armour – and the British had lost a great deal of theirs. To try to hold with infantry alone would mean that, as at Gazala, the position would be outflanked. Ritchie therefore decided, and Auchinleck agreed, that the next battle would be fought at Mersah Matruh, 170 miles east of the frontier and about halfway to Alexandria and the Nile Delta. Auchinleck instructed that Mersah Matruh was to be defended by troops of X Corps, arriving from Syria, XIII Corps and the remnants of 1 Armoured Division, while XXX Corps was to go back for another 150 miles to El Alamein, and there to reorganise and re-equip its shattered armoured regiments.

The breathing space that Ritchie had hoped for was not to be. Rommel pushed Panzer Army Africa on, and by 25 June Rommel's reconnaissance elements were probing the perimeter of Mersah Matruh. The defences of this small port had, like those of Tobruk, been long neglected. Wire had been stolen by local farmers, trenches had silted up, mines had been cleared or shifted in the sand. Even so, Ritchie's dispositions were unsound. Units were spread out with wide gaps uncovered by fire in between, which might not have mattered had he sufficient armour, or even motorised infantry with anti-tank guns to cover those gaps, but he had not. That same day Auchinleck flew up from Cairo, looked at the defensive layout, heard Ritchie's plan for the battle, sacked him, and took over command of Eighth Army himself.[*] Ritchie was no coward, physically or morally, and he was ready to fight to the last man and the last round at Mersah Matruh, but Auchinleck did not want a last stand; he knew that what really mattered was Persia and its oil wells, and that if the Eighth Army was destroyed there was no other army to put in its place. The real threat was not just to Egypt, but to the link with India, the Russian left flank and the Persian oil fields. If Panzer Army Africa could roam unchecked through the Middle East, then Britain could even lose the war, or at best find herself isolated from her empire, without a land theatre where she could oppose the Axis, and at the mercy of the Americans who might or might not be able to come to her rescue. As far as Auchinleck was concerned, if the battle of Mersah Matruh could not be a victory, then the army must be

* It was not the end for Ritchie, who re-emerged as a corps commander in Normandy.

withdrawn from it to fight again, and not be bottled up against the coast where it could be surrounded and destroyed in detail.

On the night of 25 June Auchinleck issued a series of instructions indicating how he wanted the coming battle to be fought. He emphasised the need for flexibility, for all-arms co-operation, for formations to come to the help of their neighbours without waiting to be told. Auchinleck was absolutely right, and it had been the absence of this doctrine that had been very largely responsible for the mediocre performance of the British army so far in the war, but altering the mindset instilled by years of caution could not be done overnight. On 26 June Rommel attacked two British corps and the 150 tanks of 1 Armoured Division with 100 tanks and around 3,000 German infantry. By a combination of bluff, astute manoeuvring and British subordinate commanders who were beaten before they started because they expected to be, Rommel got in between X and XIII Corps and forced the withdrawal first of XIII and then, because there was no option, of General Holmes' X Corps. By 28 June the Eighth Army was in full retreat back to El Alamein, with only the RAF preventing Rommel's armour from doing more than snapping at their heels.

Although few at the time realised it, the next clash between Rommel and the Eighth Army was to be the turning point of the war in North Africa. Auchinleck had little time to prepare the Alamein position for defence; in Cairo there was panic and the burning of records; the Mediterranean Fleet sailed from Alexandria, and most of Auchinleck's corps and divisional commanders assumed that they would be continuing the eastward movement fairly shortly. The layout of the Alamein defensive position, devised by Auchinleck and his able, if psychologically flawed, chief of staff, Major General Dorman-Smith, held, and when Rommel, at the end of a very long supply line and short of fuel and of infantry, attacked on 1 July the line held. It was the closest to Cairo that the Axis would get, and while it would be sometime before anybody realised it, it was the end of a long series of defeats and retreats for the British. The year 1942 brought Rommel promotion to field marshal, and the sack for Auchinleck.

NOTES

1. Winston S. Churchill, *Their Finest Hour*, Cassell, London, 1949.

2. Portal to Beaverbrook, quoted in John Terraine, *The Right of the Line: The Royal Air Force in the European War 1939–1945*, Hodder & Stoughton, London, 1985.

3. Martin Middlebrook and Chris Everitt, *The Bomber Command War Diaries*, Ian Allen, Leicester, 2000.

4. Sir Charles Webster and Noble Frankland, *The Strategic Air Offensive Against Germany 1939–1945*, HMSO, London, 1961.

5. T. A. Heathcote, *The British Admirals of the Fleet*, Leo Cooper, Barnsley, 2002.

6. Eric Maguire, *Dieppe: August 19*, Jonathan Cape, London, 1963.

7. Alex Danchev and Daniel Todman, *War Diaries 1939–1945: Field Marshal Lord Alanbrooke*, Weidenfeld & Nicolson, London, 2001.

8. B. H. Liddell Hart (ed) and Paul Findlay (tr), *The Rommel Papers*, Collins, London, 1953.

14

Enter the Messiah

THE EL ALAMEIN POSITION stretches from the coast forty miles south-west to the Qattara Depression. In the north the ground is open and the only features are two barely discernible ridges: Miteirya, five or so miles west of Alamein, and Ruweisat, fifteen miles south of it. Beyond that, movement gets more and more difficult until reaching the depression, an area of salt marshes, wadis, cliffs and steep escarpments that is not impassable for individual vehicles, but effectively so for large numbers, particularly if the exits are covered. The great strength of the position was that provided there were enough troops to cover the forty miles – which Auchinleck calculated as two divisions and plenty of armour – it was almost impossible to turn, which is why Auchinleck had long ago selected it as the position from which to fight the battle for Egypt.

The troops that would defend Alamein were a disparate lot: men rushed up from Iraq and from Egypt along with the survivors of Gazala and Mersah Matruh. Auchinleck believed that infantry unsupported by armour and without its own transport was useless in the desert for anything other than static defence, and even then it needed plentiful field and anti-tank artillery. He thought the divisional organisation too clumsy for desert warfare, and preferred to create brigade groups, whereby a brigade had not only its three infantry battalions but its own artillery as

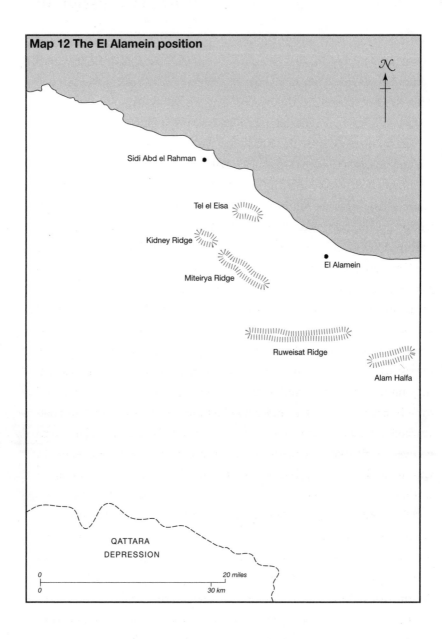

Map 12 The El Alamein position

Sidi Abd el Rahman

Tel el Eisa

Kidney Ridge

Miteirya Ridge

El Alamein

Ruweisat Ridge

Alam Halfa

QATTARA
DEPRESSION

0   20 miles
0   30 km

well. His ideas attracted opposition, most of it, sadly, based not on functional or tactical grounds, but on inter-arm jealousy and a reluctance to relinquish power to a commander not of one's own arm of the service. This was not a problem the Germans faced, where there was a higher loyalty to the army rather than to a specific regiment.

Auchinleck put only the minimum of troops necessary to hold the line in the forward edge of the position, and then only as many as could be moved by the available transport. One of the great irritants of this phase of the fighting in North Africa was that there were not enough troop-carrying lorries to lift all the British infantry, whereas Rommel's captured British vehicles (of which he had 1,135) had moved the bulk of the German and Italian infantry to Alamein. Apart from that allocated to the new brigade groups, Auchinleck took all artillery under army command, to use in both defence and attack, giving the British a powerful weapon of mass bombardment, a forgotten lesson from the Great War that they had not yet used in this; and he formed a light armoured brigade consisting entirely of units in armoured cars, intending to use it as a fast-moving reconnaissance and harrying force. Auchinleck was determined to fight a mobile defence, and while he prepared for the worst and had worked out a withdrawal to the Delta if need be, he had also planned to go over to the offensive, once the army was ready for it. First Alamein was Auchinleck's battle, but so was Second Alamein, even if Auchinleck was not there to see it.

Ultra and other signals intelligence told Auchinleck that Rommel would attack the north of the Alamein position on 1 July and when he did so, with 90 Light Division north of Miteirya Ridge and 21 and 15 Panzer south of it at 0300 hours, he was stopped by massed artillery, 1 South African Division, 18 Indian Brigade and the RAF. An attempt to cut the coast road to the east of Alamein on 3 July also failed, and meanwhile Auchinleck, guided by Ultra, began launching attacks of his own: short, controlled forays with easily identifiable objectives and aimed against the Italians in order to force the Germans to come and stiffen them, and therefore to go on to the defensive. On 10 July an attack along the coast by Australian infantry supported by Valentine tanks captured the useful hill feature of Tel el Eisa, destroying two Italian divisions in the process, and a counter-attack by 21 Panzer next day was brought to a halt by the RAF and the British massed artillery. Rommel obtained some respite when another British attack on 14 and 15 July by the New Zealand and 5 Indian Divisions, intended to recapture Ruweisat Ridge, went wrong when, due to a lack of coordination, 22 Armoured Brigade failed to support them. The infantry took and held the ridge but sustained heavy and unnecessary casualties in the process. By 17 July it was obvious to Rommel and to his superior in Italy, Kesselring, that the Axis advance into Egypt had come to a halt. Panzer Army Africa had performed near-incredible feats; they had chased the British over a thousand miles, from Gazala to within two days' march of the Nile, and they had kept pressing forward and attacking, often outnumbered and usually with the skies commanded by the RAF. But between 26 May and 20 July 1942 the DAK had lost 231 tanks, two of them Mk IVs with the 75mm gun, and fourteen the Mk III Specials. [1] The brief period of reinforcement from Italy, possible when the Royal Navy was temporarily on the back foot, was over, and resupply under the guns and bombs of the RAF was a Herculean task.

At long last some grip was being applied to the Eighth Army, but there was much still to do before it could undertake serious offensive operations. This was in part due to unnecessary feuds between individual commanders and between different arms of the service, allied to the British disposition to treat orders as a basis for discussion and a tendency to do nothing if communications broke down, rather than using initiative and seeking out something useful. Relations between the armour and the infantry were not good. The infantry resented the way the tanks shot off to the rear at night, while the armour thought the infantry were constantly panicking and screaming for help. The truth was that the armour had to replenish in a secure area by night, and that tanks were of little use in darkness anyway, and the infantry were terribly vulnerable to enemy armour in the desert in the absence of a good anti-tank gun and enough of them. It was unfortunate that the armour was all British, and most of the infantry were from the Empire, turning resentment of the armour into resentment of the British. Nor did it help that Dominion commanders had the right of appeal directly to their own governments if they disliked the orders they were given. Auchinleck's ideas about flexibility and mobility were, slowly, beginning to seep through, but discipline was not good and desertions, always a problem in an army that is constantly being beaten, were running at such a rate that Auchinleck unsuccessfully asked for the death penalty, removed by parliament in 1930 against military advice, to be reinstated.

A report by the DAK on British tactics and fighting methods for the period May to July 1942, and signed by the corps commander, General Nehring, said:

> The slowness, clumsiness and lack of initiative and tactical versatility observed up to date has not changed. There was no alteration in the planning if the battle developed in a way which had not been expected beforehand... [there was] no close cooperation between infantry and armoured formations. Tanks followed very slowly and were not really quick enough in exploiting the successes gained by the lorried infantry... the British have not yet mastered the art of handling larger formations with speed and manoeuvrability.[2]

On the other hand the Germans thought highly of the British in defence:

> There is all round defence in strongly constructed positions mined and wired in great depth... many alternative positions from which the enemy again and again offered stubborn resistance... Fighting [in enemy defensive positions] was tough and embittered and hardly ever was it possible to put the enemy to flight. Either he withdrew according to plan or defended himself until he was annihilated or captured.

and they admired the British artillery:

> ...great versatility, quick to open fire... with trained observers who fired quickly and with manoeuvrability.

Auchinleck was concerned about discipline in the Eighth Army, and the Germans had obviously noticed it too:

> ...It was found that some Australian and New Zealand troops had been drinking heavily before they attacked. Whether this was ordered as a stimulant or was due to a loosening of discipline is not known.

Auchinleck's next attempt to shift Rommel was on 21 July. The plan was sound: a left–right, starting with an attack in the south to draw in the German armour and reserves, then an attack and breakthrough in the north. It failed due to lack of urgency by commanders, units being too slow, poor navigation and the newly arrived 23 Armoured Brigade losing ninety-three of their 104 Valentine tanks when they lined up and attempted an armoured Charge of the Light Brigade and paid the penalty. As the brigade's radio net had ceased to work nobody could tell them not to do it. An attempt to renew the attack on 26–27 July failed because by then Panzer Army Africa, while realising that it could no longer advance, saw no reason why it should retreat, and had brought up such meagre reinforcements as it could and had thickened up the minefields in front of its defences. Auchinleck, too, realised that he had insufficient reserves – indeed he had none – with which to sustain continued attacks. He had stopped Rommel's advance on the Suez Canal but before he could expel Panzer Army Africa he needed time to reinforce, re-equip and, most of all, retrain Eighth Army. He and Dorman-Smith drew up plans for an eventual defeat of any further attack by Rommel, to be followed by a British offensive from the Alamein position. These proposals were sent off to London at the end of July with Auchinleck's recommendation that Eighth Army remain on the defensive until mid September. The Dorman-Smith–Auchinleck plan would be followed almost exactly in the battles of Alam Halfa and Second Alamein, but neither Auchinleck nor most of his staff would be there to see it.

For Churchill in London the suggestion of inaction – as he saw it – until September was yet another red rag to a very grumpy bull. The Prime Minister had not had a good summer. He was in the USA when news of the fall of Tobruk had come through; the Battle of the Atlantic was not going well, with 128 merchant ships totalling 618,000 tons lost from enemy action in July alone;[3] Rostov was under heavy German pressure and if the Caucasus fell, the Germans would be on the borders of Persia; long and hard negotiation had only just managed to persuade the Americans that a cross-Channel invasion of Europe was not an option for 1942 or 1943 (shortly to be confirmed by the failure of the Dieppe raid); and he had just had to face (and defeat) a motion of no confidence in the higher direction of the war in the House of Commons. He was now determined to remove Auchinleck, to whom his telegrams had been increasingly offensive, and he and the CIGS arrived in Egypt by air on 3 August as a stopover on the way to talks with the Russians.

After discussing the command arrangements with Smuts (and it is difficult to see what possible experience he could bring to bear) and the Minister of State Casey (whose military knowledge was even less than that of Smuts) and allowing his staff to pick up gossip from junior commanders trying to cover their own backs, Churchill first tried to persuade Brooke to take over from Auchinleck, then presented the CIGS with his own plan. A new command would be created by hiving off Iraq and Persia from Middle East Command, and this would be given to Auchinleck, with General Sir Harold Alexander as the new Commander-in-Chief Middle East. Alexander had been brought back from the Far East as commander designate of the British contribution to an Anglo-American landing in French North Africa, which the Americans had only just agreed to. 'Strafer' Gott would take over command of the Eighth Army, and Auchinleck's chief of general staff, Lieutenant General Corbett, his adviser and deputy chief of general staff, Dorman-Smith, and Ramsden, who had taken over XXX Corps from Norrie, were to be sacked.

Here was a most extraordinary situation. It could be argued that the appointment and removal of a commander-in-chief has a political dimension, and that the government is therefore entitled to have a say. To allow a politician, even if the head of government, to decide the fate of more junior officers, however, was setting a very undesirable precedent. It risked politicisation of the army and Brooke should never have agreed it. He did argue against the appointment of Gott, on the grounds that, fine general though he undoubtedly was, he had been in the Middle East since the beginning of the war and was tired out, but he seems to have made no attempt to prevent the utterly unfair treatment of Corbett or Dorman-Smith, although in the end Ramsden escaped, but only for the moment. Brooke's supine acceptance of the sackings that did happen presumably stemmed from his having formed a poor impression of both. Having met Corbett for the first time on 3 August, Brooke confided in his diary:

One interview with him was enough to size him up. He was a very very small man unfit for his job as CGS and totally unsuited for command of the 8th Army, an appointment which the Auk [Auchinleck] had suggested. Consequently Corbett's selection reflected very unfavourably on the Auk's ability to select men and confirmed my fears in that respect.[4]

As early as 29 January Brooke had been suspicious of Dorman-Smith's influence over Auchinleck, and in an after-note to his diary entry of that day he said of Dorman-Smith:

'...[Auchinleck] allowed himself to fall far too deeply under Chink's [Dorman-Smith's] influence. This became one, and possibly the major, cause of his downfall!

Brooke was entitled to his opinion, and it was shared by some,[*] but if junior officers had to be sacked then it should have been done by a senior officer, and Brooke should have taken a stand against interference by the Prime Minister, as he far too often failed to do.

Two things then happened that threw Churchill's plans into disarray. First, Auchinleck refused the offer of the new Persia Iraq command, on the dual grounds that it was all too obviously a sop to a beaten general, and that as an ex-Commander-in-Chief India it would be demeaning to that appointment were he to accept a command junior to it (it was given to Wilson). Instead, he would resign, which he did, returning to India. Fortunately for the course of the war in the Far East his resignation lasted only ten months until he was recalled to his old post of Commander-in-Chief India. The second spanner in the works was the death of Gott, shot down when flying back from the front. Brooke was now able to persuade Churchill that his choice for the Eighth Army, Montgomery, should be summoned from England.

Today Montgomery is the only British general of the Second World War whose name is recognised by more than a handful of the British public. National myth has it that Montgomery took over a defeated,

---

[*] Field Marshal Lord Carver in *Out of Step* (Hutchinson, London, 1989) quotes Strafer Gott as telling him that Corbett was 'well known as the stupidest officer in the Indian army – and that's saying some'; but even if a lieutenant general really would say this about another lieutenant general to a major, Gott was no great admirer of the Indians.

demoralised and badly led Eighth Army, and by his own abilities and powers of leadership won the great victory of Alamein and then went on to drive the Germans and the Italians out of North Africa in a whirlwind campaign that could not have been achieved by anyone else. We know that because Montgomery has told us so, not only by his masterly grasp of public relations at the time but in one of the most self-serving memoirs ever foisted on the reading public, and one that did immense harm to Anglo-American relations after the war.[5] Montgomery's admirers would not deny that he was cocky, self-assured, fiercely ambitious, domineering, often unsociable, desperate for success, frequently undiplomatic, jealous of the success of others, unable to admit that something had not gone exactly as he had intended, incapable of seeing how his behaviour could infuriate others, and not good at soothing the ruffled feathers of the Allies whom he offended. None of these blemishes necessarily make a general a bad commander. Montgomery's detractors would not deny that he had boundless energy, an eye for detail, complete dedication to his profession, a single-minded determination to win, the admiration – adulation almost – of junior officers and soldiers, and the willpower to resist all blandishments to attack until he was absolutely sure that all was ready. None of these qualities necessarily make a general a great commander.

Montgomery and Alamein are also remembered because Second Alamein was a victory, and the first British victory lauded to the British public and the world for a very long time. First Alamein was a victory, too, but it was not as dramatic and it was not spun, to use the currently fashionable term, by a Prime Minister who badly needed a victory, and a general who craved fame and recognition. More books have been written about Second Alamein than about any other British battle of the Second World War, with the possible exception of the Battle of Britain. It is not intended to repeat here a detailed account of what happened; the two best accounts are over forty years apart: *The Desert Generals* by Correlli Barnett, published in 1960, and *Pendulum of War: Three Battles at El Alamein* by Niall Barr, 2004. Suffice to say that Lieutenant General Montgomery had what no Eighth Army commander before him had: a Commander-in-Chief who was able to keep the Prime Minister off his back, time to prepare and train, massive reinforcement and a carefully worked-out plan put in place by Auchinleck and Dorman-Smith. There is nothing wrong with picking other men's flowers, but it is gracious to acknowledge the planters.

Churchill always had a soft spot for Harold Alexander – they were both old Harrovians, albeit not contemporaries – and as he had forced the removal of both of his predecessors, he may have felt that yet another sacking could have caused questions to be asked about his own judgement. Now that Brooke had got his nominee in post, Montgomery was going to make absolutely sure that he would be protected by the double layer of Brooke himself and then Alexander. Churchill had growled when Auchinleck said he could not go on the offensive until mid September, but Montgomery was allowed until the last week in October. On his first tour of his new command, he acquired an Australian slouch hat on which he attached numerous regimental badges, wearing it until even he realised how ridiculous it made him look, after which he took to wearing a Royal Tank Regiment black beret with an RTR badge in addition to his general staff badge.[*] By the time Montgomery had taken over and briefed Churchill and Brooke on 'his' plans (actually Auchinleck's) his boundless confidence so won over the Prime Minister that a delay that had brought Auchinleck the sack was accepted. In equipment and manpower the days of scrimping and saving and making do were over for the Eighth Army. From the end of July, before Alexander and Montgomery had arrived, men and tanks began flowing in, including the new Sherman tank from the USA, promised by President Roosevelt as a consolation to Churchill after the fall of Tobruk.

When, just after last light on 30 August, Rommel tried one final Napoleonic gamble and hooked round to the south of the British position to try to cut the coast road and then head for the Nile, just as Dorman-Smith had predicted, British armour and infantry dug in on the Alam Halfa Ridge stopped him, just as Dorman-Smith had planned; and the massive artillery that the British could now call upon, plus the greatly augmented Desert Air Force, wreaked unexpected havoc on the DAK

---

[*] I should be annoyed if I found someone wearing my cap badge when he was not entitled to it, and I should be even more annoyed if I found my general wearing someone else's cap badge to which he was not entitled.

and their Italian allies. Out of fuel, thanks to the Royal Navy and the RAF, and unable to get forward, on the night of 2–3 September Rommel had no option but to close the operation down. A British attempt to cut off Panzer Army Africa's withdrawal, Operation Beresford, failed with heavy losses. The British could fight well in defence but were still far too slow and too ill-coordinated for mobile operations. Rommel's men pulled back into their defence positions, and went on laying yet more mines, while Rommel argued with Italy and Berlin for more fuel.

On 12 October Montgomery wrote to one of his sycophants in the War Office (then a brigadier):

> My first encounter with Rommel was of great interest. Luckily I had had time to tidy up the mess (and it was 'some' mess, I can tell you) and to get my plans laid... the situation here when I arrived was really unbelievable; I would never have thought it could be so bad. Auchinleck should never be employed again in any capacity...[6]

Montgomery was beginning to lay the foundation of the myth of his own infallibility. Rightly, and supported by Alexander and Brooke, he would not launch his own offensive until he was quite sure that he had the men and equipment he needed and that the army was organised and trained as he wanted it. Although he made much of being a new broom that swept away all the old ideas, some of his changes to Auchinleck's organisational reforms were little more than cosmetic. He did abolish any idea of fighting as brigade groups, and insisted that divisions would fight as divisions, although he accepted in part Auchinleck's policy of giving infantry divisions their own integral armour. Even the dismissal of the brigade group concept was not quite the throwing out of the old that Montgomery tried to pretend: Auchinleck had only advocated brigade groups because the British army was incapable of operating and reacting quickly as divisions: smaller formations might have more success in doing so. Montgomery hoped that training would instil cohesion and flexibility into his divisions. Where he reversed Auchinleck's policy completely was in allowing once more a separation of the armour and the infantry, for he formed X Corps, entirely of armour, and had XXX Corps become an entirely infantry corps. XIII was a mix of one armoured and two infantry divisions. Auchinleck's idea had been to have all divisions mobile, with a mix of armour and motorised infantry, commanded and trained by one commander. It is what the British army does today, but in 1942 was strongly resisted by the advocates of the regimental system. By listening to those protesters against all-arms integration, Montgomery perpetuated the inability to reorganise and regroup quickly, something that was a hallmark of the German army but which, right to the end of the war, the British never mastered.

By 23 October 1942, when the Second Battle of El Alamein, Operation Lightfoot, began, the Eighth Army had received two new armoured divisions, two new infantry divisions and more tanks, guns and men than ever before. Rommel had been reinforced by one German infantry division and a parachute brigade, an Italian armoured division, two Italian infantry divisions and a parachute division. The reality was that the Italian infantry brought no transport with them; fuel in particular and all manner of supplies including rations were in very short supply, sickness rates even among the Germans were rocketing, and Rommel himself had to return to Germany on sick leave on 23 September. Relative strengths were:[7]

	EIGHTH ARMY	PANZER ARMY AFRICA
Armoured divisions	4 *	3
Infantry divisions	7	8
Tanks	1,348	560
Field guns	856	500
Anti-tank guns	1,403	850
Manpower	220,476	112,000

The bare figures do not tell the full story. Of the 560 Axis tanks, 340 were lightly armoured and undergunned Italian tanks, and of the 220 German ones only thirty-eight were Mk IVs with the 75mm gun, whereas the British had 246 Grants and 285 Shermans, all with 75mm guns. The Sherman (M4 to the Americans) was an innovation in tank design. Whereas previous tanks were beautifully and painstakingly put together by skilled craftsmen, the Sherman was designed to be constructed on the assembly-line principle, which meant a prodigious rate of production

---

* Only three were actually deployed. 8 Armoured Division was as yet incomplete so its one armoured brigade (24) was put in 10 Armoured Division.

(1,000 a month in 1942, in eleven US factories). With a cast and welded, rather than riveted, hull it had 2.5 inches of frontal armour, a range of 100 miles and a speed of 24 mph. The RAF had complete air superiority. Only in anti-tank guns did Panzer Army Africa have a fighting chance, as of their 850, eighty-six were 88mm guns, while the British total of 1,403 broke down into 554 2-pounders and only 849 6-pounders. The Axis were short of everything except mines, and between Alam Halfa and Second Alamein they laid the astonishing total of half a million, to add to the minefields already in place.

If Alamein was the position of choice for Auchinleck from which to defend Egypt because the British defences could not be turned, then equally neither could the Germans'. Auchinleck's plan, therefore, was to create diversions on the south but to break through on the northern flank, and Ramsden, commanding XXX Corps, had been working on this premise well before Montgomery arrived. It would be uncharitable to say that Ramsden's sacking by Montgomery after the Alam Halfa battle was to prevent him or anyone else taking the credit for 'Montgomery's plan'. On the night of 23–24 October 1942, behind a tremendous rolling artillery barrage, the infantry advanced on a ten-mile front. The intention was for the engineers to clear lanes through the minefields to allow the armour to cross. The tanks were then to go on the defensive until the infantry battle was over and the Axis anti-tank screen had been dealt with. Although the British initially achieved complete surprise, fierce German and Italian resistance, the depth of their defences and well-organised counter-attacks meant that this first phase took much longer than hoped, and the infantry did not reach their initial objectives in time. When the commander of the leading armoured division (Gatehouse, late of the RTR and the most experienced armoured commander in the British army at that time) objected to being asked to advance unsupported by infantry through a minefield against a German anti-tank screen, he was threatened with the sack by Montgomery unless he did. The result was entirely predictable; the leading armoured regiment, the Staffordshire Yeomanry, lost all but fifteen of its tanks and made no progress.

At one stage the attack was completely stalled, and had Rommel been there the result might have been disastrous for the British. As it was, by the time Rommel returned on the night of 25 October, the immediate crisis for the British had passed and superior resources began to tell. On 29 October the British attacked again with one division, and on the night of 1–2 November the second major offensive began. Operation Supercharge, spearheaded by the New Zealand Division and its attached 9 Armoured Brigade, struck westward north of Kidney Ridge. As many of the mines could not be lifted, in the van went a number of Scorpions, locally adapted tanks with a rotating drum fitted to the front, to which were attached lengths of chain that exploded mines ahead of the tank. After the New Zealand Division came 1 Armoured Division. There was argument and dissent between infantry and armoured commanders, there were map-reading errors, there was traffic chaos, but on 2 November Rommel came to the conclusion that clumsy and pedestrian though the British might be, they ruled the skies, they vastly outnumbered him and they had no shortage of fuel. He issued instructions for a withdrawal, and sent a signal to OKW in Berlin to tell them what he was doing. Thanks to Ultra that signal was in the hands of Eighth Army staff twenty-four hours later. OKW's reply, in actuality Hitler's reply, was that Rommel was not to retreat but to stand fast. It was too late. Rommel tried to cancel his orders for withdrawal but units were already moving and on 4 November Hitler changed his mind and gave his approval to Rommel's plans.

Second Alamein was a British victory, and it earned Montgomery promotion to general and a knighthood, but it was by no means the great triumph that the British press made it out to be, and on purely military grounds did not deserve church bells to be rung in its honour. It was, however, the first British victory over the Germans on land, albeit that they were sick and outnumbered Germans suffering from shortages of all kinds, and it was the last purely British victory of the war in the west. From now on, all British operations against Germany and Italy on land would be as part of Allied operations, in which more and more the Americans with their vastly greater population, wealth and industrial potential would move to centre stage. Finally, of course, it rescued Churchill from increasing mutterings about his direction of the war, and later on the British could talk grandiosely about Alamein being a turning point of the war. That while Montgomery was directing the activities of eleven divisions at Alamein, there were eighty-two Russian divisions fighting the battle of Stalingrad seems to have gone unnoticed.

Churchill had at least managed to convince the Americans that as a cross-Channel invasion was not yet possible, an Allied operation in North Africa was the next best thing, and would take the pressure off Egypt and the Persian oil fields. So was born Operation Torch, which as Rommel very quickly appreciated, meant the end of the war in North Africa, although if the British army had been a bit lighter on its toes and Montgomery less cautious, that end might have come rather sooner than it did. On 8 November 106,000 Allied troops landed at Casablanca in French Morocco, and at Oran and Algiers in Algeria. The Casablanca and Oran landings were entirely American, while at Algiers it was a mixed Anglo-American force with the Americans landing first as it was thought that the French were much less likely to oppose Americans than British, whom they had not forgiven for sinking their fleet and seizing Syria. For the first time British parachute troops were used other than in raids. The British elements of the Algiers landings were two infantry brigades, to be formed into 78 Division, which with the American II Corps, commanded by George S. Patton, and the British 6 Armoured Division would form the nucleus of the British First Army, commanded by Lieutenant General Sir Kenneth Anderson, a post originally intended to be filled by Montgomery before Gott's death gave him Eighth Army. Montgomery did not like Anderson, or perhaps he feared that Anderson might steal his thunder. To his mole in the War Office Montgomery wrote: '...I doubt myself if Anderson is the right man for the job', and rubbing salt in another man's wounds in the same letter, 'I feel that to make Gort a field marshal was quite dreadful...', and to the CIGS he wrote: 'It would seem that Anderson is quite unfit to command an army in the field.'[8]

Initially the Torch landings made considerable progress, although the Vichy French forces put up stout resistance, particularly the navy, until Admiral Darlan agreed a ceasefire.[*] Germany did not dither. The whole

---

[*] Darlan was assassinated on 24 December by a Frenchman who may or may not have been a Gaullist, and who may or may not have been put up to it by the British. As the assassin was tried and executed with remarkable speed, we will never know the truth, but the removal of Darlan certainly made life much easier politically for the Allies.

of France was occupied by German troops, French airfields were used to transfer troops to Tunisia and reinforcements also came from Italy.[*] Colonel General von Arnim was sent out to command what with its reinforcements of 17,000 men was now to be Fifth Panzer Army, and a convoy carrying more tanks managed to evade the Royal Navy and the RAF. British and American troops got to within twenty miles of Tunis before they were stopped and pushed back, but the Axis forces were now caught between the Eighth Army advancing from the east, and the Anglo-Americans from the west.

Two new types of tank appeared at this stage, one British and one German. The three regiments of First Army's 21 Army Tank Brigade were equipped with the Churchill, or A22 Mark VI Infantry Tank. Originally produced under the threat of invasion in 1941 it was well protected with 4 inches of frontal armour, a top speed of 15 mph and a range of eighty-eight miles, but only a 2-pounder gun. It was due to be phased out, but by the time it arrived in Tunisia initial mechanical unreliability had been resolved and to everyone's surprise it was better than any other Allied tank at going up steep slopes – useful in the hills around Tunis – and it was reprieved. The German arrival was the PzKpf VI, or Tiger, more than a match for any Allied tank of the war, then or later. Designed as a defensive tank for the Russian front it had nearly four inches of frontal armour, an 88mm gun with an effective range in excess of 2,000 yards and, despite a weight of fifty-six tons, a top speed of 23 mph and a range of 120 miles. Fortunately for the Allies, there were only twenty-five of them sent to Africa.

Montgomery began his pursuit of Rommel. On 12 November the British were in Tobruk, on the 17th they were in Derna and Mechili, and on the 23rd had closed up on El Agheila, which they did not attack until 12 December. Even then they could not trap Rommel. Try as he might, Montgomery could not cut off an army which for all its supply and manpower problems, to say nothing of the RAF's complete command of the air, was well accustomed to moving slickly and efficiently protected by a screen of anti-tank guns. On 23 January the British entered Tripoli,

---

[*] The Germans attempted to seize the French fleet in Toulon, which to its eternal credit scuttled on 27 November.

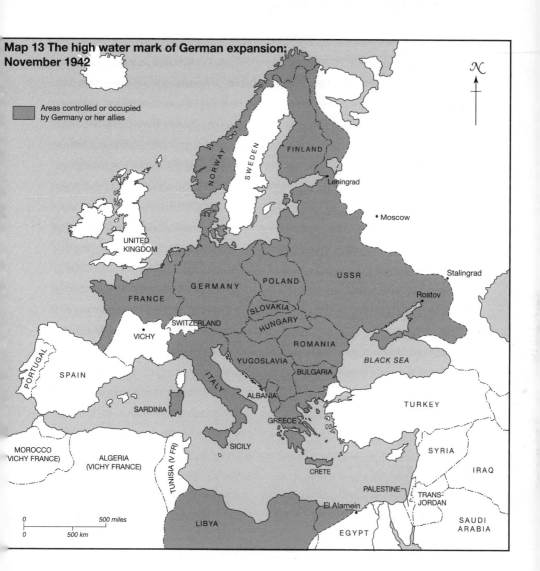

Map 13 The high water mark of German expansion: November 1942

Areas controlled or occupied
by Germany or her allies

NORWAY
SWEDEN
FINLAND
Leningrad
• Moscow
UNITED
KINGDOM
GERMANY
POLAND
USSR
Stalingrad
FRANCE
Rostov
SLOVAKIA
SWITZERLAND
HUNGARY
VICHY
ROMANIA
PORTUGAL
SPAIN
YUGOSLAVIA
BULGARIA
BLACK SEA
ITALY
ALBANIA
TURKEY
SARDINIA
GREECE
MOROCCO
VICHY FRANCE)
ALGERIA
(VICHY FRANCE)
TUNISIA (V FR)
SICILY
SYRIA
IRAQ
CRETE
PALESTINE
TRANS-
JORDAN
0   500 miles
LIBYA
El Alamein
SAUDI
ARABIA
0   500 km
EGYPT

and on 15 February Rommel was secure behind the Mareth Line in Tunisia. The Eighth Army had advanced an average of just under fourteen miles a day since Second Alamein. Fifth Panzer Army's immediate aim was to defend Tunis and to prevent the Allies from getting to the Tunisian coast, and thus cutting the Axis forces in two. A combination of bad weather, stubborn Axis resistance to the Torch forces and a counter-stroke by von Arnim against the Americans at the Kasserine Pass on 14 February 1943, which exposed all sorts of faults in training and tactics, forced the Allies to recognise that the war in North Africa was one campaign, not two. The American General Eisenhower was appointed Supreme Allied Commander Mediterranean, with Alexander as his deputy. Alexander also became commander of the newly formed 18 Army Group, consisting of the British First and Eighth Armies, and Tedder took all air assets under his command. Alexander was diplomatic, sociable and able to get on with allies, and managed to diffuse at least some of the resentment created by Montgomery's domineering manner and barely disguised contempt for American military prowess.

An initial attack on the Mareth Line by Eighth Army on 19 March 1943 failed, but another succeeded, as did an offensive against Rommel's next defence line, at Wadi Akarit. By now it was just a question of time before all Tunisia was in Allied hands, and Rommel was medically evacuated by air to Germany on 9 March. Although Germans and Italians fought doggedly and well under von Arnim and the Italian Field Marshal Messe, a final push by First Army augmented by two of Montgomery's divisions, forced the collapse of the defences of Tunis. The last isolated party of Germans surrendered on 13 May, and for von Arnim it would be his second taste of British captivity, having been captured at Mons leading a troop of German cavalry in 1914. There was to be no Dunkirk for the Axis troops, for there was no navy to take them to Sicily – about the same distance as the Royal Navy had transported the BEF in 1940 – and a quarter of a million German and Italian soldiers and airmen went into Allied prison camps.

The North African campaign was over, and as there were still insufficient men or landing craft to contemplate an excursion to France, the British lobbied very hard for an invasion of Italy, via Sicily. The Americans were unsure: they were not believers in the indirect approach; they were suspicious of British motives, and they had not come into the war to ensure that the Mediterranean remained a British lake. Churchill was an enthusiast for the Italian option: it was all part of his 'soft underbelly' strategy that he had pursued since the beginning of the Great War; it would knock Italy out of the war and it would open a second front against Germany. If it went well and Allied troops got through Italy and into the Balkans quickly, it might even make an invasion of Fortress Europe unnecessary; otherwise it would form a useful distraction from that operation. It might also forestall any Russian ambitions in the Balkans, about which Churchill was – rightly – increasingly concerned.

Planning for the Italian campaign was muddled, not least because the major participants were either still fighting the Battle of Tunisia or spread between Cairo, London and the USA while Operation Husky – the invasion of Sicily – and Operations Baytown and Avalanche – the landings by the British and the Americans on the Italian mainland – were being put together. Husky was preceded by a month's ceaseless pounding from the air by the RAF and the USAF, and was supported by a formidable array of ships: 1,614 of the Royal Navy, including six battleships and two carriers, 945 of the United States Navy and thirty-one from the navies of the occupied countries. On 9 July parachutists and glider troops attempted to seize key points and coastal defence gun batteries, although due to the inexperience of the pilots many were dropped or released in the wrong place and achieved little. The next day the British put four divisions ashore and the Americans three. Defending Sicily were 315,000 Italian and 50,000 German troops, and a further 40,000 German reinforcements were brought in from Italy. It took nearly six weeks to capture Sicily, the campaign being marked by stiff Axis resistance, an inability by both the British and the Americans to prevent the Germans and Italians from retreating in good order, and quite unnecessary antagonism between Montgomery and Patton, now commanding the US Seventh Army. On 11 August the Germans began to evacuate their troops across the Straits of Messina to Italy, an operation conducted in an orderly fashion and which the Allies were unable to do very much about. On 17 August the evacuation was complete and the Allies entered Messina.

Map 14 The Italian theatre

GERMANY

SWITZERLAND

HUNGARY

Milan

YUGOSLAVIA

N

Genoa

Bologna

GOTHIC LINE

ITALY

CORSICA

Rome

GUSTAV LINE

Anzio

Cassino

SARDINIA

Salerno

Taranto

Messina

SICILY

TUNISIA

0   200 miles

0   300 km

This should have been the time to strike straight across for the Italian mainland, but now politics intervened. Covert negotiations had been going on in Lisbon and Tangiers between the Allies and the Italians since the deposition of Mussolini by his own Fascist Grand Council on 25 July 1943, and the formation of what was effectively a military government under Marshal Badoglio. Badoglio hoped to keep the Germans at arms length and to combine an Italian surrender to the Allies and declaration of war against Germany with an Allied landing on the mainland. Negotiations continued until 3 September, and the Germans, who knew very well what was going on, were able to bring sixteen divisions into Italy during that period. At 0430 hours on 3 September 1 Canadian Division, fresh from training in the United Kingdom and having their introduction to battle, and 5 Division, which had been in North Africa since March 1943 and was relatively inexperienced, landed unopposed on the toe of Italy. At 1830 hours on 8 September Eisenhower made public the terms of the Italian surrender, and at 0330 hours the following morning elements of General Mark Clark's American Fifth Army landed at Salerno and the British 1st Airborne Division dropped to seize the naval base of Taranto. The Germans reacted swiftly. All key points including telephone exchanges, airfields, railway stations, and military and government buildings were taken over and the Italians occupying them bustled out of the way. Contrary to the agreement with Badoglio, few Italian units attempted to resist the Germans, and those that did were ruthlessly dealt with. The Americans at Salerno were very nearly driven back into the sea, and if the Germans had had just a few more battalions they would have been.

The Italian campaign now developed into a long, hard, slow slog. Political differences between the British and the Americans as to what exactly the aims were, and whether the campaign was worthwhile anyway, led to confusion and muddle further down. The country was a defender's dream and the Allies' complete air superiority was reduced by the hills and ravines that made bombing far less effective than it had been in the open desert of North Africa. Field Marshal Kesselring was a highly capable Commander-in-Chief and, as in North Africa, the Germans were always able to resist stoutly, cause maximum casualties, and then slip away to the next defended line. Bad or non-existent roads, steep mountains, foul winter weather, flooded river valleys and national susceptibilities in a command containing American, British, Indian, French, Canadian and Polish formations all added to Alexander's difficulties, as did the increasing priority given to the proposed invasion of France. Once that invasion happened, in June 1944, morale in Italy dropped as the men fighting there saw themselves forgotten by press and public at home. On several occasions the fighting in Italy, and the casualties sustained, were reminiscent of the Western Front in the First War. The four Battles of Cassino, from January to May 1944, were particularly so when the Allies tried again and again to pierce the Germans' Gustav Line. The second Battle of Cassino once again showed up the British inability to act swiftly: after much discussion the monastery dominating the mountain ridge was finally bombed and reduced to rubble, but then there was a delay of a day before the New Zealand Corps attacked, with the inevitable result that the Germans were given time to reorganise and reinforce.[*] Even when the Gustav Line was at last broken in May the Germans were not unduly discomfited: they simply melted away and began a fighting withdrawal to the next prepared positions, the Gothic Line, while the Allies involved themselves in a childish and unnecessary squabble as to who should first occupy Rome. In July 1944 there were eighteen Allied divisions in Italy (and probably another division's-worth of deserters, sitting out the war in the hills, well provided with Chianti and girls) as well as eighteen German divisions. It was hardly a distraction from Normandy.

Montgomery regarded Alexander's strategy in Italy as wrong, but then it was not Montgomery's strategy. He had escaped from that theatre before the fighting became bogged down, being ordered to return to England in December 1943 to prepare for the Normandy invasion.

---

[*] This author has been assured by an ex-officer of the Waffen SS, on his regimental headquarters staff at Cassino, that while there were conducted tours of the monastery for German officers and men in civilian clothes, at no time was it defended or used for any military purpose until it was bombed. I have no reason to think he lied.

AT SEA THE BATTLE of the Atlantic was by no means won by the end of 1943, but the balance was tilting. German submarines were still sinking merchantmen but increasingly were being sunk themselves. Better radar, improved depth charges and the escort-carrier building programme meant that the days of U-boat supremacy were coming to an end. By the beginning of 1943 the Royal Navy deployed more than 450 warships on escort duties alone, and while convoys still lost merchant ships to submarines, greater numbers of U-boats were being sunk as well. Admiral Dönitz, commander of the German navy's submarine arm, increasingly sought 'soft spots' where he could find and sink unescorted merchantmen, but increasingly swift British and American reaction forced the U-boat packs to move on. A new and greatly improved radar, that could pick up a surfaced submarine at a range of three miles, the emissions of which could not be detected by the U-boats, was coming into service. As this was the same type of radar that was being fitted to the RAF bombers, and as the Chiefs of Staff had agreed that Bomber Command should have priority, it was not until March 1943 that these devices began to make their presence felt at sea. Most German disguised raiders – merchant ships flying false colours and heavily armed – had been dealt with, and those that still lurked in the oceans of the world were increasingly the hunted rather than the hunters.

Even the embarrassment of 11–12 February 1942, when the German battlecruisers *Gneisenau* and *Scharnhorst* and the heavy cruiser *Prinz Eugen* had sailed up the Channel from Brest to German ports despite the efforts of the Royal Navy and the RAF to stop them, had reaped advantages. It had proved that torpedoes, not bombs, were the best weapons with which to attack ships under way, and the destruction of the dry dock at St Nazaire in a daring raid in March 1942 meant that even if the *Tirpitz* ventured out of her Norwegian fjord, there was nowhere for her to run to. Finally, a bold attack on the *Tirpitz* by midget submarines of the Royal Navy in September 1943 put her out of action, even if it did not destroy her completely. During 1943 more and more American troops were being conveyed across the Atlantic in liners converted to troopships; the British *Queen Mary*, *Queen Elizabeth*, *Aquitania* and *Mauretania*, the French *Île de France* and the Dutch *Nieuw Amsterdam* could carry 15,000 men at a time and travel fast enough to make the journey without escort.

Possibly the greatest British advance in the naval war was the introduction in May 1943 of new naval codes, which the Germans were unable to break, and which thus deprived Dönitz of his main source of naval intelligence. This, the ability of Ultra to decipher German navy messages and increasingly sophisticated cooperation between the Royal Navy's surface vessels and aircraft of the RAF's Coastal Command did much to counter the improvements in the U-boats' anti-aircraft armament and the introduction of what the Germans called 'milch cows' – large logistical submarines that resupplied the operational U-boats, thus allowing them to stay at sea for longer. Between June and August 1943 U-boats sank fifty-eight Allied merchantmen, mainly in the North Atlantic and the Bay of Biscay, but in that same period seventy-four U-boats were sunk or destroyed, fifty-eight by carrier or shore-based aircraft. This total included four of the milch cows, leaving the German navy with only six.[9]

In August 1943 the First Sea Lord, Admiral of the Fleet Sir Dudley Pound, returned from Quadrant, an Allied conference at Quebec, and was diagnosed with a malignant brain tumour. He resigned the following month, and died on 2 October. The obvious replacement was Admiral of the Fleet Sir Andrew Cunningham, in his second incarnation as Commander-in-Chief Mediterranean (he had been naval commander-in-chief for the Torch landings), who was the nomination of the First Lord, A. V. Alexander. Alexander was somewhat of a nonentity, having been appointed by Churchill who wanted no opposition to his theories on the conduct of war at sea, and Churchill initially rejected the recommendation, claiming that Cunningham was too old to cope with the stresses of working in the Chiefs of Staff Committee. In fact Cunningham was sixty, nine years younger than Churchill, and the real reason for Churchill's opposition to him as professional head of the Royal Navy was the knowledge that he would not be the Prime Minister's quiescent lapdog, as his sharp replies to Churchill's interference at the time of Crete had demonstrated. Churchill offered the post to Admiral Sir Bruce Fraser, commanding the Home Fleet (and only a year younger than Cunningham), who replied, 'I believe I have the confidence of my own fleet. Cunningham has the confidence of the whole navy.' Faced with the views of his own First Lord and the refusal of any other admiral to accept the post, Churchill had no option but to appoint Cunningham, and it was well that he did so. A forceful, quick-thinking and thoroughly professional officer, Cunningham was able to prevent Churchill from throwing away ships and sailors on at least some of his unrealistic adventures, even if he could not entirely keep him under control; but then no one could.

If 1943 was a rather better year for the British, it was not a good year for the Germans. Not only had they been chased out of North Africa but their chief ally in the West, Italy, was out of the war, and the quick overthrow of Russia, expected in 1941 with such confidence that no winter clothing had been provided for the troops, had not only not come to pass that year, but had not come to pass in 1942 either. If the British services were irritated by interference from Churchill, so the Germans had to put up with it from Hitler. It was unfortunate (for Germany) that Hitler had been right in the winter of 1941. Convinced that the Russians would take advantage of the reduced German mobility and launch a counter-offensive, the German generals wanted to pull back to shorten the line, and stand on the defensive until resuming the advance in the spring. Hitler was convinced that the Russians were in no state to go on to the offensive and refused to permit any withdrawal. In the event Hitler was right, which persuaded him to believe that he had strategic and tactical insight denied to his generals, and encouraged him to interfere more and more. His strategic opinions were not necessarily wrong – often he showed remarkable perspicacity as to what might be possible – but his habit of delaying to the last minute before giving a decision forced the General Staffs more and more into cobbling plans together without the time to properly think them through. Fortunately for the Germans, their army was capable of thinking on its feet and of being flexible, yet there was a limit beyond which even it could not go.

On the home front, too, Germany was being hit with far more punch than had been the case in 1942. Air Chief Marshal Harris's determination to destroy the Germans' will to fight was having its effect, even if that was not necessarily on German morale. Improvements in radar, OBOE to assist in navigation and H2S to help in target identification, and the formation from August 1942 of the Pathfinder Force, composed of some of the most competent crews, whose job it was to lead the others to the target, which they marked with pyrotechnic bombs, and the production of more and more bombers, particularly the Lancaster, all increased the number of aircraft that could be sent on a raid, and their effectiveness once they reached their targets. It took until 1943 before a definite policy was formally established regulating the length of time aircrews should fly operationally before being rotated through a training or administrative appointment. Previously it had generally been accepted that bomber crews should be relieved after thirty sorties, the squadron commander deciding what was and what was not a sortie, but there was disagreement as to how long a second and subsequent tour should be. Other types of aircrew had their tour lengths decided by the number of flying hours completed, or by the number of sorties, depending on the group they served in. From February 1943 bomber crews' first tour was thirty sorties, and second and subsequent tours were twenty sorties, except for pathfinder crews who would complete one tour of forty-five sorties, which, because they were limited in number, would take about as long as a standard crew would take to fly thirty. Day-fighter aircrew were to complete two hundred flying hours in their first tour, and night fighters one hundred.

In broad terms Bomber Command concentrated on the Ruhr, Germany's main industrial area, from March to July 1943, on obliterating Hamburg at the end of July and the beginning of August, and on Berlin from November 1943 until March 1944. The attack on Hamburg, like that on Dresden in February 1945, remains controversial. Bomber Command attacked Hamburg on the nights of 24–25 July, 27–28 July, 29–30 July and 2–3 August 1943 with a total of 3,095 sorties, and the United States 8th Air Force bombed it by day on 25 and 26 July with 526 sorties. It was the first use by Bomber Command of Window, strips of tinfoil dropped by the thousand from aircraft in order to confuse German radar, which could not distinguish a strip of tinfoil from a bomber. On this occasion the Kammhuber Line was completely overwhelmed, and could do little. A firestorm – the first time this phenomenon had been noted – occurred as a result of the raid on 27–28 July, when incendiaries caused large fires in the city. The heat generated caused a huge up-draught as superheated air rose, sucked in air from outside the burning area and spread the flames, increasing the heat and producing even fiercer winds, up to 150 mph. Temperatures were as high as 1,000 degrees Centigrade, and winds uprooted trees, tore the roofs off buildings and flung people into the flames, where they were incinerated. Exact casualty figures are unknown, but the British Official History estimates 40,000 dead. About 60 per cent of Hamburg's housing was destroyed or severely damaged and nearly a million people fled the city. The RAF lost eighty-six aircraft, with another 174 damaged in some way, and the USAAF lost forty-three.

At a casualty rate of 8 per cent in aircraft the raid was, on the face of it, highly cost effective. The expressed objection to the raid by those who protested at the 1992 erection of a statue of Harris at the RAF Church, St Clement Danes, in London, is that it burned to death 40,000 people, and that makes Harris and his crews war criminals. Apart from the fact that in law it does no such thing, would it have been alright if the raid had killed just ten people? Or a thousand? Or ten thousand? Far more people were killed in the deliberate fire-bombing of Tokyo, but where was the outcry then? Or didn't that matter – the Japanese being not only inscrutable Asians, but a long way away.

War is not just about killing enemy soldiers, sailors and airmen. It is also about destroying the enemy's will to fight, and at the time it was believed that bombing of cities would do just that. That it did not, does not mean that it should not have been tried. Morality aside, the attack had less impact militarily than was at first thought. Most of the inhabitants returned within a week of the raid, industry got going again remarkably quickly, and only about fifty working days' production was lost. Once Bomber Command switched to Berlin, improved German night fighters and the concentration of large numbers of 88mm anti-aircraft guns once more caused huge casualties in Bomber Command and to the crews of 8th USAAF, but it also forced the transfer of anti-aircraft defences and day and night fighters away from France and into the Reich itself, leaving very little for the Channel coast.

THE BRITISH HAD ALWAYS accepted that at some time they would have to return to Europe, the only question was when. The ghost of the Dardanelles still stalked Whitehall, and in particular clanked its chains around the Prime Minister, who had been forced out of office in the First War because of the Gallipoli fiasco. The British were determined not to attempt an invasion until the men, the aircraft and the ships, and particularly the landing craft, were available to carry it out. After repeated complaints from Stalin and prodding by the Americans, who always suspected that British preoccupation with the Mediterranean was an excuse for not getting on with invading France, an Allied conference at Casablanca in February 1943 agreed the setting up of a joint planning staff to prepare for the cross-Channel invasion. Lieutenant General Sir Frederick Morgan was appointed COSSAC (Chief of Staff to Supreme Allied Commander) and began to plan for what was to become Operation Overlord.

It was at Casablanca that President Roosevelt, without any consultation with the British, or even notifying them, blurted out at a press conference that the Allies would accept nothing less than unconditional surrender from Germany. The British were dismayed: this could only encourage the Germans to resist the harder and eliminated any possibility there might have been of a German overthrowing of Hitler and a negotiated end to the war. It may be that Roosevelt simply did not understand the implications of what he was saying, but it was too late to renege on it and the British had to accept it henceforth as Allied policy. At this stage the Americans still hoped for an invasion in 1943, but when that was shown to be impossible, the Tehran conference in November 1943 agreed a target date of 1 May 1944.

The appointment of a supreme commander for Overlord was a political decision, and in June 1943 Churchill told the CIGS, Brooke, that it would be him. Churchill cannot have discussed this spontaneous offer with the Americans, although at that time in the war Britain was still the senior partner and it was not unreasonable to assume that the overall commander for Overlord would be British. As planning proceeded, however, it became clear that although the British would land more men in the first phase, as the build-up of troops in Europe progressed only the United States, with its huge manpower resources, could provide the numbers needed, and the supreme commander must, therefore, be American. Brooke was told this unwelcome news by Churchill '...he offered no sympathy, no regrets at having to change his mind, and dealt with the matter as if it were of only minor importance!'[10] The Americans had originally proposed the chairman of their joint chiefs of staff, General Marshall, but President Roosevelt decided that he did not want to part with Marshall as his military adviser, and the appointment of Eisenhower was provisionally decided upon in December 1943, with confirmation in February 1944. COSSAC now had someone to present his plans to.

NOTES

1. TNA Kew, CAB 146/15 Appx 5, Captured enemy documents.

2. Ibid.

3. Stephen Roskill, *The War at Sea, Vol. II*, HMSO, London, 1954.

4. Alex Danchev and Daniel Todman, *War Diaries 1939–1945: Field Marshal Lord Alanbrooke*, Weidenfeld & Nicolson, London, 2001.

5. B. L. Montgomery, *Memoirs*, Collins, London, 1958.

6. Stephen Brooks (ed), *Montgomery and the Eighth Army*, Army Records Society, 1991.

7. British statistics from Lt Col H. F. Joslen, *Orders of Battle: Second World War 1939–1945*, HMSO, London, 1960; German from B. H. Liddell Hart (ed), *The Rommel Papers*, Collins, London, 1953, and Barrie Pitt, *The Crucible of War, Vol. III*, Cassell, London, 2001.

8. Stephen Brooks, op. cit.

9. Stephen Roskill, *The Navy at War 1939–1945*, Collins, London, 1960.

10. Danchev and Todman, op. cit.

15

To the End of the Road

OPERATION OVERLORD, the invasion of north-west Europe, would have to begin with a landing. In examining the options for a return to the Continent the joint planning team had firstly to answer four questions: how, when, where and how many? 'How' was relatively easy to answer. Experience of Crete had shown that to attempt an airborne assault alone would be to invite disaster, even if the Allies had enough airborne troops, which they had not. The only way to get a force into Europe large enough to avoid being kicked back into the sea was to take it there in ships and land it somewhere on the coast. Then it would have to be supplied, maintained and reinforced, as the force large enough to achieve a lodgement would not be sufficiently large to take the initiative by moving inland, defeating the German army in France and fighting its way into Germany.

As far as the Russians and Americans were concerned the 'when' was 'as soon as possible', but once it had been agreed that nothing could be done before 1944, the 'when' depended on weather, moon and tides. Spring, autumn and winter in the Channel are unpredictable, and even the summer can throw up brief but intense storms, which meant that the months from May to August would be best, but even then could not be guaranteed. The 'where' depended partly on the 'how many', but also, given that a port would not be assaulted directly (supposedly one of the lessons from Dieppe), on the availability of suitable beaches. There was no such thing as an undefended beach of any size. The whole of the Channel coast, nearly 3,000 miles from northern Norway to the Franco-Spanish border, had been incorporated in the Atlantic Wall, a series of gun emplacements, machine-gun posts, beach obstacles, wire, minefields and infantry bunkers built under the supervision of the Todt Organisation to prevent invasion. Fritz Todt was the engineer who had created the German autobahn network before the war, and as Reich Minister for Armaments and Munitions was the obvious man to undertake military fortifications. He was killed in an air crash in February 1942 and was succeeded by Albert Speer. Contrary to popular myth, the Atlantic Wall was not built by slave labour but by the normal system of calling for tenders and then awarding contracts to French construction companies. Before any invasion could take place these defences would have to be degraded, and the troops landing would have to have the means to get over, through or round them.

Along the Channel coast the choice of landing beaches was limited. Norway was too far from Germany, the weather could not be relied upon and the terrain would negate the Allies' preponderance in vehicles and armour. Landings in Holland or Denmark could easily be cut off and isolated, and anything south of Brittany in the Bay of Biscay would be exposed to the full rigours of the Atlantic weather and would be outside fighter-cover range from the UK. The obvious area for invasion was the Pas de Calais: it was the shortest way across the Channel from England; there were a number of ports that could be captured shortly after the invasion; it was well within fighter range and it was on the direct route to Germany. Conversely the Germans too could see that it was the most obvious crossing point, it had the most heavily fortified coastline and it was where the bulk of German armour in Western Europe was stationed. To land there would be to play into the Germans' hands, and the planners ruled it out. The only other realistic possibility that was within striking distance of Germany, had enough beaches of the right sort, was within fighter cover from the UK and was reasonably sheltered from the Atlantic weather, was Normandy, and that is where the planners decided the invasion should be launched.

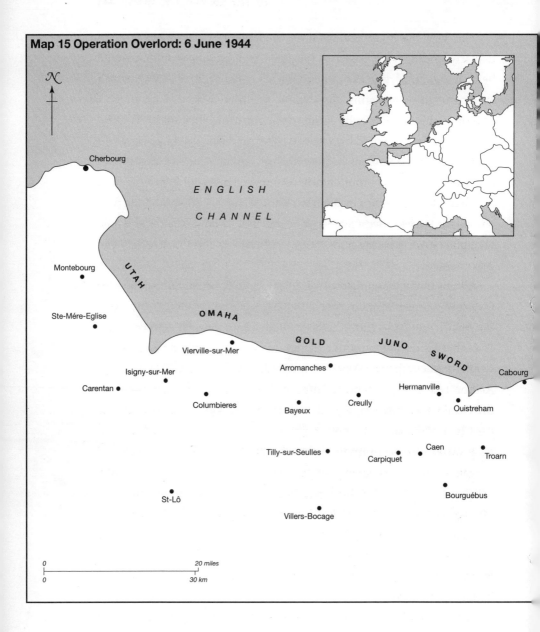

Map 15 Operation Overlord: 6 June 1944

N

ENGLISH CHANNEL

Cherbourg

UTAH

Montebourg

OMAHA

Ste-Mére-Eglise

GOLD

JUNO

SWORD

Vierville-sur-Mer

Arromanches

Cabourg

Isigny-sur-Mer

Hermanville

Carentan

Columbieres

Creully

Ouistreham

Bayeux

Tilly-sur-Seulles

Caen

Troarn

Carpiquet

St-Lô

Bourguébus

Villers-Bocage

| 0 | | 20 miles |
| 0 | | 30 km |

The 'how many' depended on the availability of men and ships, particularly landing craft. Based on the number of landing craft that would be available in spring 1944, the planners calculated an initial assault landing of three divisions, closely followed by two more, and another two once the landing craft could turn round and pick them up. Two airborne divisions would be dropped to seize crossing points over rivers inland, to provide flank protection and to take out positions that threatened the landings but could not be eliminated by bombing or by naval gunfire. Three beaches in the bay of the River Seine were identified, named from east to west Sword, Juno and Gold, and the landings would take place over a frontage of twenty miles between Ouistreham and Arromanches.

All this initial planning took place before the command structure for Overlord was established. After long and detailed discussions between the British and American Chiefs of Staff, it was confirmed in February 1944 that General Dwight D. Eisenhower of the United States Army would be the Supreme Allied Commander, with Air Chief Marshal Sir Arthur Tedder as his deputy. Admiral Sir Bertram Ramsay, architect of the Dunkirk evacuation, would command the Allied naval forces while Air Chief Marshal Sir Trafford Leigh-Mallory would command the air. As ground forces commander for the invasion Eisenhower wanted Alexander, whom he knew well and with whom he had established an excellent working relationship, but Brooke insisted that it should be Montgomery, and so Montgomery it was, while Alexander stayed in Italy. Montgomery took over Headquarters 21 Army Group in January, and immediately began replacing the existing (perfectly competent) staff with his own nominees, mostly from Eighth Army, which was left to fight on in Italy without them.

Although it is not always possible for those who have to carry out operations to have any part in their planning, on this occasion Eisenhower and Montgomery were able to look at the plans for Overlord and Operation Neptune, the naval phase, and comment upon them. They had no objection to the concept, nor to the location, but they were concerned that an assault by three divisions over twenty miles was too few men into too small a lodgement area. Their considered view was that the landings should take place over a much wider area, beginning with a minimum of five divisions, to be followed up immediately by two more, and the introduction of the thirty follow-up divisions from the UK as soon as the lodgement area could be expanded to fit them in. Three airborne divisions, rather than two, should be used to support the landings. These arguments were convincing, and the Chiefs of Staff allowed a postponement of one month while another thousand landing craft were manufactured. The date was now to be 1 June 1944, eventually altered to 'not later than 5 June' to allow some flexibility depending on the weather. The planners managed to find two more beaches, Omaha and Utah, and the naval bombardment force and the allocation of aircraft was increased accordingly. Landings would now be over a frontage of fifty miles and extend as far west as Varreville. The ground forces for the assault would be commanded by Headquarters 21 Army Group and would consist of the American First Army, commanded by Lieutenant General Omar N. Bradley, which would land on Omaha and Utah beaches; elements of what would become the Canadian First Army, commanded by Lieutenant General Crerar, would land on Juno beach; and the British Second Army, commanded by Lieutenant General Sir Miles Dempsey, would land on Sword and Gold. The commander initially nominated for Second Army was Sir Kenneth Anderson, late of First Army in Tunisia, but Montgomery vetoed his appointment: Dempsey would not steal his Commander-in-Chief's thunder, and would do exactly as he was told.

Planning for Overlord and for Neptune did not depend entirely on the troops to be landed. War was now three-dimensional, even if it took some commanders a long time to realise it, and the part to be played by the navies and air forces was critical. In the months leading up to the invasion the RAF and the USAAF were tasked to destroy the French road and railway systems, to impede German attempts to reinforce Normandy, and to target gun positions on the Atlantic Wall. Divers and midget submarine crews covertly reconnoitred beaches all along the Channel coast, and the population of Britain was asked to send in their pre-war holiday snaps taken in European seaside resorts. All this had to be done while preventing the Germans from realising where the landings were to take place, and to make them think that the Allies were intending to strike in the Pas de Calais.

The deception plan, Operation Fortitude, was one of the great – and at the time perforce unsung – successes of the war. The British were particularly good at intelligence generally and deception in particular. Perhaps this was because the British had been at it for many hundreds of years, or perhaps it was because such operations appealed to British eccentricity and love of individuality; whatever the reason the Americans recognised British primacy in this area, and although Fortitude was an Allied operation, it was British-led. Fortitude had multiple tentacles. As well as Allied agents in place, the turning of captured German agents, the construction of dummy oil installations at Dover and the scattering of blow-up rubber tanks and landing craft made of plywood around ports that faced the Pas de Calais, Fortitude convinced the Germans that there was an Allied army poised to invade Calais and another in Scotland ready to descend upon Norway. Both of these armies consisted of little more than parties of signallers sitting in hedgerows sending messages to each other pretending to be divisional commanders, formation headquarters and logistic units, but the impression given was so carefully crafted that German radio intercept was convinced that they were real. OKW intelligence discounted the Scottish army, but did not move troops from Norway, just in case. So that the bombing programme gave nothing away, for every bomb dropped in Normandy, two were dropped in the Pas de Calais, and beaches that the Allies had not the slightest intention of landing on were duly reconnoitred, with the inevitable deaths or capture of some of those sent secretly to look at them.

In Germany OKW was taken in by Fortitude. Hitler, with that extraordinary intuition that he could sometimes display, was less sure: 'The whole thing the British are doing looks like theatre to me... I can't get rid of the impression that the entire thing is an impudent charade.'[1] While the Pas de Calais was still considered to be the most likely option, Hitler thought Normandy was a possibility, and Field Marshal Rommel was sent off hotfoot to inject some urgency into the defenders of that area. The Eastern Front took up most of the attention of both OKW and OKH, and the bulk of the German army's assets were concentrated there;

indeed, by June 1944 there were 165 German infantry divisions on the Eastern Front, and only fifty-nine in France and the low countries. There were eighteen panzer divisions in Russia, and six in France. The west, however, could not be neglected. The Commander-in-Chief West was the redoubtable Field Marshal Gerd von Rundstedt, the senior officer in the German army who had been commissioned in 1893, had commanded Army Group A in the Battle of France and Army Group South in the invasion of the Soviet Union, before being sacked in November 1941 for arguing with Hitler. Rundstedt had said that while Rostov could be captured, it could not be held, and told Hitler that his orders to the contrary were 'madness'. After Hitler had actually visited the Russian front and realised that Rundstedt was right, the field marshal was recalled in March 1942 and appointed Commander-in-Chief West, with his head-quarters in Paris. To begin with this was an agreeable posting, and Rundstedt liked and got on well with the French, at least until the Torch landings in North Africa precipitated German occupation of what had hitherto been Vichy, unoccupied, France. As time went on and the like-lihood of an Allied invasion drew nearer, so the tempo increased. By early 1944 Rundstedt had under his command two army groups, A commanded by Rommel and G commanded by Colonel General Blaskowitz; Panzer Group West commanded by General of Panzer Troops Freiherr Geyr von Schweppenburg; and Colonel General Student's First Parachute Army.

Rommel's Army Group B was the formation responsible for the Channel coast, anti-invasion measures and the Atlantic Wall defences. Rommel and his Commander-in-Chief, von Rundstedt, disagreed as to how an invasion should be countered. Rundstedt had no faith whatso-ever in the Atlantic Wall, which he called the 'Propaganda Wall', and he was concerned that British and American naval bombardment would swiftly overcome shore-based coastal artillery. He wanted to allow the invasion to happen, identify the main thrust, and then use concentrated armour to defeat the enemy well inland out of naval gunfire range. Rommel, on the other hand, was convinced by his North African expe-riences that Allied air supremacy would prevent German armour from moving by day, and so he wanted to have the armour forward and to defeat the invasion on the beaches. There was merit in both arguments, but the answer, decided upon in Berlin, was an untidy compromise. Panzer Group West was designated as a training command, and thus had no operational control over its six armoured divisions. After much argument three of these divisions were placed under Rommel and Army Group B, while the other three were retained as OKW reserve, which meant that they could not be moved without the authority of Berlin, to wit Hitler personally. Of the two armies in Rommel's army group, Seventh Army (Colonel General Dollman) was responsible for Brittany and the Cotentin Peninsula to the east of the River Orne. It was this army that would face the weight of Operation Overlord, and to do it had twelve infantry divisions, of which two infantry divisions, 352 and 716, were deployed along the landing area. Of the three armoured divisions immediately available to Rommel, only 21 Panzer Division (reformed after its near destruction in North Africa) was within easy reach of what would become the British beaches, and Rommel was refused permission to put another panzer division at St-Lô, which would have placed it a few miles from the American landings.

For the first phase of Operation Overlord the British intended to land an infantry division on each of their three beaches, supported by amphibious tanks that would reach the shore at the same time. The divisions that would carry out the landing were specially tailored for the task. Coming ashore on the most easterly British beach, Sword Beach, 3 Division was composed of a divisional reconnaissance regiment in armoured cars, and three infantry brigades, each of three infantry battalions. The division had a machine-gun battalion (2 Middlesex); three regiments of field artillery with M7 Priests, 105mm guns mounted in Stuart chassis; one anti-tank regiment with 6-pounders; one light anti-aircraft regiment; three Royal Engineer field and one field-park companies; two beach groups, each based on a reinforced infantry battalion and whose task it was to secure and protect the lodgement areas while second wave troops came ashore; one provost company of Royal Military Police, there to organise traffic rather than to lock up offenders, and one field security section that had an anti-espionage and an intelligence-gathering role. In support of the division were elements of 27 Armoured Brigade (13 / 18 Hussars less two squadrons, and the Staffordshire Yeomanry) and flail, ramp, bridge-laying and track-laying tanks of 5 Assault Regiment Royal Engineers. The division had its own signals company and since late 1943 infantry battalions had radios down to platoon level. The other two squadrons of the 13 / 18th Hussars manned DD, or Duplex Drive, tanks. These were a British development that involved waterproofing the underside of a Sherman tank and fitting it with a rubberised canvas screen around the deck, which enabled it to float. Motive power was supplied by two propellers at the rear, driven by the tank engine. On hitting the beach the power was switched from the propellers to the tracks, the screen was dropped and the Sherman reverted to being a normal gun tank. The purpose of the DD tanks was to give the infantry some armoured support and firepower at the moment of arriving on the beach. On the other two British beaches the organisation was the same, except that some of the field artillery was in Sextons, rather than Priests, the former having 25-pounders rather than 105s.

On each beach the assaulting infantry would transfer from their transport ships to landing craft about seven miles offshore, which would give them a ninety-minute run-in to the beach. The landing craft were flat-bottomed, carried a platoon of thirty men and were mainly crewed by sailors or Royal Marines. With the infantry came the DD tanks, and immediately behind them the engineers whose job it was to demolish obstacles, lift mines and clear routes off the beach.

Given that Eisenhower had been instructed to invade by 5 June, that the air forces wanted a full moon and that everyone wanted good weather and calm seas, the weather and tide forecasts indicated 5 June as being suitable, and D-Day was fixed for that date. The army was keen to land at first light, thus having the cover of darkness for their run-in, and enough light to be able to see once ashore. The Royal Navy needed two hours of daylight so that they could make absolutely sure of their final bombardment. In the event, the time of landing was decided by the tides: as the beaches were covered in all manner of obstacles, including mines, it was decided to land at low tide, when the obstacles would be uncovered. This had, of course, the disadvantage of giving the infantry a long stretch of open beach to cross before getting into cover, but meant that the obstacles could be seen and avoided, before being neutralised by the engineers. Low tide on 5 June would be at 0730 hours British Double Summer Time (GMT + two hours) on the British beaches and 0630 hours on the American beaches.* First light was 0530 hours.

Herodotus tells us that Darius, King of Persia, led an army of 700,000 men in the seaborne invasion of south-eastern Europe in 511 BC, making that the greatest amphibious operation ever undertaken. Even if the entire population of Persia numbered 700,000, which is doubtful, Darius only had to worry about moving horses and men. Operation Overlord involved 7,000 ships of all types including landing craft (of the 1,213 warships 80 per cent were British), 3,200 aircraft of the RAF, Royal Navy, USAAF and US Navy, and nearly three million men, of whom a small minority were the assaulting troops. It was a masterpiece of planning, a quite incredible feat, far greater in complexity than anything attempted before or since. Getting every man, ship and aircraft to the right place at the right time was infinitely more difficult than the actual fighting. Credit for the tactical landing plan should go to General Morgan and the staff of COSSAC, for it was the sort of battle that the British could do very well: a steady, methodical, set-piece affair moving from phase to phase with a stately inevitability. Morgan did not get the credit, of course, because Montgomery claimed all of that, and Morgan disappeared from the stage to be deputy chief of staff in Eisenhower's headquarters. Although they did not realise it at the time, for the British D-Day would be their last day as leaders of the free world. They would land 83,000 men, 10,000 more than the Americans, but from then on they would be outstripped by the far greater reserves of American manpower.

The weather on 4 June and the forecast for 5 June were so bad that Eisenhower had no option but to postpone the landings for twenty-four hours. Had he not been able to go ahead then, there would not be another

---

* As the American beaches were added when it was decided to assault with five divisions and not three, there was a gap of twenty miles between the westernmost British beach (Gold) and the westernmost American beach (Utah). The tide sweeps up the Channel from west to east, hence low tide (and the time of landing) was an hour earlier for the Americans.

window when weather, tides and moon would be right for several weeks. It would have been almost impossible to keep this vast operation secret from the Germans for that length of time, to say nothing of the problems of recalling ships and unloading men and equipment. From 2300 hours on 5 June 8,000 British and 16,000 American paratroopers and glider troops took off from airfields all over southern England to be dropped into occupied France. Of all the airborne troops, from one British and two American divisions, 75 per cent took no part in the battle. They were dropped in the wrong place and got lost, dropped in the sea and drowned, or dropped in flooded fields, losing their radios and heavy weapons. Then and now everyone blames the pilots, and it is true that many of them were inexperienced, particularly at dropping paratroopers. In fairness, although the weather was better than it had been twenty-four hours before, it was still bad, and the combination of cloud, wind and rain that made navigation difficult, and anti-aircraft fire, forced the aircraft to spread out too widely. Aircraft dropping paratroopers need to fly in as tight a formation as possible so that the soldiers all land in the same area and can reorganise and get on with the job with minimum delay. When in fact they were dropped all over Normandy, men reacted in different ways. Some simply went to ground and waited until the war reached them some days later; some wandered around trying to find their way and were captured, some refused to be discommoded and headed for the nearest objective, whether it was theirs or not. Parachute operations are always planned on the sledgehammer-cracking-nut principle, because many of the troops will not get to the area of the objective, particularly at night, either because they will break ankles or worse on landing, or will land in the wrong place. Fortunately, on the night of 5–6 June there were enough paratroopers and glider troops who used their initiative, and all the objectives were taken, even if many were not taken by the men or in the manner that the planners intended.

The great fleet of ships moved through mine-swept lanes towards the coast of Normandy, one hundred miles from the English coast. Overhead, formations of bombers flew on to add a finishing touch to what they had started three months before. If a bomber formation could not find its target it was to return to the UK – there were so many aircraft in the sky that staying in the area and trying to find the target was not possible. In fact, due to the difficult weather conditions, the results of the bombing on D-Day were negligible, and by far the greater damage was done by naval gunfire. The abiding memory of all those who took part in the Normandy landings is one of noise: from aircraft flying overhead and, particularly, from the naval bombardment, ranging from the 15-inch guns on battleships to rockets from specially designed monitors, to army artillery firing from its landing ships. On the British Gold and Sword beaches the landings took place on time and as planned. On Juno, because of an offshore reef, timings were particularly critical: too early and the beach obstacles would still be covered by water; too late and the landing craft would hit the reef; even later and the tide would be coming in again and covering the obstacles. As it was, anxious to avoid the reef, 3 Canadian Division was late, the Germans had woken up and of the 306 landing craft ninety were sunk or damaged by mines, beach obstacles or German artillery. Even so, the Canadians got ashore and captured their immediate objectives.

The Germans were caught completely by surprise. The few ships of the German navy that were in the area had been told to cancel their patrol programme for the night 5–6 June because of bad weather; the senior commanders of Dollman's Seventh Army were all away in Rennes at a study period, and Rommel was on leave in Germany celebrating his wife's birthday. Even the scattering of the airborne troops worked in the Allies' favour because the Germans were unable to figure out their exact purpose and objectives. When senior commanders in Normandy and in Berlin were told that landings were in progress they believed that it was only a feint, and that the real landings would come in the Pas de Calais. It was several days before they reluctantly accepted that Normandy was the real thing, by which time it was too late.

Only at Omaha beach did the American 1 and 29 Divisions run into trouble. Omaha was always going to be difficult: it was four miles long, the longest of the invasion beaches; it was more exposed to the weather than the others, and it was overlooked along its entire length by a low but dominating escarpment. The planners knew this but reckoned it would be offset by the low quality of the defenders, who were mainly

Poles and Russians unlikely to fight very hard at this stage of the war. Unknown to the Allies, however, was the presence of 352 Division, an experienced German formation that had been withdrawn from the Eastern Front, brought back up to strength and re-equipped in Germany, and then sent to Normandy in January 1944. Ultra had failed to pick up this fact because the divisional commander had imposed radio silence until an invasion happened; the French resistance, such as it was, did not report the division's arrival because the civilian population had been moved out of the area. Stout and professional defence, and the launching of 1 US Division's DD tanks too far out, putting most of them on the bottom, led to 'Bloody Omaha', as it was named in the purple prose of the time, costing the Americans about 600 of the Allied total of 2,500 dead on D-Day. That toll was a mere pittance compared to battles in the First War, or to what it might have been in this one, but at one point it had Bradley considering diverting troops not yet landed to the flanking beaches. Fortunately the commander 352 Division, believing he had scotched attempts to land on Omaha, began to pull out his units and divert them to other threatened areas, and the Americans were able to take and hold Omaha.[2]

On Sword, the most easterly beach, the British reverted to type on landing. 3 Division was a regular division. It had fought in the Battle of France when it had been commanded by Montgomery, and it had been evacuated from Dunkirk. Since then it had been on anti-invasion duties in England, and then training for Overlord. It had not seen any active service for four years and those who had been with the division in 1940 were still defensively minded and nervous of the German soldier. The task of the division after landing was to advance inland and attack and capture Caen, supported by troops from Juno beach next door. As the centre of Caen was nine miles from the beaches, this was asking rather a lot, but to expect the division to get within striking distance of the port was not unreasonable. Although the landing was to be carried out by a heavily reinforced division on each beach, the first wave would be four companies, two from each of two battalions of the lead brigade. On Sword the lead brigade of 3 Division, 8 Brigade, was to put four companies ashore in the first wave, two each from 2 East Yorkshires and 1 South Lancashires.

Once on the beach and secure, the brigade, including its third battalion 1 Suffolks, was to push on four miles south and take up a position on Perriers Ridge, when 185 Brigade, the second brigade to come ashore, with the Staffordshire Yeomanry (Shermans) of 27 Armoured Brigade, would pass through and take part in the assault on Caen.

At first all went well, and by 0930 hours the South Lancashires were off the beach and into Hermanville, a mile or so south of the landing, although the East Yorkshires and the Suffolks were meeting increasing German resistance. Beyond Hermanville, on the approach to Perriers, the Lancashires came under fire from some German infantry and what appeared to be anti-tank guns dug in on the ridge. Knowing from his German army handbook that the standard German tactic was to put anti-tank guns forward with armour concealed behind them, the commanding officer of the Lancashires decided to wait for 185 Brigade and the tanks. That brigade had got ashore, but the commanding officer of the lead battalion, 2 King's Shropshire Light Infantry, chose not to press on until it could do so with the Staffordshire Yeomanry. That regiment was having problems getting on to an overcrowded beach, and even more problems getting off it. Eventually the KSLI were told to press forward on foot, and some while later the Yeomanry got off the beach; but it was not until around 1400 hours that 185 Brigade and its tanks reached Perriers, by which time it was far too late.

To expect one brigade and a regiment of tanks to capture a large and well-defended port such as Caen was nonsense anyway. Montgomery should have known better, but this was a time to throw caution to the winds and crack on: if the commander of 8 Brigade on the beach had thrown in the DD Shermans and pushed the KSLI on with them, then Perriers Ridge could have been taken quickly, before German armour appeared, and 185 Brigade could have been pushed through. That brigade might not have captured Caen – almost certainly it could not have – but it would have been well placed to act as the springboard for a weightier attack a day or two later. As it was, defensive-mindedness, caution and reluctance – fear almost – to depart from pre-arranged plans and orders held everyone back and the opportunity was gone.

Next day the tactical ineptitude of an army that had supposedly been at war for four and a half years was tragically demonstrated north of Carpiquet, the largest and nearest airfield to Caen and one that the RAF wanted as soon as possible, for it would add a hundred miles in range and much more time over target than was available by flying to and from the UK. The capture of Carpiquet, west of Caen and ten miles south of the beaches, was entrusted to 9 Canadian Brigade supported by the Sherbrooke Fusiliers, which despite its name was an armoured regiment equipped with Shermans. The leading elements of the brigade reached Villers-les-Buissons by last light on 6 June, and intended to push on for Carpiquet, only five miles away, next morning. It was unfortunate for 9 Brigade that the area over which they intended to advance was the forming-up place for a German counter-attack on the beaches to be carried out by 12 SS Panzer and 21 Panzer Divisions, and that 9 Brigade's axis was across the area where elements of 25 SS Panzer Grenadier Regiment had been getting into position during the night.

The Waffen SS has had a bad press. The SS was an independent organisation within the NSDAP, with wide-reaching responsibilities. It was almost a state within a state, and included the secret police (the Gestapo), the security police, the various states' criminal police forces, the state security apparatus (the SD) and the race and settlement office. It had a commercial arm, a foreign intelligence department and had publishing and educational interests. Most notoriously, the SS was responsible for the administration and guarding of concentration camps. This has led to the assumption that everyone in the SS was engaged in the gassing of Jews, which was far from the case. Members of the Waffen, or armed, SS were equipped and trained as soldiers, and came under the army for operational purposes, while retaining SS ranks, having their own training organisation and depending on the SS for administration. The men of the Waffen SS were all volunteers, or conscripts who then opted for the SS. They were highly motivated, and their units were among the most capable in the German army. At regimental level they had few equals, but at divisional level and above they suffered from a shortage of trained staff officers, leading to a number of army officers having to transfer across to the SS. By the end of the war there were thirty-eight Waffen SS divisions, but these included Norwegian, Danish, Croatian, Latvian,

Ukrainian, Hungarian, Albanian, Italian, Slovene, Serbian, Belgian, Byelorussian, Russian and French volunteers. Although the standards inevitably dropped as time went on, casualties among Waffen SS units were heavy and it is estimated that between 20–25 per cent of all Waffen SS soldiers were killed in the war.[3]

It is often claimed that 12 SS Panzer was composed of schoolboys because of its honorific title of Hitler Jugend or HJ. In fact, the most recent recruits to this division were from the class of 1925, so the youngest members of it were nineteen.[4] The regiment that the Canadians would meet on 7 June consisted of three motorised infantry battalions, a company of six self-propelled 105mm guns, an anti-aircraft company of 12 towed 20mm guns, a recce company and a pioneer company.[*] In support and under command were thirty Mk IV tanks of 2 SS Panzer Battalion. The regiment was commanded by Standartenführer (colonel) Kurt 'Panzer' Meyer, aged thirty-four, who would in time become the youngest general officer in the German army. Meyer had carefully concealed his infantry, his guns and the supporting tanks so as not to be spotted from the air. They were in orchards, in farmyards, in woods and in folds in the ground. He established his tactical headquarters in the roof of the ruined Ardennes Abbey, where with his tank and artillery commanders he could see the whole of the area and control his units by radio. Meyer watched with interest as at 0745 hours the Canadian tanks poked their noses out of Villers-les-Buissons, and moved, painfully slowly, along the minor road leading to the village of Authie. In the lead were Stuart recce tanks, then one infantry company of the Nova Scotia Highlanders in carriers, followed by that battalion's other three companies riding on the Shermans of the Sherbrooke Fusiliers. It took the leading tanks until 1300 hours to cover the two miles to the village of Authie. Caution is all very well, but had they not stuck almost exclusively to the road and ignored the woods and orchards to their flanks, they might have discovered the waiting Germans, who watched silently without firing a shot, no doubt thinking that all their Christmases were about to come at once.

[*] In the British army men of the Royal Pioneer Corps were humpers and dumpers and drawn from the less intellectually gifted brethren, or men with medical conditions, such as perforated eardrums, that made them unfit for the infantry. In the German army pioneers were skilled men more akin to field engineers.

Finding Authie empty, the Sherbrooke Fusiliers and the Nova Scotians pushed on another half-mile to the hamlet of Franqueville, less than a mile from Carpiquet airfield. At this stage the tanks and the infantry were strung out over a distance of about two miles, and it was then that Meyer, from his eyrie on the abbey roof, gave the order to pounce. Infantry and tanks hit the Canadians from hull-down positions to their front and from their left flank. By last light the whole thing was over; the Canadians were back where they started and Carpiquet would not be captured for another month. The Sherbrooke Fusiliers lost twenty-one tanks destroyed and another seven damaged. The Germans had fired just forty rounds of anti-tank ammunition. The Nova Scotia Highlanders had eighty-four men killed, 158 wounded and 128 taken prisoner. 9 Brigade reported twenty Mk IV and eleven Tigers destroyed. There were no Tigers in the area, and the Germans actually lost nine Mk IV. 9 Brigade was far too slow and used ground badly, the brigade commander failed to deploy his other two battalions when he could and should have done, and the divisional commander, Major General Keller, failed to get a grip of the brigade. German concealment, fire discipline and coordination had prevailed once again.

That night a number of Canadian prisoners were shot by men of 25 SS Panzer Grenadier Regiment, after an attempted escape. In 1945 a war crimes trial found Meyer guilty of being responsible for the shooting of eighteen of those prisoners, although not for the deaths of another thirty odd. The court sentenced Meyer to death, but this was commuted to life imprisonment by the reviewing officer on the grounds that the evidence against Meyer was 'hearsay and circumstantial'.[5] He was released in 1954 and died in 1961.*

The British had met the German Mk VI Tiger tank in Tunisia, although mercifully few of them, and they would meet it again in Normandy. A tank that they had not met before was the German Mk V Panther. By 1944 the Panther was officially the standard German main battle tank,

---

* It has to be said that this author has been told by more than one British soldier that German prisoners were shot in Normandy and after because there were insufficient men to guard them. This does not excuse the shooting of prisoners, which is never acceptable, but it does make it understandable. In the west war crimes of this nature were rare, but they were not confined to one side only.

although many much-improved Mk IVs were still in service. The Panther was designed as a result of experience in Russia, and copied the wide tracks and the sloping armour of the Russian T 34. British tanks in Normandy were the Cromwell for armoured reconnaissance regiments, the Cromwell, Sherman and the Firefly in armoured regiments, and the Churchill in army tank brigades. The Firefly was a Sherman with an adapted turret to take a 17-pounder gun, in place of the standard 75mm, and there was one per troop in armoured regiments. Comparisons of British and German tanks in Normandy were:

TYPE	WEIGHT	FRONTAL ARMOUR	MAIN ARMAMENT	SPEED	RANGE	PENETRATION AT 1,000 YDS
British Sherman	32 tons	2.59-inch	75mm gun	25 mph	130 miles	2.36 inches
Firefly	32 tons	2.59-inch	17-pdr gun	25 mph	130 miles	5.12 inches
Cromwell	28 tons	2.99-inch	75mm gun	31 mph	173 miles	2.36 inches
Churchill	39 tons	4.02-inch	75mm gun	15 mph	88 miles	2.36 inches
German Mk IV	22 tons	3.15-inch	75mm gun	25 mph	130 miles	3.03 inches
Mk V (Panther)	44 tons	3.15-inch	75mm gun	34 mph	110 miles	4.64 inches
Mk VI (Tiger)	56 tons	3.94-inch	88mm gun	23 mph	121 miles	4.01 inches

This meant that all German tanks could knock out all British tanks at 1,000 yards, whereas at the same range only the Firefly could knock out any German tanks at all, and there were only twelve Fireflies in an armoured regiment. One might wonder why all British Shermans were not turned into Fireflies, and the answer is that there was simply not enough industrial capacity to do it. When the German 88mm towed anti-tank gun is taken into account, which in its 1944 version could penetrate five and a half inches of armour at 2,000 yards – well outside the range that a British tank could hit a target, never mind knock it out – it will be seen just how inferior Allied armour still was.

Perhaps the nadir of British incompetence during the Normandy campaign was the Battle of Villers Bocage on 13 June. With the failure to capture Caen on Day One, the British tried various approaches to that city in the subsequent days and weeks. On 12 June the Americans captured Caumont, twenty miles west of Caen. The British knew from Ultra intercepts that the German panzer division in that area, Panzer Lehr (the panzer training and demonstration division) had given up the idea of counter-attacking and was now defending against an expected attack from the north, with only flank guards out to the west. Running south-west from Caen, behind Panzer Lehr's positions and as far as Villers Bocage, was a long ridge, and if the British could get on to that then perhaps they could push along it to capture Caen. Commander Second Army, Dempsey, thought that a thrust from Caumont south-east to Villers Bocage and then on to the ridge might achieve surprise, and as a secondary aim might cut off Panzer Lehr. Dempsey conferred with Montgomery and Lieutenant General Bucknall, commanding XXX Corps, who both agreed, and 7 Armoured Division, 'The Desert Rats', were ordered to Caumont. There, at 1145 hours on 12 June, Major General Bobby Erskine was briefed to go for Villers Bocage. He was able to sort out his division, take the corps reconnaissance regiment (11th Hussars) under command and get on his way by 1630 hours, which was near-incredible speed for a British division.

At this stage 7 Armoured consisted of a divisional reconnaissance regiment (8th Hussars), two field regiments, an anti-tank regiment and a light anti-aircraft regiment Royal Artillery, two field squadrons and a field-park squadron Royal Engineers,[*] divisional signals, a motor machine-gun company, one armoured brigade (22 Armoured Brigade) and one lorried infantry brigade (131 Infantry Brigade). The armoured brigade, commanded by Brigadier 'Loony' Hinde, had three tank regiments and a motorised infantry battalion in carriers and half-tracks, while Brigadier Michael Elkin's infantry brigade had one armoured regiment and three infantry battalions in three-ton lorries. For this operation Erskine reorganised his division. 22 Armoured Brigade, in the lead, would have 4 County of London Yeomanry (Cromwells), 5 RTR, 1 Rifle Brigade (motorised), 1/7 Queen's (lorried), a Field Regiment RA with self-propelled 25-pounders and an engineer troop. Their task was to capture Villers Bocage and then push on up the ridge to Point 213. 131 Brigade was to follow on and be prepared to exploit along the ridge, and would have 1 RTR, 2/7 and 3/7 Queen's (lorried) and a field regiment with towed 25-pounders. The two recce regiments would provide flank protection except for one squadron of 8th Hussars which would be with 131 Brigade.

* The Royal Engineers had just moved from companies to squadrons, for no good reason save elitism.

En route the lead brigade ran into an anti-tank ambush just the other side of Briquessard. This was cleared but by then it was about 2000 hours and the brigade commander decided to spend the night there and press on in the morning. The divisional commander agreed, and it was a perfectly reasonable decision. Tanks on the narrow, tree-lined French roads were vulnerable at the best of times, and more so at night. At 0530 hours on 13 June, just after first light, the lead elements of the brigade, 4 County of London Yeomanry (4 CLY) group, pressed on towards Villers Bocage, which they reached at about 0800 hours. Assured by the inhabitants that there were no Germans in the area, the commanding officer, Lieutenant Colonel the Viscount Cranley,[*] ordered A Squadron group to push on up the ridge to Point 213, less than a mile away. There was one road up the ridge, and it was narrow, with trees and bushes close to the road on either side. The squadron tanks, with an artillery tank and followed by A Company of the Rifle Brigade in carriers and the regimental recce troop in Stuarts, now headed up this road.

Vital ground to the attacker is vital ground to the defender too, and the Germans were more than capable of appreciating the importance of Point 213. Unknown to the British, 101 SS Heavy Panzer Battalion of Tiger tanks were on their way. The battalion had left Paris on D-Day and had experienced all manner of difficulties in getting to Normandy, including air attacks, wrecked trains and blocked roads. By 12 June, when they were in the Normandy area, they had only eighteen tanks left and they were well over the recommended limit of track mileage. Two companies were ordered to Noyers Bocage, the next village up and about five miles north-east of Villers Bocage, and a third company of five Tigers[**] to Point 213. That company was commanded by Obersturm-führer (lieutenant) Michael Wittmann, something of a legend in his battalion for his record in knocking out Russian armoured vehicles. On the night of 12 June Wittmann leaguered his tanks on the southern side of the ridge, with a piquet on the high ground. Early next morning the piquet reported the noise of moving tanks, and Wittmann, knowing that

[*] A Territorial officer and later the Earl of Onslow, he began the war as a captain.
[**] One may have been a Mk IV.

the only German tanks in the area were his, and they were not moving, walked up to the ridge from where he could see the British tanks lining up in the town. He brought his five Tigers up the hill, hid them off the road among the trees, and waited.

The County of London Yeomanry's A Squadron group motored up the road, arrived nose to tail at Point 213 and began to brew up (tea, not the tanks, at least not yet). Wittmann emerged in his Tiger, fired at the last tank of the CLY knocking it out and thus blocking the road, and then drove down the hill parallel to the road, shooting up carriers as he went. When he got into Villers Bocage he caused chaos there, too, before driving back up the hill, where the rest of his company were knocking out the tanks and other vehicles of A Squadron group. The commanding officer of the CLY went up the hill to see what was happening and got caught in the mêlée; the brigadier, Hinde, appeared, sent 1/7 Queens into Villers Bocage on foot and then disappeared, not being seen again until late afternoon. The commander of 131 Brigade, Elkins, arrived in Villers Bocage, remarked that the situation appeared hopeless and left, not being seen again by anyone until the next morning. Wittmann now reappeared in Villers Bocage in his Tiger, when his luck ran out and he was fired on by a number of British tanks and at least one anti-tank gun. His Tiger disabled, he baled out with his crew and got back to his own battalion headquarters on foot that evening.

Up on the hill, the entire CLY Squadron group ceased to exist. Altogether, including those in Villers Bocage, twenty Cromwells, four Fireflies, three Stuarts, three artillery tanks, fourteen half-tracks and two 6- pounder guns were destroyed. In the Rifle Brigade sixteen men were killed and in the Yeomanry fourteen. All the rest, including the commanding officer of 4 CLY, were taken prisoner, save one, the second-in-command of the Rifle Brigade company, who escaped. For the commander of 7 Armoured Division there was no question of pressing on, and the division withdrew from Villers Bocage over the next two days, assisted by the RAF who destroyed the town by bombing. Villers Bocage was not recaptured until 4 August. One understrength company had forced the withdrawal of an entire armoured division.

The County of London Yeomanry was not a green regiment having its introduction to battle; it had served in North Africa and its officers and men were highly experienced. True, that that experience was in the wide open desert, where engagements happened at a range of 1,000 yards, rather than in the close country west of Caen where the Germans would mount ambushes from a few yards away; but the regiment had been in France for a week and should have realised that things happened differently there. The Germans, too, were used to wide, sweeping movement and engagement at long range in the vast plains of Russia, and yet they were able to make the transition considerably more quickly than the British. It was (and is) axiomatic that in close country the infantry should dismount and go first, and if the squadron commander of A Squadron had ordered A Company of the Rifle Brigade to dismount and clear either side of the road up the hill, they would have found the German tanks and the disaster would not have occurred. If the squadron commander was incompetent, then Cranley, who saw them start for the ridge, should have ordered it. As it was, the commanding officer and the squadron commander were guilty of a tactical error that would be inexcusable in a subaltern. The Regimental History says: 'With the loss of Regimental Headquarters and one complete squadron, 4 CLY had suffered a setback from which a lesser regiment might have found it difficult to recover'.[6] One cannot help remarking that a better regiment would not have allowed it to happen in the first place.

Both brigade commanders, the divisional commander, Erskine, and the corps commander, Bucknall, were eventually (although not immediately) sacked, but one wonders why they were there in the first place. Wittmann was killed two weeks later, and, having become a legend to the British as well, was claimed by everyone from the Northamptonshire Yeomanry (who published a pamphlet about it) to the Canadians and the Poles. He was actually killed by a rocket-firing Typhoon of the RAF and is buried in La Cambe German cemetery.[*]

The Germans were not helped by political interference from Berlin. German officers were trained to fight a mobile war: withdrawal to regroup

---

[*] Many of us as subalterns dreamed of getting senior officers sacked, but Wittmann must be one of the very few lieutenants in any army who can claim the scalps of a lieutenant general, a major general and two brigadiers!

and then counter-attack was a normal tactic, and fighting to the last round in static defence was not part of the German doctrine. When it became obvious that the Allied invasion was not going to be pushed back into the sea, Rundstedt wanted to abandon the Cotentin Peninsula and fight a mobile defence back to the River Seine. Hitler insisted that Cotentin and the port of Cherbourg be defended, and when the Americans finally captured Cherbourg on 30 June the entire garrison was lost. Admittedly 4,000 of these were Russians and Poles, but 15,000 were Germans who could have been used to far greater purpose if they had been allowed to withdraw. As Cherbourg fell the Americans were also closing up on St-Lô and Rundstedt and Rommel flew to Berlin to try to persuade Hitler and OKW that if a tactical withdrawal was not authorised, the Seventh Army would be cut off and destroyed. Hitler refused to sanction any rearward move and when a German counter-attack on the River Odon on 1 July failed, Rundstedt told Keitel by telephone that all Germany could now do was to make peace. Keitel told Hitler, and Rundstedt[*] was sacked yet again, being replaced by Field Marshal von Kluge, who had been on sick leave after a vehicle accident on the Eastern Front.

The Normandy campaign dragged on, and it has to be admitted that whenever the British (or the Americans) met the Germans on equal terms, the Germans won. Of course the Allies rarely did meet the Germans on equal terms: the Allies had complete air supremacy and only when bad weather intervened could the Germans move vehicles easily by day; it may have taken three, or five, Shermans to knock out a Tiger, but the Allies could produce lots more Shermans whereas the Germans, although they could still turn out tanks and aircraft, despite the bombing of Germany, found it increasingly difficult to get them to the front.

The plan for Normandy had always envisaged the British holding while the Americans broke out on their front, the Allied advance hinging around Caen, which was eventually captured on 10 July. The American breakout, Operation Cobra, was dependent upon the British drawing the German armour on to their front and keeping it there, and to do this Montgomery intended to launch Operation Goodwood, a thrust from east of the River Orne and south past the eastern suburbs of Caen to the

---

* He was recalled yet again two months later as Commander-in-Chief West, then based in Koblenz, Germany.

Bourguébus Ridge on 18 July. There would be the heaviest carpet bombing yet seen in this war, after which three armoured divisions, supported by rocket-firing Typhoons, would advance down a narrow corridor, scattering all before them. It would be so overpowering that the Germans would have to concentrate all their armour to oppose it: they would fail and be 'written down', as Montgomery put it.

The reality was very different. Beginning at 0535 hours, more than 2,000 aircraft of various types dropped nearly 8,000 tons of bombs on an area seven miles deep by five miles wide. At 0745 hours 11 Armoured Division crossed the start line, to be followed up by the Guards Armoured Division and 7 Armoured Division. Despite bombing that in Lieutenant Freiherr von Rosen's 3 Company of 503 Heavy Panzer Battalion blew one Tiger tank upside down, drove one soldier stark raving mad and caused another to shoot himself, the Germans reorganised remarkably quickly. Fighting a mobile and elastic defence in depth they made the British look like rank amateurs. The huge preponderance of RAF fighters on call was quickly dealt with when the Germans simply knocked out the armoured vehicles that sprouted numerous antennae, used by RAF officers to direct the close air-support Typhoons. The British had insufficient infantry to deal with the German anti-tank gun defence, including the 88s that shot up the Shermans before they could get within range. By last light the attack had got nowhere near its objectives and 11 Armoured Division had lost over half its strength. Goodwood petered out on 21 July and the Germans withdrew at their own pace. The British had lost 353 tanks, the Germans seventy-five.

All would still have been well if it had not been for Montgomery's posturing. The stated aim of the operation had been to draw the German armour on to the British front. It had done just that, even if it had only 'written down' 20 per cent of it, and it did allow the Americans to break out from St-Lô. Montgomery, however, in a press conference at the close of the first day insisted that all was going well and that a breakout was imminent. Apart from the fact that Montgomery was never supposed to be breaking out, when it became clear what had really happened, and when there was an attempt to recall maps showing objectives much farther away than were actually reached, and when Montgomery continued to insist, against all the evidence, that all had gone according to his master plan, he was exposed for the fake that he was. All the boasting, the childishness, the insensitivity, the denigration of the Americans, all came to a head. This was the time when Montgomery should have been sacked, indeed Air Chief Marshal Tedder, the Deputy Supreme Commander, recommended that he should be. The most difficult operation of the war – Overlord – was a fact, and all that was needed now was a competent commander to oversee the British part in ending the war in the west. Montgomery was no longer essential – if he ever had been – and there were many others who could take over. Alexander could have been brought back from Italy, and if he had been the constant inter-Allied bickering and the vicious post-war battle of the memoirs could have been avoided. The British had made Montgomery into a hero, however, and they could not admit that they had been wrong, nor could they publicly acknowledge that the Messiah had feet of clay. Montgomery stayed, but his reputation had taken a blow from which it would not recover in the eyes of senior commanders of both Allies, and he had now lost any chance of continuing as Allied land forces commander.

While post-war Germany has tried, for perfectly understandable reasons, to create a myth of German resistance, the 20 July 1944 assassination attempt on Hitler involved only a very small number of officers, who would have taken no action at all if Hitler had continued to give them victories. Rommel's great apologist, his son Manfred, later mayor of Stuttgart, has maintained that Rommel was an anti-Nazi, and this legend has been perpetuated into the modern German armed forces, and although the memory of most of their Second War generals has been allowed to lapse, there are a number of Rommel barracks, a Rommel ship and even a Regiment Rommel. Rommel leapt on the NSDAP bandwagon to gain promotion, was one of the few senior officers to greet Hitler with the Fascist salute and his attitude to the 20 July plot was almost certainly 'if it works, count me in; if it doesn't, I know nothing about it'. Most German officers did not approve of the plot, not because they liked, admired, or even agreed with Hitler but because, as Field Marshal von Manstein said:

As one responsible for an army group in the field I did not feel I had the right
to contemplate a *coup d'état* in wartime because in my own view it would
have led to an immediate collapse of the front and probably to chaos inside
Germany. Apart from this, there was always the question of the military
oath and the admissibility of murder for political motives.[7]

The July plot, the aftermath of which swept up Rommel (recuperating
at home, having been shot up by the RAF), von Kluge, the retired field
Marshal von Witzleben and numerous other less eminent figures,
increased Hitler's distrust of the army general staff, and made any suggestion of withdrawal liable to be considered treasonable. By the end of
July, when the American Cobra advance had got as far as Avranches, it
was becoming increasingly obvious that if Seventh Army, now commanded by SS-Oberstgruppenführer (colonel general) Paul Hauser,[*] did
not withdraw it was liable to be encircled and cut off. Appeals to OKW
fell on deaf ears, Field Marshal von Kluge shot himself on the way back to
Berlin to be questioned about the July plot, and his replacement, Field
Marshal Model, only received permission to withdraw by saying that he
needed to do so to concentrate for an offensive that he had no intention
of launching. Meanwhile the Americans were pressing in from the west
and south, and the British, slowly and amid much Anglo-American
acrimony, from the north.

By the time Model could begin to extricate his army from Falaise it
was far too late; 100,000 German soldiers were in a pocket twenty miles
from west to east and ten miles from north to south. On 19 August troops
of the American 90 Division met the 20th Mounted Rifles (part of a Polish
armoured division under British command) at Montormel. 1 SS Panzer
Division Leibstandarte Adolf Hitler made valiant efforts to keep open
gaps to the west, and some 30,000 men did get away, but without most
of their heavy equipment. Hauser, the army commander, was wounded
and taken out on the deck of a tank, while 'Panzer' Meyer found a guide
to safety by putting a pistol to the head of a French farmer. But with 3,000
aircraft sorties every day the Battle of Falaise sounded the death knell of
the German Seventh Army: 10,000 were killed and 50,000 taken prisoner;

* Colonel General Dollman, refused permission to withdraw, had shot himself.

500 tanks, 700 guns and 7,000 other vehicles were destroyed or captured. On 19 August the Normandy campaign was over, and the road to Paris open. On 25 August the German garrison commander of Paris surrendered the city intact, despite being ordered to do so only as a heap of ruins. If the Seventh Army had still existed, getting across the Seine and anywhere near Paris would have been a great deal more difficult.

On 1 September Eisenhower took over command of the land forces from Montgomery, who was promoted to field marshal and reverted to command of the British 21 Army Group, while Bradley assumed command of the American 12 Army Group. Until a working port farther north on the Channel coast could be captured, all supplies including food, fuel and ammunition had to come through Normandy, and there was insufficient transport to meet the needs of the two British and the (eventual) one French and four American armies. Montgomery, supported by Bradley, wanted a concentrated thrust into Germany whereas Eisenhower preferred a safer broad-front approach. Much of this dispute was political: the Americans suspected the British of wanting to let the Russians and the Germans fight each other to a standstill after which they could decide the shape of Europe, whereas the British suspected the Americans of making concessions to the Russians in Europe in exchange for a Russian declaration of war against Japan (which never came). There was some truth in both viewpoints, and certainly the British were concerned – with good reason – to keep the Russians as far to the east as they could.

The role of 21 Army Group now was to make for Belgium and Holland, while Bradley's US army group struck towards the German border and the West Wall (the Siegfried Line). The Canadian First Army (of one Canadian and one British corps) pushed up the Channel coast, one of their aims now being to clear flying-bomb and rocket sites. The Germans began launching V1 flying bombs against England in June 1944. The RAF and the Royal Artillery learned how to shoot them down fairly quickly, although they did kill over 6,000 people. Much more serious was the supersonic V2 rocket, against which there was no defence. The Germans launched the first V2 against England in early September, and unlike the V1 it could be launched from mobile platforms. The V2 killed nearly 3,000 Londoners and the attacks went on until the end of March 1945, when the last launching areas in the Netherlands were overrun. The V weapons came far too late to affect the course of the war, but the British government was very worried about public morale, and casualties caused by V weapons were not admitted to until much later.

On 3 September the British reached Brussels, and the next day they captured the port of Antwerp, although to the great annoyance of the Royal Navy it could not be used until the army cleared the Germans out of the seaward approach to it, the Scheldt estuary, which it was not able to do until early November. Now came an operation which was so untypical of Montgomery – the meticulous, cautious plodder – that one has to wonder who put it into his mind in the first place. Between Belgium and northern Germany lay the canals and rivers of Holland, considerable obstacles that the Allies would have to cross before getting to grips with the defences of the West Wall. Montgomery's plan was in two parts. Operation Market would use paratroopers and glider troops of the First Allied Airborne Army to seize bridges over the canals at Zon and Veghel, the River Maas at Grave, the River Waal at Nijmegen and the Lower Rhine at Arnhem before the Germans could blow them up. In Operation Garden, meanwhile, the British XXX Corps would send an armoured thrust on a narrow front sixty miles in three days through German-held territory to link up with those bridges. This would outflank the West Wall and give the Allies a jumping-off spot to drive into the German industrial heartland of the Ruhr. Eisenhower agreed the plan and gave Montgomery priority for logistical support.

On 17 September the American 101 Airborne Division dropped and took the bridges at Veghel intact, and the 82nd did the same at Grave, while the British 1 Airborne Division dropped farthest away, at Arnhem. Almost immediately it all started to go wrong. The bridge at Zon had been demolished, German resistance was much stiffer than had been estimated, 1 Airborne were too slow in getting their second and subsequent lifts in, British intelligence had either not known about or had ignored reports of two SS armoured divisions, 9 and 10 SS Panzer, refitting in the area and which had just finished an exercise to test measures to deal with an airborne landing; the British landed too far away from the

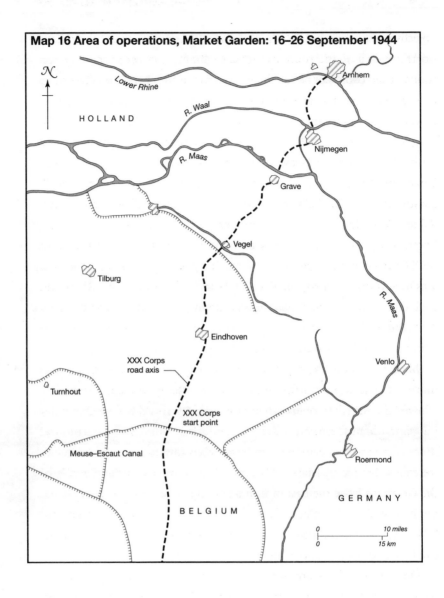

Map 16 Area of operations, Market Garden: 16–26 September 1944

objectives and while 2nd Battalion the Parachute Regiment did capture the northern end of the road bridge at Arnhem, they were quickly surrounded and could not be reinforced, and the railway bridge was blown up by the Germans. The armoured thrust was delayed by the need for the Royal Engineers to put a Bailey Bridge over the canal at Zon, but XXX Corps linked up with 82 Airborne in the evening of 18 September, and with 101 Airborne at Grave on the morning of 19 September. On 20 September the bridge at Nijmegen was captured in a joint attack by US paratroopers and XXX Corps, but the latter was now well behind schedule, XII and VIII Corps, to the west and east of XXX Corps, were moving 'depressingly slowly', as even Montgomery admitted, and in the event XXX Corps could not get to Arnhem. The best that could be done now was to withdraw 1 Airborne Division to the south side of the Rhine and evacuate them. Of the 9,000 men dropped or landed at Arnhem, only 2,300 got back, the rest being killed or captured. Total US casualties were about 3,500 killed, wounded and missing.

Market Garden was a disaster, but even if it had succeeded, it seems unlikely that a German army commanded by Model would have passively allowed the British to operate from the end of a corridor forty-five miles long and only fifteen miles wide. It could easily have been cut off and there was enough German armour in the area to do just that. As it was, the salient gained by Market Garden was of some use in the clearing of the Germans from the east of Nijmegen in January and February 1945, but it could have been equally well done at far less cost. The Allies still had to get across the Rhine, but before they could do so the Germans still had a number of shots left in their locker.

On 16 December eight panzer divisions appeared as if from nowhere out of the Ardennes, a little north of where they had done it in 1940, and fell upon the US VIII Corps like a pack of ravening wolves. Bad weather grounded the Allied air forces, English-speaking members of the Brandenburg regiment in American uniforms spread alarm and despondency behind the Allied lines, and 101 Airborne Division, which was hastily thrown in from resting after Market Garden, was surrounded at Bastogne. The Germans had achieved complete surprise for the Battle of the Ardennes, or the Battle of the Bulge, the aim of which was to capture

Antwerp and cut the Allies in two using, from north to south, Sixth SS and Fifth Panzer Armies and Seventh Army. By Christmas Eve the Germans had pushed the Americans back fifty miles almost to Dinant, before their fuel ran out and the weather allowed Allied aircraft to fly again. Montgomery took command of all Allied forces north of the bulge and Patton of all south of it, and it took until 7 February 1945 for the British and the Americans to eliminate the German salient. Montgomery could not resist infuriating the Americans yet again by claiming that he had saved them from disaster. It says much for the skill and training of the German army that even in the last few months of the war in Europe, and having suffered around 700,000 casualties in the west since Overlord, it could still mount this sort of operation – an operation that very nearly succeeded. Had it done so it would not have altered the result of the war, but by allowing the Germans to hold in the west and switch armour to the east, it would have delayed it.

The RAF's Bomber Command, actively assisted by Lieutenant General Carl Spaatz's Eighth United States Air Force, was still engaged in what Harris described as de-housing the German population. At the Allied conference at Yalta in February 1945 the Soviets asked for British and American strategic bombing to assist their Vistula offensive, aimed eventually at Berlin, and the Allies had already drawn up a plan to bomb cities in eastern Germany to do just that. Operation Thunderclap began on 3 February with raids on Berlin and Magdeburg, and on the night of 13 February 1945 796 RAF Lancasters dropped 1,500 tons of high-explosive bombs and 1,200 tons of incendiaries on Dresden. Next day the city was attacked again by 311 American bombers. The firestorm started by the RAF and fuelled by the Americans destroyed the medieval centre of Dresden and may have killed up to 30,000 people in a city swollen by refugees fleeing the advance of the Soviet armies. The Dresden raid caused adverse comment in the press, and Churchill, quick to evade the blame for his own policy, said in a minute of 28 March 1945 to the Chief of the Air Staff: 'It remains a serious query against the conduct of Allied bombing.' This comment caused understandable anger in the Air Ministry and Churchill substituted it on 1 April with one that merely called for a review of bombing policy 'in our own interests'. [8]

Even today what happened to Dresden is cited by those who believe that Harris and his crews were guilty of some awful crime, and that somehow what they did was reprehensible, or unnecessary, coming as it did only three months before the end of the war. We know now that it was three months before the end of the war, but in February 1945 the Allies had only just stopped the German Ardennes offensive, they had not yet crossed the Rhine, and the V2s were still raining down on London. Dresden was just one more raid in a long war and was totally justified.

In March, in accordance with Eisenhower's policy of a broad front, the Allied armies closed up along the Rhine. The Germans were still fighting hard, but on 7 March the American First Army seized a railway bridge at Remagen before it could be blown, and established a bridgehead on the far side; on 14 March Patton's Third Army crossed the Moselle to outflank the Siegfried Line; on 23 March the British 51 (Highland) Division and the Canadian 3 Division crossed the Rhine near the Dutch border, and by the end of the month even the French were on the east side of that river. On 4 April 21 Army Group began to clear Holland, and particularly the V2 sites. Almost as important as dealing with German troops was getting food to a population only just above starvation level.[*] On 11 April the American Ninth Army reached the Elbe, the agreed demarcation line between the western Allies and the Russians, and two days later Soviet troops entered Vienna. The German military structure in the west was now beginning to break down. Individual units continued to fight on, but on 18 April all resistance in the Ruhr ceased, and the Russians were over the River Oder and advancing on Berlin. By 28 April the Russians were in Berlin and on 30 April Hitler shot himself in his command bunker in Berlin, after having nominated Grand Admiral Dönitz his successor as head of state. On 2 May the Berlin Reichstag finally fell to the Russians. On 4 May a German delegation surrendered all German forces in north-west Germany, the German islands, Schleswig Holstein and Denmark to Field Marshal Montgomery on Luneberg Heath. Over the next few days other Germans formations surrendered to the Americans and on 7 May Colonel General Jodl signed the surrender

---

[*] The Dutch railways had gone on strike to coincide with Market Garden, which in turn led the Germans to stop the Dutch importing food by rail.

of all German forces still in the field to all the Allies. On 15 May the last German soldiers still fighting laid down their arms. The war in Europe was over.

NOTES

1. Helmut Heiber and David M. Glantz (eds), *Hitler and his Generals, Military Conferences 1942–1945*, Enigma Books, New York, 2002.

2. Omar N. Bradley, *A Soldier's Story*, Henry Holt, New York, 1951.

3. I. C. B. Dear and M. R. D. Foot, *The Oxford Companion to the Second World War*, OUP, Oxford, 1995.

4. Michael Reynolds, *Steel Inferno: 1 SS Panzer Corps in Normandy*, Spellmount, Staplehurst, 1997.

5. Ibid.

6. Andrew Graham, *Sharpshooters at War*, CLY Regimental Association, London, 1964.

7. Field Marshal Erich von Manstein, *Lost Victories*, Greenhill, London, 1987.

8. John Terraine, *The Right of the Line*, Hodder & Stoughton, London, 1985.

Epilogue

IN EVERY WAR SOMEBODY has to take on the main enemy in the main theatre and defeat him. In the First World War that was the British Expeditionary Force on the Western Front. In the Second World War it was the Russian army on the Eastern Front, for even at the height of the 1944–45 campaign in north-west Europe there was never more than 25 per cent of the Wehrmacht in the west. Had Overlord never happened the Germans would still have lost the war; indeed one could argue that in geopolitical terms the only reason for the British and Americans invading Europe in June 1944 was to ensure that the Russians did not get to the Channel coast, for if they had who knows when they might have gone home again? Germany lost the war because she took on far too much. Militarily strong though she was, even her superb soldiers could not take on the British Empire, the United States and the USSR all at once. Population, industrial base, economics and geography made that an impossible dream. Once Germany failed to invade, persuade or starve the British out of the war, and could not take Moscow in 1941 (which might have precipitated the downfall of Stalin), and then allowed Japan to drag her into war with America, she was lost; it was only a matter of time.

Britain emerged on the winning side: crowds thronged Trafalgar Square, the King and Queen were cheered, everyone blessed good old

Winnie and the general election returned a Labour government to face the harsh realities of the post-war years. And those realities were harsh: Britain had expended her treasure and her credit to stay in the war, and not until the 1980s did her economy reach its pre-war strength; indeed, the last instalment of the last dollar loan will not be repaid until 2006. The British Empire began its twenty-year process of dissolution. The Empire would have gone anyway – since the 1880s it had been a clearly stated tenet of British imperial policy that the Empire was ruled for the benefit of the governed as well as the governing, and in due course colonies would have been considered fit for independence and the British would have withdrawn gracefully. Much of the turmoil still with us in Africa and the Middle East is directly attributable to independence being granted far too early; the British knew that perfectly well, but could not meet the expense of staying.

The lessons of the First World War had been thoroughly studied by soldiers, sailors, airmen, civil servants and politicians, and some had been absorbed. The direction of manpower was far more efficiently managed in the Second War than in the first, as were the armaments and ship-building industries once they had recovered from their inter-war neglect. In the First War 8,375,000 men and a small number of women had been absorbed by the British armed forces, in the Second War 4,758,500 men and 559,390 women.[1] Of course more workers were required for a much more technically oriented weapons industry than had been required in 1914–18, but nevertheless the much smaller numbers indicate the relative ferocity and involvement in the fighting. From 1914–18 the British armed forces had 702,410 killed, or 8.4 per cent of those mobilised. Between 1939 and 1945 we lost 264,443 servicemen killed, or 5.6 per cent of those mobilised. In the First War 17,800,000 days were lost through industrial action (strikes and stoppages),[*] whereas in the Second the total was an improved 10,430,000, largely because, as a result of the First War, the government knew how far it could push the work force.[2]

Some lessons, however, had been forgotten, or never understood in the first place. The British, who invented Blitzkrieg, promptly ignored

---

[*] Why are strikes, stoppages, go slows and the other ways by which disgruntled workers can disrupt the activities of the rest of us always called 'industrial action'? Industrial inaction would be more accurate.

it and it was left to the defeated enemy of 1918 to develop and refine it. The German armed forces enjoyed, of course, the luxury of having nothing else to do but prepare for war: the British had an empire to police. Funding for military experimentation in Germany – much of it, such as the tank development in Russia, forbidden by Versailles – was not a problem; for the British any capital expenditure between the wars, from a ship to a tank, had to be argued for and fought for and was often turned down. Yet even within those restrictions mechanisation was resisted all along the way by too many British generals, whose experiences in 1917 and 1918 should have enabled them to envisage the potential development of the tank, and should have encouraged them to think in terms of shock action and manoeuvre. Part of the problem was the regimental system: funding limitations meant that if something new was needed – such as tank battalions – then something old had to go. Eventually the solution was the mechanisation of the cavalry, and whereas many cavalry officers welcomed the new role, many did not. While all-arms cooperation improved as the war went on, the British never managed to fight a truly integrated battle, nor could they ever regroup with the speed and flexibility of the Germans. Inter-service cooperation was even more difficult: radios were not compatible, ship borne commanders had difficulty talking to troops on the ground, nobody was really prepared to get down to understanding the other services' problems, but saw them as competitors for available assets and money. There was never the funding available before the war for realistic exercises involving all three services, and nobody was powerful enough to resolve the conflicting requirements of the army for air support, the RAF's belief in strategic bombing and the Royal Navy's wish for an air arm that would do what it wanted.

Politics is the art of the possible, and while we may decry the lack of realistic defence funding during the inter-war years, it has to be recognised that 'Never again' and 'Peace in our time' were very powerful slogans, and deeply ingrained in the British psyche. The views of men who did want to rearm, like Chamberlain, were stifled and by the time public opinion was ready for a change, it was too late and appeasement was the only possible policy until at least a modicum of armed strength could be built up. Even so, things need not have been allowed to get as bad as they did. If the army had been given a peg upon which to hang a doctrinal hat – an expeditionary force – then the modernisers would have had much more sway; if the government had dug its toes in and not agreed to give up naval supremacy in Washington in 1922 and if the RAF had received funding for agreed (but not implemented) expansion, then the services would have been more ready for war even if they would not necessarily have been very much bigger, nor have cost very much more.

The British army did not win the war: the Royal Navy and the Royal Air Force prevented us from losing it. The Royal Navy kept the sea lanes open, and the RAF prevented the Germans from obtaining control of the skies over Great Britain and the Channel. The army did not do well in Norway, had no chance to do anything in France, and once Germans appeared in North Africa took a very long time to do anything there, and even then was heavily dependent on Empire troops. Italy was a slogging match reminiscent of the Western Front in the First War, but without the improvements in tactical skill seen between 1916 and 1917 in that earlier conflict; the landings in Normandy were very well done, thanks to meticulous planning and the navy, but subsequently the army was too slow, too inflexible and too ponderous.

There was less change in the character of the Royal Navy during the war than there was in the army, which altered radically. Despite Washington and lack of funding, the British navy was still very big, and the dilution of hostilities-only officers and ratings did not greatly affect the naval ethos or way of doing things. This was not the case in the army, which was anyway considerably less competent in 1939 than its forbear in 1914 had been, had huge problems in training its inflow of men and machines, and which improved only slowly between 1939 and 1945. Many aspects of pre-war soldiering disappeared completely. In 1939 it was still considered that the telephone was the chief means of communication: by 1945 the Royal Corps of Signals had expanded from a body of 10,000 men to 150,000 and portable battlefield radio had revolutionised warfare, even if not everyone understood that.

The difficulty of learning relevant lessons from the Second World

War lies in the reluctance of some who fought in it to admit that there were any lessons to be learned. Immediately after the war the army established a Directorate of Tactical Investigation in the War Office, with a major general in charge, tasked with examining the lessons of the recent conflict and recommending what might be done to prepare the army for a future war. The Deputy Director, a brigadier, wrote to Lieutenant General Sir Brian Horrocks, now General Officer Commanding-in-Chief Western Command, and who had been a corps commander in Normandy, asking for any post-action reports or any analyses of operations that he might have initiated or had drawn up. On 13 May 1946 Horrocks replied:

> I never write anything, nor if I can help it ever read anything that is of an official nature. During the nine months that I commanded XXX Corps I never signed one paper, up or down, so you will realise that I am the last man to help you with reports or analyses of operations.[3]

After 1945, many officers who had had what was considered to have been a 'good war' saw little point in getting excited about peacetime exercises, and the Cold War, that was until very recently the major focus of the British army, held no great interest for men who had actually done it for real. There was an artificiality about the major British military deployment – that in Germany – from the end of the war in 1945 until the demolition of the Berlin Wall. On the surface everything was frightfully serious, but underneath training was often more of a game than serious preparation for war. Ammunition stocks were always far less than would have been needed, constantly run down as an economy measure, the British Army of the Rhine had almost as many wives and children, to say nothing of domestic pets, as it had soldiers and airmen to repel the Russian hordes, and when in 1992 it was necessary to send one armoured division to the Gulf there was hardly a tank engine or a working armoured personnel carrier left in the four British divisions. It seems to this author, with the great benefit of hindsight, that it was not until there were British generals who had not been in the Second World War, nor unduly influenced by those who had, that professionalism began to return. It is difficult to conceive of Kosovo, East Timor, Sierra Leone, or Gulfs One and Two being conducted by many of the generals of the 1960s or 1970s, or even early 1980s, not because they would not have been able to work out what to do, but because they would not have initiated the doctrine and training that enabled the army to do it.

If there is one professional lesson that comes out of the comparison of the British and German efforts on land in the Second World War, it is the importance of a doctrine understood and trained for by all. The British army is making progress, but it is not there yet. This author was recently told by one of the more forward-thinking young brigade commanders of the British army that on one of his first exercises he had ordered an immediate regrouping whereby an infantry battalion was to carry out an operation with an armoured regiment with whom it had not previously worked. There was much discussion as to how the armour might be given a number of copies of the infantry battalion's standing operational procedures (SOPs), for if not then how could the tanks conform to what the infantry wanted? The brigadier, rightly, ordered that in future there would be no individual unit SOPs, but only brigade ones, to which all units of the brigade would conform. The brigade commander was absolutely right, but everyone should be working to army, rather than brigade (or divisional, or corps) SOPs. In the German army that is exactly what happened, and why the Germans could throw together an ad hoc battle group and have it operating in no time at all.

History is written by the victors. After the First War Stanley Baldwin is reputed to have said, 'Winston has written a big book about himself and called it The Great War.'[4] Similarly, Churchill's *History of the Second World War*, published in six volumes between 1948 and 1951, was the first major serious history of the war, and was Churchill's perception of it. By getting in first he ensured that his interpretation of what happened and how it happened became the accepted version, and anyone who disagreed was written off as an appeaser, a time waster, timorous or incompetent. There is no doubt that Winston Churchill was a charismatic and inspirational leader. His rhetoric, his ability to appeal to the British public and his absolute refusal to admit that Britain was not still a mighty power with a great Empire, was an inspiration not only to Britons but to those in neutral and occupied countries too. But if Churchill was the man who won the war, as election posters in 1945 said he was, then he was also the man who by his political actions between 1919 and 1929 contributed in very large measure to Britain being unready for it, and who by his flights of fancy, his unwillingness to trust professionals and his unshakeable belief that he knew better than anyone else how this nation's efforts should be directed, was very nearly responsible for losing it. His conduct as First Lord of the Admiralty during the Norway campaign was disastrous; his demands to sink the French fleet at Mers el Kebir unnecessary, for as Cunningham showed, the French would have come to an agreement without the threat of force, and thus the Syrian campaign need not have happened and the Torch landings might not have been opposed. His insistence on sending troops to Greece when Britain was no longer under any legal or moral obligation to do so; his constant chivvying of successive commanders-in-chief Middle East to go on the offensive when all their military instincts told them to wait, and his insistence on an Italian campaign which then got so bogged down that it was neither a distraction from Normandy nor an enabler of a Balkan front, all dissipated what few assets Britain had and wasted lives to little avail.

Of course in a democracy the civil power is paramount, and that is the way it should be, but once the politicians have decided to go to war they would be very much better off leaving the job to those who have spent their lives studying warfare and practising how to wage it. Brooke and the other chiefs of staff should never have allowed the Prime Minister to dictate minor detail, nor to sack generals and admirals on a whim (the air marshals, although not unscathed, got off more lightly). Probably the worst example of picking the wrong man and backing him come what may, was in Brooke's constant support for Montgomery, who should have been dismissed once it became clear that he could not operate in a coalition environment, but whose retention soured Anglo-American relations for years after the war.

As for Germany, the horror engendered by the extermination camps has eclipsed her military traditions, and Germany is today a good member of the European Union, and almost pacifist. There is a German army, navy and air force, but they are mere shadows of what once was. In May

1949 the Federal German Republic was established to include the zones of occupation of the western allies. The new West Germany was then asked to raise an army of half a million to help defend Europe against the Russians. They were given a sloppy uniform, made to do American drill and not allowed any battle honours, nor to wear wartime medals. When, eventually, they were permitted to wear medals these were sanitised versions, and only in the past year or so have German veterans of the Second World War, all ageing now, taken to wearing the original medals that they were awarded at the time. Present-day German officers, when asked their views on any aspect of the Second World War, have no opinions until they are certain that the enquirer is not about to accuse them of burning Jews. This is a shame. Germany's armed forces, particularly the army, achieved great feats during the war that should be lessons for us all; most of their generals were true professionals, many of them far more competent than any produced by Britain. Germany is deserving of her military dignity, and should be allowed to regain it.

In this book I have argued that Britain did not perform well in the Second World War. It took forty years from the end of that war for the British army (and to a lesser extent the other two services) to regain the professionalism that it last had in 1918. Our selection methods are now better, we no longer stifle military discussion, professional debate is no longer banned in the mess, we have more thinking officers in high places than ever before. One hopes that if another major war comes along, and one day it might, that the inevitable expansion can be properly managed and that doctrine and training will enable us to wage large-scale warfare with the flexibility and effectiveness that the Germans did for most of 1939–1945. Finally, however, for all the criticisms that can be levelled at the civil and military leadership of this nation from 1919 to 1945, it must never, ever, be forgotten that Britain did the decent thing. Britain went to war and she stayed in the war, regardless of all the temptations and opportunities for withdrawing from it that there were. Nazism was an evil creed, and opposition to it cost the British their blood, their Empire and their treasure, but stick at it they did and the world is a better place for that.

NOTES

1. Figures for WWI from *Statistics of the Military Efforts of the British Empire in the Great War*, HMSO, London, 1922, and for WWII from Peter Howlett, *Fighting with Figures*, HMSO, London, 1995.

2. WWI figures from Ian F. W. Beckett, *The Great War*, Longmans, London, 2001; WWII from Howlett op. cit.

3. TNA Kew, WO 232/2 Reports of Directorate of Tactical Investigation.

4. In fact six big books: W. S. Churchill, *The World Crisis 1911–1918*, 6 Vols., Butterworth, London, 1923–1931.

Bibliography

Ascoli, David, *A Companion to the British Army 1660–1983*, Harrap, London 1983

Barnett, Corelli, *The Desert Generals*, George Allen & Unwin, London 1983

Barnett, Corelli, *The Audit of War*, Macmillan, London 1986

Baudot, Marcel; Bernard, Henri; Brugmans, Hendrik; Foot, Michael R. D.; Jacobsen, Hans-Adolf (eds), *The Historical Encyclopedia of World War II*, Macmillan, London 1981

Beevor, Antony, *Stalingrad*, Viking, London 1998

Beneš, V. L. & Pounds, J. G., *Poland*, Ernest Benn, London 1970

Best, Geoffrey, *Churchill: a Study in Greatness*, Hambledon and London, London 2001

Bethel, Nicholas, *The War Hitler Won*, Allen Lane, London 1972

Bevis, Mark, *British and Commonwealth Armies 1939–43*, Vols. 1 & 2, Helion, Solihull 2001

Bidwell, Shelford & Graham, Dominick, *Firepower*, Allen & Unwin, London 1982

Bond, Brian & Taylor, Michael (eds), *The Battle for France and Flanders, Sixty Years On*, Leo Cooper, London 2001

Bradley, Omar N., *A Soldier's Story*, Henry Holt, New York 1951

Brooks, Stephen (ed), *Montgomery and the Eighth Army*, Bodley Head, London 1991

Burdick, Charles & Jacobsen, Hans-Adolf (eds), *The Halder War Diary, 1939–1942*, Greenhill, London 1988

Butler, J. R. M., *Grand Strategy*, Vol. III, Part II, HMSO, London 1964

Butler, J. R. M. (ed), *History of the Second World War*, HMSO, London 1956

Carver, Michael, Field Marshal Lord, *Out of Step*, Hutchinson, London 1989

Central Statistical Office, *Statistical Digest of the Second World War*, HMSO, London 1951

Chamberlain, Peter & Ellis, Chris, *Tanks of the World 1915–1945*, Cassell, London 1972

Charmley, John, Churchill: *The End of Glory*, Harcourt, London 1993

Connelly, Mark, *We Can Take It!*, Pearson, Harlow 2004

Cross, J. A., *Sir Samuel Hoare*, Jonathan Cape, London 1977

D'Este, Carlo, *Eisenhower: A Soldier's Life*, Weidenfeld & Nicolson, London 2003

Danchev, Alex & Todman, Daniel (eds), *War Diaries 1939–1945: Field Marshal Lord Alanbrooke*, Weidenfeld & Nicolson, London 2001

Dank, Milton, *The French Against the French*, Cassell, London 1978

Dear, I. C. B. (ed), *The Oxford Companion to World War II*, Oxford University Press, Oxford 2001

Deighton, Len, *Blood, Tears and Folly*, Jonathan Cape, London 1993

Delaforce, Patrick, *Monty's Ironsides*, Sutton, Stroud 1995

Delaforce, Patrick, *Monty's Highlanders*, Tom Donovan, Brighton 1997

Delaforce, Patrick, *Churchill's Desert Rats*, Sutton, Stroud 2002

Demeter, Karl (trans. Malcolm, Angus), *The German Officer-Corps in Society and State 1650–1945*, Weidenfeld & Nicolson, London 1965

Dilks, David (ed), *The Diaries of Sir Alexander Cadogan 1938–1945*, Cassell, London 1971

Doherty, Richard, *A Noble Crusade*, Spellmount, Staplehurst 1999

Ellis, John, *Brute Force: Allied Strategy and Tactics in the Second World War*, André Deutsch, London 1990

Ellis, John, *The World War II Databook*, Aurum, London 1993

Farrel, Charles, *Reflections 1939–1945*, Pentland, Bishop Auckland 2000

Foot, Michael R. D., *SOE in France*, HMSO, London 1966

Forty, George, *The Reich's Last Gamble*, Cassell, London 2000

Foss, Christopher F. (ed), *The Encyclopedia of Tanks and Armoured Fighting Vehicles*, Spellmount, Staplehurst 2002

Fowler, Will, *The Commandos at Dieppe: Rehearsal for D-Day*, HarperCollins, London 2002

Fraser, David, *And We Shall Shock Them*, Hodder & Stoughton, London 1983

French, David, *Raising Churchill's Army*, Oxford University Press, Oxford 2000

Gibbs, N. H., *History of the Second World War – Grand Strategy, Vol. I*, HMSO, London 1976

Gilbert, Martin, *A History of the Twentieth Century (2 vols)*, HarperCollins, London 1997–8

Glantz, David M., *The Battle for Leningrad*, University Press of Kansas, Lawrence 2002

Goutard, A. (trans. Burgess, A. R. P.), *The Battle of France 1940*, Frederick Muller, London 1958

Graham, Andrew, *Sharpshooters at War*, CLY Regimental Association, London 1964

Gwyer, J. M. A., *Grand Strategy, Vol III, Part I*, HMSO, London 1964

Hamilton, Nigel, *Monty: The Making of a General 1887–1942*, McGraw Hill, London 1981

Hamilton, Nigel, *Monty: The Field Marshal 1944–1976*, Hamish Hamilton, London 1986

Hamilton, Nigel, *The Full Monty*, Allen Lane, London 2001

Hastings, Max, *Overlord*, Michael Joseph, London 1984

Heathcote, T. A., *The British Field Marshals 1763–1997*, Leo Cooper, London 1999

Heathcote, T. A., *The British Admirals of the Fleet 1734–1995*, Leo Cooper, Barnsley 2002

Heiber, Helmut & Glantz, David M. (eds), *Hitler and his Generals*, Greenhill, London 2002

Holmes, Richard, *Army Battlefield Guide, Belgium and Northern France*, HMSO, London 1995

Holmes, Richard, *Battlefields of the Second World War*, BBC Worldwide, London 2001

Holt, Thaddeus, *The Deceivers*, Weidenfeld & Nicolson, London 2004

Howlett, Peter, *Fighting with Figures*, HMSO, London 1995

Hylton, Stuart, *Their Darkest Hour*, Sutton, Stroud 2001

Ireland, Bernard, *War at Sea 1914–45*, Cassell, London 2002

Ironside, Edmund, *Time Unguarded*, Greenwood Press, Westport 1962

Irving, David, *Hitler's War*, Hodder & Stoughton, London 1971

Irving, David, *The Rise and Fall of the Luftwaffe*, Weidenfeld & Nicolson, London 1973

Irving, David, *The Trail of the Fox*, Weidenfeld & Nicolson, London 1977

Irving, David, *Göring*, Macmillan, London 1989

Isby, David C. (ed), *Fighting the Breakout*, Greenhill, London 2004

Ismay, General the Lord, *The Memoirs of General the Lord Ismay*, Heinemann, London 1960

Jackson, Julian, *The Fall of France*, Oxford University Press, Oxford 2003

Jackson, William & Bramall, Dwin, *The Chiefs*, Brassey's, London 1992

Jane's Fighting Aircraft of World War II, Studio Editions, London 1989

Jarrett, Philip (ed), *Aircraft of the Second World War*, Putnam, London 1997

Jenkins, Roy, *Baldwin*, Collins, London 1987

Joslen, H. F., *Orders of Battle: Second World War 1939–1945*, HMSO, London 1960

Keegan, John, *Six Armies in Normandy*, Jonathan Cape, London 1982

Keegan, John & Wheatcroft, Andrew, *Who's Who in Military History*, Weidenfeld & Nicolson, London 1976

Keegan, John (ed), *Churchill's Generals*, Weidenfeld & Nicolson, London 1991

Kennedy, Paul M., *The Rise and Fall of British Naval Mastery*, Allen Lane, London 1976

Kesselring, Albert, *The Memoirs of Field Marshal Kesselring*, Greenhill, London 1953

Kurowski, Franz (trans. Johnston, David), *Panzer Aces (2 vols)*, Stackpole, Mechanicsburg PA 2004

Leutz, James R., *Bargaining for Supremacy: Anglo-American Naval Collaboration 1937–1941*, University of North Carolina Press, Chapel Hill 1977

Liddell Hart, B. H., *The Rommel Papers*, Hamlyn, London 1953

Liddell Hart, B. H., *The Tanks: The History of the Royal Tank Regiment (2 vols)*, Cassell, London 1959

Lord, Walter, *The Miracle of Dunkirk*, Allen Lane, London 1983

Mack Smith, Denis, *Mussolini*, Weidenfeld & Nicolson, London 1981

MacKenzie, William, *The Secret History of SOE*, St Ermin's Press, London 2000

Maguire, Eric, *Dieppe: August 19*, Jonathan Cape, London 1963

Makepiece-Warne, Anthony, *Brassey's Companion to the British Army*, Brassey's, London 1995

Mallmann Showell, Jak P., *German Navy Handbook*, Sutton, Stroud 1999

Man, John, *The Penguin Atlas of D-Day and the Normandy Campaign*, Viking, London 1994

Manstein, Erich von (trans. Powell, Anthony), *Lost Victories*, Greenhill, London, 1958

Mason, David, *Who's Who in World War II*, Weidenfeld & Nicolson, London 1978

McKee, Alexander, *The Race for the Rhine Bridges*, Souvenir Press, London 2001

Mellenthin, F. W. von, *Panzer Battles*, Cassell, London 1955

Middlebrook, Martin, *Arnhem 1944*, Viking, London 1994

Middlebrook, Martin & Everitt, Chris, *The Bomber Command War Diaries*, Viking, London 1985

Milner, Marc, *Battle of the Atlantic*, Tempus, Stroud 2003

Mitcham, Samuel W. Jr., *Hitler's Field Marshals and their Battles*, Leo Cooper, London 1988

Neillands, Robin, *The Bomber War*, John Murray, London 2001

Neillands, Robin, *The Battle for Normandy 1944*, Cassell, London 2002

Nicolson, Nigel (ed), *Harold Nicolson: The War Years: Diaries and Letters 1935–1945*, Collins, London 1967

Paget, R. T., *Manstein, his Campaigns and his Trial*, Collins, London 1951

Parker, H. M. D., *History of the Second World War – Manpower*, HMSO, London 1957

Pitt, Barrie, *The Crucible of War: Auchinleck's Command*, Cassell, London 1980

Pitt, Barrie, *The Crucible of War: Wavell's Command*, Cassell, London 1980

Pitt, Barrie, *The Crucible of War: Montgomery of Alamein*, Cassell, London 1980

Pitt, Barrie, *Churchill and the Generals*, Sidgwick & Jackson, London 1981

Pope, Stephen & Wheal, Elizabeth-Anne, *Dictionary of the Second World War*, Macmillan, London 1989

Probert, Henry, *Bomber Harris, his Life and Times*, Greenhill, London 2003

Reider, Frederic, *The Order of the SS: A Pictorial History*, Foulsham, Slough 1981

Research Institute for Military History, Germany, *Germany and the Second World War (6 vols)*, Oxford University Press, Oxford 1990–2002

Reynolds, Michael, *Steel Inferno*, Spellmount, Staplehurst 1997

Reynolds, Michael, *Eagles and Bulldogs in Normandy 1944*, Spellmount, Staplehurst 2003

Rogers, Anthony, *Churchill's Folly*, Cassell, London 2003

Rohwer, Jürgen, *War at Sea 1939–1945*, Chatham Publishing, London 1996

Roskill, S. W., *The War at Sea*, HMSO, London 1954

Roskill, S. W., *The Navy at War 1939–1945*, Collins, London 1960

Roskill, S. W., *A Merchant Fleet in War*, Collins, London 1962

Roskill, S. W., *Churchill and the Admirals*, Collins, London 1977

Rothbrust, Florian K., *Guderian's XIX Panzer Corps and the Battle of France*, Praeger, New York 1990

Saward, Dudley, *Bomber Harris*, Cassell, London 1984

Scarfe, Norman, *Assault Division*, Spellmount, Staplehurst 2004

Seaton, Albert, *The German Army 1933–45*, Weidenfeld & Nicolson, London 1982

Sheppard, G. A., *The Italian Campaign 1943–45*, Arthur Barker, London 1968

Sweetinburgh, Sheila, *The Role of the Hospital in Medieval England*, Four Courts, Dublin 2004

Taylor, Brian, *Barbarossa to Berlin*, Spellmount, Staplehurst 2003

Telford, Taylor, *The March of Conquest*, Hulton, London 1958

Terraine, John, *The Right of the Line*, Hodder & Stoughton, London 1985

Terraine, John, *Business in Great Waters*, Leo Cooper, London 1989

War Office, *The Second World War – Army – Mobilisation*, War Office, London 1950

War Office, *The Second World War – Army – Signals Communication*, War Office, London 1950

War Office, *The Second World War – Army – Personnel Selection*, War Office, London 1953

War Office, *The Second World War – Army – Supply and Transport*, War Office, London 1954

Wellum, Geoffrey, *First Light*, Viking, London 2002

Whiting, Charles, *The Battle of the Bulge*, Sutton, Stroud 1999

Whiting, Charles, *The Field Marshal's Revenge*, Spellmount, Staplehurst 2004

Willmott, H. P., *Battleship*, Cassell, London 2002

Wistrich, Robert S., *Who's Who in Nazi Germany*, Weidenfeld & Nicolson, London 1982

Wood, Derek & Dempster, Derek, *The Narrow Margin*, Hutchinson, London 1961

Wragg, David, *Wings over the Sea*, David & Charles, Newton Abbot 1979

Zeigler, Philip, *Mountbatten*, HarperCollins, London 1985

Index